Becoming America's Playground

Becoming America's Playground

Las Vegas in the 1950s

LARRY D. GRAGG

University of Oklahoma Press : Norman

For Harold Gragg
I could not have asked for a better brother.

Library of Congress Cataloging-in-Publication Data

Names: Gragg, Larry Dale, 1950– author.
Title: Becoming America's playground : Las Vegas in the 1950s / Larry Gragg.
Description: Norman : University of Oklahoma Press, [2019] | Includes bibliographical references and index.
Identifiers: LCCN 2018059837 | ISBN 978-0-8061-6351-2 (pbk. : alk. paper)
Subjects: LCSH: City promotion—Nevada—Las Vegas—History—20th century. | Tourism—Nevada—Las Vegas—History—20th century. | Social change—Nevada—Las Vegas—History—20th century. | Las Vegas (Nev.)—Social conditions—20th century. | Las Vegas (Nev.)—Economic conditions—20th century.
Classification: LCC HN80.L27 G77 2019 | DDC 306.4/81909793135—dc23
LC record available at https://lccn.loc.gov/2018059837

Copyright © 2019 by the University of Oklahoma Press, Norman, Publishing Division of the University. Manufactured in the U.S.A.

Contents

Illustrations

Preface

I have been interested in the history of Las Vegas for nearly two decades. As I was researching and writing two books—*Bright Light City: Las Vegas in Popular Culture* (2013) and *Benjamin "Bugsy" Siegel: The Gangster, the Flamingo, and the Making of Modern Las Vegas* (2015)—as well as many journal and magazine articles, it became clear to me that the 1950s marked the most important decade for Las Vegas. By the end of World War II, a growing number of Americans had become aware of Las Vegas as a regional tourist town, a place to enjoy vices largely forbidden elsewhere, such as gambling and prostitution. However, few saw it as a true resort city like Palm Springs, California. Yet, in a scant fifteen years, that is just what Las Vegas became. With more than a dozen resort hotel-casinos, Las Vegas attracted nearly ten million tourists in 1960, a dramatic increase over the barely one million who visited a decade earlier. I was eager to learn how developers, investors, and civic leaders accomplished that extraordinary increase in tourism in such a short time; hence the research that led to this book.

I drew upon rich source material for this study. Books by Eugene P. Moehring, Michael S. Green, David G. Schwartz, Geoff Schumacher, John M. Findlay, Hal Rothman, Gary E. Elliott, and Ralph Roske provided a highly useful overview, even though none of them focus exclusively on the 1950s. Articles in the *Nevada Historical Society Quarterly* were particularly helpful, as its authors dealt with women's history, the impact of atomic testing on Las Vegas, civil rights struggles in the 1950s, the role of defense spending on the local economy, efforts to promote Las Vegas, and key developments in entertainment. To learn what was most important to the people of Las Vegas in those years, I thought it critical to read the city's two major newspapers of the era, the *Las Vegas Review-Journal* and *Las Vegas Sun*. While I did not read every article, I did examine each available issue of the two papers from the decade. Such an approach helped me understand the key economic, social, and political issues for residents. Because there are so many useful databases now, I was also able to look at articles about Las Vegas in newspapers in more than fifty other communities in the United

States to learn about national perceptions of the city. I drew on more than forty oral histories of Las Vegas residents and had the great good fortune to interview eight individuals who shared their recollections of that decade. Publicists Harvey Diederich and Jim Seagrave, veterans of the Las Vegas News Bureau Don Payne and Don English, and dancers Joy Garner, Judy Jones, and Joan Ryba were all helpful and a delight to get to know. Johnny Mathis indulged me with two helpful interviews and both times was gracious and forthcoming about his tough experiences performing in a segregated city. While I did not formally interview Valda and Esper Esau, we exchanged emails that always helped me to better understand Las Vegas. Conversations with Corinne Entratter Sidney were useful in developing an understanding of Jack Entratter's role at the Sands Hotel. I also had the benefit of drawing upon the material in more than two dozen manuscript collections at the Special Collections and Archives at the University of Nevada, Las Vegas. These collections run the gamut from hotel promotional material and chamber of commerce records to city commission minutes and the huge Union Pacific Railroad collection.

Many people have helped me in the four years of researching and writing this book. The staff in Special Collections at the Lied Library at the University of Nevada, Las Vegas is simply the best in the business. They know the manuscript collections so well and are always welcoming and helpful. Joyce Moore, Aaron Mayes, Cyndi Shein, Tammi Kim, Michael Frazier, Karla Irwin, and their boss Michelle Light are a great team. Delores Brownlee helped in so many ways, particularly in the selection of photographs for the book, as did Aaron Mayes. Student worker Max Gonzalez scanned some of the photos. Lunch conversations with David Schwartz, Michael Green, Barbara Tabach, Claytee White, Stefani Evans, and Peter Michel were always a treat and an informal way to learn more about Las Vegas history and UNLV. The librarians at Missouri University of Science and Technology were a great resource, particularly in acquiring needed material through interlibrary loans. June Snell was invaluable in obtaining loans of dozens of reels of the two Las Vegas newspapers, and Yuko Shinozaki at the Lied Library was great in facilitating those loans. Lisa Jacob, Kelli Luchs, and Sam Morris at the Las Vegas News Bureau helped me find appropriate photos.

My colleagues at Missouri S&T—Diana Ahmad, Michael Bruening, Robin Collier, Petra DeWitt, Pat Huber, Tseggai Isaac, Alanna Krolikowski, John McManus, Michael Meagher, Justin Pope, Jeff Schramm, and Kate Sheppard— have developed a premier department of teaching scholars, all of whom contribute to a great environment for productive work, largely because of the excellent leadership of our department chair, Shannon Fogg. Steve Roberts, who was on the faculty at UNLV for a decade, is our dean of Arts, Sciences, and Business and has always supported all that I do. Provost Robert Marley has not only supported my research and teaching but also pulled me out of retirement to head a new Center for Advancing Faculty Excellence, a job I love every day. In 2017 the two of them even treated me to a wonderful dinner at the classic Las Vegas steakhouse, the Golden Steer!

A dozen folks read draft chapters of this book—Stefan Al, Alicia Barber, Judy Jones, Joy Garner, Joanne Goodwin, Valda and Esper Esau, Peter Michel, Geoff Schumacher, Claytee White, Andy Kirk, and Steve Watts. There were also two anonymous readers of the manuscript. Collectively, their advice improved the book, but, of course, none is responsible for any of my errors. Several years ago I met Chuck Rankin at a conference, and he asked if I was working on another Las Vegas book. This is it. Chuck is the best kind of editor—encouraging while nudging me along to the finish line. Chuck's colleagues at the University of Oklahoma Press—Bethany Mowry, Amy Hernandez, and Steven Baker—have been terrific in helping me complete this project. Sarah C. Smith is not only a talented copy editor, but she also helped me recover files I thought I had lost!

I met Su Kim Chung in 2003 when I began research trips to the Lied Library. Throughout my subsequent dozens of trips, she has been a constant source of support. Because of her intimate knowledge of the manuscript collections, Su Kim has alerted me to many helpful sources that I otherwise would not have consulted. A highlight of virtually every research trip is a visit with her at Blueberry Hill for breakfast and good conversation. More important, Su Kim and her parents Al and Kelly "adopted" me, and it was always a treat to see them on research trips. Sadly, both died while I was working on this project.

Lastly, I owe the most thanks to the best person I have ever known. My wife, Doris, has read every word in this book with a sharp pencil in hand, always improving the prose. I could have finished it without her, but doing so would have meant a lesser final product.

So that's it. What follows is my effort to explain how Las Vegas became America's Playground in the 1950s with all the challenges, disappointments, and rewards reflected in that endeavor.

Becoming America's Playground

Introduction

A study of the 1950s conjures many, often conflicting images. They were the "happy days" of innocence after a long depression and global conflict. It was a decade with a war-hero president, Dwight Eisenhower, who, following the New Deal and Fair Deal programs of Franklin Roosevelt and Harry Truman, sought a "middle way between untrammeled freedom of the individual and the demands of the welfare of the whole nation."[1] It was a decade when African Americans accelerated their struggle against segregation and when the nation began paying more attention after the successful Montgomery, Alabama, bus boycott that elevated Martin Luther King Jr. to a national leader. It was a decade when the Mad Men of Madison Avenue advertising firms ever more creatively pushed product promotion in the marketplace. It was a decade when U.S. Senate committees spent millions seeking to understand the role of organized crime in American life. It was a decade that saw almost all Americans buy one or more televisions, which dramatically changed leisure time patterns, a shift that particularly hurt the movie industry. It was a decade when many women embraced the ideal of homemaker and mother, while many others, their number ever increasing, sought work outside the home or became activists in trade unions and a variety of reform movements. It was a decade when intellectuals worried about the emergence of a mindless conformity, particularly in the rapidly growing suburbs all across the land. It was a decade when the Soviets successfully launched the first satellite into orbit, a development that caused many to doubt American superiority in science and technology. It was a decade when rock 'n' roll became a force in the music industry, with a galaxy of African American, Hispanic, and white performers like Chuck Berry, Ritchie Valens, and Elvis Presley. It was a decade when America ended a war in Korea but became ever more involved in a conflict in Indochina.

For many newspaper and magazine editors, an intensifying Cold War between the United States and the Soviet Union was the preeminent story of the decade, a narrative made more ominous by the potential of communist infiltration of American institutions. In response to that threat, the Truman

3

administration conducted a thorough investigation of the loyalty of federal employees, a four-year effort that led to the dismissal of more than 1,200 and the resignations of thousands more. Drawing upon the McCarran Internal Security Act (sponsored by Nevada's senior senator Pat McCarran), Attorney General Tom C. Clark identified ninety-one groups he considered subversive. In response to House Un-American Activities Committee investigations, Hollywood production companies blacklisted hundreds of directors, writers, and actors. Some public school teachers lost their jobs, as did more than five hundred college professors, all suspected of disloyalty. Alger Hiss, a former State Department official, was found guilty of perjury. Hiss had falsely claimed that he had not known journalist Whittaker Chambers, who had told the House Un-American Activities Committee that he and Hiss had been communists in the 1930s and that Hiss had given him State Department documents. British scientist Klaus Fuchs admitted giving atomic secrets to the Russians, and the American couple Julius and Ethel Rosenberg were found guilty of conspiracy to commit espionage with the Russians. All of these developments provided opportunities for demagogues such as Joseph McCarthy to exploit.[2] The Wisconsin senator gave countless speeches, chaired the Senate Permanent Subcommittee on Investigations of the Government Operations Committee, and conducted a televised investigation of the Army, all in a vain quest to uncover what he argued was a massive communist conspiracy.[3] In 1952 McCarthy even appeared in Las Vegas, where he accused Hank Greenspun, publisher of the *Las Vegas Sun*, of being an ex-communist and his newspaper of espousing communist ideology.[4]

While most Americans likely acknowledged communism as "an internal conspiracy as well as an external reality," public opinion polls reveal that the issue mattered less to them than it meant to politicians and journalists. In 1953 and 1954, they rarely identified an internal communist threat as a problem facing the nation, and by summer 1954 only 36 percent had a favorable opinion of Joseph McCarthy. Indeed, a survey in 1955 revealed that "the number of people who said that they were worried either about the threat of Communists in the United States or about civil liberties was, even by the most generous interpretation of occasionally ambiguous responses, *less than 1%!*"[5]

Most Americans chose to focus instead upon things more immediate and satisfying. As historian William H. Chafe has pointed out, "the attention of most Americans was so riveted on the astonishing new world of consumerism and prosperity that social issues—for the moment, at least—seemed relatively unimportant."[6] There was good reason for this. The generation after World War

II experienced "an historic reign of prosperity, longer lasting and more univer-sally enjoyed than ever before in American history."[7] To be sure, not everyone shared in the bounty. Perhaps as many as 20 percent lived below the poverty line. Yet during the decade the U.S. gross national product rose nearly 40 percent, and median family income rose 30 percent, while unemployment and inflation remained low most years. David Halberstam, one of the leading chroniclers of that decade, reminded us that "few Americans doubted the essential goodness of their society."[8]

Many factors contributed to this success. Inexpensive and plentiful supplies of oil, an increased demand for goods and services triggered by the continuing baby boom, access to inexpensive credit, facilitated by the introduction of credit cards, and companies' investment in research and development of new products all played a role. Massive spending by the federal government was also import-ant. The award of large defense contracts in the wake of the escalating Cold War, a commitment to enhance the nation's infrastructure largely through the 1956 Interstate Highway Act, continued funding of the Servicemen's Readjust-ment Act of 1944 (GI Bill), and increased housing subsidies pumped substantial amounts of money into the economy. Moreover, "social programs," as Lizabeth Cohen has written, including "unemployment insurance, social security, pub-lic assistance, and minimum wage legislation . . . helped maintain purchasing power."[9]

There was such a pent-up demand to spend among a population that had endured the economic deprivation of the Great Depression and the rationing of World War II that, as cultural critic Thomas Hine has argued, many Americans expressed an "outright, thoroughly vulgar joy in being able to live so well."[10] Conspicuous consumption became the byword for the decade. "From 1950 to 1960," J. Ronald Oakley determined, "the amount spent on spectator sports admissions rose from $222 million to $290 million, that spent on radios, tele-visions, records, and musical instruments from $2.4 billion to $3.4 billion, and that on commercial participant amusements from $448 million to $1.2 billion."[11] Most importantly, Americans wanted new homes and built 13 million of them between 1948 and 1958 with a substantial assist from the federal government through Veterans Administration and Federal Housing Administration loans. More than 80 percent of the homes went up in suburbs across the nation, particularly in southwestern states where ever more Americans chose to live. In 1957 *Newsweek* magazine "pointed to a consensus among economists that 'the suburbanite is tomorrow's best customer and a firm foundation for future national prosperity.'"[12] To accommodate those eager consumers, developers built hundreds of shopping centers, almost two thousand by 1960. These new marketplaces "evolved into islands of stores surrounded by vast parking lots."[13] They were part of an extraordinary emerging culture built upon the automobile. Americans, who fell in love with cars in the 1920s, had the means to buy them in record numbers in the 1950s, 7.9 million of them in 1955 alone. Beyond shopping centers, drive-in restaurants, motels (41,000 of them by 1960), and the expanding freeway system "all catered to the person behind the wheel."[14]

In 1955 the editors of *Fortune* magazine forecast consumer spending in the near future, anticipating that "the biggest promise of new leisure expenditure lies in foreign and domestic travel." Indeed, they expected that Americans would increase spending on domestic vacations perhaps to as much as $10 billion by 1960.[15] Besides the general prosperity that gave Americans the means to travel, as well as the improving highway system and cheap gas, the editors noted, the average workweek had been reduced from almost fifty hours in the 1920s to less than forty-two by 1953, and there had been "a sharp rise in paid holidays."[16] The *Fortune* editors were spot-on. Americans embraced travel in the 1950s. "The number of annual visitors to national parks," for example, "rose from 13.9 million to 26.6 million."[17] Early on, states and communities grasped the significance of this yearning to take vacations. Just after World War II, the trade paper *Advertising Age* wrote, "Every state will be going over its terrain, its institutions, its history and its people with a high-powered microscope, trying to discover or embellish attractions which can help it dip more heavily into the tourist lode."[18] State governments and chambers of commerce poured money into promotion, and by 1950 tourism was the first or second most important source of income for several states, including California, Florida, Oregon, New Jersey, and Michigan.[19] As a result, Americans could pick from an extraordinary range of vacation possibilities. Besides visiting a multitude of national historic sites, they could ski at Aspen, Colorado, or Sun Valley, Idaho; enjoy the sun-drenched attractions of Miami Beach, Saint Augustine, Cypress Gardens, Daytona Beach, and Key West in Florida; experience the fashionable resorts of Palm Springs, California; marvel at the spectacular scenery in national parks; tour hundreds of Civil War battlefields; and "rough it" at the hunting lodges and dude ranches in the West.[20]

These were the circumstances Las Vegas faced in the postwar years. The growth of the desert community from around five thousand residents in 1930 to more than twenty thousand by the end of World War II had been heavily dependent upon the city's embrace of vice and substantial federal spending.

Nevada had legalized wide-open gambling in 1931 and had also implemented the shortest residence requirement for divorces in the nation. In addition, prostitution had been legal in Las Vegas until the early years of World War II. The federal government funded the construction of the massive Boulder Dam (later renamed the Hoover Dam) just thirty miles from the town, a decision that helped make it a regional tourist center. The establishment of a gunnery school just north of town at the beginning of the war brought thousands of airmen and employees. The construction of a magnesium plant to the southeast to provide needed metal for war effort armaments brought more than ten thousand workers to the area.

When the war ended, chamber of commerce leaders Maxwell Kelch and William Moore, unsure if such federal largesse would continue, decided to rely on tourism for their town's future, a decision echoed by those in many other states. For the next fifteen years, Las Vegas worked to develop into a premier destination locale, one that promised the best escapist fun and in the process became more than a successful regional tourist town. By 1960 Las Vegas had become the nation's favorite destination. It had become America's Playground. In 1950 a local journalist estimated that the town was attracting about a million tourists a year, but by the end of the decade almost ten million came to Las Vegas.[21] The impact of those numbers were both immediate and long-lasting. In the 1950s, Las Vegas's population more than doubled, and its residents enjoyed the highest per capita income in the nation. In the subsequent six decades, the city has built upon the foundation established by the developers, city leaders, publicists, and journalists of the 1950s to make Las Vegas one of the most visited places on earth. In 2016 nearly forty-three million tourists visited Las Vegas, and nearly half of southern Nevada workers had jobs supported by tourism.[22]

This is the story of that pivotal decade. It is about the people responsible for the promotion of the city, the circumstances that improved their chances of success, and the consequences of Las Vegas becoming a major vacation locale. I have not organized it in a traditional chronological way. Instead, the chapters address the specific factors in the successful promotion of the city and how that success changed lives in Las Vegas. In the first chapter, "Vegas Rising," I include an account of the rapid development of the resort corridor along Highway 91, increasingly known as the Las Vegas Strip. The challenges in securing funding for new hotels, the successes, and the failures are all included, as well as the drive to open a large convention center to help fill all the hotel rooms when demand for reservations lagged between weekends. I note the momentary threat that

Cuban casinos posed for Las Vegas and end with a brief discussion of how political leaders dealt with the many challenges the city's rapid development posed.
In chapter 2, "Selling Vegas," I explain how leaders in the chamber of commerce,
the Las Vegas News Bureau, hotel publicists, and self-appointed promotional
"ambassadors" crafted a winning formula for selling Las Vegas to a rapidly
increasing number of Americans. In the third chapter, "Entertainment Capital,"
I describe how hotel owners used great singers, comedians, and fantastic dance
lines to attract tourists to Las Vegas. In addition, I discuss the importance of
entertainment directors' choice of entertainers in bringing guests to their hotels.

In the fourth chapter, "Women in Las Vegas," I explain the barriers and
opportunities facing women who hoped to secure well-paying jobs in America's
most prosperous community. In chapters 5 and 6, "Struggles for Black Entertainers" and "Mississippi in the Desert," I write about the many ways black
entertainers and black residents struggled against entrenched segregation in
Las Vegas in the 1950s and their triumphs large and small. In chapter 7, "Mob
Vegas," I explain the role of organized crime in the city's success and the ways
state, county, and city leaders sought to control, if not eliminate, the mob's
influence. In chapter 8, "Atomic Vegas," I describe the ways residents responded
to and ultimately exploited the atomic testing that occurred just a few dozen
miles from Las Vegas throughout the 1950s as a promotional prop. In chapter 9,
"Rat Pack," I note the role Frank Sinatra, Dean Martin, Sammy Davis Jr., Peter
Lawford, and Joey Bishop played in promoting the image of Las Vegas that had
developed by the time they first performed together at the Sands Hotel in 1960
while filming the heist film *Ocean's Eleven*. In the brief afterword, I describe
how the trends of the 1950s continued to have an impact on Las Vegas past 1960.

One
Vegas Rising

As Wilbur Clark prepared to open his Desert Inn Hotel on April 24, 1950, he invited journalists from around the nation to witness the event, and they did not disappoint him. They came in large numbers and lavished praise on the nearly $4 million Bermuda-pink resort with three hundred rooms and a large casino. Their stories introduced many to the locale most would, by decade's end, acknowledge as America's Playground. The Desert Inn featured almost twenty acres of landscaped grounds, a large swimming pool with cabanas, a glass-enclosed cocktail lounge called the Sky Room, the Painted Desert showroom that

The new luxurious Desert Inn Hotel opened in 1950.
Courtesy University of Nevada, Las Vegas, University Libraries Special Collections and Archives, Paul J. Richert Photo Collection, Las Vegas News Bureau, and Wynn Las Vegas.

could accommodate four hundred, an oval fountain out front that could shoot water fifty feet high, tennis courts, and a children's playground and nursery. The journalists marveled at the ninety-foot bar and pink Joshua tree in the casino, the dazzling floor show starring ventriloquist Edgar Bergen accompanied by "a chorus line rivaling Manhattan's Copa Girls," and the remarkably varied opening night crowd. People arrived "wearing everything from mink capes to pedal pushers, from dinner jackets to sport shirts."[1] Todd Simon reported in the Cleveland *Plain Dealer* that besides "a gaggle of Hollywood stars," he saw Nevada governor Vail Pittman rubbing "shoulders with a crap-shooter rolling the dice with a Brooklyn accent."[2]

Yet it was Wilbur Clark himself who most impressed the reporters and columnists. His was a compelling tale of rags to riches. The "greying, boyish man" had hitchhiked from the Midwest in the 1920s to the West Coast. Starting as a bellboy, Clark had moved from crap dealer to entrepreneur, running cocktail bars in San Diego and then to ownership of the El Rancho Vegas and Players Club before pinning his hopes on a more lavish resort hotel project.[3] Designed by architects Wayne McAllister and Hugh Taylor, the Desert Inn proved to be more costly than Clark could afford, and he had to rely upon a syndicate of midwestern gangsters led by Cleveland's Moe Dalitz for the financing needed to finish the resort.

The Desert Inn's success—the hotel made an almost $2 million profit in its first year—prompted a host of other eager developers and investors to build hotel-casinos. Taxes generated by the growing number of properties became ever more important for city, county, and state governments in Nevada, and the resort industry became the most important employer in the state. As early as the opening of the Desert Inn, *Life* magazine reported that 10 percent of all workers in Nevada had found employment "in the gambling places, at an average of $4,100 a year" in salary.[4] The rapid creation of well-paying jobs in Las Vegas in the 1950s drew thousands of new residents, and the city's population grew from 24,624 in 1950 to 64,405 ten years later.

Yet the rise of the Strip, the resort hotel corridor along Route 91 that drove much of the economic development of Las Vegas and Clark County, had taken several decades. The town had begun in 1905 as a division point for the new San Pedro, Los Angeles, and Salt Lake Railroad. It was a company town that grew slowly. A quarter-century after its founding, Las Vegas had fewer than six thousand people. However, construction began in 1931 on the massive Boulder Dam on the Colorado River just thirty miles from Las Vegas. Besides bringing in thousands of workers, many of whom spent their wages in Las Vegas, the dam brought tourists in ever-greater numbers, and many spent time and money in town. As Eugene Moehring has shown, this "federal trigger" was critical in the early growth of the town, and it continued with the establishment in 1941 of an Army Air Corps Gunnery School northeast of town. The base trained thousands of gunners and pilots to operate B-17 and B-29 bombers, which were critical to the U.S. effort in World War II. The federal government also established the Basic Magnesium Industries plant at what became the city of Henderson. At one point during World War II, the plant employed more than thirteen thousand to process magnesium for use in armaments.[5] This infusion of federal spending that came with the base and the plant fueled record growth for the local economy. In a *Collier's* magazine article, Richard English reported that between 1941 and 1942 alone, Las Vegas added six thousand people to its population.[6]

After the war it remained clear that federal government spending, notably at Nellis Air Force Base and at the Nevada Test Site, seventy miles northwest of the city, would be crucial to sustaining the southern Nevada economy. After a three-year standby period, the old gunnery school base reopened in 1949, and the following year the air force named it after Las Vegas resident Lt. William Nellis, a fighter pilot killed in combat during the Battle of the Bulge. By 1954 Nellis employed about 5,500 civilian and military employees. Many also found work with the Atomic Energy Commission (AEC) at the Nevada Test Site. Beginning in 1951, the AEC conducted a series of aboveground atomic tests, a decade-long program that required a staff of five hundred. The payroll for all the employees at these two installations was about $22 million annually.[7] Chemical and metal companies at the old Basic Magnesium Industries plant provided more jobs. The five companies there in 1957 employed more than 1,900 and had an annual payroll of more than $12 million.[8]

Besides the beginning of construction on Boulder Dam, 1931 brought two pieces of important legislation for the future of Las Vegas. One new law facilitated the state's divorce business, requiring only six weeks to establish legal residence, the shortest time in the nation. Housing, meals, lawyers' fees, and court costs averaged about $1,500 per spouse and held out the possibility of a substantial economic benefit for communities that could attract those seeking the "six-week cure."[9] The second law made Nevada the only state with "wide-open" gambling. Soon after its passage, city commissioners licensed casinos in downtown Las Vegas. Although cautious in the first couple of years, city commissioners approved licenses for several by the end of the decade—including the Northern Club, Boulder Club, Las Vegas Club, Frontier Club, and the Apache Casino. In the 1940s, the number rapidly increased to include the El Cortez, Monte Carlo, Pioneer Club, and Golden Nugget. However, there was little chance of opening a true resort hotel in the downtown area; there was too little space for a resort with amenities like a large swimming pool, tennis courts, and landscaped grounds that tourists would expect. Tony, Frankie, and Louie Cornero, bootleggers from California, did briefly operate the Meadows, a small nightclub, casino, and hotel just outside town on the Boulder Highway in 1931, but a fire consumed its casino and destroyed their chances of success. Hollywood restaurant owner Bob Brooks opened the Nevada Biltmore on Main Street in 1942. Although it had a pool, attractive bungalows, a Tahitian-themed casino and bar with lush carpeting and leather upholstery, the Biltmore struggled financially because it could not compete with the larger, more luxurious resort hotels out on Highway 91.[10]

Even before William A. Clark, copper baron and U.S. senator from Montana, established Las Vegas, he tantalized investors with the promise that he would build a "magnificent" resort hotel in the new community. Because of the area's "salubrious climate," Clark believed that he could develop a successful hotel and sanitarium for those "suffering with pulmonary and other diseases."[11] The railroad man made little effort to realize that promise, but in the next three decades Las Vegas residents were always hearing about boosters' plans for a "grand tourist hotel."[12] In 1928, for example, an investment group from Cleveland promised to build the Desert Rose Hotel, a resort property with a golf course, tennis courts, swimming pool, and "a casino that will offer all the attractions given by the great continental centers of Monte Carlo and Biarritz," even though casino gambling was illegal at the time in Nevada. To promoters, such a project made great sense because of the rapid development of successful resort hotels in New Mexico and Arizona and particularly in Palm Springs, California, none of which could offer the allure of casinos. Nonetheless, all of the efforts in Las Vegas failed because too few investors were willing to assume the risks, and financial institutions remained hesitant to back hotels associated with casinos.[13] Even the four-year effort in the 1930s to open El Sonador collapsed. Backed by an investment house in San Diego, the project's promotional booklet described a hotel of "modified Spanish architecture," one sure to exude "friendly luxury and careful refinement." However, the group could only raise about half the money needed to start construction. Only when California hotel man Tommy Hull, collaborating with Los Angeles architect Wayne McAllister,

The Flamingo was the first of the plush properties on the Strip; its casino opened
in December 1946 and its hotel in March 1947. *Courtesy University of Nevada,
Las Vegas, University Libraries Special Collections and Archives, Las Vegas News Bureau,
and Caesars Entertainment Corp.*

secured sufficient funding, including a loan from a Las Vegas bank, did the town
see the opening of a resort hotel, the El Rancho Vegas in 1941.[14]

In the seven years following the opening of the El Rancho Vegas, three
more resort hotels opened. Like the El Rancho Vegas, R. E. Griffith and William Moore's Hotel Last Frontier (1942) and Marion Hicks and Clifford Jones's
Thunderbird (1948) both drew upon western themes in their designs and marketing. However, Benjamin "Bugsy" Siegel built the Flamingo, a truly luxurious
hotel-casino in 1946 and 1947, drawing upon the ideas of Billy Wilkerson, publisher of the *Hollywood Reporter* and owner of fashionable Southern California
nightclubs. Siegel's property had spectacular rooms, expensive clothing shops,
a casino decked out in green and pink, and acres of beautiful lawns with palm
trees.[15] The Flamingo became the model for the resort hotels of the following
decade, the type of properties Las Vegas needed to accommodate an extraordinary growth in affluent tourists. As Las Vegas emerged as America's Playground
by the end of the decade, there were fifteen resort hotels, thirty-eight commercial hotels, and 286 motels.[16]

While the benefits of federal jobs were obvious in a community of a little more than 24,000 in 1950, tourism truly drove the Las Vegas economy. In 1952 total tourist spending reached $122 million and increased every year, exceeding $250 million by the end of the decade. In 1952 fewer than 4,600 worked in hotels, motels, casinos, and bars, but three years later that number jumped to more than 8,000. That figure represented more than 20 percent of the jobs in Las Vegas and Clark County, and employment opportunities in the tourism industry continued to grow steadily throughout the decade.[17] As developers built more resort hotels, commercial hotels, and motels, as well as hundreds of new homes, businesses, schools, and a massive convention center, and as the city and county expanded streets and the sewer system through the decade, construction jobs proliferated. Indeed, in 1957 an editorial in the *Las Vegas Review-Journal* predicted that the construction boom would continue over the next two years with projects that would cost about $20 million, a figure that would "take care of a large group of workers for a long time."[18] Not only were jobs plentiful, but they also paid well. In 1954 average household income in Las Vegas was just over $8,000, which, according to the *Las Vegas Sun*, was "53 percent above the national average."[19] Indeed, Nevada, because of the booming Las Vegas economy, enjoyed the nation's highest per capita income.[20] The most lucrative jobs were in the resort hotels. In 1954, for example, total annual payroll of the seven resort hotels alone exceeded $21 million, a figure comparable to the total payroll for all the employees at Nellis Air Force Base and the Nevada Test Site.[21]

Between 1952 and 1958 developers opened the Sahara, Sands, Riviera, Royal Nevada, Dunes, Hacienda, Tropicana, and Stardust on the Strip; the Showboat and Moulin Rouge off the Strip; and the Fremont and Mint downtown.[22] Other than the Riviera and Fremont, the resorts were two- and three-story hotels with one hundred to three hundred rooms. A few like the Sahara and the Dunes, sought to evoke a desert theme. The Sahara had plaster camels outside, and inside were the Congo and Caravan Rooms, along with a Casbar Lounge. Atop the Dunes stood a fiberglass sultan with a flowing blue cape. At the far south end of the Strip, the Hacienda sought a niche as a family-friendly resort, with a go-cart track and huge pool instead of an elegant restaurant with nationally known headliner entertainers, an effort that earned the property the title of "Hayseed Heaven." Similarly, the Showboat, located on the Boulder Highway, sought a local clientele and budget-minded tourists with amenities like a forty-nine-cent breakfast and a bowling alley.

A suite in the Tropicana Hotel, dubbed the "Tiffany of the Strip," which opened in 1957.

Courtesy University of Nevada, Las Vegas, University Libraries Special Collections and Archives, Las Vegas News Bureau, and Tropicana Las Vegas.

The rest, however, hoped to attract well-to-do guests with luxury unexpected in a tourist town. The Tropicana, the most expensive of the new hotels, earned the title of "Tiffany of the Strip." The $15 million Y-shaped hotel-casino featured mahogany panels in the lobby, mosaic tile at the entrance, huge chandeliers throughout, twenty-four acres of lush landscaping, a sixty-foot fountain in front, and guest rooms decorated in four different styles including French Provincial and Italian Renaissance.[23] The local newspapers never tired of singing the praises of the luxurious new hotels. Two years after the Sahara opened, for example, entertainment columnist Ralph Pearl described the atmosphere at the "plush and swanky" property. "The air," he wrote, "is richly scented with expensive cigar smoke, fresh money and Channel No. 5." Everywhere he looked, Pearl claimed that he saw "full length, gaudy minks," and when he left "this Taj Mahalian palace of plenty," he found himself "surrounded by a maze of Caddys and Jaguars cluttering up the parking lot outside."[24]

One might expect such puffery from local columnists, as their newspapers depended heavily upon casino advertising, but similar hyperbole found its way into the columns of many national journalists who visited Las Vegas in the 1950s. *Life, Time, Newsweek, Saturday Evening Post*, and *Holiday* were among the dozens of periodicals that published articles about the "beautifully and tastefully furnished and landscaped" resort hotels.[25] In *Harper's* Dick Pearce told his readers about the hotels' "rich sleekness of modern design that suggests suavity and impermanence" and the "dewy lawns laid on imported soil, and painfully maintained against nature," while in the *Chicago Daily Tribune* Herb Lyon described the "posh" hotels with "elegant, richly adorned, restful guest rooms and suites, a splashy swimming pool, moderate priced dining rooms and finally a fabulous night club."[26] In 1956 John Gunther, who had gained fame for his "Inside" books about locales around the world, published a three-part series on Las Vegas in the widely circulated *American Weekly* Sunday supplement. In it, he discussed the luxurious hotels focusing upon the "magnificent" Sands Hotel. "I know," he wrote, "few hotels in the world that can match it for taste in decoration, impeccable service and pleasant atmosphere."[27] Gladwin Hill, however, waxed most poetic in his *New York Times* article "Klondike in the Desert," which became a favorite among Las Vegas promoters. He claimed that the hotels along the Strip offered "a never-never land of exotic architecture, extravagant vegetation, flamboyant signery and frenetic diversion" that created a unique holiday atmosphere and transformed visitors. "Las Vegas," he argued, "is so unlike where anybody ever came from that hometown tensions and inhibitions fall away like overcoats under the desert sun."[28] In an otherwise critical analysis of Las Vegas in *The Nation*, Julian Halevy agreed with Hill, describing the ability of Las Vegas hotel owners to provide the tourist with a remarkable "escape from reality." Halevy wrote that a visitor encounters "a luxury world . . . of Olympic swimming pools, hanging gardens, waitresses beautiful as movie stars, marble baths and bars a block long, air conditioning, deep carpets, royal buffets and obsequious waiters offering free drinks." Put simply, the hotel owners create an illusion "that we are all rich."[29]

As this approach of offering luxury lured an ever-rising tide of tourists, hotel owners seemed to always be building additional rooms or completing plans for more. By the mid-1950s it was clear to residents that "the Las Vegas vista never remains static."[30] "There is never a moment, on the Strip," Katharine Best and Katharine Hillyer wrote in their delightful 1955 book *Las Vegas: Playtown U.S.A.*, "that facades aren't being lifted, casinos enlarged, cocktail lounges

The Las Vegas Strip, c. 1960, looking north, with the Thunderbird on the lower right and the El Rancho Vegas on the left. *Courtesy University of Nevada, Las Vegas, University Libraries Special Collections and Archives, Manis Photo Collection.*

lengthened, rooms added."[31] The Sahara, for example, added 200 rooms a year after opening, the Flamingo added 92 rooms in 1958, and the Riviera tacked on 120 rooms two years later. In fall 1960 the *Las Vegas Sun* reported, "Along the renowned Las Vegas 'Strip' practically every one of the mammoth resort hotels is engaged in some sort of expansion. These range from a recently-completed 14-story addition at one resort, to new wings of rooms and improved dining and recreation facilities and contemplated golf courses at others."[32]

While most journalists focused upon these glittering resort hotels, for many tourists the "real" Las Vegas was downtown, along Fremont Street, which one Chicago journalist explained offered "little entertainment—just gambling." Still, it was a street that boasted "more neon signs and lights than Times Square in New York."[33] Fremont Street attracted veteran Las Vegas investors and casino managers like William Moore, John Kell Houssels, and Guy McAfee, as well as newer men like John "Jackie" Gaughan, Sam Boyd, and Texas gambler Benny Binion.

Everyone had a favorite downtown casino. For some, it was the Pioneer Club, with the iconic forty-foot Vegas Vic standing on top. Others preferred the

After World War II downtown Las Vegas remained popular with many tourists.
Courtesy University of Nevada, Las Vegas, University Libraries Special Collections and Archives,
Manis Photo Collection.

massive Golden Nugget, which claimed to have the world's largest casino when
it opened in 1946. The Horseshoe Club had many fans because of the philosophy
of owner Benny Binion, who proclaimed, "the way to get rich . . . was to treat
little people like big people." Whatever their level of play, as Binion explained, a
gambler knew what to expect at the Horseshoe: "'good food cheap, good whiskey cheap and good gamble.'" Sam Boyd at the Mint and Jackie Gaughan at the
Boulder Club and Las Vegas Club followed Binion's lead with coupon books and
free meals. While the Strip resort hotels appealed to more affluent gamblers,
men like Binion, Boyd, and Gaughan democratized the gaming experience in
Las Vegas and helped develop the allure of the town.[34]

Las Vegas soon saw the mid-twentieth-century version of a gold rush.
Developers, promoters, and investors from across the country converged on the
desert community with schemes, some truly fantastic, for the next best resort
hotel. But as with most boom town ventures, they were poorly financed, and
most of the plans never materialized. While the promoters came from all across
the country, most were southern Californians with Las Vegas partners. Movie
star Mae West headed a group that had not only drafted plans for a resort hotel

and casino but also had secured the services of local contractor Stanley Harris to build the Diamond Lil across the street from the Flamingo.[35] Other promoters included Charlie Morrison, owner of the fashionable Mocambo nightclub on the Sunset Strip in West Hollywood; Frank J. Trevillian, who owned a hotel in Santa Barbara, California; William Moore, who had made the Hotel Last Frontier a successful Las Vegas hotel for a decade; local builder Lou Davidson; Colonel H. J. Cox, an oil operator from the small town of Cranfills Gap, Texas; and a group of young successful executives from Salt Lake City known as the "uranium wizards of Utah."[36] For many of these ventures, reporters could only learn that there were many unnamed men providing financial backing. For example, the most local journalist Alan Jarlson could uncover in researching plans for a hotel to be called Kismet was that "powerful New York interests" were backing a local developer.[37] The hint in Jarlson's characterization of an organized crime element was more evident in other stories. The diligent Jarlson learned that Max Field, who promised to build a ten-story luxury hotel in 1959, had partnered with "hoodlum Joe Sica" and had been an associate of a suspect in a "gangland killing . . . of Los Angeles bookie king John Whalen."[38] Extraordinary rumors about potential backers for these ventures were common. For example, in 1950 the story surfaced that American Tobacco Company heiress Doris Duke was interested in purchasing land along the Strip for a new hotel.[39]

Some of the proposed hotels had a prosaic vision. In 1952, anticipating that Las Vegas might become a convention city, two groups disclosed plans for convention hotels. One would have 525 rooms with a meeting hall that could seat 1,600, and the other planned 1,000 rooms.[40] Most of the proposed hotels, however, offered fantastic visions of resorts that backers believed would set Las Vegas apart from other tourist destinations. William Moore's Caribbean would have been a ten-story hotel in the "South American Modern style, with great expanses of glass and sun baffles." Automobiles would have arrived under this hoped for "Eighth Wonder of Highway 91" to "discharge passengers below the lobby, to which access will be gained via escalators." The street level would have featured shops and the lobby would have been on the second level. "A lavish Sky Room" would have adorned the roof with a restaurant.[41] Texas oil man H. J. Cox had plans for the Golden West with "a huge dining room, vast swimming pool, wading pool for children, three bars, eight shops and a whopping casino— largest in town."[42] The eight-story, five-hundred-room Kismet—backed by those "powerful New York interests"—was going to be topped by "a penthouse and a sky room," along with "facilities for an entire ice show."[43]

The El Morocco, designed by Morris Lapidus, the architect who designed Miami's Fontainebleau, was going to be a ten-story, 1,000-room hotel with "Moroccan Gardens, and a series of two-story pavilion buildings, featuring rooms with terraces overlooking the gardens and pool," a large convention hall, casino, and nightclub that could seat 1,200.[44] Plans for the "modernistic" Hotel Martinique also included a ten-story structure with 700 rooms. Beyond a 2,500-seat convention hall and large restaurant theater, the hotel was to have an 8-acre patio with "a 150-foot-long swimming pool" and employ 1,000 people.[45] The ten-story Hotel Fabulous would have included "luxury suites" and "individual swimming pools," along with a charter plane service to bring guests from Los Angeles, San Francisco, and New York.[46] The Samuel Gompers would have been the largest of the proposed hotels. Named after the founder of the American Federation of Labor, the hotel's plans called for a fourteen-story building with more than 2,500 rooms and a convention hall that could seat 7,500.[47]

Unlike these gigantic hotel proposals, Charlie Morrison planned a smaller yet elegant hotel. With rumored backing from Greek shipping magnate Aristotle Onassis, Morrison's designer Don Loper described an elegant niche hotel property. With one hundred rooms "constructed in the French Regency décor," the hotel property would present "the appearance of a massive estate." A large marble entrance would lead to a "flying staircase of wrought iron and brass." A rathskeller with wines "displayed behind glass" would be below an intimate restaurant and above it a "miniature ballroom."[48] There were many other proposed hotels with names like the Saratoga, New Horizon, Trade Winds, Continental, International House, Mardi Gras, and Viva Hotel, which architectural historian Stefan Al described as "a triangular sixteen-story hotel with concave sides gradually tapering upward." Its "slanting spire stairs and neon-lined, scalloped balconies accentuated the inverted shape."[49] These fanciful schemes for resort hotels fundamentally foundered because of inadequate financing. With estimated costs ranging as high as $20 million, the promoters simply could not find the backing needed.

Few of the failed schemes surfaced after 1955, the most challenging year for the Las Vegas economy. In January it looked like another banner year for the resort hotels. Gladwin Hill characterized the economic boom "as about as subtle as the Klondike in its heyday." It seemed "you just aren't anybody in Las Vegas these days unless you're building a luxury casino-hotel."[50] Hank Greenspun, publisher of the *Las Vegas Sun*, confident in the continued growth of the community, told his readers that with the addition of more hotels, their city was "slowly evolving from the 'get-rich-quick,' shoddy promotional stage of a boom town's beginning into a stable, reputable community."[51] Developers were completing construction of four new resort hotels, and the owners of a fifth, the Last Frontier, were opening an expanded transformed hotel to be called the New Frontier. Between April 4 and May 23, 1955, the New Frontier, Royal Nevada, Riviera, Moulin Rouge, and Dunes opened with much fanfare.

By June, however, *Life* magazine asked: "Had Las Vegas overextended itself?" The magazine's reporters traveled to America's Playground and found that the new hotels were doing well on the weekends, but "on weekdays they found their rooms unbooked." To emphasize the point, the article included photos of idle croupiers who "dawdled behind their roulette tables" at the Dunes and a nearly empty lobby at the Riviera.[52] The new resorts had to lay off employees, the management at the Sands and Flamingo took over the Dunes and Riviera, and the Royal Nevada and Moulin Rouge closed by the end of the year.[53]

Over the next two years, journalists from across the country continued to question the future of the resort city. They asked: "Las Vegas Bubble . . . about to Bust?" "Was it true that Las Vegas at last was going to the wall? Was the rich vein of sucker-tourist gold running out?"[54] Part of the problem for the newer hotels was that they had attracted a different type of tourist. The established hotels retained a wealthy clientele that liked to wager substantial bankrolls. However, according to *Life*, those opening in 1955 brought in "a new breed of visitor" who "came to enjoy the good quarters, food and shows but . . . not to gamble."[55] More was at play than a changing clientele. As *New York Times* journalist Gilbert Millstein concluded, all the new hotels had been undercapitalized, with their construction costs exceeding estimates "by at least a quarter." Moreover, they had "engaged in a prohibitively costly competition for entertainment." Perhaps most significant, however, was the fact that "they seem to have been run by men experienced in standard hotel operation, but unworldly in the ways of gambling."[56]

Local and state analysts worried about the consequences of the doomed attempts of hotel operators who had tried "to swing multi-million dollar deals on shoestrings." Beside laid-off employees, local contractors suffered financial losses. The five properties that opened in 1955 collectively faced lawsuits of more than a million dollars for unpaid bills owed to "local contractors, material houses, jobbers and retail merchants." The Royal Nevada alone faced sixteen liens totaling nearly $470,000.[57] Some in local government had anticipated what happened with the rapid construction of hotels. In late 1954 Clark County Commissioner George "Bud" Albright told the local press that he worried that Las

Vegas had reached a "saturation point" in the number of tourists coming from Southern California because of the "overloaded two-lane highway" from Los Angeles. As a consequence, developers might be adding too much hotel-room capacity to the resort city. It might be advisable, he argued, to "halt any new construction" of hotels by rejecting applications for gambling and liquor licenses.[58]

Alternatively, Albright suggested that construction of a large convention center might "stabilize the economy of the entire community."[59] Before World War II, civic leaders had developed a modest convention business in Las Vegas, surprisingly attracting a few thousand conventioneers annually to a town with no resort hotels and only the downtown American Legion War Memorial building for meetings.[60] After the war, hotel owners typically could not find enough rooms for the weekend crowds from Southern California but struggled to fill them Sunday through Thursday evenings. With each new resort hotel, the problem worsened. The chamber of commerce had a convention committee with representatives from the downtown hotels, as well as the resort hotels, but aggressive boosters like Jake Kozloff, co-owner of the Hotel Last Frontier, pushed for a convention bureau.[61] The chamber of commerce complied, creating the Las Vegas Convention Bureau in 1953. Chamber veteran Elmo Ellsworth served as the first director with a budget of $35,000. During his four-year tenure, Ellsworth, usually accompanied by representatives from the resort hotels, traveled the country hawking Las Vegas as a great locale for conventions. When he stepped down in June 1957, his bureau claimed that it had brought more than five hundred conventions with 111,000 delegates to Las Vegas. For the chamber's investment of $104,000, the bureau claimed that the delegates had spent almost $10 million in the city.[62]

Richard Tully and Desmond Kelly, Ellsworth's successors, opened offices in Los Angeles, San Francisco, and Chicago, hoping to lure "big chip" conventions of 10,000 or more delegates.[63] However, to bring major conventions to Las Vegas, chamber leaders knew they had to have a large convention center. In summer 1954 veteran hotel man William Moore pitched to the Clark County commissioners the idea of a hall to accommodate up to 10,000 people. The county commissioners, led by George Albright, and the city commissioners cooperated to push through a bond issue to pay for construction of a convention center. Los Angeles architect Adrian Wilson designed a structure that offered almost 130,000 square feet of exhibit space and seating for more than 9,000 delegates.[64] Through 1958 the biggest conventions in Las Vegas had drawn between 500 and 2,500, but the new center a block east of the Strip hotels, looking like a flying saucer, enabled Las Vegas to host the World Congress of Flight with its 5,000 delegates in April 1959. By November there had been five more large conventions, bringing in a total of more than 18,000 delegates. The following year, Leonard Bernstein and the New York Philharmonic drew the first sellout crowd, and a Billy Graham crusade attracted almost 7,000.[65]

Building a mammoth hall was a critical step in attracting large conventions, but Las Vegas faced the challenge of making it easier for delegates to get to the city. The *Las Vegas Review-Journal* noted in 1958, "Delegates to the conventions in session here during the last few weeks, have declared that it is practically impossible to get fast transportation into Las Vegas from their home area."[66] When the decade began, air service came to McCarran Airport, formerly called Alamo Field, south of town. In 1950 four small airlines brought just over seventy thousand passengers to Las Vegas (on sixteen daily flights), but the numbers steadily increased to 440,000 five years later and to just over a million in 1960. Once the near-monopoly that Western Airlines had on the Los Angeles–Las Vegas route ended, major carriers like United and Trans World Airlines began adding flights (more than seventy by 1956) to Las Vegas from New York, Chicago, Minneapolis, Detroit, and Kansas City.[67] In the late 1950s, the Hacienda Hotel leased eight planes to offer inexpensive airfare-hotel packages. By 1960 Hacienda Airlines brought more than one hundred thousand passengers to Las Vegas. To accommodate the expanding number of flights, the Clark County commissioners, drawing upon successful bond issues and federal government subsidies, expanded the airport terminal, added and extended runways and taxiways, improved the control tower and night lighting, and added parking areas. When voters approved a bond issue on March 17, 1960, the airport had the funds needed to expand the runways to accommodate jet planes.[68]

That airlines rapidly eclipsed the Union Pacific Railroad as a way to get to Las Vegas is unsurprising, as passenger trains were steadily losing business across the country. In 1950 trains carried only 4 percent of intercity traffic.[69] The Union Pacific, which had seven other daily trains into Las Vegas, sought to counter that trend in late 1956 when it introduced the City of Las Vegas train. The "all aluminum aeroflyte miracle," with seven coaches, carried up to three hundred passengers daily from Los Angeles. The seventeen-dollar ticket included a free "Chuck Wagon" buffet and a "'Howdy Podner,' Bar-Lounge." Initially quite popular, with fifty-four thousand passengers in its first six months, the City of Las Vegas quickly lost its luster. The Union Pacific cut service to three days a week in 1958 and ended its run two years later.[70]

As late as 1958, buses carried more than three hundred thousand people to and from Las Vegas, but most tourists came in automobiles. John M. Findlay has concluded that "more than 85 percent of the visitors to Nevada traveled by car, and almost half of all cars headed for Las Vegas came from Southern California."[71] The journey along the two-lane road of 290 miles from Los Angeles took most motorists more than six hours to navigate. However, the 1956 Interstate Highway Act provided federal funding for 90 percent of the cost of constructing a much-improved highway. Once completed a decade later, Interstate 15, as Eugene Moehring has explained, provided a "smooth, wide road, with gentle banked curves and a center median for added safety," allowing drivers to it make to Las Vegas in less than five hours.[72]

In addition to their concerns with inadequately financed resort hotels, their drive to build a large convention center, and the pressing need to improve the transportation infrastructure, local observers also worried about the growing challenge posed by casino gambling in Cuba. When Fulgencio Batista took over the government of the island nation in 1952, he welcomed the development of casinos to expand the tourist trade to Cuba. The island was already a big draw for American tourists. As Robert Lacey described the island in the 1950s, "Cuba had the most accommodating girls, the finest cigars, the strongest daiquiris, Errol Flynn most winters, and Ernest Hemingway all year round."[73] Several elegant casinos opened between 1952 and 1958, adding to the allure of the island playground. To bring order to a corrupt and nearly chaotic casino scene, Batista paid noted gangster Meyer Lansky, who had developed a mastery of profitable casino operations with properties in southern Florida, Las Vegas, and Saratoga, New York, an annual retainer of twenty-five thousand dollars to reform gambling in Havana. Lansky not only succeeded in improving the image of the fairness of the casinos but also, through front men, opened his own casinos and hotels.[74] In 1955 Lansky added a casino and cabaret to the storied waterfront Hotel Nacional, bringing in the Desert Inn's Wilbur Clark as director and his brother Jake as casino manager. Two years later, Lansky opened the 440-room Havana Riviera. He and other men from organized crime, notably Tampa's Santo Trafficante Jr., drew upon the largesse of the Batista regime that granted tax exemptions to "all new hotels, motels, and similar establishments providing tourist accommodations" and the island's Bank for Economic and Social Development, which offered up to half of the capital needed to construct new hotels.[75] By the late 1950s, tourists could select from Lansky's hotels and many others including the Tropicana, Hotel Capri, Sans Souci, Comodoro,

Montmartre, Deauville, and the Hilton, the largest of the hotels with more than six hundred rooms. Most of the properties brought in popular headliners, many of whom also performed in Las Vegas. "In 1956 alone," Philip D. Beidler has written, "headliners were Dorothy Lamour, Maurice Chevalier, Billy Daniels, Nat King Cole, Eartha Kitt, Edith Piaf, Ilona Massey, Cab Calloway, Dorothy Dandridge, Tony Martin, Tony Bennett, Ginny Simms, Connee Boswell, and Vincent Escurdero."[76] Johnny Mathis, who performed at the Sans Souci, fondly recalled Havana as an exciting, exotic locale with large and accommodating crowds, beautiful showgirls, no concerns with segregation as long as he stayed in the entertainment corridor, and the opportunity to sing in an open-air venue.[77]

Delta and Pan-American Airlines had regularly scheduled flights to Havana, and several steamship lines from New Orleans, Miami, and New York brought an increasing wave of tourists. Their numbers grew every year, culminating with the 1957–58 season, which proved to be "the most popular ever."[78] A March 1958 *Life* magazine article, loaded with photographs, described the Havana casinos that "were collecting American tourist dollars as fast as the roulette wheels could spin and the craps dealers could rake in the chips."[79]

Shortly after the publication of the *Life* article the Nevada State Tax Commission ordered that all who held a gaming license in Nevada had to give up their operations in Cuba. Ostensibly, the commissioners worried that racketeers in Cuba would contaminate gambling in Nevada. However, the real concern was the rapidly increasing economic threat Havana's casinos posed for those in Nevada. As a consequence, some of Las Vegas's leading gambling men, including Moe Dalitz, Tom McGinty, Morris Kleinman, Wilbur Clark (all associated with the Desert Inn), and Edward Levinson, withdrew from Cuba.[80]

Other, much more mundane challenges vexed Las Vegas civic leaders during the decade of extraordinary growth. The rising number of tourists and the rapid increase in population put an enormous strain on the water supply. From the town's founding, the Las Vegas Land and Water Company, a subsidiary of the Union Pacific Railroad, had controlled the city's water. In the subsequent decades, complaints about inadequate supplies were common, but in the early 1950s the community faced a crisis. Demand for water reached sixteen million gallons a day by summer 1951, a figure the existing wells could not provide. Officials with Union Pacific wanted to ban access to any new subdivisions, arguing that it had "become obvious from engineering reports that the artesian supply simply is not adequate for further development of Las Vegas."[81] After heavy criticism from city leaders, the Nevada Public Service Commission rejected the company's request, leaving Mayor Charles Duncan Baker with little option other than to issue a proclamation limiting lawn sprinkling each summer.[82] The ultimate solution lay in gaining access to the water in Lake Mead. Voters overwhelmingly passed a bond issue in late 1953 to provide the funds to purchase the water system from the Union Pacific. The Las Vegas Valley Water District then reached an agreement with Basic Management in nearby Henderson to construct a pipeline from its factory to the city system. This enabled the city to draw upon Lake Mead for the peak demand summer months.[83]

Providing an adequate educational system was also a challenge. The number of students increased 20 percent or more annually, leading to half-day sessions and a chronic shortage of teachers, textbooks, and elementary school playground equipment, as well as deteriorating buildings. In a series of articles on education woes, one local journalist described some teachers working in "rooms lighted by bare bulbs hanging on fly-specked cords and dodging falling plaster, waiting for a building to collapse."[84] Similar challenges in other parts of the state prompted Governor Charles Russell to call a special session of the legislature, which appropriated twenty-five thousand dollars in 1954 to retain a team from the George Peabody College for Teachers in Nashville, Tennessee, to make recommendations for reform. The Peabody Report urged consolidation of the nearly two hundred school districts into one per county and improvements in school facilities and teacher salaries. In response, state officials consolidated districts, and state legislators passed a 2 percent sales tax devoted to education. This helped, as did additional bond issues, but continued rapid population growth, as school superintendent R. Guild Gray explained in 1956, meant that it would take ever more revenue "to take care of the future needs."[85]

Beyond working to meet the needs of elementary and secondary school students, Las Vegas community leaders sought to establish a college in the community. In addition to high school graduates who did not want to travel the 450 miles to the University of Nevada in Reno for their classes, many Las Vegas teachers wanted local access to graduate courses, and men based at nearby Nellis Air Force Base wanted the opportunity to attend college classes. Initially, this interest led the Reno campus to offer a few courses at the high school in 1951, but through a combination of the cooperation of administrators in Reno, increased state appropriations, and local fund-raising, the Southern Regional Division of the university opened in Las Vegas in 1957 with one building on Maryland Parkway. About three hundred students attended classes in Frazier Hall, but during the next decade, the campus added eight buildings, and enrollment reached almost four thousand.[86]

During most years in the 1950s, law enforcement in Las Vegas and Clark County struggled with increasing crime rates. In 1951 stories of burglaries, armed robberies, auto thefts, rapes, and murders led city commissioners to worry about an "increasing crime wave," and it progressively got worse. According to Sheriff Glen Jones in 1953, the crime rates in almost all categories increased by 15 percent. He was most concerned with "crimes of violence," which he noted were "increasing at an alarming rate."[87] Between 1954 and 1955, "criminal complaints of all kinds almost doubled," and murder cases increased from six to thirteen.[88] While underpaid policemen and "a lack of cooperation between the city police and sheriff's department" complicated matters, a common explanation developed for the growing crime problem. As sheriff Captain Bill Payton argued in late 1953, "transient criminals who swarm into this desert resort area from all over the United States, lured by gambling and entertainment," posed "the greatest threat to the local population."[89]

The burden of addressing this multitude of challenges largely fell on the shoulders of the Clark County commissioners and Las Vegas city commissioners, two governing bodies that seldom agreed. The prospect of consolidation of the two into a metropolitan district was the chief issue dividing them. From the mid-1940s, city officials had fought a vain battle to annex the rapidly growing prosperous Strip and surrounding properties. When city commissioners suspended sewer service to the hotels, county commissioners not only successfully pushed a bond issue to create their own sewer district, but they also established a fire department. By the mid-1950s, the county controlled McCarran Airport and the Las Vegas Valley Water District.[90] A few leaders were able to foster some cooperation, as when county commissioner George Albright gained the cooperation of city commissioners to push for approval of a bond issue for construction of a convention center. As mayor between 1951 and 1959, Charles Duncan Baker was the most effective local leader. He had formerly served as city surveyor and city engineer, a term in the state assembly, and two terms in the state senate. As an engineer, Baker had focused on infrastructure improvements in the city, so Las Vegas had an expanded and improved street network, an expanded sewer system, and a new fire alarm system at the end of his two terms.[91]

However, Pat McCarran, Nevada's senior U.S. senator, emerged as the most significant political figure for Las Vegas in the 1950s. The four-term senator had become a major power broker in the nation's capital, chairing the Senate

Judiciary Committee and Internal Security Subcommittee, and he headed the state's political machine.[92] In summer 1951 the U.S. House of Representatives began debate on a bill to impose a 10 percent tax on the gross receipts of gambling. From the moment of the bill's introduction, all in Nevada understood its significance, particularly McCarran, a man known for being a great champion for his constituents. In July McCarran wrote to Reno newspaperman and political associate Joseph McDonald: "The City of Las Vegas has come from a wide spot in the road to a community of 40,000 or more. It was accomplished by making the State of Nevada a playground to which the world was invited, and that playground has as its base gambling in all its forms." If the House and Senate approved the tax, essentially eliminating the casino's edge on all table and machine games, legal gambling in the state would end, and that would do more than dramatically reduce state revenue. While it wasn't "a very laudable position . . . to defend gambling," McCarran feared an even greater consequence. The "gleaming gulch of Las Vegas," he believed, would become "a glowing symbol of funereal distress."[93] When he testified against the bill, McCarran predicted

Nevada's influential senior senator Pat McCarran. *Courtesy University of Nevada, Las Vegas, University Libraries Special Collections and Archives, Elberts Photo Collection.*

doom for his state, claiming that "the finances of the entire state would be in jeopardy" and that nearly half the population would leave.[94] He also lobbied heavily throughout the summer, calling in all his favors. As Hank Greenspun explained to his readers, the senator "argued, cajoled, pleaded and traded" until he eliminated the tax from everything except the sports and race books, thus saving most of legal gaming for the state.[95]

This was not the last of the efforts from the nation's capital to limit legal gambling in the state. Nevada congressman Cliff Young took up McCarran's banner upon the senator's death in September 1954 and was able to block efforts by New York representative Kenneth Keating to cripple gambling in Nevada. Keating's first bill would have made "it illegal to transport money across state lines for gambling purposes," and the second would have outlawed "cashing of checks in interstate commerce for the purpose of gambling" and "interstate advertising of gambling."[96] While there were other occasional rumblings of attempts to limit gambling in Nevada, McCarran and then Young successfully protected one of the key elements in the city becoming America's Playground.

With the backing of local and state political leaders, Las Vegas had an opportunity for continued explosive growth in the 1950s. However, it fell to the city's promoters to determine the best way to present their city to a nation eager to travel. They had to make a compelling case that their community had the most appealing attractions. In other words, they had to determine the best way to sell Las Vegas.

Two
Selling Vegas

In summer 1953 Stan Irwin, entertainment director and publicist for the Sahara Hotel, ordered a new billboard to be placed at the intersection of Sunset Boulevard and Doheny Drive in Hollywood. Because southern Californians made up the bulk of the resort hotel business along the Strip, Irwin wanted to lure them to the Sahara and its new headliner, Red Skelton. The forty-year-old comic, who had starred in movies and on radio and television, was making his first nightclub appearance. To build interest and excitement for Skelton's show, Irwin ordered an expensive and unique billboard from Foster and Kleiser, California's leading billboard designers. Larry Sloan, one of Irwin's associates, promised a local columnist that the billboard would be "bigger than the atom bomb."[1] It included not only the date of Skelton's opening with singer Anna Maria Alberghetti but also a miniature version of the hotel's Garden of Allah swimming pool and eight bikini-clad "bathing beauties." Skelton even dropped by one day and leaped into the pool fully clothed. This billboard, which entertainment columnist Hy Gardner dubbed "the most startling billboard in the world," accomplished what Irwin sought. Thousands daily noticed the sign as traffic snarls developed on Sunset and Doheny. As one columnist claimed, "8 of 10 motorists gape at the sign and every third driver does a double take."[2] The billboard undoubtedly prompted many to make the trek to Las Vegas, where they helped fill the Congo Room. The opening night crowd for the Skelton show was so large that the Sahara had to turn away 650 disappointed fans. Because of the great publicity and Skelton's performances, characterized by entertainment columnist Hedda Hopper as a "smash hit," the Sahara enjoyed its "biggest business" ever.[3]

Irwin's successful promotional effort was just one example of hundreds scored by the publicists of the Las Vegas resort hotels. These men and women, working with the managers and owners of the hotels, the talented photographers and writers of the Las Vegas News Bureau, the chamber of commerce, and self-appointed promotional ambassadors made Las Vegas a "must-see" tourist destination in the 1950s. In making the nation aware of Las Vegas they collectively pitched their town as a "Fun in the Sun" resort mecca to counter the perception that the community was a hotbed of vice. Their promotions, advertising, and skillful exploitation of radio, television, and movies created what Don Payne, who served a quarter-century as manager of the news bureau, called the "halcyon days of publicity in Las Vegas."[4]

As a first step, the town's promoters had to make more Americans aware of Las Vegas, but they also had to address the negative views that existed about their community. The scale of the challenge was clear from a report provided to chamber of commerce leaders in the late 1940s. Led by Maxwell Kelch, the chamber had hired a consulting firm to survey the perceptions of Las Vegas in San Francisco, a potentially critical market for tourists. Consultants, Ltd., sent an employee to talk with travel agents in seven "leading hotels" and in eleven travel agencies to determine what potential tourists could learn about Las Vegas. Most of the travel agents either did not know much about Las Vegas or recommended other tourist destinations in the Southwest. Those who did suggest that Las Vegas might be worth a one-night stay advised that it offered little more than gambling "to appeal to the sporty crowd" and "obnoxious people from Los Angeles or the East." Moreover, visitors should be aware that they likely would encounter "a lot of loose women."[5]

Through advertisements in newspapers and magazines, on billboards, and in brochures, the chamber of commerce had worked diligently since the mid-1930s to portray Las Vegas as a tourist town that offered the hospitality one would hope to encounter in a friendly, laid-back Old West community near numerous scenic attractions. However, the organization struggled against a narrative developed by scores of national magazines and newspapers.[6] Journalists from the major media markets enjoyed regaling their readers with graphic descriptions of the town's historic embrace of vice. In 1940, for example, *Look* magazine, in a five-page article with fifteen photos entitled "Wild, Woolly and Wide-Open," characterized Las Vegas as a community that had become the "American Gomorrah" with its nineteen casinos and legal prostitution. Readers encountered a "hell-raising" town where sin was "a civic virtue."[7] Seven years later a seven-page article in *Life* argued that "the taproots of Las Vegas' prosperity" were "legal gambling, all-night drinking, two-minute marriages and six-week divorce."[8] In 1948 Richard Joseph labeled the town in *Argosy* magazine as a "Bargain-Basement Monte Carlo," arguing that it was "probably the crap-shootingest, hard-drinkingest, and high-livingest town in these United States since San Francisco's Barbary Coast shut up shop toward the end of the last century."[9]

In response to such depictions, the chamber of commerce, in just four years in the mid- to late 1940s, hired four publicity and advertising firms to assist in the promotion of Las Vegas. Among Ask Mr. Foster, the J. Walter Thompson Company, Steve Hannagan and Associates, and West-Marquis Advertising, the latter two were most helpful.[10] Steve Hannagan, who had successfully promoted Miami Beach and the Union Pacific ski resort in Sun Valley, Idaho, had the Las Vegas contract for a little more than sixteen months in 1948 and 1949. However, he established an effective approach to publicity. Hannagan created a "news" organization called the Desert Sea News Bureau with a staff of three writers and three photographers whose mission was to saturate the country with stories and photos with a Las Vegas dateline. The staff assisted visiting journalists, planted stories in major newspapers and magazines, and sent packets of photos and stories to travel editors. Jack West of West-Marquis handled advertising for Las Vegas. Although he placed ads in some national-circulation travel magazines like *Holiday*, he did not follow Hannagan's model of pushing a nationwide publicity campaign; instead, West focused on placing ads in Southern California newspapers, commercials on Los Angeles radio and television stations, billboards along California and Arizona highways, and widely distributed brochures. In the era before jet passenger planes, West believed it best to target tourists who would not have to spend much to get to Las Vegas. Indeed, West and Maxwell Kelch developed a marketing strategy that prevailed throughout the 1950s. They focused on attracting "visitors from the most logical potential markets" using "mass marketing in Southern California," developing a "selective regional market," a "highly selective national market," and a "highly selective market on all the highways leading to Las Vegas."[11]

Beyond the sustained effort to make more Americans familiar with Las Vegas, Hannagan, West, and the chamber of commerce understood that they needed to frame a clear message, one that branded their town as something other than a locale awash in sin.[12] When he got the publicity contract in spring 1948, Steve Hannagan explained to the chamber leaders that it was critical to counter the "bad news" about Las Vegas in the national press. The essential first step was to "avoid advertising the obvious . . . gambling." Americans already associated the town with gaming, and it need not be "flaunted." Instead, Hannagan emphasized that his staff would focus upon the "natural beauties" surrounding Las Vegas—Hoover Dam (known until the year before as the Boulder Dam), Lake Mead, Death Valley, and the canyon lands. Five months later, Neil Regan, the man Hannagan selected to head the Desert Sea News Bureau, clarified their approach. Evidently reacting to some concerns voiced by casino owners, Regan explained that his staff would not "detract from the gambling business which they realized was the major industry." Instead, they would focus "on the other facilities in addition to gambling, to round out an effective overall program bringing tourists into the area."[13] The success of this approach was evident in an article by Reuters news service correspondent Harold Heffernan. He quoted a "city official" who had quickly and fully embraced the Hannagan line. The man explained, "The gambling is purely secondary here. We have found many things far more substantial to sell the Hollywood crowd and the tourists who come to see us from the east. We have the most beautiful national parks. Our climate is agreeable and healthful at all times."[14] As the staff of the Desert Sea News Bureau, soon to be named the Las Vegas News Bureau, successfully planted such stories about area attractions in *Life*, *Look*, *New York Times*, *Los Angeles Times*, *San Diego Union*, and *Dallas Morning News*, Jack West added to Hannagan's message in his advertising. Retaining the prewar claim of Las Vegas as a "Last Frontier Town," West used the image of a "genial cowboy, with his thumb cocked in the air" pointing to Las Vegas, a figure he named Vegas Vic. On billboards and in brochures and magazine ads, Vic invited visitors to have "Fun in the Sun." Besides Hoover Dam and all the natural beauty in the area, Vegas Vic, West believed, would confirm the image of Las Vegas as a locale of relaxing western hospitality.[15]

Beyond planting stories in periodicals, the news bureau staff aggressively pursued a campaign focused on "hometowners, cheesecake, and stars." Photographers Don English and Joe Buck daily dropped by the resort hotel swimming pools hoping to capture images of ordinary folks having a good time. With the tourists' permission, the photographers would snap a photo, making sure to capture the name of the hotel in the background, and send it to the visitors' hometown newspaper. Describing the city's promotional approach nearly five decades later, English explained that they used these "hometown" photographs to show readers of local newspapers that Las Vegas really was not a sinful place but a healthy family resort town.[16]

Counterintuitively, English and his colleagues also used photos of scantily clad women, which they called "cheesecake," to promote Las Vegas. While these did nothing to reinforce the notion of a "family friendly" destination, the cheesecake photos, the news bureau photographers quickly learned, were an almost surefire way to get Las Vegas dateline images printed in newspapers. As Al Guzman, who became a publicist at the Desert Inn in the 1960s, argued, "A pretty girl will get an editor's attention." Once you have his eye, an editor might publish the photo, and "you've got some free publicity."[17] So English and his colleagues would use virtually any excuse, such as recognizing the Fourth of July or New Year's Day or the start of Daylight Saving Time, to send out cheesecake photos.[18]

English later regretted that sexist approach, but it was not surprising given the times. After all, hotel developers in the 1950s made extraordinary efforts to create a casino resort experience for men that featured a range of sexual possibilities. All the Strip hotels offered a line of attractive dancers, many of whom performed topless by the late 1950s. They further tantalized patrons by often requiring the dancers to sit at the bar or in the lounge between and after shows. Many clubs and casinos featured strippers in their showrooms. The nation's leading strippers—Sally Rand, Tempest Storm, Candy Barr, and Lili St. Cyr—performed in Las Vegas in the 1950s. Beyond the dancers, young women working as cocktail waitresses, shills, and cigarette girls in alluring attire could be found throughout the casino.

For those who had yet to visit Las Vegas, there were plenty of images of its attractive women in the nation's popular culture. Mainstream magazines like the *Saturday Evening Post* and *Life*, fan magazines like *Screen Stories*, and male pulp magazines routinely used photos of scantily clad women at hotel swimming pools and references to attractive available females. Movies of the 1950s depicted beautiful women dancing, lounging poolside, or sitting in the casinos. Novelists often luridly depicted provocative women in the casinos wearing dresses "that left little to the imagination."[19] It is thus no surprise that the news bureau and hotel publicists drew upon these images in their advertising copy, promotional material, and publicity gimmicks.

The news bureau staff also exploited the presence of the many celebrities in Las Vegas for show openings, weddings, or movie premieres. When English playwright and cabaret singer Noël Coward opened at the Desert Inn in 1955, the Painted Desert showroom was awash with recording artists and movie stars including Rosemary Clooney, Judy Garland, Frank Sinatra, Lauren Bacall, and Humphrey Bogart. It was a great opportunity for dozens of news bureau photos and newsreel film. Similarly, beyond Dan Dailey and Cyd Charisse, a host of stars including Jimmy Durante, Peter Lorre, Fred MacMurray, Peggy Lee, and Groucho Marx were on hand for the world premiere of *Meet Me in Las Vegas* in 1956. While none could top the publicity surrounding the Rita Hayworth–Dick Haymes wedding in 1953, news bureau photographers were on hand for the weddings of Kirk Douglas and Anne Buydens in 1954, Joan Crawford and Alfred N. Steele in 1955, and Paul Newman and Joanne Woodward in 1958. By saturating the nation with photos of celebrities, according to Joe Buck, the news bureau sought to "create the belief that if you came here you might be able to rub elbows with the movie stars."[20]

This was the promotional context in which the hotel publicists worked in the 1950s. The resort hotels attracted dozens of talented men and women to handle promotion during the decade. Many of them had degrees or had pursued a course of study in advertising, marketing, or journalism. Some had been entertainment columnists, others had worked in television or radio, some had been publicists for or managed hotels in other cities, others had operated their own public relations firms or run newspapers, and a few had worked for major newspapers in New York or in Southern California or for Hollywood movie companies. The career of Lee Fisher, who became publicist at the Dunes, illustrates their varied backgrounds. Fisher had been a press agent for RKO Pictures, had run both an advertising firm and a weekly Ohio newspaper, had been a campaign manager for Cliff Young, who failed to defeat incumbent Alan Bible in the 1956 Senate race in Nevada, and had written a column for the *Las Vegas Sun*.[21] Regardless of their background, publicists, particularly those who also served as entertainment directors, faced long days and nights in the frenetic buildup of the hotel business in 1950s Las Vegas. In a *Las Vegas Sun* story, for example, readers learned about the tasks that Vi Taylor, publicist at the New Frontier, faced in the first two and a half months in her position: "An estimated 100,000 words have rolled off her typewriter concerning the fabulous New Frontier Hotel, embracing stories, captioned art, radio and TV copy, fact sheets, biographies, promotional tie-in servicing throughout the country, column plants, etc." Beyond all the writing, her telephone rang "incessantly," and she had to train "new girls" in her office staff.[22]

In the increasingly competitive hotel market, owners or managers of the more established properties were particularly demanding bosses, always wanting more done in the face of the opening of new hotels. Jack Entratter, the most successful of the Strip's impresarios, expected much from his longtime publicist Al Freeman. It is clear in a 1957 memo from Freeman to his boss that Entratter believed that his publicist's efforts were falling short. Freeman wrote, "I agree with you about stepping up the pace on publicity." He assured Entratter that he would not "lay down on the job" because he did not want "to be shown up by the good press agents coming in town with the new hotels."[23] The work pace, extraordinary pressure, and better job offers often led to short tenures among publicists. Ruth Brady, who worked briefly at the Desert Inn, had worked formerly at the El Rancho Vegas, Hotel Last Frontier, and Flamingo.[24] Harvey Diederich, who left a publicist job at Sun Valley, Idaho, in 1952 to work at the Hotel Last Frontier, moved on to publicize Nassau in the Bahamas, then, after a short stop with a New York City firm, returned to Las Vegas to promote the Hacienda, Tropicana, and Sahara, all by 1959.[25] Herb McDonald, who started his career promoting acts for Music Corporation of America, was publicist for the El Rancho Vegas, Club Bingo, the Last Frontier, and Sahara between 1946 and 1960. He even had a three-year stint as the managing director of the Las Vegas Chamber of Commerce.[26]

The most successful of the publicists—Stan Irwin, Harvey Diederich, Herb McDonald, Al Freeman, and Eugene Murphy—were good writers, but they also knew how to cultivate friendships with syndicated columnists and journalists with the wire services and then exploit those connections. Diederich, for example, recalled becoming "close and friendly" not only "with the Los Angeles print media" but also with United Press, International News Service, and Associated Press. He would meet with them and persuade them to come to Las Vegas and "of course, wherever they went," they got free rooms and meals.[27] Al Freeman, at the Sands from its opening in 1952 until his death twenty years later, likewise courted columnists, both those who were syndicated and those who wrote only for their local papers. Freeman almost always provided free rooms at the Sands for journalists or at the reduced "press rate." Knowing about this practice in Las Vegas, some columnists even offered a quid pro quo, promising "page one mileage" in return for a room. Freeman, like other publicists, also provided press releases that some columnists under deadlines willingly printed verbatim.[28] Jim Seagrave, who arrived in Las Vegas in 1961 as a journalist for the *Las Vegas Review-Journal*, quickly learned the value of this successful courtship of columnists when he became a publicist. Seagrave discovered that when they needed coverage of a headliner's opening or a major event at their hotel, publicists like Freeman, Diederich, Murphy, and McDonald "could pick up a phone and have Walter Winchell out here on the next plane. They could have Leonard Lyons out here on the next plane. They could have Earl Wilson and Jim Bacon[,] just to cite a handful of maybe a universe of fifty journalists who were syndicated."[29]

Identifying and attracting big gamblers was another key task for publicists. As Lee Fisher at the Dunes reported in 1961, "All selling approaches will reflect the important objective of attracting better monied people rated as good casino customers."[30] At the Sands, Al Freeman aggressively pursued a wealthy clientele in Texas and California. For example, he drew upon chamber of commerce reports on Bakersfield, California, and determined that the city of 150,000, home to a thriving oil industry, offered two potential markets: a "class market" and a "public market." The former included more than 1,100 members of two country clubs, about 1,000 businessmen, and more than 2,000 "large farm owners." Most of the rest of the population, the "public market," however, were "workers in the semi-skilled and laborer class, and thus a lower income class." His analysis of the potential of the community encouraged him to push "Weekender" packages of inexpensive airfare and rooms to bring twenty-eight "substantial business prospects" at a time to the Sands. Freeman's analysis revealed the Sands' overall approach. While the hotel continued to buy advertising on radio and television and in newspapers to attract the "public market," management, through Freeman, worked diligently to attract ever more gamblers from the "class market."[31]

Publicists also understood the value of attention-grabbing stunts in creating Las Vegas dateline stories. Stan Irwin, who pulled off the successful Sahara billboard stunt, had earlier captured attention for the new Sahara hotel when he hired Karl Carsony. One of three brothers who made up the Carsony Brothers acrobatic team, a popular backup act on the nightclub circuit, Karl agreed to perform a one-arm handstand first with his finger in a wine bottle and then on a cane on top of the fifty-foot Sahara sign, all while the wind was blowing furiously. Of course, Irwin had alerted photographers and newsreel cameramen, all of whom captured the stunt atop the name of the hotel.[32] Harvey Diederich, while working at the Hacienda in 1956, came up with a gimmick to promote its new lighted golf course. Diederich had an attractive showgirl in the slightest of negligees pose for a photo at night swinging a club on the first tee of the course with the name of the hotel in the background. The caption read, "Night-Tee-Time."[33] Believing that successful publicity often revolved around entertainers, Diederich developed a variety of stunts to get their photos, along with his hotel's name, published across the nation. In 1954, when he learned that actress Marilyn Maxwell planned to bring a tiger named Britches onstage during her finale at the Last Frontier, Diederich knew he had rich possibilities for publicity. He alerted *Life* magazine, which published a two-page story with seven photos about what turned into a fiasco for Maxwell but a gold mine for the publicist. The two-hundred-pound animal was supposed to sit beside her during her last song, but the tiger's handlers had given it sixteen pounds of meat before it went on stage, and under the hot lights, it just lay there with a full stomach despite

Maxwell's tugging on its collar. Diederich thought it would be a good idea the following day to pose Maxwell in the hotel's swimming pool with Britches. As photographers snapped away and a newsreel cameraman caught the action, the tiger panicked and in escaping the pool scratched Maxwell's leg. All of this appeared not just in *Life* but in newspapers across the country, and the copy invariably identified the Hotel Last Frontier as the locale for all the action.[34] When singer Abbe Lane was appearing at the Last Frontier with her husband, bandleader Xavier Cugat, the rumor spread that she took baths in coffee to darken her complexion. Diederich swiftly took advantage and persuaded Lane to do just that with the press in attendance.[35]

As good as Irwin, Diederich, and the others were at producing successful stunts, almost all Al Freeman's contemporaries agreed that he, as the Sands Hotel publicist, was the best. Dick Odessky called him "the uncrowned king of Las Vegas publicists," and Bill Willard concluded that he was "the big daddy of all Las Vegas Strip publicists."[36] His two best stunts drew extraordinary attention for the Sands Hotel. In summer 1953 Jack Entratter signed crooner Dick Haymes to perform for two weeks at the Sands. According to *Billboard* magazine, Entratter made the decision not because he thought Haymes would necessarily be a great draw; instead, the Sands impresario believed that Rita Hayworth would be at the Sands during Haymes's run and "would be a plus box office attraction."[37] One of the most popular film stars of the 1940s and 1950s, Hayworth had divorced Prince Aly Khan in 1951. Two years later, she had begun a very public affair with Haymes before he divorced his third wife Nora Eddington. Shortly after her arrival to be with Haymes, Hayworth had become "the object of reams of newsprint and news photos with her Las Vegas sojourn being televised for CBS, and with a number of fan magazines flying in writers and cameramen, this town," columnist Alan Jarlson predicted, "will be getting plenty of copy."[38]

Hours after a Las Vegas judge granted Haymes a divorce, he and Hayworth married in the Gold Room at the Sands on September 24. Al Freeman choreographed it all, including photos of Haymes right after the judge granted the divorce decree, his walk with Hayworth to the license bureau, and their wedding the following morning with only ten guests but almost thirty photographers and reporters.[39] The flood of publicity that resulted gave the Sands, which had opened only nine months earlier, remarkable visibility. The *Time* magazine article noted the Sands six times, the *Life* magazine article included a photo of Freeman standing next to the cake the hotel provided for the wedding with "The

Sands" printed across the top in big letters, and many newspapers, including the *Los Angeles Times*, put the story on the front page.[40] According to syndicated columnist Erskine Johnson, the wedding was a stunning promotional event. "The Sands Hotel," he wrote, "thanks to Rita, racked up more publicity than any of her expensive movies."[41] The lavishly covered nuptials also elevated Freeman's stature in the field of promotion. He was in three of the *Life* magazine photos and one in *Time*, and the reporter who crafted the latter article wrote, "Never in Hollywood history had there been such a sample of matrimony-by-press agent." Indeed, after the short wedding ceremony and lunch that followed, the assembled journalists raised a glass to toast the Sands publicist.[42]

Freeman also came up with the most memorable image of Las Vegas in the 1950s. Ironically, given the collective effort to avoid using gambling in the promotion of the city, Freeman's iconic stunt photo was the floating craps game. In 1954, inspired by the running gag of portable craps tables in the popular musical *Guys and Dolls*, Freeman had three table games, including a craps table, placed in the Sands Hotel swimming pool, along with three slot machines at the edge of the pool. Las Vegas News Bureau photographers took photos and filmed the action. The most often used photo focused on employees in swimsuits surrounding the craps table in the foreground, and in the background one sees the Sands marquee. Because of the global exposure of this iconic photo, it became, in the words of Don Payne, "a signature photo for Las Vegas" in the 1950s.[43]

While hotel publicists usually worked in the background; that was not true of two self-appointed "ambassadors" for Las Vegas. Abe Schiller and Wilbur Clark embraced serving as the face and voice of their growing resort town, and both thoroughly enjoyed the national stature their efforts brought them. Born in Detroit in 1904, Schiller, according to publicist Dick Odessky, "grew up as a hustler," a young man who "caught the eye of some underworld bosses." Schiller became a "booking agent" and talent scout before serving in World War II. When hostilities concluded, Schiller moved to Las Vegas, where he worked at the El Rancho Vegas for Sanford Adler, and Schiller followed Adler when he purchased the Flamingo in 1947. Schiller had a number of titles while working at the Flamingo through the 1950s—publicist, entertainment director, and vice president. However, he fundamentally was a greeter of guests to the hotel, particularly celebrities, whom he invited to the Flamingo and then alerted the press of their impending arrival. An avid sportsman, Schiller often took celebrities fishing, with cameramen in tow, on the Flamingo's lavish boat on Lake Mead.[44]

In a quest for a distinct, readily recognized identity and in deference to Las

Floating craps table in the Sands Hotel pool, 1954—an iconic photo of the resort town.
Courtesy University of Nevada, Las Vegas, University Libraries Special Collections and Archives,
Sands Hotel Collection, Las Vegas News Bureau, and Sands Corp.

Vegas promoters' longtime effort to persuade tourists that they were visiting a "last frontier" town, Schiller decided to dress as a cowboy. In doing so, he followed the example of Elmo Ellsworth, who, when he headed the Chamber of Commerce Visitors Bureau, would often welcome arrivals at McCarran Airport wearing a Stetson hat and western shirt. Schiller began wearing gaudy western outfits when invited to be grand marshal of the Calgary Stampede in

1955 and continued to do so the rest of his career. By 1960 Schiller, according to one report, had an estimated "$6,000 worth of sequined shirts, 30 of them, 14 brilliant hats and 25 pairs of boots, plus a western Tuxedo."[45]

Over time, Schiller became more than a flack for the Flamingo. He became the unofficial goodwill ambassador for the town. Columnists could always count on Schiller for a great quote. For example, Leonard Lyons wrote, "A noted New Yorker asked him, 'Is it possible to go to Las Vegas and not gamble?' According to Lyons, Schiller responded, 'Does anybody ever go to a burlesque show just to listen to the music?'"[46] But Schiller most liked to take his message on the road. He traveled frequently to the western states and occasionally to the Midwest to speak before civic organizations. He most enjoyed riding in parades, whether it was the inaugural parade for Dwight Eisenhower, the Tournament of Roses Parade in Pasadena, or the Calgary Stampede, always decked out in his flashy western gear. Like the publicists, Schiller was more than willing to engage in stunts. During the 1953 Rose Parade, he tipped the driver of the City of Las Vegas float "to pull the choke . . . just as it was passing the TV cameras and attendant announcers. This stalled the float and before the drivers could get it started again the announcers, having to find something to talk about, interviewed all six of the lovelies who rode the float."[47] By 1960 Schiller was known across the nation as "Mr. Las Vegas," or, as columnist Bob Considine labeled him, the "bon vivant" of the Las Vegas Strip.[48]

However, there was a face and voice more widely known than Abe Schiller. "If there is one person above all else who can be called our top salesman," Hank Greenspun claimed in 1953, "I would have to give my vote to Wilbur Clark."[49] The former San Diego busboy and bellhop thoroughly embraced the role as the most visible spokesman for the Desert Inn and Las Vegas, and he did so with panache. Clark was always a picture of sartorial splendor with designer suits and dazzling jewelry. He even had his name stamped on the ashtrays and towels of his Desert Inn and had more than three thousand silver dollars made featuring his likeness, which he spread around the country, including to President Truman.[50]

Reporters, columnists, and cameras attracted him like magnets. Clark enjoyed being interviewed by all, whether it was a syndicated columnist like Hal Boyle or a journalist like Richard English or newsmen like Drew Pearson and Edward R. Murrow. In fall 1953 on a trip to New York to attend the World Series and to see Rocky Marciano defend his heavyweight title against Roland La Starza, Clark appeared on several television programs "to boost Las Vegas."[51]

When he appeared on Drew Pearson's daytime television show *New Horizons*, the always upbeat Clark proclaimed, "I think the whole world would like to come to Las Vegas." He focused on the region's pleasant climate, the opportunities for swimming and skiing, "the greatest shows in the world," and that the Desert Inn had one of the "greatest golf courses in the world." When Pearson coaxed him into discussing gambling, Clark was quick to point out that because the state tax commission monitored gaming, it was run on a "very high plain." During the interview, there was a short video of the Desert Inn featuring its luxurious rooms, fine restaurants, pool, golf course, and entertainment, with only a passing reference to the casino.[52] Similarly, when a reporter with the *Chicago Herald* interviewed him, Clark championed the virtues of Las Vegas, arguing that gambling had not had a negative impact on the town's culture. "I've never seen more than three or four drunks in the year and a half I've had my place open—and we run 24 hours a day," he said. And he claimed, incorrectly, "There's practically no crime in our town and no arrests to speak of."[53]

Clark also corresponded with many leading political and public figures, including John and Jackie Kennedy, Lyndon Johnson, Richard Nixon, Reverend Billy Graham, and Wallis Simpson, Duchess of Windsor, some of whom stayed at his Desert Inn. Clark enjoyed the association with prominent people but also understood that this was a way to gain goodwill for his hotel and Las Vegas. Billy Graham, for example, thanked Clark for the opportunity to stay in the home of a "living legend" and appreciated Clark's "explanation of gambling which was most enlightening."[54] Clark particularly sought a close relationship with the Kennedys. When the young Massachusetts senator visited Las Vegas in 1956, Clark welcomed Kennedy into his home, and as a delegate to the Democratic National Convention that year, he supported Kennedy's bid for the vice-presidential nomination. Kennedy stayed at the Desert Inn in September when campaigning for the Stevenson-Kefauver ticket and again in November 1957.[55] Variously labeled as "Las Vegas' Golden Boy," as the man "most likely to become the 'Ziegfeld of the Desert,'" and "the Strip's ranking citizen," Wilbur Clark was a critical figure of Las Vegas promotion because of his successful and "inordinate passion for publicity."[56]

Clark and his publicist Eugene Murphy, with the blessing of Moe Dalitz, the real boss of the hotel and golf enthusiast, were also responsible for the successful Desert Inn's Tournament of Champions golf tournament beginning in 1953, the most effective sustained hotel promotion of the decade. They worked with Walter Winchell, who promoted a cancer research fund on behalf of his friend

Wilbur Clark, front man for the Desert Inn Hotel and avid promoter of Las Vegas, with Massachusetts senator John F. Kennedy, who frequently visited Las Vegas. *Courtesy University of Nevada, Las Vegas, University Libraries Special Collections and Archives, Wilbur and Toni Clark Photo Collection.*

Damon Runyon, a sportswriter, author, and columnist who had succumbed to throat cancer. The tournament, which attracted the nation's premier golfers, raised a little more than three hundred thousand dollars for the Runyon Fund by the end of the decade.[57] It also attracted a bevy of celebrities. The highlight for many was the putting duel between Winchell and actor Bob Hope that kicked off the tournament. More important for the hotel, the tournament regularly attracted big crowds, usually more than three thousand, and they filled the rooms not only at the Desert Inn but also at the other resort hotels, which helped underwrite the event. NBC televised the tournament, and several dozen radio stations broadcast part of the event. All major newspapers sent their golf columnists to cover the tournament and the city hosting it. "There is no doubt," John Cahlan, the managing editor of the *Review-Journal*, wrote in 1957 about the Desert Inn event, "the Tournament of Champions publicity does more for the city of Las Vegas than any other one event. It is an event which gives the world the idea that there is something else besides gambling tables in the city."[58]

While not as successful as the Tournament of Champions, the resort hotels devised a wide range of other promotional schemes. The Sahara held an annual fall trapshooting tournament and a cup race on Lake Mead in addition to an airline Christmas party that attracted employees of all the domestic air carriers to Las Vegas.[59] The Royal Nevada set up table games in its Beverly Hills office "to teach Angelinos how to gamble when they come to Vegas." *Time, Newsweek, Life*, and the wire services, along with CBS News, all contributed to the "harvest of national publicity" that the effort produced.[60] Several of the hotels also staged anniversary parties. In 1950 the Flamingo hosted nearly seventy disc jockeys from around the nation who had "been singing the praises of Las Vegas" as a prelude to a "big anniversary celebration" and open house.[61] Likewise, Wilbur Clark had several celebrities on hand in 1951 to celebrate the first anniversary of the Desert Inn. News bureau photographers captured photos of Jane Russell, Victor Mature, and Vincent Price who were on hand for the festivities while taking a break from their filming of the Howard Hughes production *Las Vegas Story*.[62]

The Sands Hotel, under the guidance of Jack Entratter and Al Freeman, topped them all. Each December they brought back headliners from the past year and invited a small army of Hollywood celebrities to be on hand for the entertainment columnists that Freeman brought in to cover the event. The 1956 event reflected their best effort. One wire service reporter proclaimed, "This Babylon of the desert has had some mighty celebrations in its time, but I've never seen anything quite like the current festivities to mark the fourth anniversary of the Sands hotel."[63] On December 14 Danny Thomas, Jerry Lewis, and Frank Sinatra were all on hand to perform (though laryngitis kept Sinatra from singing at the second show) in front of a packed house that included Marlene Dietrich, Jayne Mansfield, Lucille Ball, Desi Arnaz, Loretta Young, Liberace, Esther Williams, Mitzi Gaynor, Peter Lorre, and the Ritz Brothers. The next day, in front of newsreel cameras, Jerry Lewis and Danny Thomas went aboard a floating birthday cake in the Sands pool to serve the people crowded around. The highlight was when Jayne Mansfield climbed aboard and Lewis pushed her in and she returned the favor. For what Jack Entratter called the "greatest show of the century," the Sands paid more than a hundred thousand dollars to bring in the entertainers, celebrities, and journalists. The payoff was worth it. Besides great headlines, a newsreel shot for Movietone News played on one hundred television stations across the country.[64]

Publicists and their bosses became adept at exploiting all the available media to promote their properties. Newsreels of current news long had been a staple for movie theaters which aired them between feature films and later for television. There were newsreels covering a time capsule burial at the Sands Hotel in 1953, Noël Coward's opening at the Desert Inn in 1955, Elvis Presley at the New Frontier and Liberace at the Riviera in 1956, and Jane Powell at the Desert Inn in 1957. There were also short films about the town, including *A Last Frontier: Las Vegas, Nevada*, part of Bengal Pictures' *Know Your Land* historical films for television, and *Fabulous Las Vegas, U.S.A. 1954*, a Twentieth Century Fox color film narrated by actor Dan Dailey, who two years later starred in the musical *Meet Me in Las Vegas*.[65] In 1956 the Desert Inn funded a slick sixteen-minute color film entitled *Las Vegas Recreation Unlimited* depicting Las Vegas and especially Wilbur Clark's hotel as a destination of "glorious days and glamorous nights." At the hotel one can see a glittering array of "famous personalities of the entertainment world" such as Noël Coward, Johnnie Ray, Ray Bolger, Gordon MacRae, Eddie Fisher, Debbie Reynolds, Walter Winchell, Bing Crosby, and Bob Hope either at the pool or on the golf course. It also featured the Painted Desert Room with the Donn Arden dancers, the Lady Luck Lounge, and the Sky Room Lounge for dancing. At no point did the viewer see any gambling.[66]

In 1956 the news bureau staff, with funding from the chamber of commerce, collaborated with Warner Brothers to produce *Las Vegas: Playground U.S.A.*, the most widely distributed film about Las Vegas. While it does in passing acknowledge gambling, the narrator reassuringly noted that it "is conducted under the supervision of the Nevada State Tax Commission." The rest of the full-color film is focused upon the scenic beauty around Las Vegas, the chance to experience the nation's "last frontier," and the luxurious resort experience, including the great entertainers and dance lines awaiting tourists in this "Broadway of the desert." Throughout, the film the narrator is careful to remind viewers that Las Vegas truly is "the city of daytime sun and nighttime fun" and "the entertainment and fun capital of the world." Besides distributing it to television stations, the chamber of commerce utilized the film to attract conventions.[67]

As upbeat as most of these short films were, they did not have the same promotional value for Las Vegas as did motion pictures and television. Almost twenty movies included scenes in or about Las Vegas in the 1950s. Whether they were dramas, musicals, or comedies, the news bureau and hotel publicists often saw these films as great opportunities to promote the tourist community. Some had their world premiere in Las Vegas, events that attracted dozens of entertainment columnists. Notably, between 1950 and 1956, eight films—*My Friend Irma Goes West, Painting the Clouds with Sunshine, Sky Full of Moon, Las Vegas Story, The Girl Rush, Las Vegas Shakedown, Hollywood or Bust,* and *Meet Me in Las Vegas*—gave movie fans intimate looks at the Strip hotels and Fremont Street casinos. Beginning with a 1951 episode of the crime series *Racket Squad,* Las Vegas became a popular locale for television series, variety shows, and news programs. Shows as various as detective series *Boston Blackie* and *Mike Hammer,* comedy series like *My Little Margie,* the *Red Skelton Show,* and the *Lucy-Desi Comedy Hour,* and dramas like *Alfred Hitchcock Presents* and the *Twilight Zone* found it useful to feature the resort town. Variety shows like the *Gisele MacKenzie Show, Jimmy Durante Show,* and the *Ed Sullivan Show* exploited the presence of all the headliners performing in Las Vegas. Both Eric Sevareid and Edward R. Murrow broadcast news programs from Las Vegas. Radio personalities like Mitch Miller, who also had a popular television program *Sing Along with Mitch;* Dorothy Kilgallen, also known for her appearances on the television program *What's My Line* and for her nationally syndicated newspaper columns; and Frank Farrell, whose *Lunch with Frank Farrell* show was popular nationally, likewise saw ratings advantages in broadcasting from Las Vegas.

Film, television, and radio far exceeded the traditional ways of publicity and advertising offering the opportunity to reach millions with positive images and descriptions of the resort town. For example, in 1955 syndicated columnist Dorothy Kilgallen and her husband Richard Kollmar broadcast their *Breakfast with Dorothy and Dick* show for four days from the Sands Hotel. This was a real coup for publicist Al Freeman because the program on WOR was the highest rated morning program all along the East Coast.[68] Even more impressive, when Ed Sullivan decided to televise his popular variety show from the Desert Inn in summer 1958, the *Las Vegas Sun* reported, "forty million Americans got an inside TV glimpse yesterday of Las Vegas, its people, schools, churches, hospitals and homes."[69]

Hotels and their publicists worked diligently to assist, even subsidize the cost of productions to gain greater visibility for their property. In 1951 the Flamingo persuaded Jack Benny to broadcast his popular radio program from nearby Nellis Air Force Base. According to Al Cahlan at the *Las Vegas Review-Journal,*

"Don't think it was just an accident—that Benny decided he'd like to do a broadcast from here, chose the locale for his script and proceeded to broadcast." It took a lot of work and persuasion, and "the boys at the Flamingo" deserved a big hand because the program "did an outstanding chamber of commerce job for the entire area."[70] Jack Entratter and Al Freeman at the Sands were the best at luring production companies. Freeman, for example, worked diligently with Dick Kollmar to set up his radio broadcast, including covering production costs and providing accommodations for Kollmar, Kilgallen, and their staff. He even sat alongside during the broadcasts should they need anything.[71] With Entratter's blessing, Freeman also assisted NBC producers for the Sands segment of the network's *Wide, Wide World* broadcast on December 4, 1955. In addition to a $7,500 subsidy to help offset production costs, the Sands provided lodging and meals for the camera crew of twenty. In return, the Sands got eighteen minutes of the ninety-minute program, which aired live on more than 150 stations and reached perhaps thirty-five million viewers. The segment featured Frank Sinatra, Nat King Cole, Freddie Bell and the Bellboys, Copa Girls, and Antonio Morelli and his orchestra.[72]

In his memoir, producer John G. Stephens explained the eagerness with which Entratter responded to possible filming at the Sands. Stephens wrote that in 1959 he had a script for a Las Vegas–themed episode of CBS's *The Millionaire* series. "We were going to film in Vegas for two days," Stephens explained, "and come back to the studio for one day. The Sands chartered an airplane, put us up in the hotel, fed us three meals a day, and paid all of the company's expenses. They couldn't have been nicer." Entratter demanded only three things from Stephens: "the sign of the Sands to be displayed in the show, a credit after the show, and nothing in the script involving gangsters or the mob. We wholeheartedly agreed to the whole package."[73]

The greatest opportunity to exploit both the film and television industries came with the filming and release of the musical *Meet Me in Las Vegas*. The film starred Cyd Charisse as a ballet dancer performing at the Sands and Dan Dailey as a cowboy who always loses at the tables until he meets the dancer. Joe Pasternak decided to have the world premiere of the movie, filmed in part at the Sands, in Las Vegas. Not satisfied with that development, Jack Entratter persuaded NBC to telecast the *Milton Berle Show* live from the Copa Room the night of the premiere. At the gala affair, a long list of celebrities arrived at the Sands where Berle interviewed Charisse and Dailey and showed a clip from the movie during his show. Afterwards, a sports car caravan took all the stars

World premiere of popular 1956 film *Meet Me in Las Vegas* at the El Portal Theatre.
Courtesy University of Nevada, Las Vegas, University Libraries Special Collections and Archives.

downtown to the El Portal Theatre, where Shirley Thomas interviewed them for NBC *Monitor* radio.[74]

Meet Me in Las Vegas produced exactly what Entratter and Freeman wanted. First, more than forty million viewers saw a live television program from the Sands. Second, the nearly eighty reporters, columnists, and cameramen covering the event saturated the nation with copy and photos of the film, the Sands, and Las Vegas. Third, reviews of the movie were most gratifying. The reviewer for *Variety* concluded that "Las Vegas has never had a better film showcasing or more valuable advertising, and the Sands Hotel particularly provides a glittering background for the romantic tale." "For the price of a ticket," Bosley Crowther wrote in the *New York Times*, "the wary traveler can find himself taking a giant leap to the Monte Carlo of the West, putting up at the fantastic Sands Club and living like a Texas oil king." Crowther concluded, "Oh boy—what an ad for the Sands!" Sam Lesner, in the *Chicago Daily News*, wrote, "If you have even one drop of gambler's blood in your veins, it's going to be hard not to hop the next train or plane for Las Vegas after seeing M-G-M's lavish musical, 'Meet Me in Las Vegas.'"[75]

Hank Greenspun could barely contain himself. "The film," he wrote, "is not only tremendous entertainment but is probably the greatest commercial a town ever received. From start to finish, it is a glorification of Las Vegas and the Sands Hotel beautifully done in an unusually authentic setting."[76] To top it all off, Al Freeman reported that although the film was released in February, he was still getting hundreds of letters in June from fans who had seen it and now wanted to make reservations at the Sands![77]

As eager as hotels and the chamber of commerce were to assist productions that would benefit Las Vegas, they were just as resolute to stop those they believed would be detrimental. In the late 1940s, producer Frank Seltzer wanted to shoot scenes in Las Vegas for a movie about organized crime's control of the race wire service. When they saw the script, leaders of the Las Vegas Chamber of Commerce found too many "objectionable and untrue references to Las Vegas" and refused to cooperate, as did the resort hotels. This concerted opposition prevented Seltzer from shooting on-location in Las Vegas for his film *711 Ocean Drive*.[78] A decade later, the chamber's Promotion Committee, which included hotel publicists and staff from the news bureau, and chamber president Sam Boyd, the first person from the gaming industry to head the chamber, successfully blocked the production of two television series—*Las Vegas Beat* and *Las Vegas Files*. They opposed the proposed detective series, which would have aired during the 1961–62 season, because chamber leaders thought the programs would have portrayed Las Vegas as a town plagued by violence and crime.[79]

The aggressive promotional efforts in Las Vegas during the 1950s were part of a nationwide effort to capture part of the growing tourist market. In the prosperous postwar years, travel appealed ever more to Americans. This prompted chambers of commerce around the country to pump money into tourism promotion. In 1953, for example, local governments' collective spending on promotion exceeded $9 million, with communities in Florida and California leading the way.[80] The Las Vegas Chamber of Commerce funded its efforts through an annual drive called the Livewire Fund. Although most members contributed, the resort hotels largely subsidized the drive. During the 1950s the fund fluctuated between $80,000 and well over $100,000 to carry out the functions of the news bureau and pay for advertising the town.[81] In addition, hotels had their own advertising and publicity budgets. According to one Las Vegas columnist, "One hotel is known to have provided an unlimited expense account for publicity and promotion alone."[82] Often hotel publicists and the news bureau staff cooperated on ventures. One critical annual example of this included assisting Trans World Airlines when it brought dozens of editors of newspaper and magazine travel sections to Las Vegas. The hotels' publicists arranged their complimentary rooms, meals, and shows, and the news bureau made all the arrangements.[83] The news bureau formalized the working relationship with the publicists when it combined the latter's Publicity Directors' Association with news bureau staff and formed the Las Vegas Chamber of Commerce Promotion Committee, which took on the task of approving the chamber's advertising brochures, helped promote a convention center, and collaborated on copy for newspapers and periodicals.[84]

Publicists, news bureau staffers, and unofficial ambassadors Abe Schiller and Wilbur Clark consistently worked their magic, selling Las Vegas to America. Their promotional campaign drew ever more tourists to Las Vegas, and their collective efforts justifiably earned high praise from the local press. "Combine our paid publicists with the efforts of the Las Vegas News Bureau and an alert Chamber of Commerce," one journalist concluded in 1957, "and you achieve a continuing and successful promotion program."[85] However, the fulsome praise masked a growing fissure between the Strip properties and many in the chamber of commerce who bemoaned the growing apathy the resort hotels exhibited for "community enterprises" like the annual fund-raising drives for the Red Cross and Community Chest. It seemed to some that the "majority of the resort industries" had turned their backs on "cooperative" ventures to advance the entire community and instead focused too often on their own bottom lines.[86]

Three
Entertainment Capital

In October 1953 Richard English, a veteran Las Vegas observer, wrote a hyperbolic yet incisive piece in the *Saturday Evening Post* on the entertainment scene in America's Playground. He reported that Milton Berle, Red Skelton, Betty Hutton, and Vic Damone, four of the biggest celebrities of the era, "were all working casinos at the same time this past summer." That made Las Vegas, English contended, "dizzier than Broadway was during its lurid speak-easy era." Hershey Martin of the William Morris Agency had told English, "Show-business-wise, there's never been anything like it." The Las Vegas hotel-casinos had become the firm's "biggest market." After talking to hotel bosses, the local press, and entertainers, English concluded that the town long known for gambling and easy divorces was now "convinced that in using show-business names it has at last hit the publicity jackpot." The men running the seven resort hotels along the Strip believed that spectacular entertainment would drive the tourism market to new heights. The celebrities had become, in English's words, "dazzling crap-table lures."[1] English was not alone in the conclusion he had drawn about the city's emergence as the nation's entertainment center. In the *New York Times* Gladwin Hill told readers, "The wayfarer arriving in Las Vegas during any given week has a wider choice of top-banana talent than the average New Yorker," and syndicated entertainment columnist Jim Bacon proclaimed that Las Vegas had become the "night life capital of the U.S."[2] Articles in *Newsweek*, the *Wall Street Journal*, *Life*, and *Look* echoed this storyline. An article in *Time* colorfully described the critical role hotel headliners now played for the growing town. They were the "gold-horned Judas goats who lure the herds of tourists to the gaming tables."[3] A good part of the lure lay in the fact that these stars performed in small, intimate showrooms. As singer Paul Anka explained, it was "as if you were right up there with them." The 1950s in Las Vegas, he argued, was "an era that is totally gone now." As far as the entertainment scene was concerned, "there never has been anything like it, and never will be again. It was a time of incredible buzz, of fashion, everyone on display, egos to the max."[4]

Throughout the decade, eager tourists responded enthusiastically to the remarkable diversity of great talent from nightclubs, movies, and television in the resort hotel showrooms that created the exciting milieu Paul Anka described. The biggest draws were the singers, and Las Vegas attracted the best in the land, most of whom were veterans of the nightclub circuit. They had polished their acts at the 500 Club in Atlantic City, the Chez Paree in Chicago, Ciro's and Mocambo in Los Angeles, and the Latin Quarter and Copacabana in New York. Nat King Cole, Rosemary Clooney, Lena Horne, Tony Bennett, Eddie Fisher, Tony Martin, Patti Page, Johnny Mathis, Judy Garland, Billy Eckstine, Harry Belafonte, Julie London, Paul Anka, Ella Fitzgerald, Vic Damone, Dorothy Dandridge, and Bobby Darin were among the many who appeared in the showrooms or lounges. All these performers garnered great reviews and filled the showrooms, but they all worked in the shadow of two performers, one of whom was not a singer.

Liberace and Frank Sinatra dominated in the Strip showrooms in the 1950s. Between 1944 and 1954, Liberace appeared at the Last Frontier two dozen times, fashioning a performance style that never failed to please his loyal fans. Initially a concert pianist, Liberace's nightclub performances featured a mix of what he called *Reader's Digest* versions of classical music along with show tunes and "boogie-woogie." He had a candelabrum on his piano and stroked the keys with rapid exaggerated hand movements. Between pieces he ad-libbed with the audience and always performed in a tuxedo, black initially, but when he opened at the Riviera in 1955 he sported first a white tux and then one covered in sequins.[5] From that point, working on the belief that Las Vegas had an "ever-better-onward-and-upward attitude," Liberace continually performed in ever more "excessive" outfits covered in beads and rhinestones. By the end of his career one critic called Liberace "a kitsch pianist with a scullery maid's idea of a regal wardrobe," a "synonym for glorious excess."[6] Still, his fans never tired of his shtick.

After two engagements at the Desert Inn, Sinatra began a fourteen-year relationship with the Sands. The hotel's Copa Room became "His Room." An Oscar winner and a huge success with Capitol Records, Sinatra was at the peak of his influence in the 1950s. As freelance writer Richard Gehman wrote in 1961, "in the vernacular of show business," Sinatra is "the greatest of them all in every field into which he thrusts his talents—recordings, radio and nightclubs, television and films."[7] Most importantly for the Sands, Sinatra emerged as the premier attraction for Las Vegas in the 1950s. Doc Stacher, one of the gangster

Liberace riding with chamber of commerce leader and auto dealer Jim Cashman
before the performer's opening at the Riviera in 1955. *Courtesy University of Nevada, Las
Vegas, University Libraries Special Collections and Archives and Las Vegas News Bureau. Publicity,
personality, and likeness of Liberace are property of The Liberace Foundation, all rights reserved.*

owners of the Sands, explained that "The object was to get him to perform there
because there's no bigger draw in Las Vegas. When Frankie was performing, the
hotel really filled up."[8] More simply, as Paul Anka put it, "Frank ruled."[9]

Many comedians, from Red Skelton and Herb Shriner to Milton Berle and
Red Buttons, also filled the showrooms. Joe E. Lewis, however, was the gamblers' favorite. The deadpan comic, who always appeared in a tuxedo with a
drink in hand, was a master of self-deprecating humor, discussing his struggles
with alcohol and gambling and often telling audiences, "I am working under
a terrible handicap tonight. I have no talent."[10] Owner Beldon Katleman frequently booked famed stripper Lili St. Cyr as an opening act for Lewis in the

Opera Room at the El Rancho Vegas. Lewis offered a classic line after one of St. Cyr's acts. She was known for bathing in a glass-walled tub, riding in a cable car above the audience, and tossing her "scanties" inscribed "love from Lili" to adoring fans.[11] After one of her scintillating performances, Lewis ambled to the footlights and, according to columnist Dorothy Kilgallen, "pointed accusingly at a young man at a ringside table, and said with a shake of his head, 'I saw you eating while Lili St. Cyr was working. I hope I never get that hungry in my life.'"[12] In the late 1950s Don Rickles, the "Merchant of Venom," packed the lounge at the Sahara with a new style of comedy for Las Vegas. Local columnist Ralph Pearl was amazed that "this bald, naked-faced man who stands up there screaming imprecations and insults" at his audiences could have such an enthusiastic and appreciative following. Tourists and celebrities alike enjoyed being a target of his rants. As Pearl wrote in August 1959, "It is truly a wondrous sight to see a heavy-set lady sitting ringside hold her sides and howl with glee just because Don said she was an illegitimate member of the whale family."[13]

Band leaders like Benny Goodman, Harry James, Paul Whiteman, and Jimmy and Tommy Dorsey drew those nostalgic for the disappearing swing era. For example, when clarinetist Artie Shaw performed in the Casbar Lounge at the Sahara in 1954, he broke the hotel's attendance records. "Not only is there no seating room in the lounge," columnist Les Devor explained, "but there is no standing room either."[14] Opera stars like Helen Traubel and Jan Peerce consistently drew packed houses. One notably successful act was the pairing of Metropolitan Opera star Robert Merrill and jazz trombonist Louis Armstrong. Entertainment columnist Dick Odessky labeled it "a suicide booking before they opened," but after seeing the duel between jazz and opera he called it "one of the finest shows ever in our town."[15]

There were other surprise headliner successes. Some tourists were lucky to see Betty Hutton in summer 1953. The star of big movie hits like *Annie Get Your Gun* and *The Greatest Show on Earth*, Hutton had turned to performing in nightclubs after a contract dispute with Paramount studios. The super-charged Hutton's opening night of song and dance at the Desert Inn had thrilled the audience and prompted entertainment columnist Erskine Johnson to call Hutton's the "greatest one woman act ever seen in show business."[16] A year later, veteran actress Mae West made her nightclub debut at the Sahara. The sultry "blonde and curvaceous" West introduced "beef cake" to the Las Vegas showrooms with eight "muscle bound weight-lifters . . . prancing around in brief shorts." Amid whistles and catcalls, West responded "with her usual shoulder and hip wiggles and risqué songs:" "I'd Like to Do All Day What I Do All Night" and "Take It Easy, Boys." In response to one of the weightlifters who said, "I'd walk through fire and flood for you," West responded, "Make it fire, honey. I'd rather you were real warm than all wet!" West's appearance shattered all attendance records in the Congo Room and propelled her to a seven-week run at the Latin Quarter in New York, where she likewise broke attendance records. West did nothing to diminish her appeal when columnist Les Devor asked how her sexy personality had worked such magic with the audiences at the Sahara. She replied, "I guess I've always had 'it,'" and when you do, "you know what to do with it."[17]

Whether they were surprises or predictably successful veteran nightclub performers, management at the Strip resorts had quickly learned the value of the headliners to the bottom line. When the El Rancho Vegas and Hotel Last Frontier opened in the early 1940s, the western-themed hotels had showrooms but modest budgets. Maxine Lewis, who booked the acts for the Last Frontier, according to *Billboard* magazine, simply tried "anything which . . . will please the public."[18] That meant no major headliners; instead, the Round-Up Room at the El Rancho and Ramona Room at the Last Frontier offered acts on the night-club circuit who were typically opening acts for the "big-name" performers.

In 1944 Lewis, now with a budget of a hundred thousand dollars, began to sign more notable celebrities like singer-songwriter Gene Austin, rhythm and blues group the Delta Rhythm Boys, and an emerging star pianist named Walter Liberace.[19] The following year, *Billboard* labeled the Last Frontier a "big-bracket operation" after Lewis signed nightclub stars Harry Richman and Sophie Tucker.[20] Al Fischler explained in *Billboard* in 1946 that the owners of the El Rancho Vegas and Hotel Last Frontier, as well as the downtown El Cortez and Nevada Biltmore, had quickly come to realize the value of using big-name entertainment as an "attraction to gaming rooms." This was the critical moment for resort hotel owners. While all their competitors offered gambling to tourists, adding name entertainers appeared to be the key to continued expansion of their business. Thus, hotels were willing to offer three thousand to five thousand dollars a week for the likes of Tucker, Richman, Liberace, and jazz singer Arthur Lee Simpkins. Indeed, they developed a model that prevailed through the 1950s. Book a popular headliner to attract people, but implement a policy "for short and sweet offerings, so that the customers are those who come in for dinner and drinks, stay to see the show, then adjourn to dens of chance."[21]

When Bugsy Siegel opened the Flamingo Casino in December 1946 the rush to sign big-name entertainers truly began. For the first two weeks he had popular comedian Jimmy Durante, bandleader Xavier Cugat, and singer Rose Marie. After them, Siegel brought in Lena Horne, the Andrews Sisters, Abbott and Costello, and Joe E. Lewis.[22] Siegel's bold move prompted the other hotels to sign big-name headliners as well. To compete with the Flamingo's opening night lineup, the El Rancho Vegas brought in the Ritz Brothers, slapstick comics of both movie and nightclub fame, and singing sensation Peggy Lee; the Nevada Biltmore countered with the popular Mills Brothers. One of the nation's most widely syndicated entertainment columnists Bob Thomas, after sitting in on the glittering opening of the Flamingo, argued that Las Vegas was rapidly emerging at the best locale in the West for "good, live entertainment."[23] Throughout the late 1940s and early 1950s, readers of newspapers, magazines, and novels encountered echoes of Thomas's characterization. Visitors to Las Vegas would find "top-billed floor shows," indeed "some of the best night club entertainment in America."[24]

Proof that the star approach worked lay in the crowds the celebrities attracted. Columnist Dick Odessky reported in spring 1953 that the Sands Hotel had to turn away more than two thousand people for one Saturday's shows. That same evening, the Desert Inn experienced a "near riot" when it had to disappoint "hundreds of people" hoping to see its 1:30 A.M. show, and the Flamingo and El Rancho Vegas had "capacity houses."[25] The next year, when Tommy and Jimmy Dorsey played in the Ramona Room at the Hotel Last Frontier, they shattered the old crowd record of 464 by drawing nearly 600 people "with many standees," and Nick Kelly, the host at the Sands Copa Room, had to turn down more than 5,000 requests for seats each week a revival of the Ziegfeld Follies played at the hotel.[26] Through the early 1950s, these developments were commonplace. As a local columnist explained in April 1953, all along the Strip, "the walls are bursting at the seams, the tables are packed like sardines."[27] The second part of Alan Jarlson's comment was critical to the casino owners; the people drawn by the entertainers were at the table games afterward.

In 1956 Hank Greenspun discussed what had become common wisdom in Las Vegas hotel circles about what drove the increasing tourism numbers:

> Las Vegas had been in existence for many years, with no resounding success, and it wasn't until word got around the country that you could come here and for the price of a good meal or a drink, see performers like Danny Thomas, Donald O'Connor, Ken Murray, Marie Wilson, Tony Martin, Nat King Cole, Liberace, Phil Silvers, Henny Youngman,

Sammy Davis, Jr. and other tremendous top personalities of show business, that the tourist impetus started. Las Vegas now has the reputation of the greatest show town in the country.[28]

Greenspun briefly alluded to what was as remarkable to tourists as the glittering array of celebrities they could expect to see. If they got in to the showrooms, the cost was nominal. Until the mid-1950s there were no minimum or cover charges. As a journalist explained in *Harper's*, people fortunate enough to make it into the showrooms could see the "movie stars, singers, funnymen, and Broadway folk" for the "price of a bottle of beer."[29] Even when some of the hotels began levying a cover charge, it posed no significant barrier to access. Journalist John Gunther wrote that Las Vegas was the only entertainment venue where people could "have an hour or so of Liberace or Frank Sinatra, to say nothing of Tallulah Bankhead or Lena Horne, for a $2 minimum."[30]

The headliners, particularly on their opening nights, always attracted a gaggle of celebrities from Southern California. For example, when English playwright and cabaret singer Noël Coward opened at the Desert Inn in summer 1955, Frank Sinatra chartered a plane in Los Angeles and brought along David Niven, Judy Garland, Humphrey Bogart, Lauren Bacall, Joseph Cotton, Zsa Zsa Gábor, Joan Fontaine, Laurence Harvey, and Jane Powell to see the performance. It became common for tourists to encounter a "large Hollywood entourage" that had come to Las Vegas to "get away from it all."[31] The chance to see great shows, gamble, get a tan poolside, and be seen was irresistible for many celebrities. After spending several days in Las Vegas, actress Marlene Dietrich told a local columnist, "This is like Paris, when it was really Paris. How could anyone ever leave this wonderful place?"[32] Noël Coward loved the entertainment along the Strip. The floor shows were "very well put on, very well lit, very efficient musically." The talent was "great," and the girls were all "incredibly beautiful." The atmosphere up and down the Strip was one of a holiday. "The bands are playing swing, jazz, progressive and retrogressive and the people move from hotel to hotel" playing the slots, blackjack, and roulette, all "having a whale of a time."[33]

During a December 1955 episode of his live NBC program *Wide, Wide World*, broadcast from the Sands Hotel, Dave Garroway told the audience that the resort had become "the playground of the stars" and while tourists would not encounter celebrities when visiting Hollywood, "you will at the Sands."[34] A columnist agreed, telling readers that in Las Vegas "the man or woman

beside you at the roulette wheel may be a movie director, a star or a producer."[35]
According to singer Vic Damone, the casino managers encouraged headliners
to gamble so that the hotel guests could see him or Dean Martin or Jerry Lewis
"gambling next to them, and it gave them a thrill, something to talk about when
they got home."[36] He was right. James Perkins, who was stationed at the nearby
Nellis Air Force Base, frequently wrote to his parents about going to shows
along the Strip and was always amazed at seeing celebrities nearby in the bar
or lounge. One evening, while attending a Dick Haymes performance at the
Flamingo, Perkins "reached for a stool at the bar, but someone beat me to it and
it was Jane Russell."[37] Tourists also encountered famous people who were not
performers in the hotels and casinos, including in 1959 the Duke and Duchess
of Windsor, "who did the town" and "were greeted with enthusiastic applause,"
and Ernest Hemingway and his wife Mary, who dropped by the Sands to see
Johnny Mathis perform.[38]

The performers in the Las Vegas showrooms likewise found the intimacy
of the showrooms, the presence of so many luminaries, and the charged atmosphere appealing. Joel Grey, who first appeared at the El Rancho Vegas in 1952,
described the hotel "filled with West Coast society and celebrity types, such as
those that went to the exclusive Racquet Club in Palm Springs. In Vegas, they
came to gamble as well as be entertained and fed." Eddie Fisher, who was the
opening act for the new Tropicana in 1957, found "a mecca of neon lights, gambling, and beautiful girls. It had become *the* destination for high rollers from
everywhere in the world, an American Monte Carlo." Vic Damone loved the
atmosphere he encountered in Las Vegas. Beyond the "packed" houses, it was
"the combination of money and sex and electricity that you could practically
smell that made Las Vegas what it was."[39]

Knowing that the headliner policy had created this enticing atmosphere for
tourists, entertainment directors, with the approval of their bosses at the resort
hotels, as early as 1950, went on "a name binge." That year, the five Strip hotels
spent $2.5 million "for name attractions." However, hotel operators were already
claiming at this early date that there weren't "enough names to go around."
Most signed headliners for two-week runs. Unless they brought them in for
multiple appearances, each hotel needed twenty-six name talents to keep the
crowds coming. For the existing hotels that meant they collectively needed more
than one hundred headliners a year.[40] Complicating matters was the explosion
of building that went on in the subsequent eight years. Nine new properties—
Desert Inn, Sahara, Sands, Royal Nevada, Riviera, Dunes, Hacienda, Tropicana,

and Stardust—opened on the Strip and the Showboat and Moulin Rouge off the Strip between 1950 and 1958, all offering entertainment. As Al Cahlan, managing director and columnist for the *Las Vegas Review-Journal*, explained, the essential dilemma "is not filling the rooms in the hotels with customers, it's filling the dining-room stages with entertainment in keeping with the high standard already being set."[41]

The resort hotels facing these challenging circumstances needed effective entertainment directors. They came from a variety of backgrounds: dancer, singer, comedian, music arranger, orchestra conductor, entrepreneur, interior decorator, lawyer, and nightclub bouncer. Some, like Bill Miller, Jack Entratter, Monte Proser, and Herman Hover, had considerable experience as entertainment directors in other cities. Because it was such a demanding position, turnover was common, particularly at the financially strapped Hotel Last Frontier (later renamed the New Frontier) which had several: Eddie Fox, Sammy Lewis (twice), Garwood Van, and Bill Miller. Regardless of where they worked or their financial backing, most days for entertainment directors were packed and stressful. Al Freeman, Jack Entratter's publicist, described the demands on his boss's time in a "typical" day. Up by 11:00 A.M., Entratter signed performers' checks, answered calls from friends for room accommodations, met with journalists, signed letters while watching rehearsals, dealt with problems posed by the show's choreographer and stage manager, talked to the maître d' to determine who would get the valued "ringside" tables for the shows, talked with agents about future performers, dressed for the evenings' two shows, and, at 1:30 A.M., watched the rehearsals for the next show before finally getting to bed at 5:30 A.M.[42] Entratter told Richard English that finding talent was most critical of his daily tasks, "Here I am, making as many as a hundred and eighty calls a day when I'm setting a new show. And when I'm not making calls, I'm flying to catch a new act."[43]

Among the small army of entertainment directors (some used the title "producer," or both titles), five had the greatest impact. Hal Braudis, born in Rochester, New York, in 1898, got involved in the entertainment field in his teen years, initially working at a variety of backstage jobs, an experience that gave him a clear sense of what was involved in putting together a successful show. He moved on to producing shows in the Midwest and then in Nevada and Arizona, including a stint as entertainment director at the Hotel Last Frontier. Braudis joined the Thunderbird Hotel when it opened in 1948 and compared to the other resort hotels had "a comparatively small budget." He told a local columnist in 1953 that his situation prompted him to avoid "big name talent which is known to everyone."

Instead, he developed shows "around an entertainer who is new to" Las Vegas, particularly up and coming stars like Rosemary Clooney, Nat King Cole, Les Paul and Mary Ford, and the Ink Spots. His success, thus, was built upon providing "a new, fresh brand of entertainment for local first nighters." Between 1952 and 1954, Braudis also booked "attractions of unusual interest" like the Dancers of Bali, the Agnes de Mille Dancers, and the Lecuona Cuban Boys. The approach worked for Braudis, who developed a loyal following for the Thunderbird.[44]

Like Braudis, Frank Sennes was an independent booker who declined to work with Music Corporation of America or the William Morris Agency, which provided most of the talent for the Las Vegas showrooms, but he did not have the budget problems the Thunderbird entertainment director endured. From Ohio, Sennes had found talent for Moe Dalitz in Cleveland and over in Newport, Kentucky, at the Beverly Hills Country Club. In 1950, while running the Colonial Inn in Hallandale, Florida, formerly owned by Meyer Lansky, Sennes became the entertainment director of Dalitz's Desert Inn in Las Vegas. Three years later, while maintaining offices in New York, Miami, Cincinnati, Cleveland, and Beverly Hills, Sennes opened the Moulin Rouge, the nation's largest nightclub, in Los Angeles. By 1960 the consistently successful Sennes was handling the entertainment at the Desert Inn and Stardust. While he certainly brought in headliners, Sennes was best known for lavish production shows staged by his protégé Donn Arden at the Stardust and later at the Desert Inn.[45]

Maxine Lewis first came to Las Vegas in 1941 as a vocalist for the new El Rancho Vegas. The following year, R. E. Griffith and Bill Moore, who built the Hotel Last Frontier, offered her the position of entertainment director. She recalled having a "rough time booking from the very start," not just because she had a limited budget, but also because "talent was not as plentiful in those days." In 1947 Lewis moved on to work for Bugsy Siegel at the Flamingo and stayed there a decade before switching to the new Tropicana Hotel. She not only booked many big-name performers, from Tony Martin, Danny Thomas, and Lena Horne to the Andrews Sisters and Louis Armstrong, but also introduced new performers like Keefe Brasselle and Liberace to Las Vegas.[46] Besides the challenge of traveling to major cities to scout new talent, Lewis explained in 1954, "you try to anticipate what the public likes and go on from there. You can never be sure." She recalled booking composer and orchestra leader David Rose, whose "music and orchestrations were perfect yet he only drew average." Then she brought in frenetic madcap bandleader Spike Jones, "and for a month we were turning people away from the door."[47]

Bill Miller and Jack Entratter were the most influential of the entertainment directors. Miller, a Russian immigrant, was a vaudeville dancer before becoming a talent agent booking acts for resort hotels and nightclubs. He had a nightclub in Manhattan before buying the Riviera in Fort Lee, New Jersey, just after World War II. Miller booked the biggest names in show business for his lavish yellow and blue nightclub, which he called the "Showplace of America," just over the George Washington Bridge from Manhattan. Frank Sinatra, Tony Martin, Dean Martin, Jerry Lewis, Peggy Lee, the Will Mastin Trio with Sammy Davis Jr., and Vic Damone were among the stars, with dance lines choreographed by Donn Arden and Ron Fletcher, who drew big audiences to the nightclub in appearances between 1946 and 1953. When Lena Horne opened in 1953, for example, *Jet* magazine reported, "The Riviera was packed for two shows with more than 3,500 in the audience that cheered Lena for ten minutes. She did 15 encores."[48] Miller's successful run ended when the state of New Jersey needed his property for its construction of the Palisades Parkway. Before he closed the Riviera in late 1953, Miller was already booking shows for the Sahara in Las Vegas. He had struck a deal with owner Milton Prell for a 10 percent share of the property to become entertainment director.[49] He lasted with the Sahara for only two years before heading a group to take over the struggling Royal Nevada, a venture that ended in the closing of that hotel on the last day of 1955. Miller then became general manager of the Dunes Hotel in March 1956. He sold out to Major Riddle nine months later, spent some time investing in the Riviera in Havana and trying to develop another resort hotel in Cuba, then returned to Las Vegas as entertainment director of the New Frontier in 1959.[50]

When Miller began booking for the Sahara, he quickly discovered that the other resort hotels, notably the Sands and Flamingo, already had commitments from most of the biggest headliners, and he quickly adopted Hal Braudis's approach of seeking new talent. As he said in early 1955, "In the past year of Sahara bookings 14 new night club personalities appeared here. The moral of the story is to create them . . . not to pirate them."[51] Among his breakthrough signings were movie stars Ray Bolger, Donald O'Connor, Marlene Dietrich, and Mae West. He also experimented with other entertainment formats. When at the troubled Dunes, he rejected using headliners for an "experiment of dine and dance" that did not work, but his exploitation of lounge acts brought him great success particularly at the Sahara with Louis Prima and Keely Smith.[52]

Jack Entratter, who had competed with Bill Miller for talent while heading the Copacabana in New York, rapidly emerged as the major power in Las

Vegas entertainment in the 1950s. Born in New York in 1914, Entratter began working at nightclubs in New York and Miami when he was only twenty-two. He quickly rose from reservations clerk to bouncer and then manager of the new Copacabana in 1940 under the watchful eye of Monte Proser, who later became an entertainment director at the Tropicana. By his mid-twenties, the handsome six-four Entratter had become a celebrity among devotees of New York nightclubs for successfully promoting new talent like singer Johnnie Ray and the team of Dean Martin and Jerry Lewis. More important, he attracted the biggest stars of the postwar years to perform at the Copacabana, notably Frank Sinatra. Entratter also established the famed dance line the Copa Girls. Because of his rapid success, Entratter became a co-owner of the club, though the real boss was gangster Frank Costello, who sent Entratter to Las Vegas to produce shows at the Sands Hotel in 1952.[53]

Entratter rapidly made the Sands' Copa Room the premier venue for performers. Entratter booked some "package shows" like *Gentlemen Prefer Blondes*, the *Student Prince*, and a revised version of the long dormant *Ziegfeld Follies*, but they didn't always succeed. The *Student Prince*, for example, which he booked for three weeks, did so poorly that Entratter had to close it down after one week and scramble to find singer Billy Eckstine to fill in the schedule. Entratter also brought in some new talent like Johnny Mathis in 1958, but quickly landing established nightclub headliners proved to be most critical in Entratter's approach. Beginning with Danny Thomas, his opening act, he locked in most of the stars of the era. In 1955 and 1956, for example, Entratter gained commitments from Lena Horne, Nat King Cole, Frank Sinatra, Danny Thomas, Jerry Lewis, Dean Martin, and Louis Armstrong to perform in the Copa Room for between three and ten weeks annually for three years.

The competition among the entertainment directors for headliners who could bring in the gambling crowd led to a bidding war for the biggest draws. In 1953 Betty Hutton, Red Skelton, and Milton Berle all got paychecks for more than $20,000 a week, prompting columnists in the *Oakland Tribune* to call it the "lushest price war in U.S. entertainment history."[54] To secure popular vocalist Kay Starr, the Flamingo signed her to a five-year contract with a guarantee of $20,000 a week for eight weeks each year, and the new Riviera topped them all by paying Liberace $50,000 to be its opening act in 1955, a year when the Strip hotels collectively spent $20 million on talent, twice as much as in 1954.[55] Flamingo publicist Abe Schiller openly worried about the trend. "By the time you pay Liberace $50,000, plus a band, a line of girls, supporting acts and small combos for the bar," he explained, "you've got a $90,000-a-week bill. And that doesn't include the cost of publicity and exploitation."[56] In 1954 Al Gottesman, co-owner of the soon-to-open Dunes Hotel, agreed, "The constant demand for name talent at increasing salaries has got to stop somewhere. The hotels have created a Frankenstein monster that could easily destroy them."[57]

In response to such fears, the hotels occasionally pursued a variety of collective agreements to control costs. When price ceilings did not work, they tried a different approach in 1954. According to an article in *Billboard* magazine, the hotel operators agreed that none of them would "compete for an act or an attraction if the latter was in the midst of negotiations with another hotel," and "any act or attraction that played one hotel would not be bought by a competitor for at least six months after the expiration of the first date, without written approval from the first hotel."[58] These approaches always largely failed because Jack Entratter, the biggest player in the quest for talent, refused to abide by them, and others quickly followed his lead.

With those failures, many entertainment directors turned to what some called "curiosity acts," primarily motion picture, television, and opera stars who had little or no nightclub experience. In addition to Mae West in 1954, some succeeded. Van Johnson, who had danced in several Broadway productions and had been in more than three dozen films, took the first week's pay for his appearance at the Sands in advance and hired a writer and choreographer to develop an act that *Billboard* surprisingly characterized as a "real act" with songs and some soft shoe dancing.[59] The agent of Ronald Reagan, a struggling actor who had had no movie script for more than a year and who had rejected the idea of work on television and Broadway, suggested that Reagan try a nightclub act in Las Vegas. Reagan later claimed that his reaction was to run "for cover, yelling over my shoulder, 'You must be kidding!'" His wife Nancy explained, however, that "the money was good and we were broke." So, Reagan performed with a popular comic singing quartet called the Continentals at the Last Frontier in 1954, offering a monologue and joining them in a few skits. Attendance at his shows were solid, and the critics gave him good reviews.[60]

Because Las Vegas nightclubs paid much better than opera houses, and entertainment directors wanted big-name performers, a string of opera's best came to Las Vegas.[61] Mimi Benzell, Lauritz Melchior, Ezio Pinza, Helen Traubel, Jan Peerce, Robert Merrill, and John Charles Thomas had successful runs along the Strip in the 1950s. Pinza was particularly popular during his performances at the Sands. As local entertainment columnist Alan Jarlson explained, Pinza's "natural charm, robust, yet sweet voice and his magnetic personality—conveyed such completeness to even the most hackneyed listener, as to assure a success unparalleled even for Las Vegas."[62] British playwright Noël Coward was one of the biggest surprise successes. While he had developed a popular cabaret act in London, no one really knew how well American audiences would respond. However, his four-week run at the Desert Inn in 1955 produced rave reviews in the local press as well as in *Variety*, the *New York Times*, and *Los Angeles Times*. More important, throughout the month, his shows packed the Painted Desert Room, including a glittering array of Hollywood celebrities.[63]

There were failures as well. Actor and cabaret singer Maurice Chevalier had a four-week engagement at the Dunes in late 1955 and early 1956 and drew "slack" attendance throughout the run.[64] Hollywood star Jeff Chandler performed at the Riviera in 1955, and the reviewer for *Billboard* wrote that Chandler "should have stayed in Hollywood" because his singing was awful.[65] In summer 1955 comic actor Wally Cox, who had just completed a successful three-year run in the television series *Mr. Peepers*, in which he portrayed a meek schoolteacher, opened at the Dunes. Critics quickly noted that he "laid an egg" with weak material and dismal attendance. The fired Cox, in a guest column for the *Las Vegas Sun*, explained that the hotel's management was so frustrated that it even "offered to drive me away from the club in an AMBULANCE, saying that I had a high fever!"[66]

Famed tenor Mario Lanza, who had starred in *The Great Caruso*, was the biggest bomb. Amid much fanfare the New Frontier Hotel had signed him to appear in April 1955. However, his consumption of barbiturates and alcohol and opening night jitters caused Lanza to refuse to go on stage in the new Venus Room, and he left town without singing a note.[67] Even Elvis Presley stumbled in his initial performance in Las Vegas in 1956. Presley, whose "Heartbreak Hotel" had become his first number-one hit, had appeared on Tommy and Jimmy Dorsey's *Stage Show* and the *Milton Berle Show* on television earlier in the year and had just signed a seven-picture movie deal. His manager, Colonel Tom Parker, negotiated an appearance for his emerging star at the New Frontier as an "added attraction" to headliner Freddy Martin and his orchestra and comedian Shecky Greene. His high-energy gyrating style did not work for the "older, more sedate nightclub crowd" that showed up for his appearances in the Venus Room. Elvis later recalled, "After that first night I went outside and just walked around in the dark. It was awful."[68]

As they struggled to address the headliner conundrum, the Strip and Fremont Street hotels exploited the possibilities they saw in the cocktail lounges. After their midnight shows in their main rooms, hotel owners wanted to keep the gamblers on their property and in 1953 saw an opportunity to do so by not only expanding their lounges but bringing in more big-name performers. By early 1954 owners calculated that popular lounge acts might bring in more than a million dollars a year in additional gambling revenue.[69] The Sahara began it all by bringing in Cuban pianist José Melis, who later became the bandleader on *Tonight Starring Jack Paar*, to perform in the Casbar Lounge. The El Rancho Vegas soon after countered with Steve Gibson and the Red Caps, a popular rhythm and blues combo, in the Cabaret Room. The impact was immediate. "A huge volume of repeat business was the reward at both the Sahara and El Rancho," according to a Las Vegas columnist. Adding to the attraction of these hot lounge acts was the presence of "the show folks . . . in nightly attendance."[70]

The Last Frontier followed with the popular Mary Kaye Trio, who had performed in the Ramona Room as headliners in the Gay Nineties Bar with a small stage and room for two hundred. The trio quickly "became an object of devotion by showfolk and locals alike."[71] Other hotels, including the downtown Hotel Fremont with its Carnival Room, soon upgraded their lounges, and in 1955 the El Rancho Vegas added "all night dancing." As with the battle for headliners in the main rooms, a "second front" emerged in the lounges, and the Sahara upped the ante by bringing in Artie Shaw, the "King of the Clarinet." By the end of the decade Billy Daniels, Shecky Greene, Harry James, Roberta Sherwood, Don Rickles, and Della Reese were performing in the lounges. *Variety* magazine began providing reviews of these performers and the *Las Vegas Review-Journal* began running a weekly column called "Loungin' Around" with updates on current shows.[72]

Tourists could come to Las Vegas, see a dinner show and late show featuring headliners, then head to the lounges, where some acts performed from six in the evening until dawn. By the mid-1950s, most were inevitably drawn to the Sahara to see Louis Prima and Keely Smith, the superstars of the lounges. By 1954 Prima, a forty-four-year-old trumpet player, had long toured on the nightclub circuit, released several successful records, and composed "Sing, Sing, Sing," Benny Goodman's signature tune, but by the early 1950s his career was in a lull. He had married singer Keely Smith in 1953 and, seeking jobs, called Bill Miller at the Sahara.[73] Miller had no slots open in the Congo Room but offered to let Prima play in the Casbar Lounge. While disappointed, as he had been a headliner at the El Rancho Vegas, Prima accepted. He and Smith were so successful that they enjoyed a five-year stay at the Sahara. Prima called their music "hot jazz, swing, progressive jazz, Dixie and rock n' roll all rolled into one."[74] As he played his trumpet, Prima jumped and danced about the small stage while his backup group, Sam Butera and the Witnesses, supplied "a wild, relentless, driving beat that punched through the lounge's smoke and chatter and left crowds in awe."[75] Amid this cacophony of sound, Smith looked on as if bored by it all, but then broke in to sing in a beautiful "smoky voice."[76] Their energetic and exuberant style created a fanatic following. Whenever they were performing, everyone, notably celebrities and high rollers, wanted to see them. People lined up hours before their first show. As *Time* reported, "the space between lounge and gambling room piles up ten deep with waiting fans," and they would wait around until the fourth or fifth show of the early morning hours to see them.[77]

Dancers and showgirls emerged as the last critical element in the developing Las Vegas entertainment scene in the 1950s. Dance lines, from the Desert Inn's Donn Arden Dancers and the Thunderbird's Katherine Duffy Dansations to the Sands' Copa Girls and the Flamingo's Ron Fletcher Dancers, had always added glitter by opening and closing the shows for the headliners. "The seven plush show palaces on Strip 91," local columnist Alan Jarlson wrote in 1953, "boast snappy chorus lines, dressed to perfection and showing to the utmost advantage, a precision that could" equal the famed Radio City Music Hall Rockettes "were they equal in number."[78] The dance lines gained great visibility in popular culture. Two films during the decade, *Girl Rush*, starring Rosalind Russell, in 1955 and *Meet Me in Las Vegas* with Dan Dailey and Cyd Charisse in 1956, included several numbers performed by the dance lines at the Flamingo and the Sands. Novels and pulp magazines of the era also contributed to the "lure" of the hotels' dancers, a "curvy parcel of the world's most gorgeous gals."[79] In 1957 Lloyd Shearer, in *Parade*, the widely distributed Sunday magazine, claimed that Las Vegas had the most "chorus girls" of any city in the country."[80] While most choreographers wanted only experienced dancers in their lines, occasionally an entertainment director like Jack Entratter and choreographer Barry Ashton chose beauty over experience. As Ashton explained in 1960, "I don't care whether they dance great or not. I can teach them. We can put gorgeous gowns on them and teach them."[81] Regardless of their background, dancers faced production numbers that usually involved a substantial amount of preparation in the selection of wardrobe, music, dance sequence, and rehearsal, and it paid off as critics rarely panned a dance line's numbers.[82]

Because of their popularity, entertainment directors, particularly at the newer hotels, began to consider offering "production shows" built around the dancers and showgirls as an alternative to the headliner model for Las Vegas shows for the most obvious of reasons. As *Time* magazine pointed out in 1955, most of "the stars were already sewed up in three-year deals by the established hotels."[83] Al Gottesman, co-owner of the new Dunes Hotel, made clear to the entertainment press that he intended to produce "spectacular revues, with a sizeable chorus line" as a way to lure in the tourists.[84] In spring 1955 he brought in British producer Robert Nesbitt, known for staging successful spectacles, to offer "Magic Carpet Revues" for the Dunes like "New York-Paris-Paradise," the opening production with a cast of sixty.[85] That effort flopped, but Major Riddle, who succeeded Gottesman at the Dunes, partnered with entertainment director Bill Miller to offer a Harold Minsky production in 1957. Best known for shows featuring comics with baggy pants and striptease dancers, Minsky created a production show called "Minsky Goes to Paris," which, according to Esper Esau, who worked on the stage crew, was "a quasi-vaudeville effort with slapstick comics, production numbers" and "a large cast of male and female dancers."[86] The show was a hit. In summer 1958 "Minsky Goes to Paris" drew nine thousand a week to the Dunes.[87]

The Dunes' productions were a prelude to the true breakthrough production show. In summer 1958 the Stardust premiered "C'est Magnifique." With sixty performers, Pierre Louis-Guerin and Rene Fraday brought their famed Lido de Paris production to Las Vegas. This move by Stardust entertainment director Frank Sennes introduced Las Vegas to Margaret Kelly's Bluebell Girls, directed by Donn Arden. He was known for staging "the world's best night club shows" at the Desert Inn, Hollywood's Moulin Rouge, Paris's Lido, and New York's Latin Quarter. "Before I got there," Arden later explained, "Vegas had . . . no high-class girl shows," but according to fellow choreographer Barry Ashton, the Arden touch, with a "heavy accent on lavish line productions," transformed Las Vegas entertainment. His dancers had to be classically trained, and he "used tall girls because you can't put headdresses on little girls, and besides, they are lost on those huge stages. I'm into glitter. I'm very expensive. I can't work with rags."[88] Usually adorned in G-strings, fishnet tights, high heels, and large headdresses, the showgirls' role was not to perform complicated dance numbers but to move gracefully about the stage, adding elegance to production numbers.

The Stardust's spectacular Continental Theater had a stage with six hydraulic lifts, a swimming pool, and an ice rink for more than sixty performers. There

Valda Boyne, one of Madame Bluebell Margaret Kelly's dancers in the Lido de Paris show at the Stardust. *Courtesy University of Nevada, Las Vegas, University Libraries Special Collections and Archives, and personal collection of Valda and Esper Esau.*

were singers and a comedy team, but the Bluebell Girls were the big attraction. As one reviewer wrote, they were "a bevy of semi-nude beauties" who weaved "in and out of dazzling production numbers." In the *Dallas Morning News* Tony Zoppi predicted that the Lido show "will introduce an entire new trend of entertainment in Las Vegas."[89] He was correct. The El Rancho Vegas and Thunderbird added "French-revue" productions, and the Tropicana added the famed "Les Folies Bergere."

Besides the great production values of these shows, topless showgirls added to their allure. However, that element led to opposition from the management at the Sahara and the Sands, who rejected nudity in their shows, and to complaints from church leaders in Las Vegas as well as local politicians.[90] The state legislature even threatened to ban topless shows in 1959. Opposition was futile. In June 1960, *Life* magazine included a feature on three of these shows—"'Folies-Bergere' at the Tropicana, the 'Lido de Paris' at the Stardust, and 'La Parisienne' at the Dunes"—showgirl extravaganzas with "some girls gaudily overdressed, others blatantly underdressed." Most importantly to the hotels' owners, they were a spectacular success, collectively attracting "30,000 customers a week."[91]

By the end of the decade, Las Vegas columnists could not resist noting the decline of nightclubs around the country as their city's showrooms flourished. Typically, Ralph Pearl reminded his readers in 1959 that Las Vegas had "eleven major showrooms on the Strip" while "in Hollywood there is really only one night club, the Moulin Rouge. The other clubs are intimate and seat under 100. In Chicago the only nitery is the Chez Paree. In Manhattan there are two, the Copa and the Latin Quarter."[92] Because offering great entertainment had become a successful way to attract the biggest gamblers, resort hotel owners had made Las Vegas the nation's entertainment capital.

Four
Women in Las Vegas

On November 5, 1958, the Lido de Paris show "C'est Magnifique" drew a standing-room-only crowd to the Café Continental at the Stardust Hotel, as it had since opening in July. The show had amazed the critics. Hedda Hopper called it the "most spectacular I've ever seen," and Erskine Johnson labeled it "probably the greatest night-club show ever seen in the United States."[1] More important than the adulation of veteran columnists was the fact that the Lido de Paris, along with the Minsky show at the Dunes and the dance lines at the other hotels, represented a remarkable opportunity for hundreds of young, talented, and attractive women to make good money in the booming entertainment field in Las Vegas in the 1950s.

However, that same evening, about thirty women hoping to hold their jobs as dealers in the casinos learned to their frustration and disgust about the barriers to their ambitions in a resort town tightly controlled by men. In front of a packed chamber, city commissioners unanimously voted to ban women as dealers. One of the four hundred male dealers in attendance offered a rationale for the action that all had heard throughout their lives, indeed one deeply rooted in the American experience. He explained that permitting female dealers would lead to lower wages for the men, which in his view could be disastrous because "men are the basis for sound economy. A man when he gets married should support his wife and the children that he has." To Eddie Draper, who offered the commonly held notion of separate spheres for men and women, it was quite simple: "We favor men over women because men are the head of the family."[2]

Such was the milieu facing women who sought jobs in Las Vegas in the 1950s. As Joanne Goodwin has shown, women encountered "both restrictions and opportunities" in the resort town.[3] Compared to their counterparts across the nation, a higher proportion of women worked outside the home in Las Vegas because most jobs, though sex segregated, paid so well in the growing economy. It was a struggle for most in a community where men dominated the city and county government as well as the resort hotels. Culturally, Las Vegas and Nevada had long been known, as political activist and suffragette Anne

Martin wrote in *The Nation* in 1922, as a masculine locale, one that had easily embraced the pleasures of gambling, drinking, and prize fights.[4] Visiting journalists agreed. It was, according to Harper Leech in 1928, "the last refuge of the American male from the matriarchate."[5] When women were first made eligible to serve on juries in Clark County in 1921, many Las Vegas attorneys opposed seating them. "They are totally unfitted, mentally, to try the issues of a case," one attorney told a local journalist, "and their feelings are swayed not by the evidence presented, but by their emotions."[6] Las Vegas changed little in the intervening three decades, as Emilie N. Wanderer, the town's first female attorney with her own practice, learned. Shortly after she arrived in 1946, Wanderer interviewed with the firm of Jones, Wiener, and Jones. Partner Cliff Jones, then lieutenant governor of Nevada, offered her a job as a secretary, not as a lawyer. For a lawyer's position, she remembered him saying, "We wouldn't hire a woman."[7] So women in Las Vegas had to push constantly against widely accepted notions about the proper work for their gender. A few found success in male-dominated vocations, but the best opportunities for women were in the city's resort hotels and entertainment business. Many were willing to embrace well-paid jobs even if it meant that they had to accommodate "themselves to the commercialization of the female body."[8]

Occupational segregation dominated the work lives of women in America through the 1950s. Most who joined the workforce found opportunities largely in traditional "women's work," jobs with low pay, minimal opportunities for promotions, and few chances at supervisory positions. Moreover, the gap between women's and men's pay grew larger during the decade. Women unable to attend college usually found jobs in sales, clerical work, housekeeping, or on an assembly line manufacturing textiles. Those with college degrees overwhelmingly went into nursing or teaching, usually at the elementary school level. These kinds of positions, *Life* magazine argued in 1956, reflected "long-standing notions about the work she should do." "Household skills," for example, "take her into the garment trades; neat and personable, she becomes an office worker and saleslady; patient and dexterous, she does well on repetitive, detailed factory work; compassionate, she becomes teacher and nurse."[9] Most women sought jobs to supplement their family's income rather than to pursue careers. Having grown up during the deprivations of the Great Depression and the disruptions of World War II and now facing the uncertainties of the Cold War, most Americans in the 1950s sought refuge in the nuclear family. There, as Elaine Tyler May has shown, Americans believed they would find not only security but also "a vision of abundance and fulfillment." They married earlier, had more children, and enjoyed more stable marriages than the generation that preceded them. In troubling times, Americans were increasingly "homeward bound."[10] In that context, surveys in the 1950s that measured women's ambitions found that most gained greater satisfaction as housewives than in holding jobs.[11]

Nonetheless, the Las Vegas economy in the 1950s drew thousands of women eager for good jobs. "Average spendable income per household in Las Vegas is $8023," the *Las Vegas Sun* proclaimed in 1954, which was far above the national average of $5,246. By the next year, more than 8,000 people, many of them women, had jobs in the hotels, motels, casinos, and bars on Fremont Street and along the Strip. Indeed, 44 percent of Las Vegas women held jobs, compared to about a third of women nationally.[12] While the pay was good, most women in Las Vegas worked in jobs traditionally considered feminine—as housekeepers, waitresses, cashiers, clerks, nurses, and teachers.[13] Want ads in the local papers illustrated the pattern. In the "Help Wanted (Female)" section, employers predictably most often offered positions in housekeeping, babysitting, sales, typing, and waiting on tables. The situation was scarcely different in the "Situation Wanted (Female)" ads. Women, many of whom wished to work at home, largely sought jobs ironing and babysitting or as clerk-typists or practical nurses.[14]

In the hotel-casinos along the Strip, women found jobs serving drinks, food, or cigarettes and as change girls. Journalist Ed Reid discovered that pay could be quite good for some cocktail waitresses, as much as "two to three hundred a week." Indeed, some cocktail waitresses believed that theirs was "the top job in Vegas." However, "one had to have 'juice' to get such a job, which means knowing someone of importance, be it a pit boss or a hotel executive."[15] African American women had no such opportunities, as they faced the twin barriers of race and gender. They did find work along the resort corridor but only in "back of the house" positions. Typically, they worked as maids, dishwashers, kitchen help, or linen room attendants. However, the hundreds of African American women who had migrated from southern communities like Tallulah, Louisiana, and Fordyce, Arkansas, appreciated the dramatic increase in pay in Las Vegas. Lucille Bryant, for example, arrived in 1953, soon got a job cleaning rooms at a Strip hotel, and was delighted to make $8 a day, which was so much more than she had made as a domestic or working in the cotton fields in Tallulah. Still, African American women rarely found other opportunities in Las Vegas in the 1950s.[16]

A few bold women challenged the male monopoly on some of the best-paying jobs in the casinos but quickly discovered the formidable barriers to their quest. Keno was one of the more popular casino games in the 1950s, and keno writers, those who worked at the front of keno lounges recording wagers, made good money. Clara Garner was one of the first women who worked as a keno writer. However, although Garner trained many men, some of whom became her bosses, she never got promoted. When women began working as bartenders, usually because they and their husbands owned saloons, public officials and the Bartenders Union collaborated to block them from employment. Undersheriff Lloyd Bell claimed that female bartenders posed a law enforcement problem because they were unable to control customers who drank to excess, while union leaders explained that their opposition was not because "women are a problem 'per se'" but because "the employment of women endangered the salary scale being paid male bartenders."[17]

Male dealers in clubs made a similar argument as the Bartender's Union in opposing women intruding upon their work. They contended that once casinos in Reno began hiring female dealers, wages began dropping for men and women. It is true that from the early months of World War II, women had gotten jobs as dealers in casinos in Reno and at Lake Tahoe. In 1952 all Reno casinos had female dealers, and casino owners had successfully rebuffed efforts at both the state and local levels to keep women from the tables. As Raymond I. Smith, manager of Harold's Club in Reno, argued in opposition to a state ban, women "are better in every way than men" as dealers. By the early 1950s, women had become a majority of the dealers in Reno casinos and clubs. Yet Las Vegas casinos opposed the trend. Downtown clubs like the Monte Carlo, Las Vegas Club, and Nevada Club hired a few, but on the Strip, dealing at the tables remained a male domain.[18] This was true despite most dealers joining the Mutual Clerks and Gaming Employees Union, whose charter guaranteed "no discrimination against women dealers." Women were supposed to enjoy the same wages and benefits as men.[19]

At the November 5, 1958, city commission meeting, there was much debate about the impact women had on the pay for all dealers. Almost all the men who spoke at the commission session argued that "the women would work for less money and scuttle the economy of the area." One of the dealers claimed that "a similar situation in Reno 'wrecked' the gambling economy there."[20] Eddie Forsine, for example, told the city commissioners that he had been dealing in Reno until 1950 but fled to Las Vegas because "the girls drove me out." There indeed had been reports in Las Vegas papers in late 1953 that the "employment of transient women" in Reno casinos had prompted an exodus of male dealers to Las Vegas. Women in attendance countered with claims that they had worked for the same pay as men and had been working in Las Vegas for several years. A few claimed that they were the sole support for their families.[21]

In the wake of these contentions, the *Las Vegas Sun* published the results of a survey conducted among Reno dealers, players, and casino owners. It revealed that most of them rejected the Las Vegas dealers' arguments for a ban on women. One Reno pit boss argued, "They add a respectability and an honesty to the games that no man can give," and one longtime Reno gambler contended that a female dealer "softens up a house and takes gambling out of the basement and backroom atmosphere and brings it into the open." Moreover, members of the Reno city council indicated that they would reject such an ordinance if introduced.[22]

Nonetheless, the Las Vegas city commissioners bowed to the will of the hundreds of male dealers who filled their chamber and approved a resolution "that no women be employed as 'dealers,' . . . within the gambling clubs and houses of the City of Las Vegas."[23] The commissioners struggled to justify their vote to deprive women of access to well-paying jobs. Their only defense was that they had acted "for the protection of public morals." In their judgment, a woman dealing cards might lead to "bad publicity for the area," and they tended 'to induce people to gamble who would not otherwise.'"[24] An angry waitress wrote to *Las Vegas Sun* that the argument that women were taking men's jobs made her "boil." If the debate over women dealers represented a "war with sexes," she was "for it, if it will mean that I can work at the job I spent years training for." Further, she found it ironic that when women seek jobs, men "run shrieking and shrilling to the city pops. . . . Men, poor men."[25] Hers was not the only voice to ridicule the city commissioners' decision. The *Las Vegas Review-Journal* ran a front-page political cartoon lampooning their decision with a figure representing city commissioners trampling on "equal rights," the "constitution," and "employer rights" while painting signs saying "Women go home" and "A Woman's Place Is a Cocktail Waitress but Not a Dealer."[26] The city leaders' decision effectively confined women, as Eugene Moehring accurately put it, "to the so-called girl's ghetto of such lower-paying, low-prestige jobs as Keno runner, cocktail waitress, and cashier" until the 1970s.[27]

Despite the defeats in seeking jobs behind the bars and gaming tables, women in Las Vegas were able to break through in other areas of employment. Outside the resort industry, women were able to move beyond traditional entry-level jobs. At the Southern Nevada Telephone Company, for example, a few women who began as operators became supervisors, quality control clerks, and customer service representatives. One also landed a position as an engineer.[28] A few women secured positions as auditors at the resort hotels, but real estate provided better opportunities. When the Las Vegas Board of Realtors organized in 1946, only three of its forty members were women. For several years brokers usually used their few female employees to manage rental property rather than to sell houses and commercial properties. However, by 1960 more than a third of the 216 agents and real estate brokers in Las Vegas were women.[29] Amid the blitz of construction in the boom town, two women, Chris Fisk and Kitty Rodman, became building contractors. When Rodman moved to Las Vegas in 1952, she first found work as a secretary, but by the end of the decade she had established both the Sierra Construction Corporation and RKR Construction.[30]

Women found opportunities in journalism as well.[31] Ruthe Deskin, a graduate of the University of Nevada, who had worked as the women's editor at the *Reno Evening Gazette*, on radio, and in advertising and publicity in Las Vegas, accepted a position at the *Las Vegas Sun* as editor of its Sunday edition. Along the way, she became not only a trusted assistant to publisher Hank Greenspun but also a columnist for the paper.[32] Florence Lee Jones, who had a degree in journalism from the University of Missouri, became a court reporter for the *Las Vegas Review-Journal* in the 1930s and became its women's editor in 1951. Maisie Gibson became an assistant to Jones in the "society department" and eventually replaced her when Jones retired in 1953.[33] Dorothy Dorothy wrote columns for both Las Vegas newspapers in the 1950s from her home in Pahrump before moving to Las Vegas in 1958. Alice Key, who had worked for the *Los Angeles Tribune*, came to Las Vegas in 1955 as a publicist for the Moulin Rouge resort hotel. Key soon became a cohost with Bob Bailey of a television program called *Talk of the Town* on KLAS, channel 8, in Las Vegas. She also was involved in the *Voice*, an important black community newspaper.[34]

Several women secured positions in the public sector. None won election to the city commission, and only Maude Frazier was a member of the chamber of commerce's board of directors. Still, Ada Bassett headed the county welfare department, Dora Lord secured the position of assistant city manager in 1952, and Georgia Butterfield became postmistress eight years later. Sally Murphy was on the hospital board, and Peggy Hyde served on the school board. A few women held key positions for more than a decade. Mary Kennedy was nurse supervisor at Southern Nevada Memorial Hospital for fourteen years, Shirley Lodwick served as city clerk for the same number of years, and Helen Scott

Reed held the post of county clerk for seventeen years.[35] Some were in state government. Lawyer Emilie N. Wanderer served on a panel to reform state probate law.[36] In 1959 Governor Grant Sawyer appointed Dorothy Dorothy to the state parole board, and Helen Herr and Maude Frazier represented Las Vegas in the state assembly.[37] Frazier, an educator who served six years as the deputy state superintendent of schools and two decades as superintendent of Las Vegas schools, won election five times to an assembly seat during the 1950s and worked tirelessly for school reform and better funding for education. In 1960 the *Las Vegas Sun* remarked upon her success in the male-dominated legislature: "Frazier should be particularly honored and revered by those of the so-called weaker sex, who strive for more recognition in a man's world." Frazier had demonstrated, as an increasing number of women had done in other fields in the 1950s, that "a woman can hold her own . . . , and on occasions prove herself superior, to the men folk with whom she works in making our laws."[38]

In the resort hotels women found opportunities for not only good pay but also supervisory or executive roles, albeit often in positions considered feminine. Some, like Ann Kelsey at the Last Frontier and Darlene Larson at the Sans Souci, were hostesses for the dinner shows. Peggy Godwin was the head cocktail waitress at the Sahara, and Betty Singer was the social director at the Sands. In his daily column Les Devor described Singer's many duties. Besides "setting up luncheons and parties for organizations," Singer was on the scene to help all guests get reservations for shows at other hotels, find babysitters, or just hold on to "a winner's earnings."[39] A 1956 article in the *Las Vegas Sun* also dealt with this new reality for women. Beyond the hundreds of "housekeepers, waitresses and general office workers," readers learned, many women held "executive positions in the hotel setups," working as "executive secretaries and assistants" as well as "reservation managers and publicity directors." For example, Florence Ladd served as Gus Greenbaum's executive secretary at the Riviera, and Margaret Moore was an administrative assistant at the New Frontier. Charlotte Ellsworth was the reservations manager at the Flamingo, and Elinore Wiley was reservations manager at El Rancho Vegas.[40] Seven women—Ruth Brady, Bea Ratcliffe, Dorothy Gunn, Geri Nolan, Marge Friend, Vi Taylor, and Maxine Lewis—all served as publicists, a profession that attracted ever more women across the country.[41] Lewis emerged as the most visible hotel executive. She held many posts, including entertainment director at the Flamingo and El Rancho Vegas and publicity director at the Tropicana.[42] The most important breakthroughs, however, occurred in 1956 at the Hacienda Hotel at the south end of the Strip.

Owner Warren Bayley selected two women for key positions. He picked Bonnie Dorland as maître d', making her the first woman in Las Vegas to hold that post. Bayley also tapped Melba Moore, who had worked two years at his Fresno, California, Hacienda, to head operations at the Las Vegas location. As the press release made clear, Moore had the responsibility to "oversee all phases" of the property.[43]

The entertainment needs of the resort hotels provided many opportunities for women. Among the approximately eight hundred musicians playing in the casino orchestras of the hotels in the late 1950s, there were a few female harp and string players.[44] The proliferating lounge acts often included women, usually as vocalists. Some, notably Mary Kaye and Keely Smith, were huge successes and became fixtures in the lounge scene. Of course, dozens of women headlined shows along the Strip. At times female headliners at the major resort hotels outnumbered men. In early June 1959, for example, headliners Patti Page, Eydie Gormé, Marlene Dietrich, Connee Boswell, and Jayne Mansfield outnumbered Ted Lewis (who had equal billing with Marie McDonald), Mickey Rooney, Harry Belafonte, and Nat King Cole.[45] Female headliners often received paychecks comparable to those of their male counterparts. In the first two years of the decade at the Flamingo, female headliners averaged $5,400 a week, while male headliners averaged about $700 more. As compensation for headliners skyrocketed through the rest of the decade, female headliners shared in the bounty. By 1954 Kay Starr was making $20,000 a week, Betty Hutton $25,000, and Marlene Dietrich $30,000.[46]

There were also jobs to be had behind the scenes of the fabulous dance lines at the resort hotels. By 1960, as James Kraft has shown, many had found well-paying jobs as wardrobe workers. "Every large resort," he explained, "employed a dozen or more seamstresses and costume makers, even those that purchased readymade costumes from outside sources." They "also helped dress performers for shows and assisted them with quick changes of clothing during performances." Mae Burke's experiences illustrated the possibility for promotion as a "wardrobe mistress." After jobs at the El Rancho Vegas and Royal Nevada, Burke moved on to the new Tropicana in 1957. There she became head of wardrobe. In addition to managing a large staff during performances, Burke "inventoried the wardrobe, ... ordered repairs or supplies as necessary," "prepared work schedules, distributed payroll checks, and dealt with grievances."[47] Similarly, Madame Pauline, the wardrobe mistress for the Copa Girls at the Sands Hotel, played a critical role for the dance lines there. When the young women chosen at auditions arrived in Las Vegas, Madame Pauline took all their measurements, sent the results to a New York company that made the costumes, and completed the "final fittings" for the new dancers once the garments arrived. Copa Girl Judy Jones remembered Madame Pauline as "the star of her room and all the scissors and material scraps and spilled glitter" as her "stage set." It was "a fabulous room."[48]

As the number of resort hotels rapidly expanded, there was an ever-greater need for choreographers for the dance lines, which typically changed their routines with the arrival of each new headliner. Some choreographers, like Sonia Shaw, were married to other choreographers. With her husband, Bill Hitchcock, Shaw started Shaw-Hitchcock Productions, and the couple managed many of the dance lines at the Sahara and El Rancho Vegas. As a *Las Vegas Sun* columnist noted in 1959, they typically were responsible "for the ideas, choreography, staging, music, lyrics, scenery and costume concept and personnel of the dance productions."[49] Ruth Landis and her husband, George Moro, had two dance lines in Las Vegas and one in Reno, and they ran a dance school in Las Vegas.[50] Dorothy Dalton was the choreographer for the Dottie Dee Dancers, and her husband Don Tomlin managed the dance line that performed at the El Rancho Vegas.[51] Renee Stewart was a partner with Bob Gilbert at the Sands, but others like Jean Devlyn, Gale Robbins, and Dorothy Dorbin worked alone. Most came to Las Vegas with a substantial background in dance. Dorbin, for example, had started her career as a dancer in Chicago in the mid-1930s. During the next fifteen years, she moved from dancer to choreographer to entertainment director before moving to California, where she started dance lines at hotels in Los Angeles and San Francisco. Dorbin also choreographed dances for television's *Colgate Comedy Hour* and Hollywood films. This rich background enabled her to produce "superlative line productions at the New Frontier" in 1956.[52]

Because sexuality was the lure for so many men who visited Las Vegas, many women found work that made them simply a commodity. Novels and articles in newspapers and magazines frequently focused on the city's strippers and prostitutes. In 1955, for example, the pulp magazine *Pose* offered a typically misogynistic characterization of some of the women at work in Las Vegas. "Amid the plush, neon-lit casinos and fabulous hotels, Boulder Dam, sage brush and cactus," the article noted, "there is an abundance of women, all kinds of women; buxom hausfraus, bulging in blue jeans, cocktail waitresses who can be talked into working after hours, strip-tease girls and out-and-out harlots who cruise about in Cadillac convertibles.[53] Critics of Las Vegas charged that publicists skillfully sold these "hazy outlines of sexuality," creating "a vision of

Las Vegas that casino owners hope is burning in the minds of people across the continent."[54]

Burlesque, featuring the "strip-tease girls" of Las Vegas, was "part of the entertainment menu from the Strip's beginnings, though at first the gals wore pasties or dropped their tops at the end of a song, just as the spotlight blacked out," Mike Weatherford has written. Although burlesque was diminishing across the country in the 1950s, it flourished in Las Vegas.[55] Early in the decade, the Embassy Club in North Las Vegas thrived, featuring performers like Doreen Manos, "The Red Headed Bombshell"; Tracy Randall, "The Blond Venus Head-liner from Hollywood"; Lily Lamont, "The Alaskan Heat Wave"; and Ricki Covette, "Tallest Girl in Burlesque, 6 Feet–8-In. Exotic Tower of Loveliness."[56] A fire destroyed the abandoned club in 1956, but there were a couple of short-lived venues on the Strip. Briefly, in 1953 there was the Hi-Ho Club in what had been the Grace Hayes Lodge on the west side of the Strip. County commissioners rejected owner Michele Marchese's request to call the place Strip City. Indeed, they approved a license on the understanding that Marchese would not stage "girlie" shows. Although he assured them that would not be the case, Marchese soon had "bump and grind dollies . . . snapping their G-strings," which inevitably led the commissioners to suspend his license, and Marchese left town.[57] Between the Flamingo and the Sands, Monte Gardner, a veteran of burlesque shows in the East, opened Monte's with a "Girl's A-Poppin" revue. In summer 1957 Monte's "well-stacked stable of robust dress-droppers" quickly developed "a land office business" with four shows a night. According to local entertainment columnist Ralph Pearl, "the big brass of Vegas" tried several times to shut it down. Finally, in February 1958 county commissioners obliged by revoking Monte's liquor license because of repeated complaints about "B-girl operations, padded bills, drugged drinks and service to minors" at the establishment.[58] There were other venues for burlesque, or parodies of burlesque. For a short time on Boulder Highway, the Club 7th One had a show with "No Cover: That's Exactly What We Mean!" On New Year's Eve 1956, the Showboat featured Chili Bon Bon, Sweet as Candy, and Camille, "An Exotic Personality." The Silver Slipper had many such shows like "Girlesk Follies of 1957," the Sans Souci had an "Adults Only" show called "Paris Scandals" with "14 Gorgeous French Models," and in 1959 the Westside El Morocco Club offered "Miss Wiggles," the "Toast of the Coast."[59]

Amid the plethora of burlesque dancers, three emerged as stars in the 1950s, making between $2,000 and $5,000 a week. Candy Barr always packed the house at the El Rancho Vegas, Silver Slipper, and Desert Spa. After watching Barr's "G-string gyrations," columnist Ralph Pearl described her as "that nerve shattering Texas tornado who shakes and shimmies like a gal dancing on a hot stove."[60] Tempest Storm, "a sultry, red-haired burlesque strip teaser," first performed in Las Vegas at the Embassy Club in 1952 and had become a huge draw by 1957, when she helped the Dunes Hotel "set an all time attendance record." In three shows with the Minsky Revue, Storm "played to 2,115 with more than 600 turned away."[61] As in his review of Candy Barr, Ralph Pearl could not resist hyperbole in describing Storm's performances. "Sensuous and as nude as a jay bird at birth," he wrote in 1958, "the orange haired, attractive Tempest Storm indulges in brief but cyclonic bits of undress to music." Storm almost turned the Dunes "into the most glamorous garage in history by a G-string no larger than is legally necessary."[62] Lili St. Cyr gained the greatest fame, appearing regularly at the El Rancho Vegas, most often with comedian Joe E. Lewis.[63] St. Cyr developed several seductive routines, but the finale to her 1955 performances gained the greatest attention. Katharine Best and Katharine Hillyer described it in their 1955 book *Las Vegas, Playtown U.S.A.*: St. Cyr "appears on stage in such radiant undress that audiences are rendered not only speechless but gaspless. Her appeal is particularly demonstrated by the finale of an act called 'Bird in a Gilded Cage,' in which she soars out over the audience in a gilded cage dropping beaded panties, frilly garters, and sequined bras on the hands-outstretched spectators below."[64] One of St. Cyr's appearances got her into legal trouble. In 1951 District Attorney Roger D. Foley attended one of her shows, watching her "disrobe except for a towel and climb into a bathtub on the hotel stage." The following year Foley successfully prosecuted St. Cyr on a nuisance charge, and she ended up paying a $200 fine.[65]

In early 1960 Hank Greenspun complained about a particular category of female workers, the "call girls" frequenting Las Vegas hotels. He claimed, "For every girl picked up by the sheriff's department, I can point out 10 that got away."[66] Prostitution had been part of Las Vegas from its beginnings. City founders had sought to restrict it to the infamous Block 16 downtown. In 1918 a *Los Angeles Times* travel columnist described to his readers how he had wandered into that "strange and restricted district and decided to take myself away from there at once, escaping from a buxom lass of doubtful color and antecedents at great peril to my coat tails."[67] Block 16 remained the center of a thriving business for almost another quarter-century. There were nearly forty prostitutes in Las Vegas in the 1920s largely servicing travelers, railroad workers, and ranchers, but their numbers increased dramatically in the early 1930s as the large crews working on Boulder Dam came to town on weekends.[68] In World War II the U.S. Army forced the town to close its red-light district after establishing a gunnery school just outside Las Vegas. This added federal government pressure to local entrepreneurs' efforts to close down prostitution so that they could redevelop Block 16. After the war, community leaders tried to eliminate prostitution throughout Clark County. However, as late as 1954 there were still at least four brothels in the county, notably Roxie's Four Mile Motel just beyond the city limits, and there were still "street hustlers" working downtown and along the Strip.[69] After county commissioners approved an ordinance prohibiting prostitution and a California federal court found Edward and Roxie Clippinger, Roxie's operators, guilty of violating the Mann Act, authorities finally were able to shut it down.[70]

Still, the business remained profitable, and the number of prostitutes grew. In early 1953 the sheriff's office reported that ever more "ladies of easy virtue" were "flocking to this area on the weekends to work the resorts which are crowded with tourists." Moreover, "several taxi drivers" were "making a lucrative killing through steering the visitors to the proper places," and "some bellboys" were "picking up a few fast bucks by accommodating the roving males with proper room numbers."[71] Court appearances, trials, numerous "vice raids," and undercover operations in the 1950s revealed much about the work of prostitutes. During the Clippingers' trial in 1954, the sheriff's office revealed that they had records on one hundred prostitutes. Six years later, when deputies arrested Mrs. Irene Rusignuolo on charges of grand larceny they found that she had four books with names and phone numbers of prostitutes' "alleged customers" and the amount paid by them. The books included the names of men across the nation and "several prominent Las Vegans."[72] During the 1950s, prostitutes in Las Vegas made between $50 and $200 "for their favors," though they normally had to pay part of their income to those who arranged their work. By 1960 those apprehended claimed that they made between $500 and $2,000 a week at their work.[73]

A different kind of "commercialization of the female body" captured the nation's attention in the 1950s as most noticed the spectacular emergence of the dancers and showgirls at the resort hotels. Las Vegas attracted these talented women, as celebrity columnist Lloyd Shearer noted in 1957, because the city's hotels have "the most publicized and photographed chorus girls in the country." Shearer claimed Las Vegas had become "the garden spot in the world" for dancers and showgirls with between 200 and 300 "out of a national total of fewer than 900."[74] The publicity truly was grand. *Life* magazine, which built its reputation on great photography, had a particular fascination with Las Vegas chorus girls. A 1960 article, one of several in *Life*, featured three Strip showgirl shows—"'Folies-Bergere' at the Tropicana, the 'Lido de Paris' at the Stardust, and 'La Parisienne' at the Dunes." In addition to a brief narrative, the article included full-color photos of the shows' dancers and showgirls.[75]

Besides the extraordinary publicity, great compensation lured talented dancers and showgirls to Las Vegas. While it was common for them to make less than $70 a week in Paris and London and about $100 a week at the Latin Quarter in New York, those in Las Vegas made much more. In 1948 and 1949, Nancy Williams Baker made $75 a week at the El Rancho Vegas, but by the early 1950s, she was making $100 a week at the Flamingo. The Copa Girls at the Sands each made $128 a week in 1954, a figure that rose to $150 three years later. By 1961 Ed Reid contended that pay for some dancers at the resort hotels had reached $225 a week.[76] Moreover, most hotels provided accommodations for their dancers at a reduced rate. Dancers at the El Rancho Vegas at the beginning of the decade paid less than $15 a week, and although rates went up over time, most paid no more than $6 or $7 a night. More important for the dancers from overseas, accommodations in Las Vegas were vastly superior. They had their own rooms with hot showers, air conditioning, and television. They also got some of their meals either free or at a substantial discount.[77] When not rehearsing and on their occasional days off, dancers had some free time during the day for sunning at the pool, horseback riding, boating on Lake Mead, skiing on Mount Charleston, or playing the slot machines. About 10 percent were married, and a few did volunteer work during the day. On the rare evenings they were not performing, their stage managers could usually get them into other shows.[78]

For many of the dancers, the most exciting aspect of their job was seeing and meeting all the celebrities who either performed in or attended the shows. Joy Blaine Garner remembered "all the famous people" who would "sit right in front of us." In particular, she recalled an evening when Marilyn Monroe "was sitting ringside and I looked down, and she was absolutely gorgeous." Monroe "looked up at each girl and smiled at each of us individually. It was just so endearing."[79] It was a remarkable thrill for these dancers to meet the top celebrities of their era, like Jerry Lewis, Gary Cooper, Lucille Ball, Clark Gable, and Jimmy Durante, or to drop by the lounges after work to see the hottest acts. Occasionally, they had dates with celebrities. Jane Ryba, for example, dated Elvis Presley.[80] Most headliners also treated the dancers well. Some would do a special third show on

a day other than Saturday for the dancers at the resort hotels who had to perform in a third show that night. Headliners like Frank Sinatra often arranged
welcome dinners for the dancers when they returned to perform at the hotels.
Virginia James recalled Dean Martin treated all the dancers "just like family."[81]
But it was Sammy Davis Jr. who the dancers appreciated the most. When he
performed in Las Vegas, Davis occasionally dropped by during their rehearsals,
usually invited all the dancers to watch movies in the Gold Room at the Sands,
sent them roses, and gave each a gift at the end of his run.[82] The glamour of it all
was addictive. The great music and choreography, along with "lovely showgirls
adorned in Austrian Crystals, Ermine and Mink," were breathtaking to those
who had the chance to dance in Las Vegas in the 1950s.[83] The crowds, likewise,
were elegantly dressed. "When people came to Las Vegas," Gail McQuary
recalled, "it was like going to a gourmet restaurant . . . where you had to dress
up and you had to act the part." Even if those in the audience were not wealthy,
"they dressed up because this was the place to come to dress up."[84] Those who
came to the dinner show and the midnight shows in their best gowns and suits
were also appreciative of what they saw. Joan Kerr told entertainment columnist
Earl Wilson in 1953 that, unlike the crowds in California and New York, those
in the Las Vegas resorts were "friendly and warm."[85]

While dancing in Las Vegas had made many advantages, there was much
work to do. For almost all the dance lines there were two shows a night and
a third on Saturdays. Then there were the rehearsals. Nancy Williams Baker,
who began at the El Rancho Vegas in 1948, explained, "We were always rehearsing because the shows changed every two weeks." To Williams, it seemed like
they spent their lives "practicing and rehearsing." To be precise, most weeks
dancers rehearsed from four to six hours a day.[86] Choreographers were not just
demanding; they could be downright tough on the dancers. Donn Arden had
the most notorious reputation. "He was imperial in manner and expectation,"
Betty Bunch recalled. Often "caustic, sadistic, and extremely confident," Arden
could terrify his dancers. Yet, according to Bunch, they "would also do almost
anything to gain his approval."[87]

Beyond what many saw as a "grueling" schedule, all the resort hotels expected
their dancers, after both the dinner show and second show, to "mix" with the
clientele at the bar, in the lounge, or in the coffee shop. They could not dress
casually but had to wear cocktail dresses. As Nancy Williams Baker explained,
the bosses told their dancers, "You girls have to dress up the joint!" Or, as Gail
McQuary described their role, "you had to make a presence in the hotel, to look

pretty, to make everything nice."[88] Casino managers often asked the dancers to chat, have a drink, gamble, or have dinner with one of the gamblers, but usually, Joan Ryba explained, "there was no pressure" to do so. A typical example involved Copa Girl Judy Jones. The stage manager asked her and another dancer to have dinner with the famed gambler Nick Dandolos, better known as "Nick the Greek." Occasionally, a dancer refused to "mix" and quit a show, but most enjoyed it as the experience made them feel like celebrities. Gail McQuary liked getting "dressed up" and having people ask for an autograph.[89] However, Margaret Kelly, better known as "Madame Bluebell," refused to permit her dancers at the Lido de Paris show at the Stardust to mix.[90]

Most who danced in the 1950s called Las Vegas "the chorus girl's Shangri-La," a "pot of gold at the end of this neon-lighted rainbow."[91] Years later they invariably still recalled their experience in glowing terms. Denise Miller, who danced at the Flamingo, Last Frontier, and Thunderbird, called Las Vegas a "paradise." After struggling to make a living as a secretary in Los Angeles, she believed that in her move to Las Vegas, she "had found heaven."[92] Valda Esau and Tracy Heberling, who danced at the Stardust, likewise felt fortunate to have been in the Lido show. As Heberling put it, "we all feel that we did have the best of it."[93] While it seemed that she was working all the time, Gail McQuary "loved every minute of it," and Judy Jones could not have imagined working at a better place than the Sands in the 1950s. Betty Bunch fondly recalled everything about her time in the shows. "We were paid very generously," she explained, "and we were well treated and it was a glamorous, elegant job—a culmination of a lifelong dream to come work with the major stars."[94]

According to author Linda Chase, some might see the Las Vegas dancer or showgirl "as a sad, degraded creature, a piece of meat paraded before the mostly male audience."[95] Pulp magazines of the 1950s aggressively pushed this perspective. In 1958 *Real Men* published an article with ten photos of showgirls. "When these talented showgirls make the rounds of the Vegas night spots, even the dice tables empty in a hurry." One photo caption proclaimed, "Girls, choruses and choruses of them! Enough beauty to set men's imaginations afire round the entire world!" Every night, "this bevy of beauties has set the town on its ear!"[96] The dancers and showgirls understood, Fluff LeCoque explained, that "the intent of the producer was to idealize the female form." The dancers knew that audience members wanted to admire them and came to expect physical "perfection" in their appearances on stage. Local entertainment columnist Bill Willard pondered this in 1952, when he asked, "Does the general public attending shows at our resort hotels want to see these elaborate and danceworthy productions, or do they merely want girls to ogle?"[97] Yet none of the dancers interviewed for the Las Vegas Women Oral History Project saw themselves as "a pawn or a victim" in their shows. Rather, they perceived "a kind of power in the showgirl image; one available only to women."[98]

Las Vegas Sun publisher Hank Greenspun emerged as the most visible and vocal man to offer a perspective on the changes happening for women in the workforce in the community rapidly emerging as America's Playground. A self-proclaimed rebel, Greenspun never shied from taking on the powerful, whether it was Pat McCarran, Nevada's longtime senior senator; Joseph McCarthy, the Wisconsin senator who called the publisher a communist; or the mobsters in Las Vegas. Greenspun was also one of the few white voices in Las Vegas advocating equal rights for blacks. But he, like most other men of the era, did not extend that argument to women. Like the male dealers, who argued in 1958 that men should have access to the best-paying jobs because they were the heads of households, Greenspun asserted that it was important to maintain separate spheres for men and women. "It was planned by some power higher than a Las Vegas city commission," he wrote, "that woman's work should be confined to those tasks which they can do gracefully, skillfully, ably and with all the talents which are peculiar to women alone." Greenspun spoke for many men when calling for "full equal rights and suffrage," but only "within the confines manifested by the natural laws." And those natural laws dictated that men keep "women up on a pedestal" and don "a suit of armor to fight for their chastity."[99]

This perspective led Greenspun to condemn the "immorality" associated with both strippers and topless dancers. "They are distasteful to me," he wrote in 1960, "whether served up in the guise of art or just downright bump and grind."[100] Prostitution, however, most appalled him. Greenspun wrote in an often reprinted column, "A community that tolerates prostitution provides an insatiable market for the procurer who recruits prostitutes. It provides an ideal business background for the exploiters, the pimps, who live on the earnings of this racket."[101] As to the dispute over female dealers, he could not imagine that a woman could "remain sweet and angelic with a can of beer in one hand, a cigarette dangling from her lips and dealing blackjack with the other hand."[102] He did "firmly believe that there is a place for women in the commercial, industrial and artistic fields." Yet that role should be "more intellectual, artistic, social and even commercial." For example, while Greenspun believed that the gaming tables were no place for women, he did champion the appointment of Muriel

Joy Blaine Garner, who danced at the El Rancho Vegas, Riviera, Tropicana, and the Sands. *Courtesy Las Vegas News Bureau and Joy Blaine Garner.*

Tsvetkoff as the first director of the Las Vegas Better Business Bureau. "From the way men have been handling things," he wrote in 1955, "it might be for the better."[103]

In contrast to Greenspun's dismissive tone in the debate over women dealing in Las Vegas casinos, dealer Connie Delaney spoke bluntly for other women about jobs men considered off limits for women. She asserted simply, "We deserve the right to work."[104] Lawyer Emilie N. Wanderer, who certainly would have agreed with Delaney, was one of the few voices in Las Vegas to challenge the widely held perception that women should marry and remain at home. Wanderer argued, as she had shown was possible, that women should aspire to a career while having a family.[105] As she reflected upon the significance of the opportunity to perform in Las Vegas, dancer Joy Blaine Garner offered an even more compelling perspective, one that most men could appreciate. She understood that the rapid growth of Las Vegas in the 1950s provided unusual opportunities for financial success. Born in nearby Boulder City, Garner quickly discovered the world of entertainment in Las Vegas offered her a remarkable chance that few women in America enjoyed in the 1950s: to become economically independent. Dancing at the El Rancho Vegas, Riviera, Tropicana, and ultimately in the Copa Room at the Sands ("*the* place to work"), Garner "made as much money as most men made back in those days." At the time, "I was supporting my mother, my brother, myself and my son." She became "the man in the family." Garner was able to buy a house "for $900 down and a hundred a month." Garner's characterization of her achievement reflected a slowly growing reality for women in Las Vegas and is evident in her use of personal pronouns: "I made the living, I went out and worked, and it afforded me independence."[106]

Five
Struggles for Black Entertainers

On the evening of September 24, 1957, the National Broadcasting Company (NBC) telecast the *Nat King Cole Show* from the fabulous Copa Room in the Sands Hotel in Las Vegas. Cole, a jazz pianist with a silky smooth baritone voice, had become one of America's favorite singers with several hit singles like "Mona Lisa" and albums like his 1957 release *Love Is the Thing*. His success had led NBC to make him the star of a variety series in fall 1956. It began as a fifteen-minute program but expanded to a half hour in summer 1957.[1] In the process Cole became the first African American to host a nationally broadcast network television program. However, there were several challenges for him and the network. While nearly eighty NBC affiliates picked up the program, many stations in the South "either never carried it or soon dropped the show," not wanting to offend their white viewers.[2] The same fear made it impossible for NBC to attract national sponsors, and the network had to rely on regional sponsors like Rheingold Beer in New York and Gallo Winery in Los Angeles.

While most of the shows aired from New York or Los Angeles, NBC broadcast four from the Sands Hotel when Cole was performing there in late September and early October of 1957. Near the end of the September 24 program, Cole introduced the staff in the Copa Room, including host Nick Kelly, maître d' Jess Kirk, the seven showroom captains, waiters, busboys, waitresses, chefs, and entertainment director Jack Entratter. When the camera panned the dozens of employees, as well as the audience, viewers saw only white faces.[3]

There is little doubt that Cole consciously revealed to a national viewing audience that he was performing in a segregated casino-hotel. He had first performed in Las Vegas at the Thunderbird Hotel in 1949. While Mort Ruby, his white road manager, had a suite at the hotel, Cole had to stay, according to Ruby, at "a motel on the other side of the tracks." Moreover, Cole could not enter the hotel except through the kitchen.[4] Cole's humiliating experience was typical for most black performers in Las Vegas in the fifteen years after World War II. For these accomplished artists it was a frustrating and often surreal experience. It was, as singer Johnny Mathis explained, "almost like watching a sad, sad movie."[5]

Given these degrading conditions, why would so many black singers and musicians perform in Las Vegas resort hotels, knowing the discrimination they would undoubtedly face? Singer Harry Belafonte explained simply, "How could we do otherwise, when the choice was taking maybe $5,000 a week to play the Apollo or taking $25,000 to $50,000 for a week in Vegas." Lena Horne agreed, "It was and is where the big money is for a cabaret entertainer. . . . The lure is only money."[6] The lucrative contracts were not a product of the altruism of the hotel owners. Rather, they reflected the ever-greater demand for headliners along the Las Vegas Strip, and the escalation of their paychecks reflected the reality that black headliners could reliably draw good crowds. The meticulous records of Maxine Lewis, entertainment director at the Flamingo, reveal that her twenty-eight headliners in 1950 included Louis Armstrong; the Charioteers, a pop and gospel group; Steve Gibson and the Red Caps, a rhythm and blues combo; vocalist Arthur Lee Simpkins; and Lena Horne. The white Flamingo headliners received an average of just over $4,500 a week, while their black counterparts earned on average just under $3,700 a week, with Horne getting $7,900.[7] Over the next three years, leading black headliners commanded much more. Billy Eckstine got $10,000 a week at the Sands, Josephine Baker topped that with $12,500 at the Last Frontier, and when Lena Horne moved to the Sands, they paid her $13,000 a week.[8] Nat King Cole, however, saw the biggest jump in pay. At the Thunderbird in 1949, he earned $4,500 a week. Less than a decade later, he was making more than any other Las Vegas headliner. In 1956 his three-year contract at the Sands guaranteed him $500,000 to perform ten weeks each year.[9]

Black headliners also enjoyed great publicity when performing in Las Vegas. Large advertisements with hyperbolic copy announcing their performances filled the two local newspapers, and their names covered billboards along the Strip. When she first appeared at the El Rancho Vegas in 1954, Eartha Kitt was pleasantly surprised on her way from the airport to the hotel to see her name in "letters taller than I" on a sign.[10] Local entertainment columnists invariably gave glowing reviews of the black artists' shows. For example, the reviewer for the *Las Vegas Sun* described Lena Horne after her opening at the El Rancho Vegas in 1951 as "one of the great dramatic song stylists of all time," and *Las Vegas Sun* columnist Ralph Pearl dubbed Dorothy Dandridge "one of the top song stylists in America today."[11] Performing in the "Entertainment Capital of the World," particularly at the signature showroom on the Strip, the Copa Room at the Sands, was also a big boost to a young performer's career. Johnny Mathis

Johnny Mathis performing in the Copa Room, 1958.
Courtesy University of Nevada, Las Vegas, University Libraries Special Collections and Archives, Las Vegas News Bureau, and Johnny Mathis.

had been performing largely at colleges before appearing in the Copa Room and saw his 1958 engagement there as "a wonderful opportunity."[12]

Even though the pay and exposure were often fantastic, the circumstances black performers faced were in turns irritating, insulting, and humiliating, constant reminders of their perceived second-class status in the prosperous tourist center. The first challenge was always to find a place to stay while performing. The Delta Rhythm Boys were the first black group to perform in Las Vegas. The popular quartet signed with the Hotel Last Frontier in 1944. Carl Jones, first tenor and arranger for the group, later recalled that hotel management would not let them stay on the property. Instead, "they put us in a little shack downtown that had been the Red Light district," a reference to Block 16 that had been designated for legal prostitution in the town's early years.[13] Frustrated by the shabby treatment by the management of the Hotel Last Frontier, the four men signed with the El Rancho Vegas, demanding "that they be quartered at the hotel." They also demanded that they could "eat in the main dining room with all of the other guests and have the run of the entire place." The Delta Rhythm Boys had successful runs in Las Vegas, all the while generating plenty of positive publicity. A reporter for the *Plaindealer*, a black newspaper in Kansas City, Kansas, contended they quickly became "favorites of the ritzy social colony" of "eastern socialites and Hollywood celebrities."[14] From that point, the Delta Rhythm Boys specified that they would perform only in hotels where they could also stay.[15]

In the late 1940s and early 1950s, the Delta Rhythm Boys' success was uncommon. Most black performers encountered a degrading experience during their time in Las Vegas. They may have arrived in town eager to have a chance to sing or dance in the great showrooms, but upon reaching the hotel that had signed them, typically the hotel manager would tell them that they could not stay there, though their white road managers had complimentary suites. Most found themselves staying on the segregated Westside of Las Vegas. Black performers consigned to that neighborhood all recalled the shabby housing and the unpaved streets that created a depressing "Dust Bowl."[16] Sammy Davis Jr. remembered that when he first performed in Las Vegas with the Will Mastin Trio, as the taxi carrying them approached the boarding house where they were to stay, he saw "a three-or-four-year-old child, naked, . . . standing in front of a shack made of wooden crates and cardboard."[17] Harry Belafonte, who had signed to perform at the Thunderbird in 1952, remembered being taken to a "colored motel" on the Westside that could best be described as "a filthy fleabag motel."[18] Although not true in either Belafonte's or Davis's case, most of the black entertainers stayed in rooms owned by Genevieve Harrison or Alma Shaw. Harrison began renting rooms in her bungalow on Adams and F Street in 1942 and over time added rooms to her home. By 1954 the "Shaw motor court" had expanded to thirteen units with kitchens to accommodate the ever-increasing number of black performers.[19] An editorial in the Westside newspaper *The Voice* described the two facilities as "fairly decent," though the owners charged "exorbitant prices."[20]

Regardless of the quality of the accommodations on the Westside, these artists faced essentially the same question best posed by Johnny Mathis. When he performed at the Sands in 1958, Mathis was the hottest singer in America. The twenty-three-year-old had the nation's best-selling album, "Johnny's Greatest Hits," and he played in front of "packed houses" in the Copa Room. As one entertainment columnist described his run, Mathis was "a socksational hit."[21] Moreover, his warm and friendly manner, according to a local columnist, had "quickly won him the respect . . . of everybody in the Sands from the busboys on up to owners." Yet he had to stay on the Westside. He appreciated the quiet and comfortable room, one with a kitchen where he prepared his own meals. However, Mathis confronted the same quandary as all the other performers: "The first thing that came to mind was: why can't I stay at the hotel?"[22] Occasionally, black performers found accommodations in a cheap motel along the Strip or in a trailer behind the hotel. Dinah Washington, for example, when performing at the Sahara Hotel in 1955, stayed in a trailer and even had to change clothes there. While Stan Irwin, the hotel's entertainment director, was proud of the "marvelous trailer park type of accommodations" for black performers near the Casbar Lounge, Washington was so outraged at the restriction that she vowed never to return to Las Vegas. She did return to Las Vegas in 1960 but stayed in the home of one of the leaders in the local branch of the NAACP.[23]

Exacerbating their frustrations, black performers encountered the reality that "there were rules" concerning their access to the property where they performed.[24] Most of the hotels required that black performers enter only through the kitchen door. They could not go into the restaurants, coffee shops, casinos, lounges, or the swimming pools. Their dressing rooms were usually makeshift affairs, often, as in the case of Nat King Cole at the Thunderbird in 1949, "a sitting room that was fixed up adjoining the kitchen."[25] There were rare exceptions. Johnny Kirkwood, Louis Jordan's drummer, remembered that during breaks from performing at the Sands Hotel, the musicians could remain but "had to go to a booth and sit there. We were allocated a waiter so that we didn't mingle with the guests."[26] And that was the point: management did not want them to socialize with patrons of the resort hotels. They were there to entertain, not to mix. As Eartha Kitt vividly recalled her first time in Las Vegas as part of the Katherine Dunham Company when it performed at the El Rancho Vegas in 1948, "none of us were allowed through the front doors: through the kitchen to our dressing rooms was the path, and no mingling. Immediately after our show we had to return to our quarters in the black area."[27] Some hotels did not even want black performers mixing with the women in the dance lines. Betty Bunch, who performed at the Sahara in the mid-1950s, was shocked when a pit boss informed her and the others in the dance line that they were not, under any circumstances, to have any interactions with the Treniers, a singing group of five brothers.[28] The impact of the seclusion was predictable. Pete Kameron, who managed the folk group the Weavers, was in Las Vegas while Harry Belafonte performed at the Thunderbird and noted, "Next to his dressing room, which was quite small, the management gave him another room. Here he could eat, relax, receive friends. This was his isolation booth. It bugged him, made him edgy and depressed him."[29]

Just as management at the hotels made clear the restrictions on their properties, black performers likewise found the Las Vegas business community unwelcoming. As Sammy Davis Jr. learned his first time in Las Vegas, the movie theaters were segregated. After a performance at the El Rancho Vegas, Davis went downtown to see a Mickey Rooney movie. Before the film began, he recalled, "A hand gripped my arm like a circle of steel, yanking me out of my seat, half dragging me out to the lobby." A man with a badge and "big Western hat" asked, "'What're you, boy? A wise guy?'" An unknowing Davis protested that he did not understand the rough treatment. The man then pointed to a sign that read "Coloreds sit in the last three rows" and told Davis, "Mind our rules and you'll be treated square."[30] Others, like vocalist Gwen Weeks and a friend, dined in a Las Vegas restaurant only to have, as in Weeks's case, the manager ask them not to return because "their appearance would hurt his business with white people."[31] When Welsh singer Shirley Bassey appeared at the El Rancho Vegas in 1957, she and her white agent Michael Sullivan went out to other nightclubs until Beldon Katleman, the owner of the El Rancho, told Sullivan, "White men and black women should not be seen together in public." As Sullivan recalled the meeting, Katleman contended that recently "a white man [had] dated a coloured singer here and he got beaten up."[32]

Black performers were accustomed to discrimination in many parts of the country, including the Southwest and mountain states. Two studies in the 1950s found that as the black population increased in those regions, discrimination increased with it. Whether it was Bisbee, Arizona; Pocatello, Idaho; Cheyenne, Wyoming; Butte, Montana; Albuquerque, New Mexico; or Salt Lake City, Utah, blacks faced segregated public accommodations. The situation in Nevada, however, was particularly egregious. One of the studies found the situation to be "almost on par with that of the deep South."[33] "Oldtimers" in Las Vegas told journalist James Goodrich in 1954 that the problem lay with "the early gamblers" who "were from the South and brought racial prejudice with them." *Pittsburgh Courier* columnist William Nunn's research led to a similar conclusion. He argued that those who established the Jim Crow regime in Las Vegas were from Texas, Oklahoma, Arkansas, and Mississippi—"whites with those 'oil' bankrolls." Hank Greenspun, publisher of the *Las Vegas Sun*, would have acknowledged that the visiting journalists had an accurate grasp of the situation. After living for a decade in the city, he wrote in 1955 that "Las Vegas has long been a backward town in its attitude toward civil rights and race relations."[34] Governor Grant Sawyer described the situation similarly. When he won election in 1958, Sawyer was eager to attack "civil rights abuses." However, he encountered a gaming industry resolute in its opposition. He claimed that the hotel and casino owners "had an obsessive fear of being forced to permit blacks to enter casinos" because they assumed that "would drive away white patrons."[35]

As Sawyer's assessment demonstrates, many of those running the hotels and businesses in Las Vegas deflected the responsibility for their discriminatory actions to the attitudes of tourists in town. As Louis Jordan's trumpeter Aaron Izenhall recalled about his experience performing at the Thunderbird in 1949, management told him and his fellow musicians that they could not go into the casino because "they had gamblers in there from Texas and Mississippi."[36] Major Riddle, owner of the Dunes, said that whenever he had permitted blacks into his hotel, he encountered "resentment about Negroes in our hotel." In fact, he claimed, his white guests "virtually rebelled."[37] Sportswriter Roger Kahn, who covered the New York Giants for the *New York Herald Tribune*, heard the same explanation when he witnessed an incident involving the Giants' great centerfielder Willie Mays and a security man in a casino in 1954. The Giants had played the Cleveland Indians in an exhibition game in Las Vegas, and that night several of the players went to a casino. Kahn observed the security chief ask Mays to move along from the gaming tables, saying, "We don't want him mixing with the white guests." When Kahn started arguing with the man, a casino vice president and his assistant took the writer aside and explained that they didn't care if Mays played the slots, but "there's a lot of body touching around the crap tables. People brushing up against each other real close." More directly, they told Kahn, "We're really in the South here. We get a lot of customers from Texas."[38]

Given the pervasive discrimination at the resort hotels, along the Strip, and downtown, some black performers pursued the path of least resistance, a retreat into their own solitude. In the late 1940s, Sammy Davis Jr. and Dorothy Dandridge spent most of their free time alone reading, sleeping, and listening to music. A decade later, Johnny Mathis likewise "spent many, many, many hours listening to music and learning my craft by listening to Broadway productions and motion picture soundtracks," hoping to find "songs I wanted to sing."[39]

Others sought a sense of community on the Westside. Beyond a place to stay, Westside nightclubs and casinos gave black performers a place to relax, gamble, and enjoy jam sessions. There were beauty shops and barber shops that they frequented and neighbors to visit. When he stayed at Harrison's rooming house, Nat King Cole liked chatting with the children along the sidewalk as he smoked outside.[40] The Westside became an even more appealing place with the mid-1950s arrival in Las Vegas of Dr. Charles West, the community's first black physician, and Dr. James McMillan, the first black dentist. They purchased homes in the new middle-class housing development known as Berkley Square which bordered the Westside. Both men had swimming pools and often invited visiting entertainers to use them. When vocalist Joe Williams, saxophonist Frank Wess, and trombonist Benny Powell performed in Las Vegas in 1957, they rented a house near those owned by West and McMillan. Williams recalled that they not only swam in their pools but also found it to be a neighborhood where they "could feel comfortable and have our privacy and guests."[41] For the children of the neighborhood, it was a remarkable opportunity. As Jarmilla McMillan-Arnold, Dr. McMillan's daughter, recalled, she had "the most outrageous childhood because of the entertainers she got to meet. Singer Dinah Washington stopped by her house and Harry Belafonte played football on the streets with neighborhood boys."[42] Black performers demonstrated their gratitude by dropping in at popular night spots on the Westside like the Town Tavern. They also pitched in at various fund-raisers.[43]

In one instance, the local branch of the NAACP tried to assist black performers as they sought to secure accommodations at the hotels where they were performing. In 1948 the Hotel Last Frontier signed Josephine Premice for two weeks. However, the management refused to provide the twenty-two-year-old Broadway singer and dancer and her accompanist with accommodations because they were black. Premice's sister was the secretary of Gloster Current, an official at the NAACP national office, and on behalf of the young singer Current wrote to the Reverend William H. Stevens, president of the Las Vegas branch. "I do not know whether or not hotels in Las Vegas deny accomodations to Negroes. I'm referring this matter to you in the hope that you or the NAACP will be able to secure accomodations for her."[44] Stevens, minister at the Zion Methodist Church on the Westside, learned that the Hotel Last Frontier "usually sends its colored entertainers to the Westside." However, he called Jimmy Dugan, the hotel's public relations man, who, Stevens explained, did not know that he "was colored." Stevens said simply that he was a minister "requesting that Miss Premice be allowed to stay at the hotel." Stevens drew upon an argument that he thought would appeal to a publicist. "There were many liberal citizens" in

Las Vegas, he pointed out, "who would approve of such actions." Dugan readily agreed, got entertainment director Hal Braudis' approval, and persuaded hotel manager Bob Cannon to approve the request. Stevens called Premice to let her know the good news. However, the hotel manager later informed the singer that while she was welcome to stay there, she could not dine in the restaurant. So, not wanting to "be a prisoner in her room," Premice opted to stay at Harrison's rooming house.[45]

There were also occasional instances of white performers interceding for black performers. In 1946 comedian Joey Bishop took his act to Las Vegas while family friend Arthur Lee Simpkins was to perform at the Hotel Last Frontier. When management refused to allow Simpkins to stay at the hotel, Bishop declined his own room and stayed elsewhere. The two of them tried to order a meal at a drive-in restaurant, but a waitress refused to serve them. When Bishop protested another customer came over to his car and hit him with a serving tray.[46] Intervention by whites was no guarantee of success. In the late 1950s, Al Freeman, the publicist for the Sands Hotel, accompanied Nat King Cole and black singer and local television personality Bob Bailey to the new Tropicana Hotel at the south end of the Las Vegas Strip. According to Bailey, "they turned us around at the door and would not allow us in. Al got in a fight with the security guard." "When Al said, 'that's Nat King Cole,' the security guard checked with someone and explained, 'I don't care if it is Jesus. He's Black and he has to get out of here. Both of them.'"[47] Still, there were the rare successes. On the closing night of his stint at the Riviera in 1959, comedian Red Skelton violated the "rigid Jim Crow policy" of the hotel by having "as his guests, front row, ringside, Lionel Hampton and his wife Gladys, and all the members of the Hampton band." According to *Jet* magazine, Skelton's bold gesture led to "a lot of 'red faces' in the main dining room."[48]

Frank Sinatra emerged as the most influential white performer who sought to break down the segregation barriers. In 1961, at the height of his influence in popular music, films, and Las Vegas, Sinatra gave a short monologue at the end of one of his performances at the Sands Hotel. In the Copa Room, Sinatra told his audience that when he began performing in Las Vegas, he learned that "black performers . . . were living on the other side of the town." Not understanding that bigotry, Sinatra claimed, "I began to make noise about it. A few threats like: I'll walk, I'll go back to L.A." He noted that the situation had changed over time, and he took credit for it. "I did make some demands on some people and said, 'Listen, if they all have to live on the other side of town, then you don't need me.'

I think a few other entertainers began to pick up on that too and they hollered, but I guess I was the biggest mouth in the town."[49]

A victim of ethnic bigotry when growing up in New Jersey, Sinatra had early in his career become an opponent of discrimination. Near the end of World War II he spoke often about racial tolerance, and in 1945 he made a short film targeting bigotry called *The House I Live In* that won a special Oscar. He visited Benjamin Franklin High School in New York City, a school experiencing significant racial strife, and gave a speech condemning religious and racial intolerance. He also traveled to Gary, Indiana, and called for an end to the white students' boycott of the integrated high school there, calling their action "shameful."[50] In a 1958 *Ebony* magazine article, Sinatra continued to denounce bigotry and to call for tolerance and acceptance. "A friend to me," he explained, "has no race, no class and belongs to no minority."[51]

Sinatra also used his celebrity clout on occasion to persuade nightclubs to hire black performers to open for him, particularly those with whom he had developed strong friendships. As James Kaplan has explained in the case of Sammy Davis Jr., who was part of the Will Mastin Trio, "in 1947, when Sinatra headlined at the Capitol Theatre in New York, he demanded that the management hire the Mastin Trio to open for him, at five times their usual salary."[52] Once he became a fixture in Las Vegas, Sinatra continued his campaign against bigotry, particularly when it involved Davis. Sinatra refused to perform at the Sands unless Davis could stay there, gamble, and use the steam room along with white performers. In 1960, while he and Davis were having a drink in the lounge at the Sands, they observed security personnel escorting two black couples from the property for no apparent reason. According to author Alan Pomerance, "Sinatra flew into a rage, called top management to the scene, and invited both couples to stay at the hotel as his guests."[53] Sinatra had some successes because the entertainment director at the Sands, Jack Entratter, was more willing than most of his peers to accommodate the demands of his star headliner. Both Billy Eckstine and Las Vegas entertainment columnist Forrest Duke agreed that Entratter was a leader in permitting black performers not only to stay on his property but also to dine in the restaurants and gamble in the casino. Nat King Cole biographer Daniel Mark Epstein argued that "Entratter's hotel became an oasis of sanity in a desert of prejudice" in the mid-1950s.[54] Still, there were limits to what Entratter could or would do. Johnny Mathis recalled him as a "very kind" man who was "sort of a father figure" during his first appearance at the Sands in 1958. Yet, Mathis's manager had not negotiated full privileges for the young singer, and Mathis understood his "place as a performer would be to stay in the background."[55] Lena Horne often challenged Entratter, arguing that, as a headliner, she should be able to enter the Sands through the front door.[56]

The efforts of Sinatra, Entratter, and other whites produced at best only sporadic results and brought no truly significant change. Black performers gained access to all the facilities of the resort hotels largely through their own efforts or the initiative taken by their agents. Those who understood their star power and the great need hotels had for headliners and, more important, who were willing to push for the end of discrimination in public accommodations usually got what they wanted. Jazz singer and pianist Hazel Scott, popular veteran of Hollywood and the nightclub circuit, signed to play at the Hotel Last Frontier in spring 1952. As *Jet* magazine noted about her two weeks in Las Vegas, "Jim Crow reluctantly took a brief holiday" because Scott would perform only "on condition that she be given full guest privileges."[57] This was nothing new for Scott, who had a well-earned reputation for fighting discrimination in accommodations, notably three years earlier when she sued a Pasco, Washington, restaurant that refused to serve her.[58] On the heels of Scott's appearance at the Hotel Last Frontier came an even greater force for change. Josephine Baker had agreed to perform only if the hotel management accepted her "now-mandatory nondiscrimination clause." The civil rights activist was widely known for boycotting segregated nightclubs, and hotel manager Jake Kozloff, eager to have the famed celebrity performing in the Ramona Room, yielded and even relented to her demand that her musicians stay in the hotel.[59]

After his humiliation at the Thunderbird three years earlier, Harry Belafonte would sign with the new Riviera Hotel in 1955 only if management agreed to a contract that stipulated that he and "his accompanist would be guaranteed a suite of their choice at the Riviera" with "guaranteed access at all times to any and all public spaces at the resort." Unlike the dismissive treatment of just a few years back, the hotel staff treated him "like royalty." Belafonte recalled, "I'd settle into the hotel's largest suite, overlooking the Strip and desert beyond, do my two shows, then stroll into the casino, still wearing my red satin toreador's shirt, tight black pants, and mohair jacket."[60]

Nat King Cole became equally assertive. In 1953 Beldon Katleman, the owner of the El Rancho Vegas, sought to sign the star vocalist. Cole had his personal manager Carlos Gastel explain to Katleman, "We will work it, providing Nat and the boys can live, eat, gamble, drink or whatever they want to do on the premises

of the El Rancho Vegas, without any prejudice shown against them whatsoever."
An eager Katleman complied with all the conditions.[61] A couple of years later,
Gastel, who wanted to have Cole perform in the more prestigious Copa Room,
negotiated a similar understanding with Jack Entratter at the Sands.[62]

In a rare moment of candor for Las Vegas entertainment columnists of the
era, Forrest Duke asked Cole in 1955 "his views on the Vegas Jim Crow situation," which, Duke told his readers, "surprises most newcomers." Cole, ever the
gentleman, diplomatically told Duke that several black performers including
Lena Horne and Harry Belafonte "have done much to improve public relations
here." Still, "we have a long way to go, but we'll make it."[63] Despite his success
in eliminating the discrimination for his appearances, Cole, like other black
performers in Las Vegas, faced considerable criticism when he appeared before
all-white audiences. Cole explained why he did so. "The whites come to applaud
a Negro performer like the colored do. When you've got the respect of white
and colored," he argued, "you can ease a lot of things. . . . I can help to ease the
tension by gaining the respect of both races all over the country."[64] That was
Cole's consistent approach. As Johnny Mathis explained, "because of his stature
and his carriage and the way he was, he would never put himself in a situation
where he was a negative person."[65]

Following the assertive approach of Scott, Baker, Belafonte, and Cole who
demanded contracts that guaranteed no discrimination, some black performers like Joe Williams and his musicians simply ignored the "directives" they
encountered in resort hotels. For example, Williams enjoyed strawberries and
cream and simply went to the hotel's coffee shop for the dessert. If someone
refused to serve him, according to his biographer Leslie Gourse, Williams would
say in a loud voice, "THIS IS JOE WILLIAMS. I WANT TO BE ACCOMMODATED."[66]

Because of the successes of these assertive performers it became common
for more black headliners to have accommodations at the hotels where they
were performing. Eartha Kitt had stayed on the Westside when she was with the
Katherine Dunham Company in 1948. However, when she returned in 1954 as
the headliner at the El Rancho Vegas, she explained, "I was taken to my cabin
of luxury that was just like a regular little house, everything included. A bottle
of champagne waited in a bucket. Flowers scented my room. I felt strange and
alone, but wanted."[67] The management at the Hotel Last Frontier agreed to let
Dorothy Dandridge stay in the hotel in 1953, and Shirley Bassey, when she headlined at the El Rancho Vegas in 1957, enjoyed "a beautifully appointed wooden
cabin" on the grounds.[68] Restaurants and coffee shops more readily welcomed

black performers, at least when entertainment columnists were interviewing them or when white performers accompanied them.[69]

Yet management at these properties often either insisted that performers like Dorothy Dandridge stay away from the swimming pool or resorted to subterfuge to keep black performers from the water.[70] Hazel Scott's experience is instructive. In 1952 her contract with the Hotel Last Frontier included assurances of "full privileges" while she performed there. However, when Scott indicated that she would be using the hotel's swimming pool, management decided it was time to repaint the facility, and it remained closed for a few days. As Scott neared the end of her two-week run, the painters finished the job, and the singer went swimming. According to a story in *Jet* magazine, "indignant Southern guests" complained, and management again closed the pool. As Scott explained the situation, in the first instance "they might have been painting the pool and legitimately, but after I finally did get to go in, they closed the thing off again for chlorination. That's the longest chlorination job I've ever seen around a pool—three days!"[71] Harry Belafonte had a bold but simple solution for the ban on the access to the swimming pools. During his 1952 run at the Thunderbird, Belafonte simply jumped into the pool. Half a dozen white guests quickly climbed out, but instead of a confrontation with security for violating the rules, no trouble developed because some white youngsters came over to Belafonte asking for his autograph, and parents asked if they could take pictures with him and their kids. The singer called his direct action "my private act of revenge against their bullheaded prejudice."[72]

As black performers struggled to gain access to the hotels and those properties' facilities, black residents of Las Vegas and black tourists had almost always found the shows off limits to them. Black residents who knew men like Jack Entratter could call, and, as local entertainer Bob Bailey explained, Entratter "would give an OK from the doorman all the way through the 'check points' to let me in."[73] There were also instances when bold black residents challenged the segregation policy by simply walking into the hotels. Predictably, they would encounter security personnel who would tell them, "You're not supposed to come here." Yet Lubertha Johnson explained that she and friend Mabel Hoggard would "finally talk our way in" and not leave.[74] Moreover, in his investigation of Las Vegas in 1954, journalist James Goodrich discovered that "there have been instances where light-skinned Negroes 'passing' for white have fooled the club owners and gained admittance."[75] Yet, these were truly the exceptions and not the rule.

Hazel Scott, for one, found it unacceptable to perform to all-white audiences if there were black residents who wanted to see her. Consequently, she invited a group from the Westside to attend her performance in the Ramona Room at the Hotel Last Frontier. When Bob Cannon, the hotel's manager, said that it would be "impossible to seat them," Scott told him that either her friends would attend or "there'll be no second show." Cornered, Cannon yielded to the singer.[76] Scott's action was only a prelude to that of Josephine Baker—at least that was the prediction of local entertainment columnist Bill Willard, who wrote to a friend, "Josephine Baker will not only have full privileges of the hotel, but will see that Negro residents come out from 'behind their iron curtain' (Las Vegas' Westside sharply divided from the rest of the town) and attend her nightly soirees."[77]

Indeed, Baker informed Jake Kozloff, "she would perform for an interracial audience, or she would not perform at all." She asked two leaders of the local branch of the NAACP, Lubertha Johnson and Woodrow Wilson, to select individuals to sit at a reserved table for six at each performance. On opening night, according to David Hoggard, Kozloff would not let them in, which prompted one of them to contact Baker. She reminded Kozloff that if there were no black guests there would be no show, and the hotel manager yielded. After the tense opening night, all the people NAACP leaders sent to the Hotel Last Frontier "were treated well."[78] Sammy Davis Jr. likewise demanded that the Hotel Last Frontier permit his grandmother, stepmother, and sister to attend one of his performances. In his review of that night in summer 1955, *Las Vegas Sun* columnist Ralph Pearl wrote, "I couldn't help but think how important are the Sammy Davises all over the country who have a hand in helping to hurl aside the unsurmountable barriers facing their race."[79]

As some performers enjoyed hard-earned triumphs, a potential comprehensive solution to discrimination at the resort hotels emerged in the early 1950s. Hotel developers and the investors they attracted noted the growing black population in Las Vegas (nearly three thousand in 1950), and, more important, an increasingly large untapped potential market nearby in Southern California. As journalist James Goodrich wrote in 1954, "Negro civic leaders in Vegas have tried to convince local white business people that they are missing out on a bonanza trade by their Jim Crow methods. The argument is that since most of Las Vegas' tourists come from California and particularly Los Angeles, a big Negro market is going untapped. The Los Angeles area, in actuality, has more than 300,000 Negroes."[80] The first halting steps at exploiting these local and regional markets came in 1949 when an entrepreneur sought to keep a struggling hotel in business. The Nevada Biltmore, a property with a hotel, showroom, and casino, had opened in 1942 near the train depot downtown. During the next seven years the property changed hands several times. When bandleader Horace Heidt owned the Biltmore, it became a showcase for premiere nightclub talent like the Mills Brothers, Martha Raye, fan dancer Sally Rand, and Chico Marx. However, the various owners always struggled financially.[81] In 1949 Homer W. Snowden, a Dallas oil executive, purchased the Biltmore and had Stanley Hunter, a seventeen-year veteran of Nevada gambling, apply for gaming and liquor licenses and manage the hotel. Hunter explained that the Biltmore had "been dying on its feet," so he and Snowden decided that they would strike out in a new direction and seek the "colored trade exclusively."[82]

Hunter's announcement prompted Mayor Ernie Cragin to convene a special meeting of the city commissioners, who quickly revoked the Biltmore's liquor and gambling licenses. Local members of the NAACP, notably branch president Woodrow Wilson, protested, calling upon city leaders to "respect minority rights in the Biltmore matter," but city leaders would not reverse their decision. A defiant Hunter moved forward, proclaiming the Biltmore would remain open for business and that "all personnel will be Negroes." Black guests could not gamble at the Biltmore, but they could enjoy the rooms, swimming pool, and meals (including alcoholic beverages if they brought their own bottles). However, Hunter could not attract enough business and closed the hotel after only five weeks of operation.[83]

Three years after Hunter's experiment, the *Las Vegas Review-Journal* reported that the Clark County planning board had approved "a tentative map submitted by Hugh Macbeth, Los Angeles attorney, for the construction of a Westside city to be known as International Village."[84] In June 1952 Macbeth, known in the black press as a leader "in the fight against racial prejudice," had incorporated International Village in Nevada. Three months later, Macbeth purchased 160 acres, with plans for a $5.5 million luxury hotel and casino to anchor his expansive project. His intent, and that of his fellow investors, notably Studio City, California, furniture store owner Morris Gaylord, was to "cater" to an interracial clientele with a focus upon "Negro, Chinese, and Mexican" patrons.[85] However, the Securities and Exchange Commission later determined that the money raised by the sale of securities was "largely dissipated or diverted to the personal benefit of promoters," and the project died.[86]

Macbeth began again in November 1953 with International Spa Incorporated, focused exclusively on plans for an integrated luxury hotel and casino. This second version of his vision, so dramatically different from the segregated resorts at the time in Las Vegas, never progressed beyond the planning stages because Macbeth had, according to government regulators, "no information as to the number of persons who might be expected to avail themselves of such facilities in the Las Vegas area." Because of the absence of thorough market research and Macbeth's "misapplication of funds," the SEC issued a stop order on further sale of stock, effectively killing Macbeth's grand venture for an interracial resort in Las Vegas.[87]

In late summer 1954 news broke about two more resort hotels with plans to welcome "any race, creed or color." Developers, led by Lester L. LaFortune of Las Vegas and Norman O. Houston, president of the Golden State Mutual Life Insurance Company in Los Angeles, planned to construct the Las Vegas Continental between North Las Vegas and Nellis Air Force Base. News releases about the Continental included descriptions of a six-story tower with 250 rooms at an anticipated cost of $5 million.[88] The planned two-hundred-room Tangiers was to be "in the heart of the new Westside." Developers promised a resort hotel and casino with an Olympic-sized swimming pool and a nine-hole golf course. In neither case, however, were developers able to raise sufficient funds to begin construction.[89]

Another entrepreneur named Will Max Schwartz, convinced that an interracial resort could succeed in Las Vegas, purchased land on Bonanza Road near the Westside community in 1954. When the city commissioners approved a zone variance for Schwartz's planned Moulin Rouge resort, Massie Kennard, editor of the city's black newspaper, *The Voice*, could scarcely restrain his excitement about the prospects for "the first cosmopolitan hotel in the state of Nevada." Not only would it offer "a resort hotel comparable in all aspects of luxuriousness to the Strip Hotels," but he believed it "will provide the incentive for other investors to come into our community."[90] The difference between the Moulin Rouge and the other proposed integrated resorts was that Schwartz was able to complete construction on the project. He attracted two major partners, Alexander Bisno, a Beverly Hills realtor who had invested in apartments in Las Vegas, and Louis Rubin, the owner of Chandler's Restaurant in New York City. Among the twenty-five investors approved by the state tax commission, including boxing champ Joe Louis, who served as a host for the hotel, Bisno and Rubin had 60 percent of the stock.[91] As construction proceeded, there was a swirl of rumors about entertainers who would perform in the showroom. In December 1954 Joe Louis reported that the management team had made offers to Lena Horne and Sammy Davis Jr., along with promises of a glittering array

Moulin Rouge Hotel, the first interracial resort hotel in Las Vegas, opened and closed in 1955. *Courtesy University of Nevada, Las Vegas, University Libraries Special Collections and Archives and Las Vegas News Bureau.*

of other talent including Count Basie, Duke Ellington, Nat King Cole, Dorothy Dandridge, Harry Belafonte, and Pearl Bailey.[92]

While they were not able to sign most of the stars promised, Schwartz, Bisno, and Rubin nonetheless spared no expense in building the luxurious resort that cost $3.5 million to construct. The 210-room wood-framed hotel and casino with pink stucco had a large neon "Moulin Rouge" sign and a brick tower adorned with another neon sign. There were two swimming pools, a gourmet restaurant, a lounge, and gift shops.[93] A visiting journalist described the hotel rooms as elegant with "warm walnut" furniture and "fine prints of French scenes" on the walls.[94] Bob Bailey, who served as emcee for the shows, recalled "bright and colorful" carpeting, "mahogany paneling," "leather and velvet" furniture, and "crystal chandeliers." The Café Rouge, the showroom at the Moulin Rouge, had nearly five hundred seats, "sophisticated lighting and sound equipment, and perhaps the most modern projection booth in the city."[95] It truly was spectacular, and contemporaries saw it as the equal of the Strip resorts.

More important than its opulence was what it meant as an experiment in interracial gaming. While Joe Louis was the only black investor, there were many black men on the management team. Besides Louis, who was a hotel host, the owners hired Sonny Boswell, the former Harlem Globetrotter basketball star who had managed properties in Chicago and Los Angeles, as the hotel manager. Clarence Robinson of New York Cotton Club fame was the producer and entertainment director, and jazz legend Benny Carter was the musical director. Jimmy Gay served as personnel director, Pat Patterson was the maître d', and Bob Bailey was the emcee for the shows.[96] Several white men with considerable gambling experience were in charge of the gaming, notably George Altman, formerly a pit boss at the Last Frontier, who became the casino manager.[97] The staff—bellboys, waiters, waitresses, cigarette girls, cooks, and dealers—included white and black employees, a striking departure from the practices of all the other resorts in Las Vegas. The biggest difference was the talented all-black dance line directed by Clarence Robinson. The dancers performed the cancan and a Watusi number that captured the attention of reviewers and that graced the cover of *Life* magazine's June 20, 1955, issue.

Local black residents were thrilled with the opening of the Moulin Rouge because there they faced no barriers to a spectacular floor show, to a gourmet meal in the Deauville Room, or to staying in a luxurious resort room. They saw it as "truly a milestone of progress," an establishment where all in attendance "felt that that they all were of one race." In summer 1955 it was common for residents on the Westside to take friends to the Moulin Rouge for dinner parties and to have out-of-town guests stay at the hotel.[98] *Las Vegas Sun* publisher Hank Greenspun hailed the opening of the Moulin Rouge as "a positive, affirmative act toward the belief that all men are created equal."[99] Alan Jarlson, one of the *Sun* columnists, agreed: "The keynote of the Moulin Rouge, of course, is that it's inter-racial—open to people of all races. The owners are deserving of orchids for the magnificent job they accomplished in introducing a new and pleasant atmosphere to the resort world."[100]

Columnists with black newspapers were excited about the prospects for Las Vegas with the opening of the Moulin Rouge. Al Monroe wrote in the *Chicago Defender* that the opening of the resort had revolutionized Las Vegas "whites' way of thinking and acting at the sight of black faces. For the first time in the long history of this town of dollars, dice and cards dominos were rolling as potently, as freely and sometimes as profitably for Negroes as for whites." In Monroe's judgment, as far as Las Vegas was concerned, "old man Jim Crow is felled and actually trampled."[101] William Nunn of the *Pittsburgh Courier* agreed, arguing that in the Moulin Rouge "the forces of segregation and discrimination are taking a helluva walloping."[102] In *Jet* magazine, Gerri Major claimed that the action at the Moulin Rouge proved "that people of all colors can eat, drink and lose their money in the same room without 'incident.'"[103]

Pittsburgh Courier columnist Evelyn Cunningham offered the most compelling argument about the significance of the opening of the Moulin Rouge. "Being a member of a race that is alternately persecuted and slandered," she wrote, "I felt like a crazy mixed-up kid as I stretched out on the terrace of the Champagne Pool at Moulin Rouge and ordered a nice young boy to bring me a Planters Punch." At this new resort she did not feel "downtrodden at all." Rather, Cunningham explained, "the Moulin Rouge gave me the biggest bang because it took me completely away from all that downtrodden business and made me feel like I was rich—not colored—but rich."[104]

Amid the initial euphoria there were widely shared high hopes that the Moulin Rouge would set a new pattern of integrated life for Las Vegas, at least in public accommodations. Moreover, many entertainers, including major headliners, black and white, from the Strip resorts found the Moulin Rouge a congenial place to gather after their second shows because the Moulin Rouge offered a nightly third show at 2:15 A.M. Bob Bailey recalled that the Moulin Rouge quickly became a "hangout for everyone from chorus girls to major entertainers." The local press called it the "show peoples' show." One early morning in June, Nat King Cole, Sammy Davis Jr., Kay Starr, Jack Benny, George Burns, Gracie Allen, and Herbert Mills of the Mills Brothers were in the audience. Frequently, the assembled stars, dancers, and musicians would "give impromptu performances" before standing-room-only crowds.[105] In August, during a performance by Lionel Hampton, no one was surprised when Nat King Cole popped up on the stage and sang "Lady Be Good."[106]

But the Moulin Rouge faced problems from the beginning. Unfortunately for the owners, they began operation at the very time that the Royal Nevada, Dunes, and the Riviera opened for business on the Strip and the Hotel Last Frontier premiered as a much larger New Frontier. This gave Las Vegas a total of sixteen resort hotel-casinos in addition to several casinos and hotels downtown, and most of the new properties struggled. The number of tourists continued to increase, but they did not gamble as much.

Beyond the general struggle for business in the city, Bisno, Schwartz, and Rubin were woefully undercapitalized. Before they even opened the Moulin

Rouge, the owners faced a lawsuit from a construction company claiming that the owners owed more than forty-six thousand dollars for labor and materials. In late July a Beverly Hills investor demanded repayment of a $150,000 loan, sparking a decision to reorganize "the financial structure" of the resort.[107] The owners exacerbated their financial problems by a hiring an enormous staff to provide a luxurious experience for guests. When it opened, the Moulin Rouge had more than 500 employees, including, according to *Jet* magazine, "65 uniformed waiters, 10 tuxedoed captains, 75 uniformed waitresses, [and] 20 glamorous cocktail waitresses." With such high labor costs, the property had an overhead of eighteen thousand dollars a day and "was losing money from the beginning."[108] During the summer and early fall, troubling signs continued to appear in the local press. In September rumors circulated that Louis Rubin, "the principal operator" of the hotel, was going to sell his interest in the Moulin Rouge, particularly after the owners of the Sands announced that he would manage the kitchens and restaurants at both the Sands and Dunes.[109]

While the hotel did bring in a few notable performers like Earl "Fatha" Hines, Dinah Washington, the Platters, and Lionel Hampton, "the entertainment policy" of the Moulin Rouge, as the *Pittsburgh Courier* saw it, lacked "name power" in most of its shows and could not consistently "lure the tourist trade away from the main drag" in its first two shows each evening. For example, in the first week in September, Lena Horne, Pearl Bailey, Billy Daniels, and Billy Eckstine were performing on the Strip, not at the Rouge.[110] The owners belatedly responded, bringing in veteran Strip choreographer George Topps to stage the shows as part of "a new accelerated entertainment program" featuring Les Brown and his orchestra in October.[111]

By late summer those staying at the hotel and attending the shows were spending ever less. One bell captain reported that one day his staff "made only $1.50 on tips in six and a half hours."[112] Over time, occupancy in the hotel dropped. This was due in part, according to *Pittsburgh Courier* columnist George E. Pitts, to the reality that there were not "enough Negroes within reasonable traveling distance of Las Vegas." There simply was not a sufficient number "who could afford both the trip and expense of living at the plush spot for any length of time."[113] One unidentified official with the hotel affirmed Pitts's conclusion: "Negroes did not patronize the place." Though he likely overstated the case, he contended, "ninety-two per cent of our business came from white people."[114] When the hotel closed in October, barely half of the rooms were occupied.[115]

The owners took several steps to try and stanch the mounting losses. They reduced the staff by about half, lowered prices, and sought (unsuccessfully) a loan of $750,000 to keep the business open. They even tried vainly to get black stars Billy Eckstine, Billy Daniels, and Louis Jordan to invest in or perform at the Moulin Rouge.[116] Nothing helped. Rumors abounded by early October that the hotel would soon close, and on October 10 it did. There was not enough money on hand to meet the payroll, and the booking agent for Les Brown reported that the Moulin Rouge had only paid two-thirds of the $50,000 owed to Brown.[117] By early January the dimensions of the Moulin Rouge's financial problems were fully evident. More than 300 creditors had filed claims, 185 of whom were local businessmen. The total claims exceeded $1.7 million. The owners also owed $210,000 in federal, state, and local taxes and had bank overdrafts of $115,000.[118] In 1957 the Moulin Rouge reopened under the ownership of a man named Leo Fry, but it was never profitable and ultimately failed as an experiment in interracial business.[119]

Some have sought a nefarious explanation for the short life of the Moulin Rouge. There was a rumor at the time that someone was skimming the profits from the count room at the casino. While that is possible, given that skimming was happening at many of the Strip casinos, historian Gary Elliott found "no evidence of it." Many, author Earnest Bracey has noted, offered a different explanation. They "thought the closing of the Moulin Rouge was a white conspiracy" among the Strip resorts to eliminate a successful competitor.[120] Although that was a widely shared perception, as with Elliott's comment on skimming, there is no direct evidence of such a conspiracy. While the collective historical memory offers conflicting explanations for its demise, the Moulin Rouge, at least for a few months, promised to solve the accommodations problem for black performers, but true success did not come until 1960.

Six
Mississippi in the Desert

Although journalists filed an abundance of stories with major national newspapers, magazines, and wire services about the attractions in America's newest playground, they rarely reported on the segregation that developed in Las Vegas. The African American press, however, regularly lambasted the entertainment and gambling city in the 1950s for its "lily-white" policies in their "swank resorts and gambling spots." In the April 1954 issue of *The Crisis*, the official magazine of the NAACP, Franklin H. Williams, western regional director of the organization, published a powerful description of the challenges facing black residents living in a "misplaced southern jim-crow town."[1] James Goodrich published an even harsher assessment of segregated Las Vegas in *Ebony* magazine. He claimed that "no other town outside of Dixie has more racial barriers" than Las Vegas. Indeed, "the Negro finds little welcome anywhere." A journalist for the *Chicago Defender*, quoting the local branch of the NAACP, called it the "Mississippi of the West because of its primitive racial attitudes."[2] Because segregation had become "a respected institution" in the city, William G. Nunn of the *Pittsburgh Courier* called Las Vegas the nation's "racial hell-hole" in 1955.[3]

Las Vegas had not always been a "racial hell-hole." Black construction workers helped establish the town in 1905 and there were 16 black people among the 945 residents five years later. Albeit slowly, their numbers grew to 128 in a population of 5,165 in 1930. Most lived downtown, and the men usually found jobs with the Union Pacific Railroad as machinists, porters, or on track repair crews, though there was a scattering of ranchers, barbers, and carpenters. One man worked in a couple of gambling clubs. A few of the black women worked as maids. In the 1920s black residents could purchase property downtown, patronize the few restaurants and saloons there, attend dances with white residents, and play on the integrated Union Pacific–sponsored baseball team.[4] Lucretia Stevens, who moved to Las Vegas in 1923, recalled four decades later that it "was a friendly town" back then. Clarence Ray likewise remembered a community that rarely discriminated against its black residents.[5] In 1930 Charles "Pop" Squires, editor and publisher of the *Las Vegas Age*, lauded the law-abiding "colored people" of the community. "The records of the court," he argued, "will show that the proportions of serious crimes committed by them is much less than with whites." Squires saw the black population as a model that whites should emulate.[6]

Still, there were signs of discrimination and racism in Las Vegas before 1930. In 1909 Walter Bracken, the vice president of the Las Vegas Land and Water Company, worried that as their population grew, black residents would "be scattered all through the town." As a consequence, he tried but failed to restrict them to one block downtown.[7] After 1916 blacks worshiped in congregations separate from whites at Zion Methodist Church and Pilgrim Church of Christ Holiness, blacks could not frequent the brothels in the town's famed Block 16, and black employees of the railroad could rarely gain promotions.[8] In 1921 there was a more ominous development when the Ku Klux Klan began organizing in Las Vegas in response to citizens' concerns over a rising crime rate in the small town. Four years later the KKK organized a march, eighty strong, down Fremont Street, concluding with an initiation ceremony at the fairgrounds. The Klan then openly endorsed candidates for mayor and the city commission—men they claimed possessed "advanced racial, moral and intellectual standards"—though only one, who ran unopposed, won election. While they exhibited little evidence of overt racism, focusing instead on law and order, the Klan's presence in Las Vegas well into the 1930s sent an unmistakable message to the town's small black population.[9]

Ever more barriers developed as the number of black residents grew during the next two decades. Thousands of desperate men and their families descended on Las Vegas in 1930 and 1931 in hopes of securing jobs as news spread across the nation about the massive Boulder Dam construction project. Among them were many black men and their families, though few of them got jobs at the dam. In summer 1934, the more than five thousand workers included only fifteen black men.[10] The outbreak of World War II brought an enormous investment of federal money into Las Vegas and Clark County. The Las Vegas Army Gunnery School, established northeast of the town, and Camp Sibert, established in Boulder City to protect Hoover Dam, employed hundreds of construction workers and more than a thousand civilian personnel by the war's end. More significant was the nearby Basic Magnesium plant, a facility that eventually employed thirteen thousand at its peak to produce bomb casings and plane fuselage components. Even more so than the announcement of the pending construction of Hoover Dam, these massive projects attracted a wave of people to Las Vegas seeking well-paying jobs, including more than two thousand black people, largely from the Deep South, who would eventually make up more than 60 percent of the production workers at BMI. Indeed, officials at the plant recruited black workers.[11] While on the job at BMI, black workers had to use separate washrooms and toilets, and it was rare for black employees to get promoted to a supervisory position because most whites did not "want to work for a black man."[12]

Indeed, black residents began facing discrimination at every turn in the 1930s and 1940s. The few who secured jobs on the dam project could not live in Boulder City, the town built for the construction workers.[13] In Las Vegas most businesses barred blacks, and the bus depot, movie theaters, hospital, and cemetery were segregated. After the governor signed an open gaming law in 1931, the city commissioners decided that even those pursuing "Lady Luck" would do so in segregated properties. They thought it best to issue licenses to applicants of "the Ethiopian Race" for gambling clubs catering "exclusively to persons of the same race only."[14] The few blacks who owned businesses downtown suffered. Increasingly, city officials would only issue licenses to black businessmen if they agreed to move west of the tracks. Even when blacks and whites chose to integrate, city officials worried. In summer 1943, for example, Police Chief Harry Miller closed the Star Bar on the Westside because its owners had encouraged blacks and whites "to congregate in the establishment promiscuously."[15]

Most distressing to black residents was the diminishing chances to purchase a home wherever they chose. Increasingly, white residents attached restrictive covenants to their deeds to make sure sales would only be to other whites.[16] There was little other recourse than to settle on the largely undeveloped Westside of the Union Pacific Railroad tracks, an area with no paved streets and few water lines. Surveyor J. T. McWilliams had initially platted this neighborhood in 1905, but the bulk of the commercial and residential development was on the east side of the tracks. The McWilliams Townsite, with no water lines or sewer, eventually gained the label of the Westside.

There was also a new racial tone in the local press. Unlike Pop Squires's complimentary remarks about the town's law-abiding black residents in 1930, readers increasingly saw negative news accounts involving their black neighbors. In 1934 Al Cahlan, the publisher and editor of the *Las Vegas Review-Journal*, endorsed the lynching of black men who raped white women. In November, when discussing a lynching case in Virginia, he wrote, "How would you feel if the same crime were committed in Las Vegas? No, lynching is not a particularly pleasant process, and yet there are times when it is the only kind of justice that fits and can be speedily meted out."[17]

The thousands of new residents who secured jobs at BMI overwhelmed the available housing units in Las Vegas and Clark County. In late summer 1942, Richard English, writing in *Collier's*, found an estimated "9,000 people sleeping in cars that have pulled off into the sagebrush, in sordid trailer camps, tent cities and clapboard houses."[18] The federal government responded with funds for the construction of segregated housing: nearly a thousand houses at Basic townsite and almost five hundred apartments in Victory Village for white workers and 324 apartments in Carver Park for black workers.[19] Fewer than eighty of the black workers were willing to move to Carver Park because they could save most of the money they were making at BMI by staying in the substandard structures on the Westside, creating a neighborhood of about four thousand residents.[20] The rapid population growth on the Westside led to appalling conditions. A local paper quoted a city official who claimed "the condition under which several hundred families are living was worse than any of the so-called slums of the nation's largest cities." The neighborhood had "no sanitary facilities, no fire protection, and whole district is a perfect set-up for an epidemic and a disastrous fire."[21] There were only slight prospects to improve the structures because local banks would not approve loans for home improvements or new construction thanks to low property assessments on the Westside.[22]

Whether it was housing, jobs, or access to businesses, black residents of Las Vegas endured a Jim Crow town, albeit one that offered good wages, particularly on federally funded projects. Yet from the early 1930s activists challenged the discriminatory practices that so shaped their lives. A Colored Citizens Protective Association formed in 1931 with nearly 250 members and in collaboration with the NAACP lobbied almost continuously for more than a year with the construction companies building Boulder Dam to hire black workers. Finally, they got the attention of Nevada senator Tasker Oddie who "took up the cudgels" and persuaded the secretary of the interior to pressure Six Companies, Inc. to employ black workers. While the number of black employees was never great (only forty-four altogether), they had learned the value of activism.[23] In 1932 three more organizations formed: a Veterans of Foreign Wars post, a Colored Democratic Club, and a Colored Republican Club. The latter two clubs, besides endorsing candidates, agitated throughout the Depression years for more jobs for their members on public works projects in Las Vegas and Clark County.[24]

In 1939 the Las Vegas Colored Progressive Club experienced one of the few victories in the fight against discrimination. That year several white residents on the Westside petitioned the city commission to prohibit blacks from their neighborhoods. In response, the club's president, R. L. Christensen, submitted a counterpetition in which he argued, in part, "We do not feel that you will hesitate now knowing without a doubt that this petition is purely prejudicial and unconstitutional." City Attorney Harry Austin agreed with Christensen, ruling "that such restrictions were in violation of the fourteenth amendment of the Constitution," which led the commissioners to reject the white residents' petition.[25]

The Las Vegas branch of the NAACP was the longest-lasting organization that challenged the discriminatory practices in Las Vegas. Arthur McCants, who helped establish the branch in 1928, was its longtime president. By the early 1940s, however, the organization had atrophied. McCants reported his woes to the national office in May 1941, explaining that the branch record book had been lost with the departure of the secretary, he had had no quorum for meetings for eight months, and no one would help him in the current membership drive.[26] The Reverend William Stevens, one of McCants's successors, faced similar challenges. His treasurer and secretary failed to carry out their duties, and as a consequence he had to postpone the 1946 annual meeting because the roster of members was lost.[27] In 1947 a contrary McCants almost caused a split in the local branch through his criticism of some expenditures and his refusal to send dues to the national office.[28]

Nonetheless, NAACP members occasionally were active, for example, holding fund-raisers and mass meetings to learn about racial injustice in states like Georgia, Tennessee, and South Carolina.[29] Most notably, in 1939 McCants supported a bill introduced into the state assembly to guarantee equal access to public accommodations. When legislators unanimously voted to postpone the measure, McCants petitioned the Las Vegas city commissioners to pass an ordinance ensuring equal access to all city-owned property, but the commissioners failed to act.[30] The collective efforts of the activists had little impact on the developing segregation in the postwar town. As Verlene Stevens argued in *The Crisis*, a black person living in Las Vegas "might just as well be in southwestern Alabama so far as jim crow is concerned."[31]

The end of the war and the shutdown of BMI did not prompt many black residents to leave Las Vegas. Many white residents had assumed, indeed hoped, that they would. Woodrow Wilson recalled whites telling him that if the black BMI workers remained, crime would increase and a growing black population would pose a "political threat." "The whole nature of the community" would be irrevocably altered.[32] Indeed, many who had migrated to Las Vegas for the wartime jobs had intended to return home when BMI closed.[33] However, during the next fifteen years, a rapidly growing job market made Las Vegas attractive not just to the former employees at BMI but also to many more black people who moved to the area. As Las Vegas became a popular tourist destination, the number of resort hotels and commercial hotels increased dramatically, and by 1959 they collectively employed more than eight thousand. For black employees that still meant mostly "back of the house" jobs as maids, dishwashers, porters, and groundskeepers, but there were also many construction jobs for black men in building the hotels and the more than fourteen thousand "residential units of all types" built just between 1950 and 1955.[34] Black workers also secured some positions at Nellis Air Force Base and the Nevada Test Site when the federal government established the latter in 1951, as well as at many of the retail stores in Clark County and the chemical and metal manufacturing firms that occupied the former BMI complex in nearby Henderson. To be sure, they were mostly working in segregated environments, but the wages were some of the best in the nation.[35]

Regardless of their income, black residents of Las Vegas remained largely confined to the Westside, a section of town that saw its population reach nearly 13,500 by 1960.[36] Those who arrived in the early 1950s found that housing conditions had scarcely improved over that of a decade earlier. A 1950 study revealed that "seventy-six percent of the units occupied by Negroes were substandard," and "65 percent had no inside flush toilet for exclusive or shared use" and "no installed bathtub or shower." A subsequent study seven years later revealed that half of the residences on the Westside still did not meet "the city codes for safe, sanitary living quarters."[37]

Oral histories from those new arrivals confirm these dismal descriptions. Arlone Scott recollected, "When I first came to Las Vegas, there wasn't too many places to live; people were living in little boarded up houses that they had put together with just board and plywood and stuff like that." It was "a poor place to live. And I didn't think much of the place because I really wanted to get away from here." Lovey McCurdy agreed that "there were hardly decent places to live on the Westside." Alma Whitney noted all the "little shacks" with dirt floors, and Marzette Lewis recalled that almost all on the Westside lived in "shacks and tents."[38]

Periodically, the city government conducted slum clearance campaigns on the Westside. In late summer 1944, for example, city crews removed seventy-five shacks "condemned by the fire and health authorities." A few months later the city building inspector targeted two hundred more structures for demolition.[39] In 1947 the city leaders established a housing authority, headed by longtime civic leader Archie Grant, to address systematically the challenges of the escalating slum conditions. This was, in part, a response to complaints from the white middle-class residents of Bonanza Village about a nearby 160-acre Westside tract owned by a developer who consistently violated zoning restrictions stipulating that each dwelling must be situated on a half-acre lot. This led to a plethora of "unsanitary and unsightly hovels" on the Zaugg Tract, named after its developer.[40]

The housing authority was unable to do much until President Harry Truman signed the Housing Act of 1949 which appropriated $1 billion to provide grants and loans for more than eight hundred thousand public housing units nationwide. A requirement that there would be the same number of demolished substandard houses as new units constructed represented a conscious effort to help eliminate slums.[41] Housing authority members selected a twenty-acre tract they named Marble Manor after 1930s mayor Harmon Marble (Archie Grant's father-in-law) to construct fifty rental duplexes for low-income residents regardless of race; they would simultaneously demolish an equal number of substandard structures. Grant and the other members of the housing authority saw Marble Manor as the "first step" in an ambitious "long-plan of slum clearance" on the Westside.[42] Because the proposed development was close to their neighborhood, Bonanza Village residents protested with petitions and angry attendance at city commission meetings in early 1951. They argued that Marble Manor would lower their property values, that it was a cynical political effort "to influence votes," and that its construction would "increase racial strife." Equally angry black residents charged that the Bonanza Village protesters were guilty of "selfish interests blinded by racial discrimination." Carpenter Curley Lockett, a wounded World War II veteran, pled with city leaders not to deny his race "housing rights normally available to members of other races."[43] As a last resort, the city commissioners appointed a Westside Housing Committee to resolve the impasse. The seven members, including local NAACP leader David Hoggard, came up with a solution satisfactory to both sides, which included the construction of a hundred-foot-wide street between Bonanza Village and the Zaugg Tract and a promise to demolish the "shack" town on the tract.[44]

Fully cognizant of the deep racial divide over the development of Marble Manor, the housing authority made it clear to journalists that forty-eight of the first eighty families to move in were white and that many were veterans.[45]

Perhaps because of Archie Grant's cautious and diplomatic approach, the new low-income housing project gained an enthusiastic endorsement from an unlikely source, the *Las Vegas Review-Journal*. The paper had often been dismissive of the concerns of black residents and typically sensationalized crimes committed on the Westside. However, publisher Al Cahlan told his readers, "Regardless of what you think of public housing projects, you'd have to be a pretty hard-hearted individual not to be thrilled beyond description to visit any of the new units there and to realize just what they mean in the lives" of the residents, many of whom had been "living . . . in paper-box or cardboard hovels of almost unbelievable bareness." A week after Cahlan published these lines in his column, *Review-Journal* journalist Jerry Smothers wrote warmly about the "neat rows of modern and smartly painted duplexes, paved streets and grassy green lawns with newly planted trees." More important, Smothers marveled at a residential area "open to all races." He found "white and colored children . . . playing together on the project's playground and in one another's yards." In a town troubled by an increasingly ingrained segregation, Smothers concluded that the peaceful mixing of the races in Marble Manor made "this tract a unique world."[46]

Despite this promising beginning, the housing authority made little progress on the long-term plan of slum clearance. Herbert Gerson, the executive director of the housing authority, reported on plans for an additional forty low-rent units in 1956, but no further action occurred until city officials learned of plans for a freeway to connect Las Vegas with the new interstate highway system.[47] The planned route of the freeway, after much discussion and debate, was to be west of the railroad tracks and through a portion of the black neighborhoods on the Westside.[48] The following year City Manager A. H. Kennedy explained that he believed this would displace no more than six hundred people and that the proposed addition to Marble Manor and "numerous private low-rent tracts" could accommodate those needing new residences.[49]

Anticipating a significant impact on the families that would face displacement, the city appointed an Urban Renewal Area Advising Committee chaired by Mickie McMillan, wife of Dr. James McMillan, the state's first black dentist and soon-to-be president of the local branch of the NAACP. It also included NAACP activists Dr. Charles West, the state's first black physician, and David Hoggard, the branch president. Through the next year, committee members met more than twenty times, including sessions with the city planning director and architects. They concluded that construction of the freeway likely would mean the displacement of 1,900 families, and they worried that the leveling of "this blighted Westside area" would lead to "a more luxurious more modern and more permanent slum." Moreover, they believed that city officials were using "the committee as a tool to create a more modern racially segregated ghetto, that will only become another slum in less than a generation." After a year of deliberations, they recommended that the best way to help Westside residents displaced by the freeway construction was to provide them with sufficient money "to economically fend for themselves in the open housing market."[50] In addition, Dr. West unsuccessfully pushed the planning commission for an "open occupancy" resolution, one that "would prevent anyone from being denied ownership or occupancy of any house in Las Vegas because of their race."[51]

Even with considerable vetting by the city planning commission and the Urban Renewal Area Advising Committee, the acquisition of more than $1.5 million in federal aid for slum clearance and construction of low-income rental units, and 96 percent approval of the residents scheduled to be displaced, city leaders faced fierce opposition once again from the residents of Bonanza Village to a planned forty-unit project adjacent to Marble Manor. Resentful that opponents had labeled them as racists, the white residents argued not only that such an addition would depress their property values but that lending agencies in the community were reluctant to loan money to them because low-income housing was so near. Nonetheless, after many boisterous public meetings and petitions from both sides, the city, by late 1960 was able to raze more than forty acres, demolish "a motley array of 40 single-family slum houses, a duplex, a triplex, a slummy 10-unit apartment building and a 19-room disgrace which seems to be a rooming house," and sign contracts for the construction of forty new low-income rental units.[52]

Beyond the protracted struggles to provide adequate low-income housing on the Westside, two housing developments revealed that an increasing number of black residents could afford more substantial residences. The Cadillac Arms featured eighty two-bedroom duplexes. Ruby Duncan remembered the complex as "beautiful" with "nice-sized bedrooms." Marzette Lewis recalled the thrill of just walking to the complex to see the yards because they had grass, not dust and sand; they were so "pretty."[53] Berkley Square was even more impressive. A development of 148 homes, Berkley Square was the product of famed Los Angeles architect Paul Revere Williams, the first black member of the American Institute of Architects. Known as the architect of Hollywood stars, Williams had designed Carver Park, the segregated village for black BMI workers, so he was familiar with Las Vegas. Las Vegas builder Harry Wyatt had "sold the idea to West Coast backers" including Thomas Berkley, a prominent black attorney in Oakland. The three-bedroom stucco houses had landscaped yards, and the subdivision included paved streets and sidewalks along with streetlights and utility lines. There were two model homes in spring 1953, and in fall of the following year, families began moving in.[54] It was an oasis of middle-class stature on the Westside. Those who could purchase a home in Berkley Square "thought they had really accomplished something."[55]

Despite these developments, much remained to be done, as is clear in a report to the U.S. Commission on Civil Rights in 1960. The investigators found that just over a fifth "of the housing currently available to white families is substandard whereas approximately 55 percent of that available to nonwhite families is substandard." Moreover, black prospective homeowners who formerly had no access to home loans now found "mortgage financing . . . readily available." However, they paid much higher interest rates (often 12 percent) than did white applicants. Finally, among the seventy real estate firms in Las Vegas, there was only one black real estate broker. Investigators learned that "the city of Las Vegas, the City Planning Commission and the State Planning Commission" had "taken no steps to integrate or segregate housing," fearing "that integration of all their projects would be dangerous to the program as a whole."[56]

Besides the challenge in finding decent housing, residents on the Westside endured inadequate city services. In 1950 there still were no paved streets and just a few blocks with blacktop covering the gravel. Predictably, most residents and visitors called the Westside the "Dust Bowl" or "Dustville."[57] The streets, such as they were, had no gutters or sidewalks and few streetlights. There was only limited bus service, and according to the residents, the buses "never were on time" anyway.[58] Mayor Ernie Cragin and city commissioners consistently argued that they could not justify authorization of vital infrastructure improvements because of the modest assessed valuation of property on the Westside.[59] Lubertha Johnson, NAACP activist who had many interactions with Cragin, saw it differently. She concluded his inaction was due to his prejudice. Not only did he have segregated seating in his El Portal Theatre downtown, Cragin, according to Johnson, was dismissive of blacks' concerns during his two terms as mayor between 1943 and 1951. "He talked down to us," she recalled, "as if we were really stupid."[60] The election of Charles Duncan Baker to the mayor's post in 1951 brought big changes. Baker believed that services had to be improved citywide and consistently supported funding infrastructure improvements on the Westside.[61] Indeed, one resident of the Westside recalled that by 1960 there was a big improvement in city services: "Sidewalks was in, streetlights, curbs, [and] gutters."[62]

These improvements took place in a part of Las Vegas that had developed a strong sense of community. As Eugene Moehring has explained, "Confined to the Westside ghetto, blacks quickly built the foundations of a community. Physically and spiritually united by the growing tide of Jim Crow, blacks patronized their own merchants who now thrived with the trade of a captive market."[63] There were grocery stores, dry cleaners, liquor stores, shoe repair shops, an auto repair shop, beauty shops, barber shops, a candy store, and restaurants. Many of these family-owned businesses developed a deeply loyal clientele. Hamburger Heaven and Mom's Kitchen were particular favorites. Agnes Marshall recalled that Mom's "had the best food there was over there." Many black entertainers such as Sammy Davis Jr., Billy Eckstine, Lena Horne, and Duke Ellington made a point of dining at Mom's when performing in Las Vegas.[64] The barber shops on the Westside were popular hangouts. As Quincy Mills has discussed in his study of black-owned barber shops, they "were among the few public spaces where African American men could congregate, socialize, and talk outside of white surveillance or a large female presence."[65]

It was the clubs, particularly those on Jackson Street and E Street, that became the focus of commercial life on the Westside. Unable to enter the casinos and clubs on the Strip and along Fremont Street, black people enjoyed gambling, dancing, and jam sessions in a handful of popular clubs. Residents later recalled "the streets full of people" and packed clubs, a Jackson Street that was always "jumping." The high point was 1955, when the Town Tavern and Cotton Club on Jackson Street, the El Morocco and Louisiana Club on E Street, the Brown Derby on Monroe, and the El Rio on North H were all thriving. Everyone had their favorite. Ruby Duncan remembered the Cotton Club as a beautiful place—"it was like an upper club"—and Nathaniel Whaley claimed the Brown Derby "had the best band," which meant "it would be packed, Jack, packed inside and outside."[66] The highlight for many was to see all the black headliners—Billy Daniels, the Mills Brothers, Lionel Hampton, the Treniers, and Sammy Davis Jr.—from the Strip hotels popping in for jam sessions or just conversations. Jerry Eppenger, for example, remembered Louis Armstrong walking along Jackson Street and chatting with everyone.[67]

Churches were an even more important element in the life of the community on the Westside. Indeed, as one scholar has concluded, "the church was perhaps the single most important institution in the African-American community." Whether residents were members of a Baptist, Methodist, or Pentecostal congregation, churches offered "a sense of identity" and "provided a forum to express their frustration and seek solutions to white oppression."[68] Zion Methodist Church, Pilgrim Church of Christ Holiness, Second Baptist Church, Trinity Temple, Saint James Catholic Church, and Church of God in Christ were among the more than fifty churches that developed on the Westside.[69]

A shared educational experience was yet another element of the developing sense of community. All the children on the Westside attended either Madison School or the Westside School through the eighth grade. Although there were a few white and Hispanic students at those schools, the overwhelming majority were black. But there were only a few black teachers, notably Mabel Hoggard, the first black teacher in Las Vegas and the wife of local NAACP leader David Hoggard. Shirley Edmond remembered Hoggard as a wonderful role model who "had such a dignified manner about her." Whether the teachers were black or white, Ruth Eppenger D'Hondt recalled, they "tried to instill in us that we could be somebody, we could do something."[70]

The collective experiences of residents on the Westside in church, school, neighborhood, and along bustling Jackson Street contributed to a tight community. Years later, as those who grew up on the Westside reflected on their youth, they had an idealized sense of that time. They noted a clear sense of togetherness in part because "everybody knew everybody," but also because the neighborhood provided an important buffer from the racism they encountered on the east side of the railroad tracks. As Jocelyn Oats explained, "everybody helped each other."[71]

Activism to enhance the lives in the close-knit community had been sporadic at best through the early 1950s. The NAACP, suffering from poor organization and inconsistent leadership, saw few triumphs. Massie L. Kennard, frustrated by the lack of success, began publishing a short-lived newspaper called *The Voice* and founded the Progressive Civic Service League "to encourage Negroes in Las Vegas to join forces politically and numerically for an all-out drive on discrimination." However, a weak response to Kennard's initiative forced the League "to give up the ship."[72] Fortunately, the local branch of the NAACP began to coalesce behind a core of strong leaders. Dr. Charles West, Dr. James McMillan, Reverend Donald Clark, journalist Alice Key, and entertainer Bob Bailey all arrived in Las Vegas in the 1950s, joining veteran activists Lubertha Warden, Woodrow Wilson, and David Hoggard, who had moved to Las Vegas the decade before.[73] Between 1953 and 1960, Warden, Hoggard, and McMillan served as branch presidents, and in those seven years the trio effectively mobilized the organization.

They called a number of mass meetings to discuss national and local issues. In October and November 1955, for example, the local branch convened several mass meetings at the Saint James Baptist Church and the Elks Hall after the brutal murder of fourteen-year-old Emmett Till, who had supposedly flirted with a white cashier in Money, Mississippi. After a jury acquitted the two suspects, Roy Bryant and J. W. Milam, branch leaders called a meeting to "map plans to force the passage of civil rights laws to protect the lives and liberty of all Americans." A month later, they had a "Mississippi Justice Protest" meeting with more than three hundred in attendance to hear several guest speakers, including the Reverend Moses Wright, with whom Till had stayed while in Mississippi.[74]

Two years earlier, there were mass meetings at the Westside Elks Club and the Bethel Baptist Church to protest the acquittal of a thirty-nine-year-old salesman who had been charged with raping a ten-year-old Westside girl.[75] Also in 1953 the local branch drew an overflow crowd to the Zion Methodist Church in support of a state civil rights bill that had been introduced by Assemblyman George Rudiak, local attorney and white member of the NAACP. Indeed, a delegation including Lubertha Warden and David Hoggard traveled to the state capitol in Carson City to lobby for the bill, which "would have made it unlawful for restaurants, hotels, casinos, theaters and other public places to refuse service to anyone regardless of race or color."[76] When the state assembly rejected the bill, Warden and former branch president Woodrow Wilson called on the city commissioners to pass an ordinance banning discrimination in public accommodations in Las Vegas. Warden told the commissioners that black residents faced "discouraging and humiliating" conditions daily. All who had "more pigmentation in their skin—no matter how intelligent, or well dressed, cannot enter most of the licensed establishments in the city, or must accept inferior Jim Crow service."[77] The commissioners directed City Attorney Howard Cannon to offer a legal opinion on the matter. A few months later Cannon concluded that the city lacked "specific Charter authority" to pass such an ordinance.[78]

In response to city leaders' refusal to pass the ordinance, the NAACP turned to a tactic that they employed evermore in the 1950s. The Las Vegas branch supported the regional office's call for "all national and west coast business, civic, social, fraternal and labor organizations" to boycott Las Vegas when scheduling future conventions and meetings.[79] Four years later James McMillan organized a successful boycott of a local dairy that led to the hiring of black delivery men.[80] In 1959 McMillan and West supported a boycott and picketing of two Westside casinos. Black dealers at Zee Louie's Louisiana Club and S. N. Fong's Town Tavern complained that the owners were hiring many more Chinese than black dealers. The boycott and picketing continued until McMillan and West negotiated an agreement that included promises that Louie and Fong would hire more black dealers.[81]

All branch leaders were unrelenting in protesting discrimination. Two cases in late 1959 illustrate this. When Karl and Leo Fry applied for a gambling license and a liquor license for their Moulin Rouge hotel near the Westside neighborhood, leaders of the NAACP testified against them, arguing that the Frys discriminated against potential black guests. McMillan and West wrote to Mayor Oran Gragson explaining that four years earlier the integrated Moulin Rouge had been a model of an "interracial hotel." Now, however, several instances of denying rooms to blacks had "created a very distasteful attitude among the residents of West Las Vegas." Although Leo Fry denied the charges of discrimination, the city commissioners refused to grant the licenses.[82] McMillan also wrote to the general sales manager of Mobil Oil wanting to know why his company permitted black oil dealers to suffer discrimination at Las Vegas hotels during their fall 1959 convention. McMillan complained that Mobil had assured the black dealers that they would not face any problems getting rooms at the Thunderbird, Stardust, and Sahara hotels, and he urged the sales manager to lodge a protest with the city and to pledge not to use "Las Vegas as a convention site until this deplorable situation has been remedied by the state of Nevada."[83]

While their leaders were taking these actions, NAACP members used a variety of media to reach larger audiences. In 1955 Bob Bailey and Alice Key cohosted a television show called *Talk of the Town* on KLAS, the only station in Las Vegas. Bailey also had a radio program on radio station KENO.[84] In April 1958 David Hoggard and James McMillan began publishing *The Missile*, a monthly newspaper they printed with their own money. In what they called the "official organ of the Las Vegas Branch NAACP," McMillan and Hoggard devoted the paper to "articles about civil rights that the city's two papers were not addressing."[85] Charles West took the lead in hosting fund-raisers for the local branch. Particularly popular were his cocktail parties at the Town Tavern, to which he invited notable black entertainers who were performing at the Strip hotels. Between 1955 and 1957 Sammy Davis Jr., Dorothy Dandridge, Arthur

Lee Simpkins, Nat King Cole, Cab Calloway, the Ink Spots, and the Platters all helped out.[86]

In perhaps their most impressive success that decade, the local branch of the NAACP changed the political culture on the Westside. As part of their annual branch report on political activity to the national office in 1960, the leaders proclaimed, "The most notable achievement was the abolishment of political prostitution among the members of the community."[87] They were referring to a nearly two-decade record of "political exploitation on the Westside." Most of the black migrants to Las Vegas in the 1940s and 1950s had come from Deep South states where they had not had the opportunity to participate in politics. As Sarann Knight Preddy explained, "They didn't know anything about it, and it was very hard to get them involved."[88] One Westside political leader explained in 1950, "Lots of them are voting for the first time when they arrive, and they naturally listen when someone gets to them."[89]

Two story lines emerged about how candidates "got to them." Given the faithfulness of Westside residents to attend church, many candidates cultivated a good relationship with ministers who would, in turn, invite them to speak to their congregations an occasion when the candidate would make a sizable dona-tion.[90] Two ministers in particular were influential. Reverend John L. Simmons of the Saint James Baptist Church had a loyal following, and his contemporaries concluded that his congregation followed his lead on which candidates to sup-port. "Anybody that wanted to be elected, Pat McCarran and all that bunch," Woodrow Wilson explained, "they'd look up Reverend John L. Simmons." Beyond letting them speak, Simmons held events for candidates, and according to George Ullom, a Las Vegas police officer in the 1940s, "those good mem-bers who attend church were complete followers of their reverend."[91] Similarly, Bishop Clyde Carson Cox of the Church of God in Christ had great influence with his congregation. Members recalled that he would thoroughly research the candidates and offer "voting guidance." Politicians knew this and courted Cox, who was in the view of some contemporaries the "voice of West Las Vegas."[92]

The other more cynical view was that candidates influenced voters through refreshments and money. A 1950 grand jury report cited instances of bribery and men throwing barbeques and standing "the rounds for the house" to influ-ence voters. Reverend Prentiss Walker agreed, explaining that "every political year the politicians used to have a barbeque and give free drinks."[93] The most egregious example of buying votes came in 1952, when George "Molly" Malone was running for reelection to the U.S. Senate. According to the *Las Vegas Sun*,

Bill Graham, owner of the Bank Club, Reno's largest casino, and a man known for lavish dispensing of money and booze, came to the Westside to secure votes for Malone. It turned into a "spending spree" with Graham "buying everybody drinks" and handing out ten-dollar bills to folks in Jackson Street clubs. Those who witnessed the spectacle concluded that he gave away at least $1,500.[94]

The NAACP attacked this corruption in the late 1950s. Since the organization could not engage in partisan politics, Charles West and James McMillan took an essential first step by establishing the Nevada League of Voters in 1957 and mounted a get-out-the-vote campaign.[95] A year later the local branch combined its legislative and political action committees, which sent questionnaires to all the candidates running for office to learn their stances on "public accommodation and fair employment practice" and interviewed candidates. In the 1959 campaign, the NAACP had weekly "Political Education" meetings in the runup to the election, lobbied to get six additional black deputy registrars and persuaded more than seven hundred to register to vote. Nearly 90 percent of those registered turned out on election day. Taking advantage of this impressive political mobilization, Charles West ran for a city commissioner position and defeated a dozen other candidates only to lose in the run off. Acknowledging their new influence in state politics, Governor Grant Sawyer appointed West to the Democratic Platform and Resolutions Committee and McMillan to the Democratic Rules and Order Committee and selected Woodrow Wilson to serve on the President's Civil Rights Committee and Jimmy Gay on the State Athletic Commission.[96]

By early 1960 circumstances favored a direct challenge to the most visible symbol of segregation in Las Vegas—the nearly "lily-white" resort hotels. First, Grant Sawyer, a new governor elected in 1958, took office determined to challenge the "shameful" discrimination in Nevada. In his 1960 message to legislators, Sawyer charged them to make sure that all of the state's citizens could live "in peace and dignity without discrimination, segregation or distinction based on race, color, ancestry, national origin as place of birth." To accomplish that, he called on them to establish a Commission on Human Relations to address problems of discrimination. He specifically wanted to do something about the "hotels and casinos that blatantly and arrogantly" barred blacks. While he initially could do little with the private sector and was not able to get the commission established in 1960, Sawyer did get a law passed that outlawed "discrimination in public employment" in the state.[97] Second, a new mayor, Oran Gragson, took office in 1959. Although Gragson had won few votes from Westside residents, he pledged to hire more blacks as city employees and demonstrated that he was willing to listen to concerns raised by black leaders.[98] Third, a sit-in movement spreading from Greensboro, North Carolina, had captured the country's attention, prompting the national office of the NAACP to urge the local branches to agitate against segregation and to call upon all blacks "not to spend their money in chain stores that refuse to let Negroes eat at lunch counters alongside white customers."[99]

Given the positive political developments and the nudge from the national office, local NAACP president Dr. James McMillan convened his executive board, men and women who had previously served as branch presidents, and they collectively decided to challenge the long-standing segregation practices of the resort hotels on the Strip and the hotels and casinos downtown.[100] On March 11 McMillan sent a letter to Mayor Gragson threatening demonstrations if the discrimination did not end by March 26. "We feel," he contended, "that such action . . . would bring most unsavory National publicity to Las Vegas, and seriously impede its progress as a convention center."[101] McMillan led the planning for the demonstrations in churches on the Westside, though most ministers urged him to move cautiously. Once the local newspapers broke the story, there was also pressure from the hotel owners to call off the proposed march. Indeed, spokesmen for the hotels, like Benny Goffstein at the Riviera, told the *Las Vegas Review-Journal*, "There is nothing to fight about." Remarkably, he and other hotel executives claimed that "they have served colored customers on the same basis as white patrons," only barring those who misbehaved. Al Parvin at the Flamingo explained that "we don't get enough Negroes to worry about," except when the hotel featured "Negro entertainers."[102] Moreover, one city commissioner, Harris Sharp, wanted to make sure that there was no talk of any city ordinances to prescribe integration. "I am against any city ordinance forcing businessmen," he explained to the press, "to allow Negroes or anyone else they choose to deem unacceptable into their establishments."[103]

McMillan met with Mayor Gragson and City Commissioner Reed Whipple, both of whom pleaded with him "to call off the demonstration," promising more city jobs and bank loans for blacks to buy homes.[104] McMillan declined and defiantly refused even to let death threats dissuade him. He learned through an intermediary that "the underworld people" from the Strip warned him to call off the demonstration or he "might be found floating face down in Lake Mead." McMillan was bluffing when he threatened demonstrations involving three hundred black residents. He had no detailed plans and was unsure of how many people on the Westside backed the proposed action, despite several meetings at churches where he and other leaders sought to galvanize support.[105] The *Las Vegas Sun* reported, "More than a thousand Negroes chipped in dimes, quarters—whatever they could afford—into a 'battle fund' to support efforts to break the color barrier in Las Vegas," but that did not necessarily translate into a commitment to take to the streets.

Fortunately for McMillan, he gained a couple of critical allies. Oscar Crozier, who owned a casino on the Westside, served as an intermediary between McMillan and the casino owners, men McMillan later characterized as "underworld people . . . involved in the Strip hotels." Fellow activist Woodrow Wilson explained that Hank Greenspun also intervened at this critical point.[106] In the past few years, Greenspun had occasionally spoken out on racial issues in Las Vegas, and in the face of the proposed demonstrations, he had made clear his support for change. On March 25, in his "Where I Stand" column, Greenspun told his fellow citizens: "I despise intolerance, I loathe all forms of bigotry. I am against any attempt to segregate people into religious or racial groups. All our citizens are human beings and there is no distinction among the breed."[107] Wanting to avoid what he believed would be destructive demonstrations, Greenspun invited McMillan to his home to devise a strategy to avoid them. McMillan would ask Mayor Gragson to call upon owners of the downtown casinos and hotels while Greenspun would talk to the Strip resort owners to end discrimination on their properties.[108] Worried about negative national publicity and the subsequent loss of business from tourists and convention delegates if they refused, almost all owners needed little further persuasion from Crozier, Greenspun, or Gragson and, regardless of what their personal views may have been, swiftly agreed to end discrimination. The owners had come to a fundamental realization, as singer Harry Belafonte explained, "On the casino floor, no one cared what color you were. The only color that mattered was green."[109]

On March 26, symbolically at the Moulin Rouge coffee shop, James McMillan and other leaders of the NAACP met with Mayor Gragson, county commissioners, the police chief, and Hank Greenspun, the hotels' spokesman, to hear the mayor announce that "we have received assurances from the majority of downtown and strip businesses that the policy of racial discrimination has ended."[110] Woodrow Wilson and Lubertha Johnson, who had long worked to see this turnaround, were stunned. "I was surprised," Johnson remembered, "at the ease with which the system fell apart."[111] Yet NAACP leaders wanted to make sure that there would be a genuine change. So black leaders dropped in at each

The March 26, 1960, agreement to integrate Las Vegas casinos. Among the many
civic and NAACP leaders, the key participants were Dr. James McMillan (center,
in glasses), Hank Greenspun (at McMillan's right), publisher of the *Las Vegas Sun*,
and Las Vegas mayor Oran Gragson (at McMillan's left). Dr. Charles West
(at Gragson's left) was the first black physician in Las Vegas and longtime civil
rights activist. *Courtesy University of Nevada, Las Vegas, University Libraries Special
Collections and Archives, Marie McMillan Photo Collection.*

hotel and bar to make sure there were no problems. Only a couple of downtown
places, the Sal Sagev and the Horseshoe, refused to abide by the agreement.[112]

While the March 26 agreement did little to change the everyday lives of black
Las Vegans, it was an important symbolic event. Jack Entratter, who had been
one of the few resort hotel officials to permit black entertainers to stay in hotels
where they were performing, led the way in accepting the obvious reality facing
a city eager to attract more tourists and conventions. He told the *Las Vegas Sun*,
more than a week before the big meeting at the Moulin Rouge, "How can we
fight it. This is a social revolution we have to accept." Entratter acknowledged
that the efforts led by McMillan reflected an important national trend: "The
changing evolution of the society of our country demands we all take a stand.
The stand is clear. We must accept it."[113] Activists had destroyed the most visible
evidence of segregation in America's Playground.

Seven

Mob Vegas

On November 15, 1950, Senator Estes Kefauver brought to Las Vegas some members of his Special Committee to Investigate Organized Crime in Interstate Commerce. Committee members questioned six witnesses at the federal courthouse on Stewart Avenue.[1] Moe Sedway, vice president of the Flamingo Hotel, attracted particular attention. The diminutive Sedway, an associate of Bugsy Siegel and Meyer Lansky for more than three decades, had been in Las Vegas for almost ten years, first at the El Cortez, then at the Flamingo. He maintained exclusive rights to the lucrative race wire service for much of that time. Robbins Cahill, who served as executive secretary of the Nevada Tax Commission in the 1940s and 1950s, remembered Sedway as a "very personable little fellow," but he acknowledged that little Moey, as most folks in Las Vegas called him, also "had the reputation of being a tough guy, or a hoodlum."[2] During his interrogation Sedway admitted that he had been associated with or knew both Siegel and Lansky, as well as most of the major gangsters of the era including Lucky Luciano, Frank Costello, Joe Adonis, Jake Guzik, Abner "Longie" Zwillman, Charles Fischetti, and Jack Dragna.[3] Sedway's testimony revealed a critical, and to many an insidious, feature about the rapidly growing resort city. In just a few years, a remarkably complex web of connections had emerged among the developers and promoters of Las Vegas hotels and casinos and many underworld figures. These "men of shady pasts," as one historian characterized them, were critical to the men who built most of the casino-hotels in the 1950s.[4] They had access to the capital that most banks would not provide, and they had the expertise to manage the ever-larger gambling operations in Las Vegas from their experiences running illegal casinos in other states. Yet throughout the decade, city, county, and state officials sought to distance legalized gambling from the taint of organized crime. The challenging effort, as one state regulator put it, was like having "a bear by the tail."[5] Fully aware that they would be licensing neither "bishops of the church" nor "pillars of the community," state and local regulators struggled during the 1950s, with little success, to keep the underworld out of the business of gambling in Las Vegas.[6]

Moe Sedway (center), flanked by Benny Goffstein and Gus Greenbaum, prominent men in the operation of the Flamingo Hotel. *Courtesy University of Nevada, Las Vegas, University Libraries Special Collections and Archives and Las Vegas News Bureau.*

This reality confirmed the worst fears of opponents of the 1931 bill to permit "wide-open" gambling in Nevada. They had warned that legalized gambling "would be an invitation for racketeers and gangsters to start operations" in the state. When Governor Fred Balzar signed the bill, the *Los Angeles Times* similarly predicted that the "big gaming-house promoters" would not be locals; rather they would be men "from the purlieus of many cities outside the confines of Nevada itself."[7] To be sure, several local residents, such as Mayme Stocker, Frank Detra, P. J. "Pros" Goumand, and Alice Morris, obtained gambling licenses in the 1930s and 1940s. John Kell Houssels, whom one author characterized as "a businessman with no whiff of a mob past," proved to be the most successful.[8] Others, like Sam Boyd, had been involved in illegal gambling elsewhere but were not organized crime figures.[9]

There were, however, men from the underworld on the scene in Las Vegas from 1931 on. The Cornero brothers were the first of the outsider "big gaming-house promoters." Tony Cornero was a legendary bootlegger from California. With the aid of brothers Frank and Louis, he had made a fortune, and journalists had dubbed him variously as the "czar of rumland" and the "king of the liquor runners." Arrested nearly a dozen times, a court finally found him guilty. He was completing a two-year sentence in spring 1931 when the Nevada legislature legalized gambling. In anticipation of a favorable vote, Frank and Louis, with their brother still in prison, had gone to Las Vegas and built the Meadows Club, a luxurious casino and nightclub outside the city limits, along the highway to the Boulder Dam construction project.[10] It took almost a decade for others to follow. In 1939 Los Angeles's newly elected reform mayor Fletcher Bowron began a campaign against the vice lords of Southern California, and a host of gamblers headed to Las Vegas. Their ranks included Milton "Farmer" Page, Bill Kurland, Chuck Addison, Tutor Scherer, and John Grayson.[11]

Guy McAfee was the most powerful of the group. Formerly head of the Los Angeles police department vice squad, McAfee, was co-owner first of a gambling ship and then the fashionable Clover Club casino on the Sunset Strip. Journalists called him the "gambling dictator" of Southern California, and historian Kevin Starr concluded that McAfee was one of the leaders of syndicates controlling "an estimated six hundred brothels, three hundred gambling houses . . . [and] twenty-three thousand slot machines."[12] After his arrival in Las Vegas in 1939, McAfee purchased the small Pair-O-Dice club on Highway 91 outside city limits and renamed it the 91 Club. Over the next six years he opened the Frontier Club and Mandalay Lounge downtown, then purchased the Pioneer Club and S.S. Rex. In 1946 McAfee opened the Golden Nugget, the largest of the downtown casinos.[13]

While men like Cornero and McAfee were intimately linked with vice and crime networks in California, they were not part of the organized crime syndicates of the East. Those men began arriving in Las Vegas in the early 1940s. Bugsy Siegel and Moe Sedway were the vanguard of this invasion. A product of the tough gangs of the Lower East Side in New York where he was born, Siegel partnered as a teenager with Meyer Lansky in the lucrative bootlegging business during Prohibition. By the late 1920s, Siegel had made at least eight hundred thousand dollars in the trade. In the mid-1930s, Siegel moved to Southern California, where he engaged in a range of gambling ventures from a race track in Culver City to Tony Cornero's S.S. *Rex* gambling ship off the California coast. In 1940 he embraced the opportunity to engage in legal gambling in Las Vegas. Siegel began by investing in the Northern Club and soon also had an interest in the Frontier Club and Las Vegas Club. Sedway managed these properties for Siegel with the help of Gus Greenbaum, a Phoenix race book operator connected to the

Chicago mob. Siegel also used Sedway to gain control of the race wire business in Las Vegas, an endeavor that made him about twenty-five thousand dollars a month. Siegel partnered with his old friend Meyer Lansky, Greenbaum, and others in the purchase of the downtown El Cortez hotel and casino.[14]

After repeatedly failing to purchase the El Rancho Vegas, the first resort hotel along Highway 91, Siegel took control of *Hollywood Reporter* publisher Billy Wilkerson's Flamingo Hotel project in summer 1946. In his quest to build a spectacular casino-hotel, Siegel had to secure some of his funding from powerful organized crime figures, notably old friend Meyer Lansky and New York crime boss Frank Costello. The casino opened in December 1946, the hotel three months later, and syndicated columnists hailed the resort complex as plush, magnificent, and "super-colossal." Erskine Johnson claimed, "the west has never seen anything like it."[15] Although someone, still unknown, murdered Siegel in June 1947, the Flamingo soon prospered under new owners.

During the next decade, the thriving hotels along Highway 91, increasingly called "the Strip," made Las Vegas an ever-greater magnet for men from the underworld and their money. These men, seeking not only profit but also legitimacy included Joseph "Doc" Stacher and Mack Kufferman from New Jersey; Frank Costello from New York; Charlie "the Blade" Tourine and Sam Cohen from Miami; Raymond Patriarca and Joseph Sullivan from New England; "Dandy" Phil Kastel from New Orleans; Johnny Roselli, Sam Giancana, Tony Accardo, Jake Guzik, Marshall Caifano, and Murray Llewellyn Humphreys from Chicago; Ed Levinson from Newport, Kentucky; George Sadlo and Benny Binion from Texas; David Berman, Charles Berman, and Israel "Icepick Willie" Alderman from Minnesota; Charlie Resnick from Detroit; Carl and Nick Civella from Kansas City; Jack and Tom Dragna from Los Angeles; and Moe Dalitz, Morris Kleinman, Sam Tucker, Thomas McGinty, and Lou Rothkopf from Cleveland. Most were adept at the "skim," scooping off a percentage of the casino's take before making an official count. David "Davie" Berman, one of the bosses at the Flamingo after Siegel's demise, let his young daughter Susan into the count room, and she recalled him "and his friends dividing the money—so much for them, so much for the government, so much for Meyer."[16] While an accurate figure is impossible to determine, there is little doubt that the mob-owned casinos in the 1950s skimmed millions annually.[17]

Just as important as the money, as syndicated columnist Bob Considine explained in 1955, some of the men from the underworld found "a measure of respectability in Las Vegas."[18] Men like Bugsy Siegel and Davie Berman believed they could shed their notorious pasts and become legitimate entrepreneurs in a state with legal gambling, and some also hoped that they could become part of the community. Moe Sedway succeeded on both counts. A little more than a year after appearing before the Kefauver Committee, Sedway died in Miami from a heart ailment, leaving an estate worth nearly three hundred thousand dollars, including a bank account of twenty-five thousand dollars and a record of being "active in civic and philanthropic affairs."[19] While investigating Sedway, the California Crime Commission found that in hopes of creating "a veneer of respectability," he had poured "money into a number of civic and community enterprises, including two different church building projects." He also gave ten thousand dollars to the United Jewish Appeal in 1947 and chaired the organization's local chapter for two years. In 1946 a local journalist, who described the five-foot, two-inch Sedway as "the Little Giant of Fremont Street," claimed that his "philanthropies are legion." Sedway also sought political office in Las Vegas, running unsuccessfully for a seat on the city commission in 1947. At his death, *Las Vegas Sun* publisher Hank Greenspun (who belonged to the same temple as Sedway) had nothing but praise for the man with the "big and charitable heart."[20]

However, crusading senator Estes Kefauver had no interest in investigating organized crime figures' quest for respectability. In early 1950, after Kefauver introduced a resolution calling for an inquiry into "organized interstate gambling," his fellow senators authorized him to chair a special committee, and his seventeen-month investigation produced eleven thousand pages of testimony. Committee members traveled to fourteen cities besides Las Vegas in a quest to determine the scope of the crime network. Newspapers reported that following their November 15, 1950, stop in Las Vegas, committee members were "shocked" over what they had learned about the apparent connections between organized crime figures, not only with casinos but also with state officials. Lieutenant Governor Clifford Jones, for example, acknowledged that he had made more than twenty thousand dollars a year from his interests in the Pioneer Club, the Golden Nugget, and the Thunderbird Hotel, and William Moore, who sat on the state tax commission that regulated gambling, had made more than seventy thousand dollars during the previous decade from his interest in the Hotel Last Frontier.[21]

While they did not do so in Las Vegas, committee members permitted television cameras during their hearings in some cities. When the hearings reached New York City in March 1951, viewers had the opportunity to watch more than forty hours of the proceedings. At least seventeen million people watched the New York hearings, more than those who tuned in to the 1951 World Series.[22] Beyond television, there was massive coverage of the hearings in documentaries and feature articles in newspapers and in magazines like *Time*, *Newsweek*, *Life*, and *Collier's*. It all made Estes Kefauver, ambitious to make a run for the presidency, a national celebrity.[23] He was on the cover of *Time* magazine, and he appeared on the popular quiz show *What's My Line?* He published not only a four-part series on the investigations in the *Saturday Evening Post* but also a best-selling book entitled *Crime in America*.[24]

Kefauver's efforts generated widespread support for his crusade against organized crime, which consistently linked Las Vegas casinos with the underworld. Kefauver argued that his investigation demonstrated that there were two national syndicates—"the Costello-dominated 'Combination' on the East Coast and the Capone Syndicate in Chicago." "Hoodlums" from these syndicates had "invaded the legalized gambling setup" in Nevada, making Reno and Las Vegas "headquarters for some of the nation's worst mobsters." While Kefauver acknowledged that the recently established state tax commission had worked "to keep out persons known to have criminal records or strong affiliations with out-of-State gambling syndicates," he claimed that it had failed "to eliminate the undesirable persons who had been operating in the State before that time."[25] Kefauver Committee members agreed that in Nevada "too many of the men running gambling operations . . . are either members of existing out-of-State gambling syndicates or have had histories of close association with underworld characters who operate those syndicates." They concluded that "both morally and financially, legalized gambling in Nevada is a failure."[26]

The Kefauver investigation prompted many muckraking journalists to explore this toxic mix of gambling and mob bosses in Las Vegas. When newspapers published article series like syndicated columnist Bob Considine's on Las Vegas in 1955, they inevitably dealt with organized crime's role. Major magazines published exposés like "What Price Gambling in Nevada?" by Dan Fowler in *Look* magazine in 1954 and "Las Vegas: The Underworld's Secret Jackpot" by Lester Velie in *Reader's Digest*. In these pieces, Fowler and Velie searched for the most colorful description of the underworld's impact on Las Vegas. Fowler claimed, "gangsters are jamming Nevada like flies in a sugar bowl," and Velie charged that "big-name gangsters are entrenched in the palatial gambling casinos in Las Vegas."[27] Investigative reporter Fred Cook argued in *The Nation* that legalized gambling had "given the powers of the American underworld a haven" and made "'fun-loving' Las Vegas virtually the capital of American crime."[28] In his 1958 book *The Great Las Vegas Fraud*, Sid Meyers described the "interlopers" who ran the casinos as parasites who had "swooped down upon Las Vegas like a bunch of hungry vultures—and have accomplished nothing either for the city or its inhabitants." Supported by "unscrupulous politicians," these hoodlums had developed a powerful political machine. Meyers asserted, "The Capone empire in Chicago, the Prendergast [*sic*] machine in Kansas City, and the Tammany machinations were mere bagatelles compared to legalized gambling in Las Vegas."[29]

All these journalistic revelations were fodder for novelists and movie and television screenwriters. Authors usually could not resist including mobsters in their story lines about Las Vegas. Representing powerful national syndicates, underworld figures sought or already had control of the city's casinos. Some, like Al Marta in John D. MacDonald's *The Only Girl in the Game*, were part of a Byzantine structured mob empire. Marta, who ran the fictitious Las Vegas Cameroon casino, took orders "from a Los Angeles district headquarters which in turn was directed, through a Chicago setup, by the national council on syndicate policy, operating on the eastern seaboard."[30] Likewise, the 1950 movies *711 Ocean Drive* and *The Damned Don't Cry* featured national crime syndicates interested in Las Vegas, as did episodes from the late 1950s on the *Mike Hammer* and *State Trooper* television series. The 1955 movie *Las Vegas Shakedown* best illustrated this trend. A vicious gangster named Al Sirago, who "the Kefauver Committee nailed," tries to take over the El Rancho Vegas, but in the end Joe Barnes, the legitimate owner, thwarts Sirago's plans.[31] The fictional versions of mob influence in Las Vegas reinforced the accounts by journalists, creating a clear narrative that challenged the legitimacy of the city's chief industry.

Amid the blitz of hyperbole about organized crime in Las Vegas, a few truly compelling stories surfaced, including those detailing the cozy relationships between underworld figures and some prominent state officials. Besides the embarrassing fact noted by the Kefauver Committee that William Moore, one of the owners of the Hotel Last Frontier, served on the governing body that oversaw gambling, Lieutenant Governor Cliff Jones's actions raised more than a few eyebrows. In 1954 Hank Greenspun's *Las Vegas Sun* published several articles on payments to the Clark County sheriff for permitting prostitution in the county. When the sheriff responded with a libel suit, Greenspun hired an undercover investigator named Pierre Lafitte to explore further corruption. Posing as supposed gangster Louis Tabet, Lafitte taped conversations with Cliff

Jones and Jones's law partner Louis Wiener, among others. Even after Tabet told them that he had a criminal background, Jones and Wiener offered to help him get a gambling license. On one tape, Wiener talked expansively of Jones's influence, particularly if Democrat Vail Pittman could defeat incumbent governor Charles Russell. "It's important to us to have Cliff in there, because there are a lot of things that Cliff can get. He knows what's going on." Once Pittman won the election, Wiener assured Tabet, Cliff Jones would be "the top dog in the state."[32] Known as "the Big Juice," Jones had developed a reputation as the man who could clear the way with state and local commissions for those seeking a gambling license, and the men he helped showed their gratitude by giving Jones "points" or a percentage of ownership of their properties. He even solicited the business of prospective operators. For example, in 1952, the tax commission learned that Jones had contacted Jake Freedman, who was seeking a license to operate the new Sands Hotel, telling him "you have the wrong lawyer," a reference to Las Vegas attorney Harry Claiborne.[33] Two years later, an out-of-town applicant for a gambling license told county commissioners that a couple of local people told him "he 'could do better' in getting commission clearance if he took Jones with him to appear before the gambling control body." As Hank Greenspun said of Jones's influence peddling, "It was common knowledge that if you wanted a gaming license, you had to see Cliff Jones."[34]

Pat McCarran, who died in 1954, was the most powerful of all Nevada politicians, and he also had a close relationship with many of the men with "shady pasts." Nevada's senior senator, frequently came to the aid of the owners of hotel-casinos in Las Vegas as he did for virtually anyone who supported him. When Bugsy Siegel was struggling to get supplies for his Flamingo Hotel project right after World War II, he noted he was "getting very good cooperation" from McCarran. After Siegel's death, McCarran interceded on behalf of Gus Greenbaum and Moe Sedway when the Flamingo had tax problems, and he helped Marion Hicks acquire scarce building materials for the construction of the Thunderbird.[35] The grateful hotel bosses did not forget the old man, providing him free rooms and meals whenever he was in Las Vegas, and the El Cortez provided free space for his 1944 and 1950 campaign headquarters.[36] They even fell in line when McCarran called upon them to withdraw their advertising from the *Las Vegas Sun* because Hank Greenspun was such a harsh critic of the senator. For example, in one of his columns, Greenspun charged that McCarran controlled access to gambling licenses. He wrote that the "scuttlebutt around town is that the New York-Chicago-Las Vegas axis, which must be reckoned with in order to procure a major gambling license, must detour through Washington for clearance."[37]

McCarran grew weary of the publisher's criticism. As one of the senator's biographers explained, he "had never known such relentless newspaper opposition in Nevada."[38] Longtime political ally Norman Biltz later explained that McCarran decided "to clip his wings." Although Biltz argued that McCarran did not act alone, the latter clearly endorsed having the Las Vegas hotels and casinos "pull the advertising away from Greenspun."[39] On May 20, 1952, seven casinos called to cancel their ads in the *Las Vegas Sun* in less than an hour, and more followed.[40] Greenspun contended that when he confronted Moe Dalitz and Gus Greenbaum about pulling their ads, the two underworld figures told him that he should stop attacking the "Old Man," a claim both men later denied. However, Benny Binion, the lone holdout among casino owners, later recalled, "They called me out on the Strip, and told me they was going to take out all the advertising out of the Sun. That the Senator was mad at him. And Gus Greenbaum said, 'We gonna bust him.'" Fred Soly and John Kell Houssels, two downtown casino owners, acknowledged to Mayor C. D. Baker that McCarran was responsible.[41] When Greenspun sued McCarran and all the hotel and casino owners who withdrew their advertising, the senator demonstrated his clout in the nation's capital. He contacted an FBI agent, asking for any negative information they had on the publisher, including anything they had "on Greenspun's association with gangsters and the like." Agents complied, reporting that Greenspun had borrowed money from men at three of the casinos.[42] Eventually, the two sides settled, stipulating that no party "would reveal terms of the agreement," which included a payment of eighty thousand dollars to Greenspun and a promise by the casino owners to resume advertising in the *Las Vegas Sun*.[43]

This titanic struggle between a powerful U.S. senator and an aggressive newspaperman further revealed the intimate connections that had developed among the underworld, key political figures, and hotel developers in Nevada. This connection was also evident in the investigation of the Thunderbird Hotel and Casino in 1954 and 1955. During Pierre Lafitte's undercover investigation, Cliff Jones's law partner Louis Wiener made a remarkable boast on tape. He claimed that the men on the state's tax commission knew that notorious gangster Joseph "Doc" Stacher was one of the investors in the Sands Hotel and that Meyer and Jake Lansky had a stake in the Thunderbird Hotel. Widespread news accounts of this episode not only forced Jones to resign as a Democratic national committeeman but also led the tax commission to investigate whether or not the Lanskys truly were involved in the Thunderbird.[44]

The commissioners focused on the two men who were the "principal partners" in the Thunderbird—Marion Hicks and Cliff Jones. Two loans were critical in their investigation. A man named George Sadlo loaned Hicks $160,000 in 1947 to help complete construction of the Thunderbird and $37,500 more the following year to help bankroll the operation of the casino. Sadlo was a Texas gambler who had been involved in Meyer Lansky's Colonial Inn casino in Hallandale, Florida. He also was a longtime associate of Meyer's brother Jake, who had used Sadlo to funnel the nearly $200,000 to Hicks. Because Sadlo and Jake Lansky had a "financially participating interest" in the Thunderbird, the tax commission ruled that Hicks and Jones should have revealed their connection to the property but had failed to do so. As a consequence, the commissioners ordered the suspension of the Thunderbird's gambling license until Hicks and Jones sold their interests in the hotel because they had allowed "eastern underworld figures to have a secret interest in the establishment."[45] Hicks and Jones appealed the decision, and the Nevada Supreme Court upheld their appeal in 1957. However, from all the investigations, hearings, and court rulings, some intriguing connections emerged. Not only was Hicks a close friend of Sadlo's, but Jake Lansky frequently stayed at the Thunderbird, and his brother Meyer was an occasional guest. Seven employees at the Thunderbird had worked for Sadlo at his various casinos around the country. Most importantly, Justice Charles Merrill, who wrote the opinion in the Hicks case, affirmed the state's power to scrutinize "the character and background of those who would engage in gambling."[46]

The shooting of Frank Costello in 1957 did more than anything else to reveal the links between gangsters and many of the city's casinos. Labeled the "prime minister of the underworld" by his lawyer George Wolf, Costello had helped fund the Flamingo and the Sands.[47] In 1949 his stature in organized crime had led *Time* magazine to put him on their November 28 cover. "Millions of newspaper readers," the accompanying article explained, "considered him a kind of master criminal, shadowy as a ghost and cunning as Satan, who ruled a vast, mysterious and malevolent underworld."[48] Late on the night of May 2, 1957, Costello was returning to his Central Park West apartment in New York City when a gunman named Vincent "Chin" Gigante, a "muscleman" for Costello rival Vito Genovese, fired one point-blank shot at him while yelling, "This is for you[,] Frank." Although it knocked him to the floor, the bullet only grazed

Costello. Nonetheless, an ambulance rushed him to Roosevelt Hospital, where physicians bandaged the old gangster and released him a couple of hours later. However, while doctors treated Costello, detectives looked through his coat and found an extraordinary piece of paper. It included a reference to "gross casino wins as of 4-27-57, $651,284." Summoned before a grand jury, Costello refused to identify the shooter or the meaning of the slip of paper and served fifteen days in jail for contempt.[49]

Investigators for New York County District Attorney Frank Hogan traveled to Las Vegas and determined that $651,284 was the same figure as the "take" at the Tropicana Hotel between April 3 and April 26. Theodore Schimberg, president of the Tropicana, "categorically denied that Frank Costello ever had, or now has, any interest whatsoever in Hotel Tropicana." However, with the cooperation of the Nevada Gaming Control Board, investigators were able to trace the handwriting on the note in Costello's pocket to an assistant cashier at the Tropicana named Michael J. Tanico, who had been a cashier at the Beverly Club in New Orleans.[50] This was the critical link: Phil Kastel, known as the "financial wizard of underworld czar Frank Costello," had operated the Beverly Club and had invested more than three hundred thousand dollars in the Tropicana in anticipation of operating its casino. However, the Nevada Tax Commission had rejected Kastel's application, and the Gaming Control Board ordered him to divest his interest after this story broke.[51] Still, readers across the country who had followed these developments, what the *Las Vegas Review-Journal* had called "a bombshell in Nevada gambling circles," understood that Costello, the nation's leading gangster, had played a key role in the opening of the hotel-casino dubbed the "Tiffany of the Strip."[52]

The revelations about the Lanskys, Phil Kastel, Frank Costello, and all the other underworld figures with Las Vegas interests posed enormous challenges for local and state officials. In the early 1950s "we were getting applications from a lot of questionable people," men "who had been associated with the rackets, or the Mob," Robbins Cahill, executive secretary of the Nevada Tax Commission, recalled. They "were beginning to look to Nevada, and Las Vegas, particularly, as an ideal place to operate."[53] In 1951 Hank Greenspun agreed, acknowledging that even "a sharp 10 year old boy" would realize that too many "men whose backgrounds were not conducive to law and order" had gotten gambling licenses.[54] Four years later, syndicated columnist Bob Considine explained their dilemma well. Nevada leaders, he wrote, knew that when "public confidence" in gambling "is shaken," or if "notoriously apparent muggs from the outside world" invaded the business, "their whole costly investment would rot away under the baleful sun and stinging sand."[55] Gambling control, however, evolved slowly in Nevada. The 1931 law authorizing most forms of gambling and an additional law fourteen years later were essentially revenue measures requiring license fees for local and state governments and then a 1 percent tax on gross gambling receipts, but they required no background checks on applicants for licenses. A 1945 law, however, did require a state license, a move that placed the state tax commission in charge of gambling. Concerned that Nevada was attracting too many underworld figures, the commissioners asked Attorney General Alan Bible to determine if they could investigate the background of applicants before deciding if they were suitable for a license. Bible complied in 1947, explaining that the tax commission had broad powers to investigate "the antecedents, habits and characteristics of the individual applying for" a license. Moreover, commissioners could deny a license to a person for "just cause, unsavory reputation, or other reasons of public interest." In essence, he made gambling a privileged industry, one in which an applicant had "to prove to the state of Nevada that they are fit persons to hold a gaming license." State legislators passed a law in 1949 that incorporated Bible's opinion, provided additional funding for investigations, and required the fingerprinting of casino employees. Subsequent legislation in 1955 and 1959 led to a two-tiered system of control with an appointed Gaming Control Board to investigate applicants and enforce gaming laws and an appointed Gaming Commission (replacing the tax commission as an oversight board) that could approve, modify, or reject licenses.[56]

Despite the development of this control structure, some local officials expressed great frustration with the sham involving "front men." For example, in December 1952, the county gambling license board was considering four men for licenses in the soon-to-open Sands Hotel. According to the *Las Vegas Sun*, after voting to approve all four, one board member, Harley Harmon, said that it made no difference who they were because "the licensees are only front men for the hoodlums." If they had rejected these four, Harmon contended, "another front man would turn up asking for approval at the next meeting." He then posed the essential question, "who does the tax commission think they're kidding?" He argued that the Sands would still have men like Doc Stacher and Mack Kufferman "and other national hoodlums in there anyway." Harmon was not alone. Another board member, District Attorney Roger D. Foley, said, "With some of the people we have licensed, we might as well bring in Al Capone. He wouldn't be any worse than what we have."[57]

In the case of the Sands, the key front man was Jake Freedman, who for years had run the illegal Domain Privee, "a tony, lush-plush casino" outside Houston, Texas. However, the diminutive Freedman angrily rejected the charge that he was a front man. "I'm not," he told the state tax commission, "going to be a stooge for anyone."[58] There were many others, like Jake "The Barber" Factor. When Tony Cornero, who had begun construction on the massive Stardust Hotel, died in 1955, Chicago mobsters Tony Accardo, Jake Guzik, Murray Humphreys, and their capable emissary Johnny Roselli "decided that the gang would finish construction and assume the debt of the Stardust in a partnership with Cleveland's contribution to Vegas, Moe Dalitz. However, the Outfit would run the operation," according to Chicago mob historian Gus Russo.[59] They selected Factor as their front. He had made a fortune in real estate, and the "Chicago Outfit" trusted him because he had been associated with that city's underworld for more than three decades. The Chicago money would be sufficient to complete the hotel construction and they leased the hotel to the Sheraton Hotel company and the casino to Moe Dalitz. However, Factor had been involved in stock, mail, and land frauds, scams that finally landed him in prison for six years in the 1940s. His record kept him from getting a state gambling license, which sent the Chicago Outfit looking for another front. They turned to John Drew, who had been a Chicago bookie and had already been granted a license to run the Golden Bank Club in Reno.[60]

Wilbur Clark was the quintessential front man. The dapper, genial Clark, who represented the interests of Moe Dalitz, Morris Kleinman, Sam Tucker, and Thomas McGinty, was the face of Las Vegas for many across the nation in the 1950s. In a feature article in *American Legion Magazine*, Joseph Stocker called him the city's "Golden Boy," the former bellhop whose name adorned the luxurious Desert Inn resort hotel. When Stocker asked Clark about being associated with "a syndicate of Cleveland and Detroit gamblers," men whose money let him complete the Desert Inn, Clark dismissively responded, "It was embarrassing at first, but they're nice guys, so what the hell."[61] Indeed, when he appeared before the Kefauver Committee in 1950, his answers revealed what made him such a valuable front. As historian David G. Schwartz characterized his performance, "he tied the committee in knots with his good-natured inability to recall many salient details about the operation of the Desert Inn, including the sources of its finances and his own official role within the organization."[62] The underworld's use of "faultless and unknown 'associates'" to "do their wheeling and dealing for them" was a constant frustration for regulators and the newspapers monitoring their success.[63]

Beyond the use of front men for their properties, gangsters across the country successfully masked their investments in the hotels and casinos. A wiretap captured Doc Stacher's explanation of their approach: "We worked out a deal that gave each group an inter-locking interest in each other's hotels and our lawyers set it up so that nobody could really tell who owned what out there."[64] E. Fransden Loomis, the lead counsel for the state tax commission who once told the press that someone from Chicago had warned him to "lay off or get a bullet in your back," agreed with Stacher. He contended in 1955 that the "biggest hoodlums are hard to catch" because it was so difficult to determine "where their money came from." A year later, after numerous investigations, Loomis saw no improvement. "At its best," he concluded, gambling "is an evil business." Without strict supervision, it "attracts evil persons—the hoodlum, the mobster, the criminal, the near criminal—that great fraternity of silent men who live on the fringe of the law, only over-stepping the line when necessary and then in a manner to divert suspicion and responsibility."[65]

Nonetheless, local law enforcement authorities sought to keep the hoodlums out. In the early 1950s, city commissioners required everyone "employed in the gambling industry, in bars, and as cab drivers, to register and be fingerprinted and photographed" to give local police a comprehensive file, which employers had to update every three months. As famed columnist John Gunther learned, that meant everyone—"from the croupiers to the girls who serve the drinks and even the chorus girls." Local authorities had the FBI check all the prints.[66] In addition, the county commissioners required all ex-felons to register at the sheriff's office within two days of their arrival or face a misdemeanor charge.[67] The two local newspapers updated readers when hoodlums slipped into town. For example, Al Cahlan noted in summer 1954, "There can be no question whatever that the head men of the nation's so-called vice syndicates gathered in Las Vegas recently."[68]

More important, the local police and sheriff's deputies regularly rousted hoodlums. When Chicago gangster Tony Accardo came to Las Vegas in January 1953 with two associates, the Las Vegas police picked them up and gave them a welcome that "was anything but cordial." The police chief assigned two officers to "keep them in line" while they were in town. Believing that they were staying at Wilbur Clark's Desert Inn to attend a meeting of "the mob," officers ordered Accardo out of town with the warning to "never set foot inside our city limits."[69] Over the next seven years, the Las Vegas police and Clark County sheriffs and deputies regularly rousted men like Tom and Jack Dragna, Marshall

Caifano, Willie Bischoff, Doc Stacher, John Battaglia, and Sam Giancana. Typically, law enforcement authorities arrested these men and charged with them with vagrancy. Once they made bail, officers told them "to get out of town and stay out."[70] In 1960 local law enforcement got help from the state when Governor Grant Sawyer supported the Gaming Control Board's creation of a List of Excluded Persons, or the Black Book. This document prohibited eleven people with substantial criminal records from entering hotel-casinos, including Battaglia, Caifano, Tom Dragna, and Giancana.[71]

Years later, those who worked in Las Vegas, those who reported on organized crime in Las Vegas, and those who were responsible for keeping gangsters away from casinos could not agree on the role of the underworld in the city's development in the 1950s. Some, like Mary Ann Culver, who worked in the casinos, contended that employees were largely oblivious of the role of gangsters. Culver contended that she had been at the Sands Hotel for five years "before somebody told me we were working for gangsters." Irwin Molasky, who became a prominent Las Vegas developer, said that he did not understand who ran what when he arrived in 1951. Molasky claimed that he came to know the "boys" essentially as business men who employed many people and helped to develop the city.[72] William "Butch" Leypoldt, who served as Clark County sheriff from 1954 until 1961, when Governor Sawyer appointed him to the Gaming Control Board, reported that "hoodlums (so called) never" caused problems. "Many of the so called Mafia," he explained, "came here for a vacation—more of a place to have fun."[73] Crusading publisher Hank Greenspun had a much different view. In a 1972 interview, Greenspun asserted that the underworld's role "was quite extensive." There were few of the crime "families that didn't have some interest. It was very hidden; it was very remote; you couldn't trace it." Ed Oncken, one of Greenspun's reporters, agreed. He firmly believed that both Meyer Lansky and Doc Stacher were running the show at the Sands, and Jake Freedman was simply their front man.[74]

Those responsible for the control of gambling on the state level had the best perspective from which to make an accurate assessment. Charles Russell, governor from 1951 to 1959, admitted that regardless of the regulatory measures taken, "You're never sure about gambling—if there is an interest. You try everywhere you can to find out where the money is coming from. It's pretty hard to find who has the money."[75] Grant Sawyer, who succeeded Russell and implemented a "hang tough" policy to try to root out all the gangsters through the establishment of the gaming commission and implementation of the Black Book, said he "questioned the alleged extent of mob influence." However, he realized that some of the men who obtained licenses in the 1950s "came out of organized criminal backgrounds."[76] Even Robbins Cahill, the longtime secretary of the state tax commission, acknowledged that theirs had been an impossible task in the 1950s. While he and his fellow commissioners had "knocked out" many of the applicants for licenses "who had been associated with the rackets," Cahill could only claim, "we were able to, I believe, keep the most undesirable people out."[77]

From Cahill's perspective, however, the risk had been worth it. His tax commission and the gaming commission licensed men who fundamentally understood the business of gambling. Most had criminal records because they had run illegal operations elsewhere. He explained that the commissioners had approved many licenses for men from hotel, insurance, banking, or advertising backgrounds, but those men knew little about managing a substantial casino. "They didn't know," Cahill explained, "how to set up an operation that could protect them, or that they could trust. They didn't know when they were being taken by either somebody from the outside or inside." Their ventures, like the Desert Spa, often failed. The "real object lesson" for Cahill and others was "that gaming was better operated in the state of Nevada in the hands of people that know the business," men who often had some connections to the underworld but otherwise had clean records.[78] To be sure, some hotel developers had no connections to organized crime, like Warren "Doc" Bayley, who opened the Hacienda on the south end of the Strip, and Milton Prell, who made the Sahara a success. Still it was the men with "shady pasts" who were most responsible for the lavish hotel-casinos.

Frequently, commentators like Cahill made a point to focus on the career of Moe Dalitz as a caution to critics tempted to make quick collective judgments about the men who had obtained gambling licenses or backed those who did. While the FBI concluded in 1964 that Dalitz had "long been one of the top hoodlums directing Las Vegas operations," a man "allegedly in close contact with numerous national and international hoodlums such as Meyer Lansky, Doc Stacher, Sam Giancana and others," Cahill argued that the man behind the Desert Inn was the individual most responsible for the success of the Las Vegas Strip in the 1950s and that he was a "good citizen," a man who "invested in the town."[79] Others have agreed, frequently noting that Dalitz did more than advance the gaming industry. Drawing in part on funding from Jimmy Hoffa's Teamsters pension fund, Dalitz partnered with Irwin Molasky and Merv

Moe Dalitz (left), here with two unknown men, was the most prominent gangster in the development of Las Vegas. *Courtesy University of Nevada, Las Vegas, University Libraries Special Collections and Archives, Wilbur and Toni Clark Photo Collection.*

Adelson to complete several commercial developments and a new hospital for Las Vegas. More than half a century later, Sunrise Hospital is one of the most comprehensive health centers in the city. Later in life, he became a major philanthropist in Las Vegas, contributing to the YMCA, a Jewish school, and the University of Nevada, Las Vegas. In the estimate of contemporary journalist John L. Smith, Dalitz "was responsible for much of the growth and prosperity the Las Vegas Valley experienced from the 1960s through the early 1980s." Indeed, Smith has argued that residents continue to remember Dalitz as the city's "benevolent godfather."[80] They may have been bootleggers, they may have run illegal gambling places in other states, and they may have been too well connected to the underworld, but men like Moe Dalitz were critical players in making Las Vegas into America's Playground.

Eight
Atomic Vegas

In early June 1957, Gladwin Hill told his readers in the *New York Times* that this was going to be "the best year in history for the non-ancient but none the less honorable pastime of atom-bomb watching" because the Nevada "test program" would continue through the summer. During World War II, Hill had been an Associated Press correspondent in the European theater. Along with reporters like Walter Cronkite and Andy Rooney, Hill was one of the first to fly on bombing missions over Germany, and he covered the Normandy campaign. The *New York Times* hired him in 1945 and after the war assigned him to their bureau in Los Angeles, where his beat included several western states.[1] The dapper, chain-smoking Hill found Las Vegas fascinating, and in filing dozens of stories about America's emerging playground, he became one the resort city's best boosters.

Even though some of the scheduled atomic tests for 1957 would be larger than the detonations over Hiroshima and Nagasaki, the seasoned war correspondent reassured readers that "there is no danger of anyone being blown up." Moreover, "there is virtually no danger from radioactive fall-out." He only cautioned that observers should not look directly at the detonation and to be careful driving because there could be some momentary blindness from the flash. For those wanting a memento of a shot, Hill reminded readers, "The fireballs from the explosions roil as long as a minute, providing plenty of time for a series of pictures." Then he threw in the key element for Las Vegas promoters: "The best base for bomb-viewing expeditions is Las Vegas, which has a couple of hundred motels and hotels of all types, with fairly standard rates."[2] Throughout the 1950s, the chamber of commerce, the Las Vegas News Bureau, and hotel publicists, largely oblivious of the health risks involved, exuberantly embraced the opportunity to exploit the atomic testing as another effective way to portray Las Vegas as a unique resort playground.

Atomic testing had begun in Nevada in early 1951. After World War II, President Harry Truman had pushed Congress to establish an Atomic Energy Commission, headed by a civilian board (though most members were from the military), to provide for the "common defense and security." Almost three-quarters of the commission's expenditures through the 1950s was for "weapons-development," meaning "that ace in the hole—the atomic bomb."[3] The AEC conducted its earliest atomic tests in the Pacific, but many soon called for continental testing for logistical and financial reasons. A few key factors drove the rapid development of tactical atomic weapons while the United States simultaneously continued to pursue development of a much more powerful hydrogen bomb with tests in the Pacific. First, there was a widely shared concern about the growing threat of the Soviet Union to American interests. As *Las Vegas Sun* publisher Hank Greenspun told his readers in spring 1952, "The atom bomb is the hope of the free world to destroy the autocratic, totalitarian Communist regimes that menace freedom."[4] Second, the Soviet detonation of an atomic bomb on August 29, 1949, added a sense of urgency to begin continental testing, as did the escalation of the war on the Korean peninsula. As nearly three hundred thousand Chinese troops entered the conflict in November 1950, both General Douglas MacArthur, commander of United Nations forces, and President Truman contemplated the use of tactical atomic weapons in defense of South Korea.[5]

Although it considered sites in North Carolina, Utah, and New Mexico, the AEC recommended conducting the tests about seventy miles northwest of Las Vegas at the Las Vegas–Tonopah Bombing and Gunnery Range. On December 18, 1950, President Truman approved the AEC's recommendation. It was a secure location away from major population centers with generally predictable westerly winds, which the AEC hoped would carry the radioactive clouds away from Los Angeles and Las Vegas.[6] The AEC moved quickly, informing senior Nevada senator Pat McCarran, Governor Charles Russell, state legislators, Las Vegas and Clark County officials, and the local press before announcing on January 11, 1951, that it would "stage test atomic explosions at the bombing and gunnery range near Las Vegas." The AEC assured the city's residents that they probably would not "see or feel the effects."[7] In the next eight years, the AEC conducted more than eighty atmospheric tests in Nevada, mainly on a flat basin called Yucca Flat. The tests came in series: Ranger (1951), Buster-Jangle (1951), Tumbler-Snapper (1952), Upshot-Knothole (1953), Teapot (1955), Plumbbob (1957), and Hardtack II (1958). Initially, aircraft released the bombs, but increasingly the AEC affixed them to wooden or steel towers of varying heights or suspended them from balloons. There was even one fired from a cannon.[8]

Early on, the Department of Defense made it clear that it wished to exploit the opportunities the tests would provide to see how troops would perform if it became necessary to use tactical atomic weapons. The AEC approved, and in fall 1951, the army ordered the construction of Camp Desert Rock, which housed nearly one hundred thousand soldiers during the 1950s. Working on the assumption that "war training . . . with new atomic weapons will save lives," army brass tested numerous scenarios immediately after detonations. For some of the tests there were as many as five thousand troops, who quickly learned that men in trenches or foxholes within two miles of a detonation could survive the blast.[9] Usually, the maneuvers commenced minutes after a radiation safety team issued a clearance. In most tactical exercises, troops advanced quickly on foot all the way to ground zero. Other times, they parachuted in. In spring 1953 nearly one hundred planes flew into mushroom clouds to carry out a variety of "simulated combat missions."[10] On March 22, 1955, twenty-eight helicopters transported nearly two thousand men "forward in a simulated attack on an enemy stronghold" in only two hours. Two months later, armored vehicles, including M48 Patton tanks and armored personnel carriers, were deployed within minutes of a thirty-kiloton detonation. Indeed, pilots from the Air Force Special Weapons Center at Kirtland Air Force Base in New Mexico, flew "B-57, F840, and T-33USAF aircraft" through many radioactive clouds "to gather samples on filter paper for analysis by scientists of the Atomic Energy Commission."[11]

Amid these various maneuvers, the army sought to discover how the detonations affected mental and physical responses to battle situations. In 1957, for example, officers ordered their men to carry out normal battlefield tasks. As one journalist described it, "They assembled and reassembled their rifles, they advanced into a simulated mine field, they crawled under barbed wire and tossed grenades at imaginary targets." All the while a team of sociologists, psychologists, and statisticians "busily gave them a series of tests to determine whether their physical and mental reactions were normal." They wanted to know if a soldier could think clearly. "Will he be able to perform a fighting mission? Will he crack up under the strain of the frightful weapon he has been so close to?" In this instance, the men "seemingly reacted calmly." When questioned by reporters, the troops almost always expressed confidence in their ability to fight under these new conditions.[12] Indeed, there were several instances of volunteer guinea pigs for dangerous experiments. In 1953 nine officers volunteered to be in a trench only 2,500 yards from ground zero and afterwards told reporters that "it would be safe to go even closer in future detonations." Four years later, five officers volunteered to stand at ground zero and be filmed under the detonation of a two-kiloton bomb![13]

As the Department of Defense carried out simulated battle scenarios after detonations, the AEC, in cooperation with the Federal Civil Defense Administration, also used the detonations as a laboratory to measure the "bio-medical effects" of the bombs on all types of animals, from rabbits and dogs to sheep and pigs. The AEC believed pigs particularly useful because of "their skin similarities to humans." The pigs in 1953 and 1958 experiments wore a variety of fabrics and were placed near the detonation sites "to help measure the possible heat, radiation, and blast" effects of detonations.[14] More interesting to journalists were the AEC experiments on the "doom towns." These involved the construction of one- and two-story brick, concrete, and frame houses at various distances from ground zero.[15] Fully furnished with televisions and appliances and stocked with canned and packaged food, some of the houses also had concrete or wood-beam bomb shelters. Inside were mannequins dressed with clothing from the local JCPenney store, representing a typical suburban American family. In 1955 one doom town even included rats, guinea pigs, rabbits, and Dalmatian dogs, "primarily to test explosion effects on organisms of different weights." Some of the doom towns also had autos outside, along with power lines and transformer substations. All this was an effort to provide "survival information": how best should communities prepare for atomic warfare? "Three of the ten test houses, one to two miles from the explosion point," Gladwin Hill reported in May 1955, "were ruined. The rest suffered mainly broken windows and battered furnishings. Indoor bomb shelters, both of the concrete and wood-beam 'do-it-yourself' types, emerged intact. Dalmatian dogs in shelters in the ruined houses were extricated a few hours later unharmed and happy."[16]

The first test shots alarmed residents of Las Vegas. "Of course we were startled," one housewife told a reporter for the *Review-Journal*. As they took place before dawn, the detonations jolted folks from a sound sleep. As *Life* magazine reported in February 1951, the first test shot "scared many right out of bed." To demonstrate how "unsettling" the experience was, the article included the observations of "a motel operator" who believed "someone was trying to tear his roof off" and a deputy sheriff who claimed his "frightened dog jumped into bed with him." There were also stories of a broken plate-glass window at a downtown furniture store and claims of cracks in ceilings and walls of homes.[17]

The anxieties associated with the first tests quickly dissipated, replaced by genuine awe and fascination. Interviews with those who lived in Las Vegas or who worked at the test site in the 1950s paint a remarkably consistent story. Those who were children recalled being awakened by parents to view the tests. It was

Aboveground atomic test at the Nevada Test Site. *Courtesy University of Nevada, Las Vegas, University Libraries Special Collections and Archives, Manis Photo Collection.*

exciting to stand on their front porch or in the yard to view the spectacle. It was a glowing, colorful, larger version of the Fourth of July. Joyce Moore remembered that it was "amazing. . . . We loved it," and Donna Smith said, "No one was afraid, you know, everybody was like, whoa, wasn't that something."[18] The tests similarly intrigued adults. Ernest Williams, who for a time was in charge of logistics at the test site, vividly remembered the detonations and the fireball, the blast, and the developing mushroom cloud. It was "an awesome thing," a "spectacular scene."[19] Soldiers posted at Desert Rock also had vivid recollections of the tests. Michael Pertschuk, a soldier who later chaired the Federal Trade Commission, described the "the moment of zero" when "all you could see was light. And at the same time, this heat across your body, right away. You got both simultaneously." Then, as the light dissipated, "you began to see this black and red boiling cloud, boiling fireball." Shortly thereafter, "the stem came down, and you began to see the mushroom form, and it was white and purple. It was incredibly beautiful."[20]

Beyond the beguiling spectacle of the detonations, opinion leaders played a key role in residents' acceptance of the atomic tests in their midst. Parents and teachers reminded youngsters how important the tests were to national security, persuading them that the effort was "noble."[21] From the beginning, state and city political leaders, including Senator McCarran and Governor Russell, emphatically endorsed the testing. Most importantly, Governor Russell and Las Vegas Mayor Ernie Cragin assured residents that "there isn't any doubt that tests can be made without any disastrous effects.'"[22] The city's two daily newspapers gave full-throated endorsements of the tests. John Cahlan, managing editor of the *Review-Journal*, explained that before the tests, he and other "news people" met with AEC officials. Cahlan remembered that they "pleaded with us to make the people of the city of Las Vegas cognizant of what was going on and the lack of danger that they could pledge to the people of Las Vegas." Cahlan and his wife, Florence Lee Jones, also a journalist with the *Review-Journal*, recalled two decades later that their paper eagerly complied and "conditioned" people in southern Nevada for the tests by printing many stories on "what could be expected and the safety measures to be employed."[23] Hank Greenspun at the *Las Vegas Sun* joined the *Review-Journal* in pitching to readers a patriotic rationale for endorsing the tests. He told his readers that they had a special opportunity to play a vital role in the Cold War struggles with the Soviet Union. "Now we have become part of the most important work carried on by our country today," he wrote in late January 1951. All residents should not only support the tests but be "thankful for the part we are permitted to play in this epoch-making period."[24] John Cahlan and his brother Al agreed, arguing that "a majority of citizens" believe "that the state of Nevada can contribute much to the war effort by having the atomic project within its boundaries." Indeed, "citizens will be proud of their ability to serve."[25] Greenspun and the Cahlans followed public opinion on this. Before these publishers typed their columns and editorials, residents had already told reporters that they saw the tests as a chance to fulfill their duties as citizens. As Flamingo blackjack dealer Bob Gans put it, "we've got the idea we're doing something a little more important for the country than just paying taxes."[26]

The strong support in Las Vegas in 1951 for the tests reflected a widely shared judgment across the country that the United States should pursue "any measures necessary to maintain atomic supremacy," a view successfully exploited by the AEC.[27] Throughout the 1950s the agency generated many press releases and invited national, regional, and local journalists to observe the tests. The initial stories filed by journalists from major newspapers gave readers astonishing accounts of the powerful phenomena. Gladwin Hill wrote, "Experiencing it gave one, despite the scientific explanation about atomic fission, a strange feeling of fleeting contact with eternal powers."[28] "No photograph," Robert R. Brunn wrote in the *Christian Science Monitor,* "ever can convey the sheer wonder of an atomic explosion or its vivid impact on the thinking of those who 'were there.'"[29] Hill and occasionally the paper's science writer William L. Laurence, covered most of the tests for the *New York Times,* and they gave consistently positive portrayals of the tests.[30] Other papers and major magazines like *Life, Newsweek, Time,* and *National Geographic* likewise carried largely favorable stories in the earliest years of testing. In 1952, for example, *Collier's* magazine featured an emphatic positive testimonial from a soldier. "I walked through an atom-bombed area," he explained. "I didn't get burned, I didn't become radioactive, and I didn't become sterile. And neither did the 5,000 guys with me."[31]

Still, it was Gladwin Hill who became the biggest champion for the tests. Some of the stories he filed reveal his continuing fascination with the phenomenon he had the opportunity to witness, as in 1953 when he saw the effects of a forty-kiloton detonation at two thousand feet of elevation. "Acres of Joshua trees, cactus and sagebrush five miles and more away from 'ground zero,' immediately under the blast," he wrote, "burst into flame in a great desert 'forest fire.'"[32] Most articles, however, reflected his effort to reassure readers about the unsettling aspects of the atomic tests. After the first round of tests, Hill wrote that all was well in Las Vegas. "Aside from the new topic of conversation," he contended, "a visitor to Las Vegas will find little change from former times." To be sure, there were hundreds of new people in town associated with the test site. "All in all," however, "Las Vegas can be described as pleased with its new acquisition."[33]

From the mid-1950s, as an increasing number of reports circulated about the health risks posed by exposure to radiation, Hill practically became a spokesman for the AEC. In 1955 he cited a decade-long study of the survivors of the Hiroshima bombing and their children born since 1945. While there were "a few stunted babies" and an "increased susceptibility to leukemia [and] to minor eye cataracts," Hill reported that the study "produced no evidence that the radiation will affect . . . descendants" of the bombing survivors.[34] Two years later, Hill drew upon an AEC press release to proclaim that after thousands of measurements of radiation triggered by the dozens of tests, there had been no "detectable injury to health" for those living around the Nevada Test Site.[35] Soon after that, trying to tamp down concerns, Hill was dismissive of all reports of illness related to the tests. While there were "a few individuals" living in small Nevada and Utah communities within two hundred miles of the test site "whose apprehensions border on hysteria," Hill claimed, "no person off the test site, as far as is known, has ever received any injury from the explosions."[36] Hill continued his "don't worry" theme in 1958, though not so absolute in his assurances: "There is little possibility that you experienced an appreciable amount of fallout radiation from last year's atomic tests in Nevada."[37]

Hill's articles must be understood in the context of a number of problems for the AEC's continuation of atomic tests in Nevada. Significant questions began to emerge about the risks of radiation in 1953. Scientists like Lyle Borst, a noted nuclear physicist at the University of Utah who had worked for the AEC at the nuclear reactor project at the Brookhaven National Lab on Long Island, warned that the tests were exposing people to "harmful doses of radiation."[38] Utah Representative Douglas Stringfellow publicly expressed concerns after a particularly dense radiation cloud triggered by a bomb dubbed Dirty Harry drifted over Saint George on May 19, 1953. The AEC had to order the decontamination of several dozen cars and had to warn the 4,500 residents to stay indoors for three hours. Not long after, word broke about sixteen Utah ranchers losing nearly five thousand sheep.[39] In 1954 newspapers worldwide reported on the death of one Japanese fisherman and the illnesses of several others on the *Lucky Dragon* following the detonation of an H-bomb at Bikini Atoll in the Pacific. There were also infrequent but recurring reports of employees at the test site suffering from "excessive radiation doses."[40]

A series of events in 1957 brought the most attention to the challenge of balancing risks and continuing the atomic tests. The two local newspapers that had reliably endorsed the tests for more than six years began to exhibit doubts. "It is a terrible thing when people lose faith in their government," a June 1957 *Las Vegas Sun* article began, "but a group of Nevadans who live and work on lonely ranches located in the path of atomic clouds from the Nevada Test Site have almost come to that point." They were all ranchers who lived less than a hundred miles from ground zero. "These are honest, uncomplicated men and women" who did not "get hysterical easy" but had "become confused and afraid." They did not know what to make of the mushroom clouds that passed overhead, "but something unseen is left behind that makes their Geiger counter go crazy. Their eyes burn and sometimes the air has a chemical taste. Their cattle are afflicted with a horrible, cancerous eye infection; one of their dogs went stone blind and another developed an ugly malignant sore." Worse, one "woman went completely bald and a young boy died of leukemia." Most worrisome was that the ranchers could not determine precisely what was causing all the afflictions. "They'd like to know, but nobody tells them anything."[41] The *Review-Journal*'s concession to skepticism was a wire service political cartoon the Cahlans decided to publish a week after the *Sun* story on the ranchers. The bold caption at the top read "Are Nuclear Tests Safe?" and below it were dozens of question marks.[42]

Beyond increasing questions, there were protests and calls for an end to the testing. In June 1957 Ammon Hennacy conducted a twelve-day picket and fast at the AEC office in Las Vegas. The local papers, the major wire services, and the *New York Times* all covered his protest. An associate editor of the radical *Catholic Worker* newspaper, Hennacy fasted "as a penance" for the United States' use of atomic weapons to end World War II.[43] Six weeks later, a group calling themselves Non-Violent Action against Nuclear Weapons staged a nonviolent demonstration at the test site. More than thirty peace activists, many of whom were Quakers, drew upon the example of the 1956 Montgomery, Alabama, bus boycott to protest the "senseless folly" of atomic testing. After speaking to area churches and distributing leaflets about their plans, eleven members of the group tried to enter the test site on August 6, the twelfth anniversary of the Hiroshima bombing, but Nye County deputy sheriffs arrested them. A local judge found them guilty of trespassing but suspended their sentences on condition that they commit no further crimes. Papers all across America, from the Cleveland *Plain Dealer* and *Los Angeles Times* to the *Chicago Daily Tribune* and the *New York Times* covered the story. The importance of their civil disobedience was magnified by the call the day before of the World Council of Churches, representing 165 Protestant and Eastern Orthodox denominations, for England, the United States, and the Soviet Union to halt nuclear testing.[44]

The cost of the tests, or at least the publicly perceived cost in the most human of terms, came in September 1957. The *Las Vegas Sun* carried on its front page a story about Martha Bardoli. She and her husband lived one hundred miles north of ground zero, and their seven-year-old son Martin had died in 1956 from leukemia. The Bardolis believed that the fallout from the atomic tests played a role in Martin's death, and Martha was preparing to send a petition to President Dwight Eisenhower with seventy signatures from neighbors. The petition asked for either a halt in the tests or an assurance that residents would be protected. Most poignantly, she appealed for "protection for our children."[45]

The lack of agreement in the scientific community on the specific dangers posed by exposure to radiation presented a challenge for both the proponents and opponents of atomic testing. On June 12, 1956, both the National Academy of Sciences and the British Medical Research Council, after much collaboration, issued reports that explained that any amount of radiation was potentially hazardous. However, the reports stunned those opposed to atomic testing when their authors concluded that thus far fallout from atomic testing had posed only a "negligible" genetic risk. Indeed, according to the National Academy report, "fall-out from weapons testing has, so far, led to considerably less irradiation of the population than have the medical uses—and has therefore been less detrimental." This led the *U.S. News and World Report* to conclude that radioactive fallout "isn't a big danger after all."[46] Yet the next year many in the scientific community called for an end to testing. Several Nobel Prize winners and nearly forty members of the National Academy of Sciences, including famed chemist Linus Pauling, were among two thousand scientists who signed a petition to Congress arguing that further tests would exacerbate the radiation threats to current and future generations.[47] The timing for this action was not coincidental: the Joint Congressional Committee on Atomic Energy was completing a series of hearings that attracted widespread media coverage with a particular focus upon the threat posed by strontium-90. The use of strontium-90, as described in an article in *Life* magazine, was "worrisome because it takes 28 years for half of any given quantity of it to disintegrate. It lodges in the bones, where it can cause bone cancer or, by irradiating white blood cells in the marrow, leukemia. Current levels are considered too minute to constitute a serious public health menace. But continued unrestricted testing by the world's major powers could cause an appreciable increase in the death rates from bone cancer and leukemia."[48]

Members of the AEC certainly worried about the public's perception of the testing. At its May 1953 meeting after the detonation of Dirty Harry, commission member Eugene M. Zuchert expressed his concern over "the recent fall-out incident at St. George, Utah, coupled with claims of livestock deaths." He believed the radioactive fallout from Dirty Harry had created a psychological "problem" for the agency, and he argued that the AEC should "be prepared to study an alternate to holding future tests at the Nevada Test Site." Given "the present frame of mind of the public," Zuchert claimed, "it would take only a single illogical and unforeseeable incident to preclude holding any future tests in the United States."[49] One of the most instructive sets of minutes comes from a meeting two years later, when members responded to a letter from Clinton P. Anderson, who chaired the congressional Joint Committee on Atomic Energy. Anderson asked if it were possible to use the Nevada Test Site for any tests other than for "small yield devices" given the concern for public safety. What followed was a brisk exchange of thoughts, with Chairman Lewis Strauss taking the most cautious positions. For example, he advocated taking the largest planned devices and loading "them on a ship" to be detonated in the Pacific. When one commissioner argued that "people have to learn to live with the facts of life, and part of the facts of life are fallout," Strauss sharply replied, "If you don't live next door to it." Specifically, he noted the residents of Saint George, Utah, which the tests "always plaster." When another commissioner argued that they could not "let anything interfere with this series of tests—nothing"—Strauss again urged caution, explaining, "I have always been frightened that something would happen which would set us back with the public for a long period of time."[50]

As is evident in the minutes of the 1955 meeting, the AEC faced two often conflicting missions. First, they had to develop tactical atomic weapons to meet the challenge posed by a hostile power that also had such weapons. Second, as Gordon Dean, then chairman of the AEC, assured President Truman when Truman approved the Nevada Test Site in late 1950, "every precaution would be taken" to conduct the tests "in such way that nobody will get hurt."[51] Yet the men who served on the AEC struggled with the challenge of how much they could share with the public about health risks before that information diminished their primary mission, and they almost always erred on the side of carrying out that primary mission.[52] As Dina Titus, leading scholar on the testing in Nevada, has explained, "this was a classic case of government setting one priority and then ignoring any objections to that priority." In essence, "everything else became secondary to winning the arms race."[53] The AEC was not alone in this regard. Notable names from the scientific community including University of Indiana geneticist Hermann J. Muller and Howard L. Andrews, who headed the radiobiology section of the National Cancer Institute, along with political leaders, like former president Harry Truman frequently reflected the AEC perspective. "Let us keep our sense of proportion in the matter of radioactive fall-out," Truman said in 1957. He acknowledged that all must be done "to keep the fall-out in our tests to the absolute minimum." However, "the dangers that might occur from the fall-out in our tests involve a small sacrifice when compared to the infinitely greater evil of the use of nuclear bombs in war."[54]

Still, the AEC worked diligently on public relations. In 1955, for example, in an attempt to counter the growing concerns about fallout, the agency issued an informational booklet. "On the basis of experiments and observations," the agency reassured readers, "it appears that—over a number of generations—radiation from fall-out from Nevada tests would have no greater effect on the human heredity process in the United States than would natural radiation in those parts of the Nation where normal levels are high."[55] A twenty-five minute

film called *Atomic Tests in Nevada* was released two years after the 1953 Dirty
Harry shot, portraying it as "routine" and "nothing to get excited about for the
residents of St. George, Utah." It stressed the national security need for the tests
and the many precautions taken to ensure the safety of those living around the
test site. Finally, the AEC fully cooperated with the editors of *U.S. News and
World Report* on a six-page article entitled "The Facts about A-Bomb 'Fall-Out':
Not a Word of Truth in Scare Stories over Tests" that debunked the fears of
radioactive fallout.[56]

Two years later, the AEC pursued an aggressive campaign to calm the fears
of those living in the counties surrounding the test site. The effort included
screening documentary films (in 1957 more than eleven thousand attended
screenings), having personnel give more than thirty talks to about a thousand
people and appear on radio and television to discuss the tests, and setting up
displays at county fairs.[57] The agency also provided "experts" to meet with the
Nevada State Board of Health to make the case that news reports on fallout
from the tests had been "exaggerated." The *Las Vegas Sun* covered that meeting and a talk given by Dr. Russell H. Morgan of the Radiology Department at
Johns Hopkins University Medical School. The *Sun* article noted that Morgan
confirmed recent "statements by the Atomic Energy Commission that radiation
from X-rays and fluoroscopy presents more of a danger to individuals than fall-
out from weapons testing here."[58]

Seemingly oblivious to all the debate and concerns over testing, the Las Vegas
publicity machine saw the tests as yet another way to promote the community as
an unparalleled resort destination. Reporters who visited Las Vegas just after the
initial tests found the community already excited about the commercial possibilities. In early February 1951, Associated Press journalist Garber Davidson visited
with many residents who told him they were delighted that the tests had "put
Las Vegas on the map in a big way." From chamber of commerce officials and
casino dealers, Davidson learned that hotel business was up because the tests had
provided "the largest advertising feat any city of this size could hope for."[59] Paul
Coates of the *Los Angeles Mirror* and Gladwin Hill similarly found enthusiasm in
Las Vegas because of the tests' economic impact. Coates chatted with Abe Schiller, publicist at the Flamingo, who claimed that there was "not a room in the joint.
Everyone's coming up from L.A. to see the excitement."[60] Hill discovered that
promotional efforts were already up and running; a "local hairdresser" had created an "'atomic' coiffure" while the news bureau was sending across the country
"a collection of pictures of bathing beauties equipped with Geiger counters."[61]

Daniel Lang, longtime staff writer for the *New Yorker*, who had a special interest in atomic weapons, journeyed to Las Vegas in late summer 1952 and found a community that not only had fully embraced the testing but also had made atomic imagery a part of the town's culture and appeal to tourists. His readers learned that residents had become accustomed to getting up early and waiting on their porches with a cup of coffee for a detonation. In just eighteen months, "the predominant attitude in Las Vegas toward the proving ground" had become "one of casualness." Beyond the atomic hairdo and atomic cocktails, Lang discovered that tourists enjoyed the "drinking and singing sessions" in anticipation of detonations. At the Desert Inn Lang learned that Ted Mossman, the pianist at the hotel's Sky Room cocktail lounge, had "improvised some boogie-woogie" he called "the Atom-Bomb Bounce."[62]

In their short visits, Lang and other journalists had only sampled the ways that atomic images permeated the community. Businessmen were not shy about exploiting the possibilities. In the 1956 telephone directory there were six "atomic" ventures, including Atomic Auto Sales, Atomic Hardware, and Atomic Liquor Store. One could sport a mushroom cloud hairstyle or purchase atom burgers and mushroom cloud-shaped cakes. Auto dealer "Boob" Jones could not resist the opportunity with a 1957 ad promising "Atom Bombs on All High Prices." The Flamingo Hotel once dumped two thousand mushrooms into its swimming pool, and a Helldorado parade float commemorated "Nevada's First Atomic Bomb."[63] Benny Binion distributed postcards for his downtown Horseshoe Club with photos of a detonation, and the cover on the 1953 yearbook for Las Vegas High School had a mushroom cloud.[64] When his star performer Lili St. Cyr married in 1955, El Rancho Vegas owner Beldon Katleman got great publicity from the event by having a cake shaped like a mushroom cloud and inscribed, "Happy wedding to the anatomic bomb, Lili St. Cyr." The New Frontier promoted Elvis Presley as the "Atomic Powered Singer" when he appeared there in 1956.[65]

As Dina Titus has pointed out, the chamber of commerce, which never missed out on a promotional opportunity, "provided tourists with up-to-date [detonation] calendars so they could schedule their visits and with road maps pointing out several vantage points around the test site." Similarly, the Las Vegas News Bureau, in its widely circulated 1956 promotional film, *Las Vegas: Playground U.S.A.*, included an early morning shot of "an atomic device," which created a "man-made sun."[66] Some "hotels packed box lunches for bomb watchers to carry to picnics at Angel's Peak, a mountain in the Charleston Range forty-five miles away."[67] In spring 1953 the Sands Hotel began to have "Atom

Watch" parties the night before a detonation and served breakfast on a terrace so their guests could see the mushroom cloud in comfort.[68]

These efforts made sense given the nation's fascination with atomic imagery in the 1950s. Dozens of songs with atomic themes like "The Wild West Is Where I Want to Be" (1953), "You Hit Me Baby Like an Atom Bomb" (1954), and "Atom Bomb Baby" (1957) hit the airwaves. One of the more intriguing titles was "Advice to Joe," released by country singer Roy Acuff in 1951 with a warning of atomic retribution to Soviet leader Joseph Stalin: "When Moscow lies in ashes, God have mercy on your soul."[69] There was a plethora of comic books with atomic themes. As one scholar has explained, "From the 1950s forward, nuclear explosions appeared on literally thousands of comic book covers." They included *Atomic War, Atomic Attack, Atomic Mouse, Atomic Rabbit*, and the *Human Torch*, who was brought back to life by an atomic blast at Yucca Flat.[70] There were even atomic-themed games like Atomic Train, Uranium Rush, which included a toy Geiger counter, and Uranium Board Game. There was also an Atomic Energy Lab and a candy called Atomic Fireball.[71] Movies and some television programs dealt with the tests. *Split Second* (1953) involved two escaped convicts taking hostages and holing up in an abandoned mining town one mile from ground zero. In the final scenes, as some hostages escape for cover in a mine shaft, the convicts and one hostage are unable to flee in a car in time to escape the detonation. The town and the car are incinerated, and as the surviving hostages slowly emerge from the mine, they see the charred remains of the town and the mushroom cloud, a sight one of them grimly describes as the "world of tomorrow." An episode of the television series *State Trooper* (1958) espoused a similarly pessimistic view of the testing. The episode, which opens with a detonation, concerns a desert zealot who sees the atomic tests as a sign of the end times.

Most movies in the 1950s about atomic testing featured radioactive monsters and mutants. *Them, The Thing, The Monster That Challenged the World, The Beginning of the End, The Incredible Shrinking Man*, and *The Beast of Yucca Flats*, all released between 1951 and 1961, were tales related to the "transmutational effect of radiation."[72] Two of the films, *The Atomic Kid* (1954) and *The Amazing Colossal Man* (1957), dealt with the Nevada Test Site. In *The Atomic Kid*, star Mickey Rooney's character is accidentally exposed to radiation in one of the doom town houses during an atomic test. Although he glowed for a time and was able to win at all the Las Vegas slot machines, Rooney's character overcomes the ill effects of radiation in the comedy. However, the officer exposed to radiation in the *Amazing Colossal Man*, after growing to an enormous height, becomes outraged and destroys parts of Strip hotels before being killed at Hoover Dam.

With this backdrop, it was a given that the gifted Las Vegas promoters would exploit the almost saturation coverage of the atomic tests to boost their community. Ken Frogley, who headed the Las Vegas News Bureau in the early 1950s, believed the tests gave him a "great break." During delays in detonations, the multitudes of reporters in town would drop by the news bureau looking for material, and Frogley's staff eagerly delivered.[73] The best promoters of Las Vegas, Sands Hotel publicist Al Freeman and news bureau photographer Don English, most skillfully exploited the opportunities to sell Las Vegas to the nation. Freeman, as he had with so many other developments, threw himself into taking advantage of ways to use the atomic tests to sell his hotel. As the Sands Hotel prepared for its opening in December 1952, Freeman "wanted to open the doors of the Sands by something resembling an 'atom bomb boom,'" but the AEC prevented it with "miles of red tape."[74] He always cooperated with the media covering the tests. When reporters for the Pacific Network of CBS were in town to cover tests in spring 1953, Freeman helped set up interviews with several employees of the hotel for human interest stories. He learned later that Douglas Edwards's CBS news program used two of the interviews, and the producer made sure to have the "Sands sign . . . very prominent in the background."[75] When he learned that some of the newsmen, led by columnist Bob Considine decided in a light-hearted moment to create the Atom Bomb Watchers Society, Freeman offered to let them meet in the Emerald Room at the Sands Hotel and provided them with food and drink. As Don English noted, "All these big shots, all the press from all over the world, would gather up there at Freeman's place."[76]

Observing the intense press coverage of the early atomic tests, Freeman saw an unparalleled chance to publicize the Sands Hotel in spring 1955. The always reliable Gladwin Hill described the upcoming Operation Cue as "the most elaborate atomic demonstration in the five years of continental nuclear tests." For the planned April 26 series of military maneuvers and monitoring of the blast effects on a doom town, the AEC invited nearly a thousand civil defense officials; local, state, and federal office holders; and about one hundred print and broadcast journalists to observe.[77] The networks sent their top on-air personalities and correspondents to cover Operation Cue: NBC sent Roy Neal, John Cameron Swayze, and Dave Garroway, host of the popular *Today Show*, and CBS dispatched Charles Collingwood, Walter Cronkite, and Dallas Townsend. British Movietone News, Paramount, Warner-Pathé, and Hearst Newsreel services sent crews. The print media was also well represented by journalists from NEA–Scripps Howard, United Press, International News Service, *Minneapolis Tribune, Los Angeles Times,* the *New York Times, Life, Newsweek,* and *Collier's.* Anticipating this media blitz around Operation Cue, Freeman persuaded Val Peterson, administrator of the Federal Civil Defense Administration, to name him "Consultant on Public Relations to the Atomic Test Staff."[78] Freeman used that advantage at a meeting of representatives of the resort hotels a month before the scheduled Operation Cue detonation. The group decided that each hotel would accommodate forty-five to sixty observers. Freeman told his fellow publicists that to meet his quota he would focus on accommodating important political figures (including Val Peterson) and the press. He soon reported to his boss Jack Entratter that he had "almost all of working national press here." As fellow publicist Dick Odessky explained, "Once he'd booked enough press into the Sands, Freeman pronounced the hotel the 'official press headquarters' for the bomb tests."[79] This approach, Freeman correctly concluded, would enable the Sands to "realize some goodwill and publicity."[80] He knew that frequently there were delays of the scheduled tests and that journalists would look for other stories in Las Vegas to cover, and he wanted to make sure that as many as possible involved the Sands.

Freeman struck gold. After repeated delays of Operation Cue, he had opera singer Marguerite Piazza, adorned with a mushroom cloud crown and dubbed "Mis-Cue." Her photo was carried on the wire services to papers all across the country. The Sands earned greater coverage when Jake Freedman, head of the hotel, canceled the reservations of "civilians" to accommodate the official observers and press who chose to stay despite the many delays of the shot. In a letter to "Our Press, Atomic Test Observers, and Government Friends," Freedman wrote, "The Sands understands the importance of this National Defense effort, and wishes to assure you that your accommodations here are yours until your mission is completed."[81] This led to ten-minute segments on both a CBS report and the *Today Show* in which Charles Collingwood and Dave Garroway interviewed Freedman about "the gesture of the Sands in accommodating Press people during emergency postponements of the A-Bomb."[82] Freeman also later secured permission to cover a couple of the blasts from the trenches along with servicemen and servicewomen and filed reports with wire services.[83]

In May 1957 Freeman provided accommodations for a host of "cameramen and writers" covering that month's test and parlayed their presence into an opportunity to get great publicity for performer Danny Thomas. As a *Review-Journal* entertainment columnist told his readers, the "funniest news

Opera singer Marguerite Piazza, styled as "Mis-Cue," in a Sands Hotel promotion during the delay of the Operation Cue atomic test in 1955. *Courtesy University of Nevada, Las Vegas, University Libraries Special Collections and Archives, Sands Hotel Collection.*

story in years to come out of Las Vegas was Danny Thomas blowing up his own A-bomb . . . in Yuk-Yuk Flats in back of the Sands maintenance department." Freeman used nine of the photos taken of Thomas's clowning around as a "mad scientist" discharging an atomic blast for a future issue of the hotel's publication, the *Sands Times*.[84]

Don English, who often worked with Freeman on publicity shots, exploited the publicity possibilities of the atom tests even more effectively than Freeman did. He and his colleagues at the Las Vegas News Bureau often assisted photographers with the wire services by offering their photo darkroom and providing photos for them when they had to leave because of delayed tests.[85] English saw all of this as a wonderful opportunity to associate with and befriend the news media from several major markets. Yet he did much more than facilitate the dissemination of atomic testing photos. English saw the tests as "unbelievable leverage for publicity."[86]

English was responsible for the most iconic of the images from the atmospheric tests in Nevada. Before newsmen began observing the tests from the famed News Nob just seven miles from ground zero, they usually gazed at the detonations from Mount Charleston in the Spring Mountains several miles northwest of Las Vegas. It was there that English had one of his greatest promotional successes, drawing upon the talents of Sally McCloskey, a ballerina and dancer in the Copa Room at the Sands Hotel. In June 1953 he persuaded McCloskey to perform a dance they called "Angel's Dance" at Angel's Peak. As he snapped shots of McCloskey performing, a mushroom cloud appeared in the distance behind her. The *Review-Journal* published eight photos of this "A-Ballet," and many wire services picked up the shots. Indeed, they became a feature in *Parade*, the widely circulated Sunday newspaper magazine. The caption to the photos in the story read, "Her task: to interpret the greatest drama of our time in dance rhythms. For high over her sinuous, leaping form rose a symbol no eye could miss: the pale, rising cloud of an atomic bomb just exploded 40 miles away."[87]

Four years later, English, knowing that newspapers "were always hungry for anything that had any kind of a different approach," tried a variation on the many "Miss A-Bomb" photos that he and his fellow photographers had produced over the years of women adorned with mushroom cloud crowns. The evening before a scheduled shoot of the Copa Girls at the Sands, English cut the shape of a mushroom cloud from cardboard and pasted cotton to it. While at the Sands the next day, he asked for a volunteer to wear the cotton mushroom cloud attached to a swimsuit. Dancer Lee Merlin agreed, and English took the photo across the street from the Sands with only desert in the background. English sent the image of Merlin with arms outstretched and dubbed as "Miss Atomic Bomb" over the wire services. It became one of the most published photos about the testing program and reminded many of the link between Las Vegas and testing.[88]

One of English's first photos of the tests had cemented that link. Sometimes

Don English's iconic photograph of an atomic test framed by two signs of Vegas Vic,
1951. *Courtesy University of Nevada, Las Vegas, University Libraries Special Collections and
Archives and Las Vegas News Bureau.*

great shots are the product of luck, and that was true of English's photo of a mushroom cloud in November 1951. The morning of a scheduled test, English overslept
and knew he could not make it to Angel's Peak in time, so he drove downtown
and decided to see if he could photograph a mushroom cloud from Las Vegas. He
climbed on top of a building, and just as he set up his camera, he saw the blast. In
moments the mushroom cloud developed, and he caught an image of it precisely
between the Vegas Vic sign and that of the Pioneer Club. *Life* magazine featured
it in their November 12 issue in an article titled "Wherever You Look There's
Danger in Las Vegas." *Life* not only selected it as the photo of the week, but this
English photo was reprinted countless times, notably on postcards.[89]

All of this was, as English explained, "a wonderful thing for Las Vegas in
terms of publicity." Yet he acknowledged that so much of what he and other
promoters did in their exploitation of the testing was "frivolous." He defended
his and his contemporaries' cavalier treatment of the gravely serious testing by
arguing, "we just didn't realize the seriousness of what was going on."[90] Others
were more critical. As Katharine Best and Katharine Hillyer wrote in 1955, some

called the promoters' attitudes "an idiot lack of sensitivity to the meaning of atom busting."[91] The indictment was not entirely fair. Few in Las Vegas or in the scientific community had a clear sense of the dangers the tests posed.

In subsequent decades, numerous studies, investigations by congressional committees and federal commissions, and litigation have demonstrated, as a congressional subcommittee in 1980 concluded, that "the government was aware of the health hazards posed to the people living downwind from the tests site" and "failed to provide adequate protection for the residents of this area during its operation of the nuclear weapons testing program."[92] Moreover, it is now clear that more than two hundred thousand people served at the test site as soldiers, air crews, test personnel, employees of the AEC, or observers.[93] Still, the studies of the direct impact on downwinders and those at the test site have been in conflict.[94] As a consequence, even those sympathetic to the plight of the thousands of veterans and civilians exposed to radiation during the atmospheric tests reach a painful conclusion. The 1995 presidential advisory committee on human radiation experiments decided that it was "very difficult to resolve whether atomic veterans as a group are at substantially elevated cancer risk." Similarly, Gary Turkak in *VFW* magazine wrote, "For atomic veterans, there simply is no way to know which maladies are a result of radiation and which are not."[95] In her recent sympathetic study of the struggles of those who lived downwind from the tests, Sarah Alisabeth Fox ultimately concluded: "Downwind residents realize they cannot prove that simply because a neighbor worked outdoors or a child drank milk from a particular dairy, their cancer was a product of exposure to radiation. Even the families of test site workers, atomic vets, uranium workers, with their direct and irrefutable link to radiation exposure, know that no matter how dramatic the evidence seems, they cannot demonstrate conclusively a causal relationship between radiation exposure and a particular cancer death."[96] As Don English said in 2005, it seemed that in the 1950s "everybody was all for it," and "we didn't know about the things that were happening with the downwind in Utah and all that until later."[97] While some in Las Vegas raised questions at the time about the health risks of the tests, for most it seemed wisest to exploit the tests to further promote their community as America's Playground. In other words, the best course was to "put the atom bomb to good use."[98]

Nine
Rat Pack

On January 20, 1960, a packed Copa Room eagerly awaited the opening-night performance of a "Summit" of headliners at the Sands Hotel. For several days, Al Freeman, the hotel's savvy publicist, had been promoting the month-long run of Frank Sinatra, Dean Martin, Sammy Davis Jr., and Peter Lawford while they filmed the movie *Ocean's Eleven*. With a tantalizing teaser—"Star-Light, Star-Bright . . . Which Star Shines Tonight"—Freeman's advertisements suggested that two or more of the entertainers would perform at each of the two nightly shows.[1] These stars, variously called the "Rat Pack" or the "Clan," along with comedian Joey Bishop, who served as emcee for the performances, turned the shows into a legendary spectacle. In their reviews, visiting entertainment columnists showed little restraint. To one, opening night was "one of the most glittering, exciting first-nights in Vegas history," and another claimed that Sinatra and his friends may have been "the night-club act to end them all." Local columnist Ralph Pearl recalled fourteen years later that among the "more than ten thousand shows" he had seen in Las Vegas, opening night of the "Summit" was "the most exciting."[2] It seemed to Shirley MacLaine, who saw several of the shows, had a cameo in the movie, and was part of the Rat Pack, that "the world came to Vegas" in 1960 to see Sinatra, Martin, Davis, Lawford, and Bishop, performers who created "an energy there that has never been duplicated since."[3]

Opening night set the tone for what was to come. With the five men seated up front, the Copa Girls performed a pleasing number, and, predictably, Frank Sinatra was first on stage to sing several songs. As celebrities Lucille Ball, Milton Berle, Cyd Charisse, Dinah Shore, and heavyweight boxing champion Ingemar Johansson watched, Dean Martin, Sammy Davis Jr., and Peter Lawford, who had moved behind stage, began to heckle the great singer. Joey Bishop followed with a monologue, and after singing "Birth of the Blues," Davis joined Lawford in a dance routine with Sinatra calling out, "What a great team. One dances and the other applauds." Martin was last on stage, playing to perfection his role as the happy drunk, mumbling a "thank you" to "Srank Finatra." While he struggled through a few songs, the others unmercifully interrupted him before

The Sands promoted the appearance of Rat Pack members Frank Sinatra, Dean Martin, Sammy Davis Jr., Peter Lawford, and Joey Bishop. *Courtesy University of Nevada, Las Vegas, University Libraries Special Collections and Archives, Sands Hotel Collection.*

joining him on stage to close, singing "Together" with Jack Entratter, the man who had organized the extravaganza. He had come up with the idea of a head-liners summit as a take on the proposed gathering of leaders of the Soviet Union, France, Great Britain, and the United States. As the six men left the stage, Bishop jumped "piggyback on Entratter's large back." The midnight show proceeded in a similar fashion but with Davis and Lawford at one point walking across the stage in their shorts with their trousers neatly folded on their arms.[4]

For the next four weeks, the Rat Pack continued this helter-skelter type of show, with ad libs, heckling, interruptions, gags, and an ever-present liquor cart. Robert Legare attended many of the performances for a feature article in *Playboy* magazine. He reported that the "fun was always free-form and zany," and it usually resulted in "general pandemonium" on stage. He argued it worked because of the charm and talent of the five men. The audiences could not get enough of them. It seemed that "every gag, every gesture, every amble across the stage by a star, had the whole place rocking with wild glee."[5] Substantial press coverage guaranteed that word got out about the shows, and the demand for tables in the Copa Room skyrocketed. Every night Nick Kelly, host of the fabled room, turned away hundreds of fans, and by early February the Sands had nearly twenty thousand reservation requests for rooms.[6]

Filming a movie in Las Vegas at the same time as their twice nightly performances added to the hectic pace for the Rat Pack. Four years earlier, Peter Lawford had purchased rights to a story about World War II veterans robbing Las Vegas casinos. No one was interested in the project until Sinatra heard about it and decided to make it the first movie for his new Dorchester Productions. He signed Lewis Milestone, veteran director of several notable films, including *All Quiet on the Western Front*, to direct the movie. On-location filming at the Sands, Flamingo, Desert Inn, Riviera, and Sahara continued as the Rat Pack performed nightly in the Copa Room. Lawford later explained, "We would do two shows at night, get to bed at four-thirty or five, get up again at seven or eight, and go to work on a movie. We'd come back, go to the steam room, get something to eat, and start all over again—two shows." According to author Shawn Levy, this made things difficult for director Milestone, who "usually got one Rat Packer at a time, occasionally two." Most were on the set for only about three hours a day.[7] Director George Sidney also used Sinatra and Martin for a scene in *Pepe*, a film starring Mexican actor Cantinflas. With film crews and extras for two movies in town, it seemed to columnist Philip K. Scheuer that Hollywood had "taken over" Las Vegas. Hedda Hopper agreed, reporting "press and photographers winging in from all over the country" to cover the excitement.[8]

When *Ocean's Eleven* premiered in Las Vegas in August, dozens of newspaper, television, and radio journalists covered the event. After a cocktail party and a dinner show featuring the Rat Pack for journalists and invited VIPs, a caravan headed downtown for the world premiere at the Fremont Theatre. To the delight of thousands of fans, many stars were on hand, including Tony Curtis, Janet Leigh, Shirley MacLaine, George Raft, director Billy Wilder, Louis Prima, Keely Smith, former Brooklyn Dodgers and New York Giants manager Leo Durocher, and famed gambler Nick the Greek. Film clips of the evening's events appeared later on NBC's late-night show *Tonight Starring Jack Paar*, and newsreel companies recorded the gala evening for distribution around the country.[9]

The Sinatra-led Clan (he did not like the "Rat Pack" label), which captured the nation's attention in 1960, was not the first such group. Humphrey Bogart and Lauren Bacall had established a Rat Pack in 1955 after an extraordinary trip to Las Vegas. For Noël Coward's opening night at the Desert Inn on June 7, Frank Sinatra had chartered a plane to bring Bogart, Bacall, David Niven, Judy Garland, Joseph Cotton, Zsa Zsa Gábor, Joan Fontaine, Laurence Harvey, Jane Powell, and literary agent Irving "Swifty" Lazar to see the renowned British playwright, composer, and actor. The group gambled, drank, and partied for four days. At the end of all that dissipation, Bacall looked at them all and proclaimed, "You look like a god damn rat pack." A month later, Sinatra bused several of these "idiot friends" to a Long Beach, California, benefit concert Judy Garland put on for special needs children. At the end of her performance, Garland called Sinatra, Bogart, and Bacall to come on stage, along with several other stars including Sammy Davis Jr. and Dean Martin. Because they had enjoyed such camaraderie, Bogart and Bacall created a group with the "Rat Pack" moniker. "In order to qualify," Bacall explained, "one had to be addicted to nonconformity, staying up late, drinking, laughing, and not caring what anyone thought or said about us." In his December 1955 *New York Herald Tribune* column, Joe Hyam reported on the Rat Pack's "first annual meeting . . . at Romanoff's restaurant in Beverly Hills." There the members elected Sinatra as "pack master," Bacall as "den mother," and Bogart as "rat-in-charge of public relations." As Bogart explained the simple mission of the group, they sought "the relief of boredom and the perpetuation of independence."[10] This was all, as James Kaplan has explained, "an elaborate put-on," a way for iconoclasts like Bogart and Bacall to thumb their noses at the smug Hollywood establishment.[11] The short-lived Holmby Hills Rat Pack, named after the western Los Angeles locale of Humphrey Bogart's home, ended with the death of the actor in 1957.

However, the following year, America learned about a new incarnation of the Rat Pack, called the Clan, in a feature article in *Life* magazine. They learned that Sinatra, who hated being alone, surrounded himself with talented but deferential people, some of whom had been in the Bogart and Bacall group. As with the

Holmby Hills Rat Pack, they were a rebellious and independent Clan. Journalist Paul O'Neil contended that their "nonconformist attitude" was best defined as "a public and aggressive indifference, not only to what the customers expect of their movie stars but also to what Hollywood expects of its own citizens."[12] Las Vegas drew them like a magnet because of the big money but also because it was the best party town. As Sammy Davis Jr. told O'Neil, "'We're in Las Vegas a lot,' to 'work or go to cheer one of our own who is working there.'"[13] For example, when Judy Garland opened at the Sands in October 1958, Sinatra summoned members of the Clan, and those who wanted to be in it, to ride in a private rail car to Las Vegas to support her.[14] By 1960 the Clan was common fodder in popular magazines and Sunday supplements in newspapers, which described Sinatra's entourage as a "gang of Hollywood fun-and-money seekers" whose "basic requirement for memberships" was to pay "homage to Mr. Sinatra."[15]

Their widely publicized performances attracted presidential candidate Massachusetts senator John F. Kennedy, whose appearance on February 7 was one of the big highlights of the Rat Pack's run at the Sands. Near the end of the first show that evening, Sinatra introduced Kennedy, who was sitting at a front table. "We are also delighted to have in our audience," Sinatra proclaimed, "the brightest man in the political world in this country or any other country today. I personally feel that I am going to visit him in that house one day very soon." After the senator took a couple of bows, the Rat Pack shtick kicked in. Joey Bishop, with his arm around Sammy Davis Jr., mumbled, "You son-of-a-gun, you got the Jewish vote" and later said, "If you get in, Frank has to be ambassador to Italy and Sammy to Israel. I don't want too much for myself—just don't let me get drafted again." At one point, Martin, in his role as Drunk Dean, wandered over in front of the microphone and asked, to the delight of the senator and the rest of the crowd, "What was his last name again?"[16]

Kennedy's appearance illustrated a remarkable nexus of Hollywood and national politics. The senator knew his run for the nomination would be challenging and was fascinated by the "glittering world of Hollywood," so he sought the help of the celebrity world to broaden his appeal. There was no one more important in that world in 1960 than Frank Sinatra. As Steven Watts has shown, for Sinatra, a lifelong Democrat who had strongly supported Franklin Roosevelt, Kennedy "represented social respectability, political power, and genuine public influence," all of which the singer craved.[17] As a consequence, Sinatra and his Rat Pack pals spent much of the year working for the senator's election, including appearing at the Democratic Party nominating convention.

Kennedy had been in Las Vegas briefly a week earlier on his way to Reno. He had visited Peter Lawford, who had married Kennedy's sister Patricia, and had dropped in on the cast during shooting for *Ocean's Eleven*.[18] In Reno to meet with labor union business agents, Kennedy found only one from Las Vegas and had his staff arrange a reception for him in Las Vegas at the convention center to shore up his support with organized labor there. He also asked to meet with Bart Lytton, finance chairman of the California Democratic Committee, to talk about his chances in that state's primary.[19] Those political activities took place after his evening in the Copa Room, all of which gave him great visibility. Moreover, some, like Peter Lawford, contended that the hotel bosses gave big donations to the Kennedy campaign during the senator's brief stay in Las Vegas.[20] In addition, Kennedy, who had for decades been a womanizer, enjoyed the company of beautiful women. An FBI memo to director J. Edgar Hoover reported that a private investigator claimed that the senator had engaged in "certain sex activities" while in Las Vegas. In part, the investigator based his report on word from Beldon Katleman, owner of the El Rancho Vegas, who contended that "while the Senator, Sinatra, and Lawford were there, show girls from all over town were running in and out of the Senator's suite."[21] Two reporters who were in Sinatra's suite following one of the shows saw young women there and left because "we sensed that Jack and Frank and a couple of the girls were about to have a party."[22] One of them was Judith Campbell, who claimed to have had an extended affair with Kennedy while simultaneously being involved with gangster Sam Giancana.[23]

From the distance of six decades it is evident to some observers that the triumph of the Rat Pack illustrated the opportunities for multiethnic success in America. One was an immigrant, and three were the sons of immigrants. None had completed high school. They did not represent establishment America. Their high visibility, Max Rudin has argued, helped redefine the meaning of class in America. They were, after all, "one black, one Jew, two Italians, and one feckless Hollywoodized Brit."[24] All frequently reminded the audiences of this, including the closing show when, just before leaving the stage, "Sinatra and Martin held up a placard with 'Italy' on it. Sammy and Bishop had an 'Israel' card and Lawford . . . had 'Great Britain' on his."[25] During that last show, the Rat Pack invited Bob Hope on stage. The famed British comedian, looking at Martin and Sinatra, said, the "Italians are taking over the world, especially television. The NBC peacock is now a guinea hen." Joey Bishop was more to the point, reminding the audience of the widely held association of Italians with organized crime. Normally, when he introduced Martin or Sinatra, Bishop promised they were "gonna come out and tell you about some of the good work the Mafia is doing." Once, when Bishop asked Sinatra, "How about the good the Mafia does?" Sinatra cheerfully responded, "Fine organization." Ironically, as they joked about the Mafia, a story surfaced in the local newspapers about the deliberations during a meeting of leading organized crime figures in Apalachin, New York, three years earlier. *Life* magazine picked up the story and reported that mobsters at that gathering expressed the hope that they would be able to control political leaders in Nevada so that they could "tap 25 major casinos in Las Vegas and Reno." Behind the scenes, the state's Gaming Control Board was preparing to assemble a list of persons with organized crime connections whom owners would have to bar from their casinos. The board issued its famous Black Book in June.[26]

The release of *Ocean's Eleven* in late summer brought another reminder of the organized crime connection. Sinatra had cast Cesar Romero to play Duke Santos, a man with underworld connections, and in one scene he meets with the bosses of the Flamingo, Sands, Sahara, Desert Inn, and Riviera to discuss what to do after Danny Ocean's gang has robbed them. They were concerned about the "partners we have to answer to," leaving little doubt that they were discussing mob partners.[27]

The presence of Sammy Davis Jr., however, drew the most commentary from the others. In the context of a city and nation struggling with segregation, the white performers made frequent references to their acceptance of Davis and took jabs at America's prejudiced culture. One evening, for example, Sinatra told the audience as Davis danced, "there'll be no segregation here."[28] This could well have been an effort by Sinatra to lend support to the local NAACP effort to integrate the casinos and hotels in Las Vegas in early 1960. During another Davis performance, Sinatra said, "I'd like to see them try this in Little Rock," a reference to the Arkansas city where President Eisenhower had sent a thousand troops to ensure the integration of the community's Central High School in 1957. Most compelling was an exchange between Lawford and Davis while they danced. When the former said, "Sam, I'm not prejudiced," Davis responded, "I know your kind. You'll dance with me, but you won't go to school with me." Several scholars have hailed the Rat Pack's "liberated views on race," noting their "full inclusion of Davis in the troupe" and the instances of their commentary that demonstrated their "contempt for bigotry."[29]

Still, some of their "irreverent mockery" of prejudice was offensive. As Nancy Sinatra wrote in her biography of her father, the Rat Pack's "racial and ethnic gags" were "awful" as well as "wonderful."[30] For example, it became a standard moment during the shows for Martin to pick up Davis, walk to the microphone, and say to the audience, "I'd like to thank the NAACP for this trophy." As Dave Calvert has characterized Martin's move, Davis was "physically, professionally and verbally diminished by the action."[31] Similarly, when the house lights went low Sinatra often would say, "You better keep smiling, Smokey, so we can see where you are." Sometimes when Davis was performing, one of the Rat Pack would call out, "Hurry up, Sammy, the watermelon is getting warm."[32] Native Americans fared no better in their gags. In early February, between shows, the five dined with Jack Entratter and planned a new gag for the midnight show based on the native-inspired production number the Copa Girls were performing. They tapped almost all the stereotypes about natives in their largely impromptu performance. As Bishop introduced the other four, they came out "in Indian regalia," including feather headdresses, tomahawks, and blankets that proclaimed they were from the Sands reservation. Sinatra explained that theirs was a "'Summit meeting. Indian style, with popcorn' and that he was 'big chief running water.'"[33]

The Rat Pack particularly targeted gay men. If someone got too close to them on stage, it was standard practice for one of them to say, "Want to meet tomorrow and pick out furniture?" One of the others would often ask Joey Bishop if he had "a fairy godmother." His standard response was, "No, but we got an uncle we keep a close eye on." On February 7, when they invited comedian Milton Berle on stage, he referred to the Rat Pack as "all these fags," and as he approached Dean Martin, Berle blew him a kiss and said, "Boy, if I ever switch you're first." During one performance, Sinatra interrupted a Dean Martin song as Sammy Davis walked in front of the singer and asked, "Did you see the Jewish colored doctor recently turned fag come by here?" Another evening, Martin called Davis the "African Queen."[34]

To those in the Rat Pack, this was just "clowning" around, offering a parody of the bias they saw in their culture. In that regard, the performer's antics likely reflected the views of most of those who attended their shows because the audiences laughed at virtually anything the Rat Pack did. However, to some their commitment against bigotry seemed neither deep nor wide. By the time the Rat Pack performed again in August, the evening of the *Ocean's Eleven* premiere, Ralph Pearl reported that many fans had had enough. "Several *Sun* readers as well as many locals who attended" told Pearl "that the boys horsing around has finally gotten out of hand. They say that race and religion is bandied about much too roughly to be fun anymore."[35]

Likewise, younger performers differed in their views of the Rat Pack. Paul Anka, who began singing in Las Vegas in 1958 as an opening act for Sophie Tucker at the Sahara, recalled that he saw Sinatra, Martin, and Davis as "little gods in black tie and patent leather shoes." Anka envied them because they could act without restraint. He recalled, "They didn't talk like other people, they didn't behave like other people, they didn't have to play by the rules the way other people had to." Anka remembered that he and Bobby Darin, another young star singer, idolized the Rat Pack and sought to "be like those guys" because they "were the coolest, suavest cats on the planet."[36] However, Johnny Mathis, who followed the Rat Pack in the Copa Room when they finished their run, recalled that in 1960 he had no interest in "staying up late, boozing, hanging out with Frank Sinatra, Sammy Davis, Jr. and Peter Lawford." He had "heard that they were pretty rowdy" and "had nobody to check" what they said and did.[37]

Other commentators have agreed that too often the five men stepped over the line and that what they offered to audiences was little more than the tasteless antics of juveniles with all the gags, ribbing, and drinking. For example, one night, the audience could hear Martin's voice off-stage interrupting a Sinatra song with, "Who's the wise guy who locked me in the men's room?"[38] Sinatra biographer James Kaplan has been particularly critical, arguing in one instance that "most of the humor was Neanderthal, if not antediluvian, at least by twenty-first-century standards" and in another that "there was a hollowness to all this misbehavior." The Rat Pack performances at the Sands were "infantile, the grown-up equivalent of fart jokes."[39]

Many contemporary newspaper and magazine articles, film clips, memoirs, and accounts written decades later chronicle the performances in the Copa Room and the days filming *Ocean's Eleven*. From them a narrative has emerged that portrays the Rat Pack phenomenon, whatever it represented, as a watershed for Las Vegas, a moment when the world truly took notice of the city for the first time. Yet much of what happened during those four weeks in early 1960 and during the world premiere of *Ocean's Eleven* the next summer is best understood as the culmination of developments throughout the 1950s in America's Playground.

To gain maximum publicity for the performances of the Rat Pack, Sands publicist Al Freeman, with the backing of his boss Jack Entratter, did what all good publicists in Las Vegas in the 1950s had learned would work. Like Harvey Diederich, Stan Irwin, Lee Fisher, Eugene Murphy, and Herb McDonald, the other great publicists of the decade, Freeman worked the phones to bring in a small army of entertainment columnists who spread the word of the month-long escapades. To add to the excitement on stage, he drew upon his and Entratter's entertainment connections to invite top celebrities to sit in front-row tables. All the big names awaited being introduced from the stage so that they could take a bow and hear the applause from adoring fans before taking their seats. Freeman succeeded. According to *Variety*, "The 'Meeting at The Summit, probably attracted during its four weeks more ringsiding celebs than any other show in history."[40] When major headliners opened in Las Vegas it had become routine for several celebrities to be in the audience to add dazzle to the evening, and on some occasions, as when Noël Coward performed in the Painted Desert Room at the Desert Inn in 1955, celebrities were on hand for each performance of his four-week run. Depending upon the night, people in the audience could see not only the famed British entertainer perform but also admire stars like George Burns and Gracie Allen, Jack Benny and Mary Livingston, Jeanette MacDonald, Cole Porter, Joseph Cotton, Tallulah Bankhead, Ethel Merman, Van Johnson, and Kay Thompson.[41] The successful world premiere of *Ocean's Eleven* in Las Vegas followed the model of previous promotions of films—*My Friend Irma Goes West* (1950), *Las Vegas Story* (1952), *Meet Me in Las Vegas* (1956), and *The Joker Is Wild* (1957)—which typically included cocktail parties at Strip hotels, a gaggle of entertainment columnists, parades to either the El Portal or Fremont Theatre downtown, appearances by the casts, and the distribution across the nation of newsreel films of the festivities, all demonstrating the emergence of Las Vegas as the nation's entertainment capital.[42]

There were many precedents for the sardonic ad libs and heckling that characterized the Rat Pack performances. As Garry Boulard has shown in his biography of Louis Prima, headliners like Frank Sinatra, Dean Martin, Sammy Davis Jr., and Red Skelton would often come from other Strip hotels to the Louis Prima–Keely Smith lounge shows (which Boulard characterized as "uninhibited forays into musical madness") at the Sahara after their shows and would "make their presence known in the audience. Sometimes they'd even get involved in the act, other times they'd happily wave and joke to the performers onstage."[43] Beginning in 1959 with his appearances at the Sahara lounge, Don Rickles had become a hit with his insult humor, which often triggered heckling from an audience that usually included several celebrities. Indeed, Rickles was performing while the Rat Pack was at the Sands. Sinatra, Davis, Bishop, and Lawford were on hand for his opening night, and Rickles could not resist picking on Sinatra: "Don't be shy. Be yourself. Hit somebody!" He continued, "Why do I have to pick on him? Because I heard him sing."[44] In 1958 Sinatra and Martin interrupted Judy Garland's performance in the Copa Room. James Kaplan described the scene: "As Garland paused between numbers, Dean, in drunk persona, called a rude remark from his seat; the audience tittered. Frank chimed in. Finally, she summoned the two of them." They climbed on stage with drinks in hand and joked and sang with Garland. Martin even fell to the floor once. To entertainment columnist Mike Connolly, "It was a wild, swingin' ad-lib affair."[45] Most importantly, all of the Rat Pack except Peter Lawford had performed many times in Jack Entratter's nightclub, and it was common for other celebrities to be onstage with one or more of them during the hotel's anniversary parties each December.

Even the appearance of John F. Kennedy was nothing new. He had become familiar with Las Vegas while campaigning for Adlai Stevenson in the latter's unsuccessful 1956 run for the presidency. He spoke before a large crowd at the Royal Nevada and stayed at the home of the Desert Inn's Wilbur Clark. Kennedy returned the following year for a couple of days to meet with local Democrats, leading the *Las Vegas Sun* to note that "the Massachusetts Senator has been prominently named as a possible candidate for the Presidency on the Democratic ticket in the next general election."[46] What was new and what gained the quintet such attention was their willingness to perform together for an entire month. That precedent-setting decision, along with simultaneous filming of *Ocean's Eleven*, is what caused all the buzz.

While they may have made some awkward and at times contradictory statements about bigotry, the Rat Pack's ultimate message about Las Vegas was much simpler. It was a message that Las Vegas promoters had been developing throughout the 1950s. "One day Frank laid it on the line," Sammy Davis Jr. recalled Sinatra's reason for their performing at the Copa together while making the movie. "The idea is to hang out together, find fun with the broads, and have a great time."[47] There is little doubt they succeeded. To those who saw the shows, as Robert Legare reported, no matter what gag or put-down came their way, it was clear that "the performers were genuinely enjoying themselves."[48] Martin later said that he and his buddies had "more laughs than the audience." Lawford said he "couldn't wait to get to work" because "it was all so much fun." Bishop claimed that performing with his pals in 1960 "was the greatest time of my life." Sammy Davis Jr. was most effusive. "We were the headliners," he explained, and "the ladies were the most attractive, the cats the coolest, the booze the best, [and] the celebrities the highest profiles." Joy Garner, a Copa Girl at the time, fondly recalled the four weeks of performances and movie filming as all "great fun." Perhaps entertainment columnist Ralph Pearl's characterization best captures the essence of their performances: "It all was a great romp."[49]

Journalists of the time suggested that the Rat Pack's "immense popular appeal" was likely due to their "devil-may-care nonconformity," behavior "that millions envy secretly or even unconsciously."[50] Many commentators in the past three decades have agreed with that assessment. They have described those in the audiences as people largely living mundane lives in a conformist culture defined by "'square' social norms," enjoying, however briefly, the freedom to identify with celebrities who did not have to endure "the constraints of fidelity, monogamy, sobriety, and dreary obligations to show up at a job every morning."[51] Richard Lacayo argued in *Time* that middle-class men of that era "wanted to cut loose, the way Sinatra wore his tie—undone, a sign of his narrow escape from a workaday world."[52]

Angie Dickinson, who portrayed Sinatra's wife in *Ocean's Eleven* and who saw many of the shows, concluded that the five men "were at the top of their game, the top of their pleasure period. I mean, they loved Vegas."[53] So did millions of Americans who were becoming "increasingly preoccupied with the consumption of leisure" in the two decades after World War II.[54] To be sure, there were many other vacation magnets for prosperous Americans, notably Disneyland, which had opened amid much fanfare in 1955. The imaginative theme park with its popular "lands"—Frontierland, Main Street U.S.A., Fantasyland, Adventureland, and Tomorrowland—within a year had drawn more than five million visitors. Walt Disney had envisioned an amusement park that would offer guests a chance, as John Findlay noted, to "forget day-to-day concerns."[55] Families could visit a happy and reassuring place that showcased the traditional values of turn-of-the-century small-town America. It was a nostalgic respite in the stressful Cold War era, all wrapped up in "an integrated juvenile world's fair of fantasy."[56]

Many journalists called Las Vegas the adult Disneyland. In 1958, for example, screenwriter and critic Julian Halevy, after visiting both locales, concluded "that both these institutions exist for the relief of tension and boredom."[57] Yet Las Vegas had crafted a wildly successful appeal dramatically different from that of the amusement park in Anaheim, California. Journalists in the 1960s who visited Las Vegas tried to grasp the essence of the city's appeal and generally reached the same conclusion. Writing in *Holiday* magazine, Caskie Stinnett told travelers "there is absolutely nothing else in the world like Las Vegas."[58]

Charles Champlin, the arts editor for the *Los Angeles Times*, agreed, arguing that among the city's "restorative qualities" was its ability to offer the traveler a "release from mundane cares." He knew of no other locale "where one can see two major shows and three or four lounge acts, get some sun and pool-time and have at least one gourmet quality meal, and thus cram a week's worth of vacation pleasures into an overnight stay."[59] Stinnett found that "vast numbers of people" saw this travel destination as "endlessly irresistible," a "glittering and gay and totally uninhibited" place. In short, "Las Vegas is fun."[60]

Because their performances gained so much national attention with their focus on irreverent, outrageous fun, the Rat Pack solidified Las Vegas's claim as America's Playground. No other destination offered a vacation experience that included such extraordinary nightclub acts, opportunities to rub elbows with celebrities, legal gambling, a resort hotel experience, beautiful women, Hoover Dam, atomic detonations, the Grand Canyon, and perhaps the chance to see a notable gangster. It all reflected the opportunity for carefree days and nights. Typically, while in Las Vegas, visitors did not concern themselves with alarm clocks and newspapers or think about obligations they had back home. Instead, they embraced this unique escapist, even hedonist destination, where they need not worry about propriety. Drawing on Lauren Bacall's characterization of the original Rat Pack is helpful in understanding Las Vegas's fundamental appeal. In a short vacation, visitors could do what they wanted to do whenever they chose to do it and not care "what anyone thought or said" about them.

Las Vegas Strip, 2002, looking north from Mandalay Bay, revealing the
many massive luxury hotels built after Steve Wynn opened the Mirage in 1989.
Photo courtesy of Aaron Mayes, photographer.

Afterword

In the 1950s the promoters, developers, and civic leaders in Las Vegas built a solid foundation for the continued growth of their vacation city. To be sure, they and their successors encountered troubling recessions in later years. Notably, the 1973 national fuel crisis stalled the increase in visitor numbers, as did the terrorist attack on September 11, 2001. However, the trajectory in visitor numbers was always up—21 million in 1990, 36 million in 2000, and a peak of 43 million in 2016.[1] The elements that explained that prolonged success mirrored those of the 1950s: an increasing number of appealing resort hotel-casinos, a dazzling entertainment scene, a chance to spend a few days and nights without a care, and a crafty roster of promoters selling those features.

Hotel developers of the 1950s quickly learned the magic of offering affordable luxurious accommodations, but in 1966 a new trend developed: the thoroughly themed hotel. Jay Sarno, who had built a Roman-themed hotel in Palo Alto, California, visited Las Vegas in 1963 and decided to bring this fantasy motif to the Strip after concluding that the resort hotels along the famed boulevard were unimaginative. Three years later, Sarno opened Caesars Palace, which featured a fourteen-story tower with a long driveway lined with fountains, statuary, and cypress trees. Inside, the hotel had marble pillars, a huge chandelier in the casino, the Circus Maximus Theater, Cleopatra Barge Nightclub, and a gourmet restaurant called the Bacchanal Room. Cocktail waitresses wore short togas, and the stationery in the rooms resembled Roman parchment.[2] Another developer named Kirk Kerkorian soon after added another element to the evolution of the Las Vegas resort hotel. In 1969 Kerkorian opened the International, the world's largest hotel. Designed by Beverly Hills architect Martin Stern, this megaresort featured a Y-shaped triform tower with more than 1,500 rooms.[3] Although *Time* magazine dubbed Kerkorian's hotel the "pinnacle of preposterousness," he opened an even larger hotel, the MGM Grand, four years later.[4] In 1989 Steve Wynn, the city's most imaginative hotel developer, combined the innovations of Sarno and Kerkorian in his Mirage Hotel. Just north of Caesars Palace, the South Seas–themed $600 million Mirage was larger than the MGM

Grand. Wynn's hotel transformed the vacation city as developers opened more than a dozen massive "Disneyfied" themed properties in the next two decades: Excalibur, a new MGM Grand, Luxor, Monte Carlo, Treasure Island, Mandalay Bay, New York–New York, Bellagio, Paris, Venetian, Wynn Las Vegas, Palazzo, Encore, Aria, and Cosmopolitan (three of these developed by Wynn himself).[5] While the rooms were no longer "loss leaders" in attracting guests, most of the hotels still offered luxurious accommodations at reasonable prices.

Similarly, the nature of entertainment, the critical draw for the resort hotels, evolved over time. Jack Entratter was able to continue the Rat Pack phenomenon through 1966, at least with Frank Sinatra, Dean Martin, and Sammy Davis Jr. In April 1966 "hundreds of people" still got "turned away" each night.[6] Yet entertainment directors struggled to find headliners who could consistently attract big gamblers to their hotel. They booked standards crooners, pop artists, country singers, and stand-up comics, hoping for that next Liberace or Sinatra who would be sure to fill the hotel for two weeks. While their quest often ended in frustration, entertainment directors did find two headliners in the 1960s who had the magic needed to connect with audiences. For many fans, the true king of Las Vegas began his reign on July 31, 1969. That night, thirteen years after his disastrous debut at the New Frontier, Elvis Presley started a seven-year run of sellout performances at Kirk Kerkorian's International Hotel. He sang his 1950s hits "Heartbreak Hotel," "Blue Suede Shoes," and "Love Me Tender," as well as more recent ones like "Suspicious Minds" and "In the Ghetto." Virtually every selection triggered standing ovations. Reviewer Richard Goldstein wrote that "he looked so timeless up there." Presley, the best-selling artist, "was still the boy that makes little girls weep. Still the man of the people, even though the people had moved to the suburbs."[7] The aura only grew. Three years later, *Los Angeles Times* critic Robert Hilburn wrote, "If there was one show I'd recommend someone seeing in Las Vegas, it would have to be Presley's show. He's a legend and everyone should see him."[8]

Wayne Newton became the longest-running headliner on the Strip. Newton, along with his brother Jerry, started performing as a teenager in a downtown Las Vegas lounge in 1959 and opened as a headliner at the Flamingo five years later. In the 1970s Newton was attracting twenty thousand fans a week, and by 1992 fifteen million had seen his show. He sang a combination of hits "Danke Schoen" and "Red Roses for a Blue Lady" and easy listening, pop, and country songs in a voice one critic described as "a husky, laid-back, low-key, good-ol'-boy, southern frat-rat, beer-brawl drawl," all the while playing several different instruments. As he sang and danced, Newton engaged in a patter with his audience and winked at all his fans. As early as 1979 most fans referred to him as "Mr. Las Vegas," and by one journalist's account, Newton had become the "highest paid cabaret entertainer ever."[9]

Because headliners had become so expensive and so few were as reliable as Newton, Sinatra, or Liberace, the *Chicago Daily Tribune* reported in 1965 that "more and more Strip hotels are abandoning big-name entertainment in their main rooms in favor of production shows."[10] Beyond the "Les Folies Bergere" at the Tropicana and the "Lido de Paris" at the Stardust, a host of new shows enlivened the Strip after 1960. The "Casino de Paris" at the Dunes, "Hallelujah Hollywood" at the MGM Grand, "Jubilee" at Bally's, "Thoroughly Modern Minsky" at the Thunderbird, "Hello America" and "Pizzazz" at the Desert Inn, and "Splash" at the Riviera were popular feather and fishnet shows, which collectively became the dominant format for Las Vegas shows for a couple of decades.

Other types of entertainment eventually emerged first to supplement, then to replace these production shows. Starting with "Mystere" at Treasure Island in 1993, Cirque du Soleil, founded by Guy Laliberte in Quebec, opened several permanent shows: "O," "Zumanity," "Ka," "The Beatles Love," "Criss Angel Believe," and "Viva ELVIS." They featured large casts of acrobats, sophisticated soundtracks, and colorful costumes. Almost all were remarkably successful, even though what they offered often was "metaphysically confusing," as critic Peter Bart wrote in *Variety*. While audience members seldom could "define precisely what" a Cirque show was "all about, or what it's telling us . . . it works."[11] Magicians such as Doug Henning, Lance Burton, Siegfried and Roy, David Copperfield, and Penn and Teller developed such loyal followers that Mark Wilson, president of the Academy of Magical Arts, called Las Vegas "the world capital of magic."[12] The proliferation of Cirque shows and magicians slowly but steadily crowded out the dancers and showgirls. "Jubilee," the last of the showgirl production shows, closed in 2016 after a thirty-five-year run.

Early in the twenty-first century, popular Canadian singer Celine Dion restored the significance of the headliner when she signed a long-term contract with Caesars Palace, which constructed a $95 million Colosseum with a capacity of 4,100 for her. Between 2003 and 2005, Dion almost always sold out the room, and she brought in nearly $250 million in revenue for the hotel.[13] Other successful pop singers like Elton John, Cher, and Barry Manilow also signed long-term contracts, moves that restored the headliner as a critical part of the entertainment offerings along the Strip.

While hotel developers enjoyed the great press coverage of their spectacular properties and their appealing entertainment options, stories about gangster influence in Las Vegas continued to be a nagging problem through the 1980s. Dozens of journalists covered the mob story line, but four were particularly influential. Ovid Demaris, a novelist and the author of a biography of Lucky Luciano, coauthored *The Green Felt Jungle* with Ed Reid, an investigative reporter for the *Las Vegas Sun*. Released in 1963, *The Green Felt Jungle* remained on the *New York Times* best-seller list for almost six months. Sandy Smith, a longtime nemesis of the mob in Chicago, published many articles in the *Sun-Times* and *Tribune* as well as a major two-part series for *Life* magazine in 1967. Wallace Turner covered organized crime for the *New York Times* from the 1960s to the 1980s and also released a book in 1965 entitled *Gambler's Money: The New Force in American Life*.

The story line that had developed in the 1950s about gangsters' roles in Las Vegas remained front and center in the accounts of Demaris, Reid, Smith, Turner, and many others. Hoodlums from New York and Chicago to Detroit and Kansas City still used front men to obtain gambling licenses, drew upon the Teamsters Union pension fund to build and expand properties, and continued to skim millions from the casino count rooms. Stories about skimming gained increased credibility from illegal FBI wiretaps in Las Vegas casinos in the early 1960s. The Justice Department leaked some of its information to Sandy Smith, who told readers in the *Chicago Sun-Times* that just five casinos in Las Vegas had skimmed more than $6 million in one year and through couriers had dispatched the money to "crime syndicate gangsters around the country."[14] In response, the state's gaming commission conducted a quick investigation and reported finding no evidence of "substantial money" being skimmed, "no evidence of concealed ownership," and "no evidence that money was transported from any gambling casino to out-of-state persons who were not licensed owners of that casino."[15] The commission's efforts persuaded few outside Las Vegas.

At that point Howard Hughes arrived in Las Vegas. A reclusive aviator and movie producer who had controlling interest in Trans World Airlines, Hughes had been a frequent visitor to Las Vegas for more than two decades. According to biographer Geoff Schumacher, "In the '40s and early '50s, he gambled, dined, and watched shows amid thousands of other tourists."[16] On November 27, 1966, to avoid heavy California taxes after the sale of his TWA stock, Hughes moved to Las Vegas, booking the top floor of the Desert Inn Hotel. When the owners wanted him out so they could accommodate high-rolling gamblers, Hughes bought the hotel. Shortly thereafter, Hughes bought the Sands, Castaways, Silver Slipper, Frontier, and Landmark hotel-casinos. Gaylord Prather, the president of the chamber of commerce, was delighted, believing this would eliminate many mobsters. "If Hughes is in," he pointed out, "our image has to look better." Visiting syndicated columnist Bob Considine, facetiously agreed in early 1968, "I've been here for six hours and have yet to see a broken nose, a cauliflower ear or hear a 'dese' or even a 'dem.' Where did the Old Guard go? Back to Detroit? Cleveland? Miami?"[17]

Yet gangsters remained, and a new round of investigative reports put Las Vegas under a cloud again between 1975 and 1986. Journalists focused upon the Kansas City mob, led by Nick Civella, with its control of the Tropicana Hotel, and the Chicago mob's control of the Fremont and Stardust hotels. The point men for the Chicago mob were Frank "Lefty" Rosenthal and Anthony Spilotro, the "reputed watchdog for the underworld's money in Las Vegas."[18] Investigations by the federal government and the state's gaming commission provided fodder for a seemingly unlimited number of articles on how deeply the mob was involved in Las Vegas gaming. Finally, federal indictments of more than twenty mobsters for their roles in controlling the Fremont, Stardust, and Tropicana led to trials that concluded in 1986 with twenty convictions.[19] To the relief of Las Vegas promoters and civic leaders, the aggressive federal prosecutions broke the power of the mob, and a new narrative emerged about Las Vegas and organized crime. As one journalist explained in 1991, "Though in the popular imagination Las Vegas is still associated with the Mafia, it's been years since an organized-crime figure was hauled in on casino-related charges."[20]

As Las Vegas struggled to eliminate the mob, African American residents carried on an even more significant struggle, one to build on the 1960 breakthrough at the Moulin Rouge that had permitted them to enter the resort hotels and casinos. They wanted to have jobs in the industry beyond the low-paid "back of the house" positions. Under the leadership of reforming Governor Grant Sawyer, the state legislature had created a Commission on Civil Rights in 1961 and passed a civil rights act four years later that forbade discrimination in employment on the basis of race. In addition, the state gaming commission had a policy of nondiscrimination in issuing gambling licenses. Still, change proceeded at a glacial pace. In 1966 only one African American dealer worked in a Strip casino. The following year, the local chapter of the NAACP, led by attorney Charles Kellar, joined the National Labor Relations Board in filing a complaint against almost twenty hotels for their lack of progress. Although they pledged to hire more African Americans in key casino positions, four years later only 5 percent of dealers in Strip hotels were African American, and not even 1 percent of floor managers were African American. In 1971 the two sides finally agreed to a consent decree that required that 12 percent of all types of positions in casinos go to qualified African Americans. Enforcement was difficult. Discrimination continued, and hotels frequently resorted to subterfuge to make it appear they were complying. For example, Jeffrey Sallaz has shown that "African Americans were hired only temporarily in order to meet reporting quotas."[21] Women faced similar challenges. After being banned as dealers in 1958, no woman had a job as a dealer on the Strip until 1970. Eight years later they made up about a quarter of all dealers but filled fewer than 4 percent of blackjack supervisor positions. Finally, in 1981 nineteen hotels agreed to "an out-of-court settlement . . . to end all sexual discrimination in hiring, training, and promotion."[22]

Amid all these challenges, veteran hotel publicists remained energetic in their promotional efforts. Al Freeman was a force until his death in 1972, and Harvey Diederich worked for several hotels until retiring in 1988. New talent, like Jim Seagrave, arrived in the early 1960s. Like their predecessors, new publicists had an eye for stunts that would gain exposure for their hotel as well as Las Vegas. In 1972 Seagrave, then Flamingo's publicist, alerted the press about a safe under the desk in his office that dated back to Bugsy Siegel's construction of the hotel. Dick Odessky, one of Seagrave's contemporaries, recalled that "speculation on the contents included millions of dollars in cash, stolen jewels, even body parts." With reporters from the wire services and a television crew recording the event, a locksmith finally opened the gangster's safe. Although there was nothing inside, Seagrave had given great visibility to the Flamingo.[23] Las Vegas News Bureau photographers, led by the legendary Don English, continued to be key allies for publicists, flooding the nation with images of Las Vegas—more than 175,000 by the early 1990s—when the Las Vegas Convention and Visitors Authority (LVCVA) took over the news bureau. The LVCVA, in partnership with R&R Advertising, developed the most successful marketing slogan ever for the city. From the "Last Frontier Town" and "Daytime Sun and Nighttime Fun" in the 1940s and 1950s, promoters had always used slogans to brand Las Vegas. In 2003 the LVCVA saturated the nation with the tagline "What Happens Here, Stays Here" and its variation, "What Happens in Vegas, Stays in Vegas," an enticement to enjoy freedom without restraint while in southern Nevada, just as the Rat Pack once did.[24]

The hint of hedonism in the LVCVA marketing campaign met with criticism. But that has been a common response to what Las Vegas represented. Bruce Bégout, a French student of contemporary urban life, reflected the views of many critics of Las Vegas, calling it a "superficial, shallow town." "When all is said and done," he concluded, "the leisure and social experience offered by Las Vegas, with all its attractions and shows, casinos and cabarets, amounts to practically nothing in anyone's life. A fleeting excitement of the senses, a frenzy of buying and escapism that very quickly borders on persistent nausea."[25] Ironically, in his critique of Las Vegas, Bégout identified what the promoters of the 1950s had been able to establish. Whether they were publicists for the hotels or employees of the Las Vegas News Bureau, the promoters effectively made the case that their city offered the ultimate escape.

One can see their success in the words of famed author Mario Puzo, who became a big fan of Las Vegas. Internationally known as the author of the remarkably successful novel *The Godfather*, Puzo published *Inside Las Vegas* in 1976. In it he argued that Las Vegas provides for the world-weary "a dream world of pleasure, supplying one of the basic needs of human nature."[26] Anticipating Bégout in a positive sense, Puzo argued that the city had "nothing to do with reality. It is a sanctuary from the real world, real troubles, real emotion, and it's somehow fitting and proper that the city of Las Vegas is surrounded by a vast desert. A desert which acts as a *cordon sanitaire*."[27] Puzo claimed that Las Vegas offered a vacation experience like no other. "On a three-day visit to Vegas," he wrote, "you can have one of the best times of your life. To do that you have to forget about great museums, the pleasure of reading, great theater, great music, stimulating lectures by great philosophers, great food, great wine, and true love. Forget about them. Just for three days. Believe me, you won't miss them. Ye shall be as little children again."[28] Puzo topped the hotel publicists in promising tourists that they would be enchanted by the magic they would encounter in casinos that "have a mistlike, fairytale quality about them."[29]

In 1991 Rob Schultheis, writing in the National Geographic Society's magazine *Traveler*, echoed Puzo's argument. In his visit to the southern Nevada city, Schultheis discovered that in Las Vegas "the far-fetched is commonplace, and anything can happen." He also concluded that it was a magical place. "Las Vegas," he wrote, "the City of Sin, the Oasis of Unimaginable Delights, of Instant Riches (and Ruin), where everyone's dreams, however foolish and reprehensible, have a chance of coming true."[30] Novelists and television script writers often fed this theme. One of the better examples was in the popular series *Las Vegas*, which had a five-year run on NBC. In one episode, a character pointed out, "In Vegas people do things that they would normally not dream of," and at the end of the show's opening episode, one of the characters enthusiastically proclaimed the escapist theme of the series, "Vegas. Legal gambling. Bars that never close. World class food and entertainment. 24/7 action. God, I love this town."[31]

The promoters and civic leaders of Las Vegas in the 1950s successfully branded their city as the ideal escape for most twentieth-century Americans. Tourists came to love it as a place where they could gamble, enjoy luxury accommodations, see famed performers, and be irresponsible, and maybe a little wicked, for a few days. Edward Allen, an author and literature professor, perhaps captures that element of the city's appeal better than any other. In a 1992 *Gentleman's Quarterly* article, Allen wrote that gambling in Las Vegas "invites me to take an hour's recess from adulthood." He explained that it gave him a chance "to play in a well-demarked sandbox of irrationality and to look at the world as a magical place, which of course it is when the light hits it at the right angle."[32] That, in essence, is what has made Las Vegas America's Playground.

Notes

INTRODUCTION

1. Eisenhower quoted in Heather Cox Richardson, *To Make Men Free: A History of the Republican Party* (New York: Basic Books, 2014), 234.

2. J. Ronald Oakley, *God's Country: America in the Fifties* (New York: Dembner Books, 1986), 48–75.

3. There are many biographies of McCarthy. A good place to start is David M. Oshinsky, *A Conspiracy So Immense: The World of Joseph McCarthy* (New York: Free Press, 1983).

4. "McCarthy Loses Face in Verbal Fire," *Las Vegas Sun* (October 14, 1952), 1; "Publisher Denies Red Charges; Puts Up $1000," *Las Vegas Review-Journal* (October 16, 1952), 3.

5. John Patrick Diggins, *The Proud Decades: America in War and in Peace, 1941–1960* (New York: W. W. Norton, 1988), 175; George H. Gallup, *The Gallup Poll: Public Opinion, 1935–1971*, vol. 2 (New York: Random House, 1972), 1118, 1166, 1167, 1199, and 1263; Samuel A. Stouffer, *Communism, Conformity, and Civil Liberties: A Cross-Section of the Nation Speaks Its Mind* (Gloucester, Mass.: Peter Smith, 1963), 59.

6. William H. Chafe, *The Unfinished Journey: America since World War II*, 8th ed. (New York: Oxford University Press, 2015), 105.

7. Lizabeth Cohen, *A Consumers' Republic: The Politics of Mass Consumption in Postwar America* (New York: Alfred A. Knopf, 2004), 122.

8. Oakley, *God's Country*, 246; James T. Patterson, *Great Expectations: The United States, 1945–1974* (New York: Oxford University Press, 1996), 312; David Halberstam, *The Fifties* (New York: Random House, 1993), x.

9. Cohen, *Consumer's Republic*, 118. See also Patterson, *Great Expectations*, 313–16; Oakley, *God's Country*, 229.

10. Thomas Hine, *Populuxe* (New York: Alfred A. Knopf, 1986), 4.

11. Oakley, *God's Country*, 250.

12. Cohen, *Consumers' Republic*, 195.

13. Andrew J. Dunar, *America in the Fifties* (Syracuse: Syracuse University Press, 2006), 171.

14. Oakley, *God's Country*, 9; Diggins, *Proud Decades*, 184. Both John M. Findlay and David G. Schwartz have argued that these developments had a profound effect on the design of the resort hotels along the famed Las Vegas Strip, properties that reflected the emerging automobile culture of Southern California and the nation's suburban sprawl. See John M. Findlay, *People of Chance: Gambling in American Society From Jamestown to Las Vegas* (New York: Oxford University Press, 1986); David G. Schwartz, *Suburban Xanadu: The Casino Resort on the Las Vegas Strip and Beyond* (New York: Routledge, 2003).

15. Editors of *Fortune, The Changing American Market* (Garden City, N.Y.: Hanover House, 1955), 213.

16. Ibid., 204. In 1950 the Department of Labor estimated that at least 80 percent of wage and salary workers were allotted paid vacation days. See Richard K. Popp, *The Holiday Makers: Magazines, Advertising, and Mass Tourism in Postwar America* (Baton Rouge: Louisiana State University Press, 2012), 63. According to William Leuchtenburg, "By 1963, paid holidays had risen to eight a year (double the 1946 figure)." Moreover, "the typical vacation ran at least two weeks" by the early 1960s. See William Leuchtenburg, *A Troubled Feast: American Society Since 1945* (Boston: Little, Brown, 1983), 58.

17. Oakley, *God's Country*, 259.

18. Quoted in Popp, *Holiday Makers*, 107–8.

19. John A. Jakle, *The Tourist: Travel in Twentieth-Century North America* (Lincoln: University of Nebraska Press, 1985), 188.

20. Joe Alex Morris, "Aspen, Colorado," *Saturday Evening Post* (October 14, 1950), 27, 172–73, 176, and 178; "Tourist Florida," *Life* (February 4, 1946), 48–54; Neil Morgan, *Westward Tilt: The American West Today* (New York: Random House, 1961), 126; Hal K. Rothman, *Devil's Bargain: Tourism in the Twentieth-Century American West* (Lawrence: University Press of Kansas, 1999), 113–42.

21. A. E. Cahlan, "From Where I Sit," *Las Vegas Review-Journal* (February 27, 1950), 10.

22. "Stats and Facts," Las Vegas Convention and Visitors Authority, accessed January 15, 2018, http://www.lvcva.com/stats-and-facts/visitor-statistics/.

CHAPTER 1

1. "Wilbur's Dream Joint," *Time* (May 8, 1950), 16–17.

2. Todd Simon, "Desert Inn's Opening is Studded with Stars," Cleveland *Plain Dealer* (April 25, 1950), 1.

3. "Wilbur's Dream Joint," 16–17; Erskine Johnson, "Bones of the Desert," *Salt Lake Tribune Magazine* (April 23, 1950), 4.

4. "Nevada Brings It into Open and Gets Rich," *Life* (June 19, 1950), 101.

5. Eugene P. Moehring, *Resort City in the Sunbelt: Las Vegas, 1930–2000* (Reno: University of Nevada Press, 2000), 13–40.

6. Richard English, "The Boom Came Back," *Collier's* (August 22, 1942), 36.

7. Ray Mills, "Vegas Defense 'Silver,'" *Las Vegas Sun* (February 14, 1954), D1.

8. Charles N. Stabler, "Fades and Factories, Las Vegas and Reno Want More Industry to Back Dice Tables," *Wall Street Journal*, reprinted as "LV 'Healthy' Says Wall St.," *Las Vegas Sun* (January 27, 1957), 19. To promote further industrial development "businessmen and labor unions here have formed the Southern Nevada Industrial Foundation, an agency aimed at interesting expanding companies in Clark County plant sites." See "LV 'Healthy' Says Wall St."

9. Mella Rothwell Harmon, "Getting Renovated: Reno Divorces in the 1930s," *Nevada Historical Society Quarterly* 42, no. 1 (1999): 50.

10. Jeff Burbank, "Meadows Club," *ONE: Online Nevada Encyclopedia*, 2010, accessed January 28, 2018, http://www.onlinenevada.org/articles/meadows-club; Wesley Stout, "Nevada's New Reno," *Saturday Evening Post* (October 31, 1942), 69; Nevada Biltmore

Hotel Collection, 1942–1986, Special Collections and Archives, University Libraries, University of Nevada, Las Vegas.

11. "W.A. Clark's New Hotel," *Salt Lake Tribune* (September 25, 1904), 14.

12. "Whittemore Promises," *Las Vegas Age* (September 2, 1905), 1; "Las Vegas in 1906," *Las Vegas Age* (December 23, 1922), 2.

13. Larry Gragg, "'A Long Struggle and Many Disappointments': Las Vegas' Failure to Open a Resort Hotel, 1905–1940," *Nevada Historical Society Quarterly* 58, nos. 1–4 (2015): 44–65.

14. Larry Gragg, "El Sonador and the Struggle to Develop Resort Hotels in Las Vegas in the 1930s," *Nevada in the West* 6, no. 1 (2015): 4–9.

15. Larry Gragg, *Benjamin "Bugsy" Siegel: The Gangster, the Flamingo, and the Making of Modern Las Vegas* (Santa Barbara, Calif.: Praeger, 2015), 113–31.

16. "Economy Boom Continues in Vegas," *Las Vegas Sun* (May 31, 1959), 1.

17. "Where I Stand," *Las Vegas Sun* (December 22, 1952), 1; Perry Kaufman, "Best City of Them All: A History of Las Vegas, 1930–1960" (Ph.D. diss., University of California, Santa Barbara, 1974), 164; "Tourists Dump Total $164 Millions Here," *Las Vegas Sun* (July 10, 1955), 1; "Employment, Unemployment Figures Indicate Vegas Boom Leveling Off," *Las Vegas Sun* (August 10, 1956), 4.

18. "It Seems To Us," *Las Vegas Review-Journal* (October 22, 1957), 4.

19. "Vegas among Nation's Boom Towns," *Las Vegas Sun* (April 11, 1954), 10.

20. "Nevada Top in Income," *Las Vegas Sun* (September 26, 1955), 1.

21. "Vegas Growth Outlined in Prospectus," *Las Vegas Review-Journal* (April 4, 1954), 1 and 3. The Las Vegas commitment to the tourism industry reflected a similar state-wide effort. See Mary Ellen Glass, *Nevada's Turbulent '50s: Decade of Political and Economic Change* (Reno: University of Nevada Press, 1981), 47.

22. The best study of the development of resort hotels along the Strip is David G. Schwartz, *Roll the Bones: The History of Gambling, Casino Edition* (Las Vegas: Winchester Books, 2013), 218–42.

23. George Stamos Jr., "The Great Resorts of Las Vegas: How They Began!," *Las Vegas Sun Magazine* (August 26, 1979), 6. For a good recent account, see David G. Schwartz, "The Tiffany of the Strip," *Vegas Seven* (March 30, 2017), accessed September 17, 2017, http://vegasseven.com/2017/03/30/tropicana-the-tiffany-of-the-strip/.

24. Ralph Pearl, "Vegas Daze and Nites," *Las Vegas Sun* (April 10, 1954), 9.

25. Lucius Beebe, "Las Vegas," *Holiday* (December 1952), 107.

26. Dick Pearce, "Pleasure Palaces," *Harper's* (February 1955), 81; Herb Lyon, "Fantastic Las Vegas," *Chicago Daily Tribune* (November 29, 1959), 110.

27. John Gunther, "Inside Las Vegas," *American Weekly* in *Washington Post and Times Herald* (August 26, 1956), AW13.

28. Gladwin Hill, "Klondike in the Desert," *New York Times* (June 7, 1953), SM14 and 65.

29. Julian Halevy, "Disneyland and Las Vegas," *Nation* (June 7, 1958), 511.

30. "Beehive of Activity in Strip Building Shown Pictorially," *Las Vegas Sun* (July 4, 1954), 10.

31. Katharine Best and Katharine Hillyer, *Las Vegas: Playtown U.S.A.* (New York: David McKay, 1955), 75.

32. "Flamingo Opens $1 Million, 92 Room Annex," *Las Vegas Sun* (August 30, 1958), 1; "New Addition Opens at Riviera Hotel," *Las Vegas Sun* (May 15, 1960), 14; "Tremendous Building Boom Continues in Las Vegas Area; Millions Invested," *Las Vegas Scene Sunday Magazine* (September 4, 1960), 4.

33. William W. Yates, "'Vegas; 1957: Slot Machine Resort Booms," *Chicago Daily Tribune* (February 10, 1957), D4.

34. Schwartz, *Roll the Bones*, 254–55; Gary E. Elliott, *The New Western Frontier: An Illustrated History of Greater Las Vegas* (Carlsbad, Calif.: Heritage Media Corp., 1999), 47–57; Doug J. Swanson, *Blood Aces: The Wild Ride of Benny Binion, the Texas Gangster Who Created Vegas Poker* (New York: Viking, 2014), 180–81.

35. "Mae West Said Planning Resort," *Las Vegas Review-Journal* (May 29, 1950), 1; "Work Starts Today on 'Diamond Lil' Resort," *Las Vegas Sun* (August 16, 1950), 1.

36. Ralph Pearl, "Vegas Daze and Nites," *Las Vegas Sun* (March 3, 1955), 28.

37. Alan Jarlson, "On the Town," *Las Vegas Review-Journal* (June 1, 1953), 5.

38. Alan Jarlson, "Hoodlum Link Disclosed in 'Deauville' Promotion," *Las Vegas Sun* (December 14, 1959), 1.

39. "Doris Duke Said in Hotel Deal," *Las Vegas Review-Journal* (May 7, 1950), 1.

40. "New $5,000,000 Hotel Planned Beyond 'Strip,'" *Las Vegas Sun* (July 30, 1952), 1.

41. "Place Big Building Material Order for 'Hotel Caribbean,'" *Las Vegas Sun* (October 5, 1951), 1; Alan Jarlson, "Inside Las Vegas," *Las Vegas Sun* (November 24, 1953), 12.

42. "Still Another Las Vegas Resort Hotel Contemplated," *Las Vegas Sun* (August 9, 1952), 1.

43. Alan Jarlson, "On the Town," *Las Vegas Review-Journal* (June 5, 1953), 5.

44. "Break Ground for Still Another Big Strip Resort Hotel," *Las Vegas Sun* (February 11, 1955), 1.

45. "$15 Million 'Martinique' Planned," *Las Vegas Sun* (April 4, 1955), 9.

46. "Another Strip Hotel Planned," *Las Vegas Review-Journal* (August 8, 1955), 3; "Fabulous Hotel Plans Revealed," *Reno Evening Gazette* (August 9, 1955), 10.

47. "New Hotel Is Being Planned for Strip Area," *Las Vegas Review-Journal* (July 1, 1955), 1.

48. "Morrison Says He Will Build New Strip Hotel," *Las Vegas Sun* (November 15, 1954), 1; "Mocambo Hotel Due to Be Plushiest Hostel on Strip," *Las Vegas Review-Journal* (November 18, 1954), 1.

49. Stefan Al, *The Strip: Las Vegas and the Architecture of the American Dream* (Cambridge, Mass.: MIT Press, 2017), 103 and 105.

50. Gladwin Hill, "The 'Sure Thing' Boom at Las Vegas," *New York Times* (January 30, 1955), X29.

51. "Where I Stand," *Las Vegas Sun* (January 26, 1955), 1.

52. "Gambling Town Pushes Its Luck," *Life* (June 20, 1955), 20–27.

53. For a good account of this tough year see David G. Schwartz, "The Long, Hot Summer of '55," *Vegas Seven*, August 6, 2015, accessed July 28, 2017, http://vegasseven.com/2015/08/06/long-hot-summer-55/.

54. Bill Becker, "Las Vegas Bubble . . . About to Bust?" *Southland Magazine, Independent Telegram* (Long Beach, Calif.) (January 15, 1956), 3; Paul Weeks, "Las Vegas, Very

Much Alive, Resembles Monstrous Jukebox," *Oregonian* (January 22, 1956), 11.

55. "Town Pushes Its Luck," 25; Becker, "Vegas Bubble," 3.

56. Gilbert Millstein, "Cloud on Las Vegas' Silver Lining," *New York Times Magazine* (March 18, 1956), 64.

57. "Seek To Curb 'Shoestring' Resort Promotions Here," *Las Vegas Sun* (June 28, 1955), 1; "Eye Effect of Debts of New Resort Hotels," *Las Vegas Review-Journal* (August 19, 1955), 1; "Records Belie Big Hotel Debt Claim," *Las Vegas Sun* (July 2, 1955), 1.

58. "Demand Convention Hall to Continue Hotel Boom," *Las Vegas Sun* (December 16, 1954), 1.

59. "At Long Last," *Las Vegas Sun* (December 22, 1954), 14.

60. Larry Gragg, "Selling 'Sin City': Successfully Promoting Las Vegas during the Great Depression, 1935–1941," *Nevada Historical Society Quarterly* 49, no. 2 (2006): 91.

61. "Conventions to be Sought for Las Vegas," *Las Vegas Review-Journal* (August 22, 1952), 3.

62. "Ellsworth Quits Bureau Job for New Hotel Post," *Las Vegas Sun* (June 12, 1957), 1.

63. "C-C to Expand Plans to Lure Conventions," *Las Vegas Review-Journal* (November 7, 1957), 2.

64. "Convention Hall Bonds Approved," *Las Vegas Sun* (March 21, 1956), 1; "Groundbreaking for New Convention Hall Slated," *Las Vegas Review-Journal* (October 27, 1957), 1.

65. Joe McClain, "5000 Delegates Arrive in LV to Open Gigantic Air Congress," *Las Vegas Sun* (April 12, 1959), 1; "The Critics Can't Argue with Facts," *Las Vegas Sun* (November 3, 1959), 8; "Thousands Hear Noted Orchestra," *Las Vegas Sun* (August 30, 1960), 1; "Big Crowd On Hand for Graham," *Las Vegas Review-Journal* (December 7, 1960), 3.

66. "It Seems to Us," *Las Vegas Review-Journal* (May 5, 1958), 4.

67. *Las Vegas Report* (Las Vegas: Las Vegas Research and Statistical Bureau, 1959), 10; Record of Passengers Enplaned and Deplaned, McCarran Airport, 1966, Box 2, Folder 6, Dunes Hotel Collection, 1955–1991, Special Collections and Archives, University Libraries, University of Nevada, Las Vegas (hereafter Dunes Hotel Collection); "TWA Schedules Major Service to Las Vegas," *Las Vegas Sun* (October 1, 1958), 9.

68. Daniel K. Bubb, *Landing in Vegas: Commercial Aviation and the Making of a Tourist City* (Reno: University of Nevada Press, 2012), 48, 49, 55, and 57.

69. John F. Stover, *American Railroads* (Chicago: University of Chicago Press, 1997), 219.

70. *1959 Vegas Report*, 10; Les Devor, "Vegas Vagaries," *Las Vegas Review-Journal* (November 21, 1956), 5; Union Pacific ad, *Las Vegas Sun* (December 12, 1956), 10; Union Pacific City of Las Vegas brochure, author's collection; Gene Tuttle, "L.A. Train Trip Very Different These Days," *Las Vegas Review-Journal* (June 23, 1957), 14; "It Seems To Us," *Las Vegas Review-Journal* (November 28, 1960), 12.

71. *1959 Vegas Report*, 10; John M. Findlay, *People of Chance: Gambling in American Society from Jamestown to Las Vegas* (New York: Oxford University Press, 1986), 140.

72. Moehring, *Resort City*, 246.

73. Robert Lacey, *Little Man: Meyer Lansky and the Gangster Life* (Boston: Little, Brown, 1991), 224.

74. Ibid., 227.

75. Ibid., 231; Eduardo Sáenz Rovner, *The Cuban Connection: Drug Trafficking, Smuggling, and Gambling in Cuba from the 1920s to the Revolution*, trans. Russ Davidson (Chapel Hill: University of North Carolina Press, 2008), 92.

76. Philip D. Beidler, *The Island Called Paradise: Cuba in History, Literature, and the Arts* (Tuscaloosa: University of Alabama Press, 2014), 116.

77. Johnny Mathis, interview with author, November 8, 2017.

78. T. J. English, *Havana Nocturne: How the Mob Owned Cuba—And Then Lost It to the Revolution* (New York: William Morrow, 2007), 152–53 and 238.

79. "Unhappy Cuba's Cockeyed Week," *Life* (March 10, 1958), 32.

80. "Hint Vegas Gamblers To Obey Quit Havana Edict," *Las Vegas Sun* (April 26, 1958), 1–2; Lacey, *Little Man*, 256.

81. "Water Company in Move to 'Freeze' Las Vegas Progress," *Las Vegas Sun* (July 18, 1951), 1.

82. "Rescind Vegas Water Ban Order," *Las Vegas Sun* (November 30, 1951), 1; "Water Bans into Effect Here Today," *Las Vegas Review-Journal* (June 15, 1953), 1.

83. "Water Construction to Start in 1954 after Bond Approval," *Las Vegas Review-Journal* (October 1, 1953), 1; Michael S. Green, *Nevada: A History of the Silver State* (Reno: University of Nevada Press, 2015), 289.

84. Jeff McColl, "Low Salaries Discourage Teachers in Vegas Area," *Las Vegas Review-Journal* (December 27, 1953), 12.

85. Green, *Nevada*, 291; "Vegas Still Confronts Crowded Schools, Despite Big Expansion," *Las Vegas Review-Journal* (February 24, 1956), 1.

86. Eugene P. Moehring and Michael S. Green, *Las Vegas: A Centennial History* (Reno: University of Nevada Press, 2005) 159–60; Eugene P. Moehring, *The University of Nevada Las Vegas: A History* (Reno: University of Nevada Press, 2007), 3–6; Ralph J. Roske, *Las Vegas: A Desert Paradise* (Tulsa: Continental Heritage Press, 1986), 110; Office of Institutional Analysis, University of Nevada Las Vegas Enrollment Trends and Selected Institutional Characteristics, 1979, accessed October 8, 2017, https://ir.unlv.edu/IAP/Files/Fall_1978_Factbook.aspx.

87. "City Dads Study Ways to End Increasing Crime Wave in Vegas," *Las Vegas Review-Journal* (December 20, 1951), 1; "Crime in Clark County Increases 15 Per Cent," *Las Vegas Review-Journal* (January 21, 1954), 11.

88. "Let's Find Out Why," *Las Vegas Sun* (January 4, 1956), 4.

89. "Sheriff's Deputy Issues Grim Warning of Increase of Crime," *Las Vegas Review-Journal* (November 3, 1953), 6; "City Dads."

90. Eugene P. Moehring, *Reno, Las Vegas, and the Strip: A Tale of Three Cities* (Reno: University of Nevada Press, 2014), 51–54.

91. Moehring, *Resort City*, 100–102.

92. The two major biographies of McCarran are Jerome E. Edwards, *Pat McCarran: Political Boss of Nevada* (Reno: University of Nevada Press, 1982); Michael J. Ybarra, *Washington Gone Crazy: Senator Pat McCarran and the Great American Communist Hunt* (Hanover, N.H.: Steerforth Press, 2004).

93. Pat McCarran to Joseph F. McDonald, July 3, 1951, Patrick McCarran Papers, Box 54, Nevada Historical Society, Reno.

94. "Statement by Sen. McCarran before Finance Committee on August 15, 1951," *Pioche (Nev.) Record* (September 6, 1951), n.p., McCarran Papers, Box 41.

95. Hank Greenspun, "Where I Stand," *Las Vegas Sun* (October 26, 1951), 1.

96. "Nevada Officials to Testify on Gambling Bill," *Las Vegas Review-Journal* (June 9, 1954), 2; "Keating Tries Again on Anti-Gambling Bill," *Las Vegas Review-Journal* (January 10, 1955), 1.

CHAPTER 2

1. Dick Odessky, "Talk of the Town," *Las Vegas Sun* (April 14, 1953), 8.

2. Aline Mosby, "Live Las Vegas Billboard Stops Hollywood Traffic," *Las Vegas Review-Journal* (July 15, 1953), 10; "Hy Gardner's Featurette," *Parade* (September 13, 1953), 29.

3. Hedda Hopper, "Looking Over Hollywood," *Springfield (Mass.) Union* (July 24, 1953), 22; Alan Jarlson, "On the Town," *Las Vegas Review-Journal* (July 15, 1953), 5.

4. Don Payne, interview with author, August 2, 2005.

5. Spot Survey in San Francisco, Las Vegas Chamber of Commerce Records, 1911–2014, Box 12, Folder 2, Special Collections and Archives, University Libraries, University of Nevada, Las Vegas.

6. See Larry Gragg, "Selling 'Sin City': Successfully Promoting Las Vegas during the Great Depression, 1935–1941," *Nevada Historical Society Quarterly* 49, no. 2 (2006): 83–92.

7. "Wild, Woolly and Wide-Open," *Look* (August 14, 1940), 21.

8. "Las Vegas Strikes It Rich," *Life* (May 26, 1947), 99.

9. Reprinted in the "Fame Spread," *Las Vegas Review-Journal* (April 26, 1948), 16.

10. For a full account of these efforts, see Larry Gragg, "'Avoid Advertising the Obvious . . . Gambling': The Chamber of Commerce Promotion of Las Vegas in the 1950s," in *All In: Gambling in the Twentieth Century United States*, ed. Jonathan D. Cohen and David G. Schwartz (Reno: University of Nevada Press, 2018), 73–96.

11. Jack West Interview Notes, 1972, Perry Kaufman Papers, 1930–1974, Box 1, Folder 29, Special Collections and Archives, University Libraries, University of Nevada, Las Vegas (hereafter Kaufman Papers); Remarks by Maxwell Kelch, January 15, 1953, Kaufman Papers, Box 1, Folder 2.

12. Alicia Barber has discussed similar efforts at "place promotion" in explaining the efforts of civic leaders around the country who sought to create a positive image of their town "to overturn an earlier, less agreeable image." See Alicia Barber, *Reno's Big Gamble: Image and Reputation in the Biggest Little City* (Lawrence: University Press of Kansas, 2008), 5–6. Jonathan Foster also has a useful study about a trio of cities, including Las Vegas, that sought to address the negative images associated with their communities. See Jonathan Foster, *Stigma Cities: The Reputation and History of Birmingham, San Francisco, and Las Vegas* (Norman: University of Oklahoma Press, 2018).

13. Las Vegas Chamber of Commerce Board of Directors Meeting Minutes, May 20, 1948, 2–4, Las Vegas Chamber of Commerce Records, 1911–2014, Box 1, Folder 5; Special Meeting of Chamber of Commerce Publicity Committee, October 27, 1948, Las Vegas Chamber of Commerce Records, 1911–2014, Box 12, Folder 2, Special Collections and Archives, University Libraries, University of Nevada, Las Vegas.

14. Harold Heffernan, "Las Vegas Playground of Movie Folk," *Post-Standard* (Syracuse) (December 19, 1948), 29.

15. Jack West Interview Notes.

16. Don English Interview Notes, 1972, Kaufman Papers, Box 1, Folder 29.

17. Al Guzman quote in Ned Day, "The Selling of Las Vegas," *Las Vegan Magazine* (August 1984), 97.

18. Colin McKinlay, "Here's the Latest from Fabulous Las Vegas," *Nevadan* (March 11, 1990), 4T.

19. For a full discussion, see Larry Gragg, *Bright Light City: Las Vegas in Popular Culture* (Lawrence: University Press of Kansas, 2013), 158–79.

20. "'Noel Coward Wows 'Em in Café Town': The Impact of Noel Coward's 1955 Performance at the Desert Inn," *Nevada Historical Society Quarterly* 53, no. 2 (2010): 115; "Actors Greeted by Glittering Lights, People," *Las Vegas Review-Journal* (February 22, 1956), 3; Joe Buck Interview Notes, 1972, Kaufman Papers, Box 1, Folder 29.

21. "Lee Fisher to Head Dunes Public Relations," *Las Vegas Sun* (September 18, 1957), 9.

22. Photo caption: "3:00 A.M. and All's Well," *Las Vegas Sun* (April 4, 1955), 24.

23. Al Freeman to Jack Entratter, March 15, 1957, Sands Hotel Collection, 1952–1979, Box 7, Folder 2, Special Collections and Archives, University Libraries, University of Nevada, Las Vegas (hereafter Sands Hotel Collection).

24. "Desert Inn Gets New Publicity Chief; Ruth Brady Resigns," *Las Vegas Sun* (August 10, 1950), 2.

25. Photo caption, "Harvey F. Diederich," *Las Vegas Sun* (September 6, 1952), 3; Dick Kanellis, "Once a Tourist," *Las Vegas Sun* (June 27, 1959), 7.

26. "McDonald Takes New Job at Last Frontier," *Las Vegas Review-Journal* (January 19, 1951), 2; "Herb McDonald Resigns from Chamber Post," *Las Vegas Review-Journal* (January 4, 1957), 1.

27. Harvey Diederich, interview by Leta Ver Hulst, May 30, 1997, in Leta Lafay Ver Hulst, "The Creation of the Las Vegas Image: A Case Study of Harvey Diederich" (master's thesis, University of Nevada, Las Vegas, 1999), 67.

28. See Larry Gragg, "'Never Accorded the Recognition He Deserved': Al Freeman, Sands Hotel Publicist, 1952–1972," *Nevada Historical Society Quarterly* 51, no. 1 (2008): 28–30.

29. Jim Seagrave, interview with author, April 1, 2006.

30. A Report from the Public Relations and Advertising Department, 1961–1962, Dunes Hotel Collection, Box 22, Folder 10.

31. Al Freeman to Jack Entratter, October 3, 1956, Sands Hotel Collection, Box 7, Folder 3.

32. *The Carsony Brothers: From Vienna to Las Vegas*, dir. Barbara Weissenbeck and Gerald Benesch (Filmwerkstatt Wien, 2014), accessed December 14, 2016, https://www.youtube.com/watch?v=1ANgN1bsYak; Katharine Best and Katharine Hillyer, *Las Vegas: Playtown U.S.A.* (New York: David McKay, 1955), 105.

33. Harvey Diederich, interview with author, August 10, 2005.

34. "Taunted Tiger Mars Marilyn," *Life* (September 6, 1954), 22–23; "The Lady and the Tiger," *Morning Advocate* (Baton Rouge) (August 25, 1954), 1; "Tiger Gashes Marilyn, Gets Fired," *Evening World-Herald* (Omaha) (August 25, 1954), 15.

35. McKinlay, "Latest from Las Vegas," 13T.

36. Dick Odessky, *Fly on the Wall: Recollections of Las Vegas' Good Old, Bad Old Days* (Las Vegas: Huntington Press, 1999), 85; Gragg, "Never Accorded," 51.

37. "Haymes Affair Has MCA and Sands Hotel in Frenzy," *Billboard* (August 15, 1953), 12.

38. Alan Jarlson, "On the Town," *Las Vegas Review-Journal* (September 10, 1953), 5.

39. "An Unfrumptious Wedding," *Time* (October 5, 1953), 45.

40. Ibid.; "Nevada Wedding," *Life* (October 5, 1953), 35; Marvin Miles, "Haymes Marries Rita Mid Studio Set Glare," *Los Angeles Times* (September 25, 1953), 1.

41. Erskine Johnson, "Hollywood," *Kingsport (Tenn.) Times* (October 2, 1953), 4.

42. "Nevada Wedding"; "Unfrumptious Wedding"; "Hayworth, Haymes Wed In Ceremony at Sands Hotel," *Las Vegas Sun* (September 25, 1953), 2.

43. Photograph of a floating craps game in the Sands Hotel swimming pool (Las Vegas), 1954, Dreaming the Skyline, Special Collections and Archives, University Libraries, University of Nevada, Las Vegas, Digital Collection, accessed December 28, 2016, http://digital .library.unlv.edu/u?/sky,213; Gragg, "Never Accorded," 50; Odessky, *Fly on the Wall*, 82.

44. Odessky, *Fly on the Wall*, 77–79; "In the Armed Forces," *Billboard* (January 16, 1943), 17; Al Bine, "Paging 'Mr. Las Vegas,'" *California Living* (February 4, 1973), 4; Abe Schiller Interview Notes, 1972, Kaufman Papers, Box 1, Folder 29.

45. "Flack Lends Color Note," *The Oregonian* (June 9, 1960), 39.

46. Leonard Lyons, "In and Out of the Lyons Den," *Sunday Oregonian* (September 19, 1954), 44.

47. "Publicist 'Not Only Sells Flamingo Hotel, But Vegas,'" *Las Vegas Sun* (April 9, 1953), 20.

48. Bob Considine, "The Only Sport 'On Strip,'" *Boston Sunday Advertiser* (April 24, 1955), 37.

49. "Where I Stand," *Las Vegas Sun* (October 5, 1953), 1.

50. Hal Boyle, "Meet Wilbur, De Luxe Gambler and Mayor of Las Vegas," *Morning World-Herald* (Omaha) (October 8, 1953), 14; "Wilbur's Dream Joint," *Time* (May 8, 1950), 17; Richard English, "The Million-Dollar Talent War," *Saturday Evening Post* (April 14, 1953), 21; Joseph Stocker, "Las Vegas' Golden Boy," *American Legion Magazine* (December 1953), 46–47; Casey Shawhan and James Bassett, "Las Vegas Lords Harvest Millions at Gaming Tables," *Oakland Tribune* (July 20, 1953), 18.

51. "Where I Stand," *Las Vegas Sun* (October 5, 1953), 4.

52. "Desert Inn with Wilbur Clark," YouTube, accessed December 30, 2016, https:// www.youtube.com/watch?v=WubDvwD-7qM.

53. Quoted in "Wilbur Clark Explains Views on Vegas Gaming," *Las Vegas Review-Journal* (November 7, 1951), 11.

54. Billy Graham to Wilbur Clark, December 13, 1960, Wilbur and Toni Clark Collection, 1947–1991, Box 1, Folder 4, Special Collections and Archives, University Libraries, University of Nevada, Las Vegas (hereafter Wilbur and Toni Clark Collection).

55. David G. Schwartz, "JFK in Las Vegas," *Vegas Seven* (July 2, 2013), accessed December 30, 2016, http://vegasseven.com/2013/07/02/jfk-las-vegas-2/. He even gave Jacqueline Kennedy a portable television. See Jackie Kennedy to Wilbur Clark, no date, Wilbur and Toni Clark Collection, Box 1, Folder 4.

56. Stocker, "Las Vegas' Golden Boy," 24; English, "Talent War," 69; "Las Vegas: Nice People Live on Divorce, Gambling," *Newsweek* (April 20, 1953), 32; Paul Ralli, *Viva Vegas* (Culver City, Calif.: Murray and Gee, 1953), 141.

57. "Desert Inn with Wilbur Clark."

58. "It Seems To Us," *Las Vegas Review-Journal* (April 22, 1957), 4.

59. Les Devor, "Vegas Vagaries," *Las Vegas Review-Journal* (October 8, 1958), 14; December 10, 1958, 16.

60. Ralph Pearl, "Vegas Daze and Nites," *Las Vegas Sun* (April 22, 1957), 4.

61. "Flamingo Hotel Host to 65 Disc Jockeys," *Las Vegas Review-Journal* (June 12, 1950), 2.

62. "Fetes First Birthday Today Wilbur Clark's Desert Inn," *Las Vegas Sun* (April 24, 1951), 4.

63. "Have a Hilarious Time Special at Sands Hotel Celebration," *Illinois State Journal-Register* (Springfield) (December 16, 1956), 10.

64. Ibid.; General Information Memo, December 12, 1956, Sands Collection, Box 10, Folder 4; Aline Mosby, "1200 Gamblers Wait in Line to See Las Vegas Hotel Anniversary Show," *Lowell (Mass.) Sunday Sun* (December 16, 1956), 11; Arthur A. de Titta to Al Freeman, December 27, 1956, Sands Hotel Collection, Box 65.

65. *A Last Frontier: Las Vegas, Nevada*, prod. Phil E. Cantonwine (Bengal Pictures, 1950), 12 mins., YouTube, accessed January 4, 2017, https://www.youtube.com/watch?v=9361U5Sd81A. Because it focused on gambling (which the narrator contended attracted tourists like "moths to a flame") and divorce (Las Vegas was "a place where good marriages go to die"), the film did little to enhance the positive image that all were trying to promote.

66. *Las Vegas Recreation Unlimited* (MacDonald Film Productions, 1956), YouTube, accessed January 4, 2017, https://www.youtube.com/watch?v=jnsj_f8PLzY.

67. *Las Vegas: Playground U.S.A.* (Las Vegas News Bureau, 1956), YouTube, accessed February 1, 2017, https://www.youtube.com/watch?v=5029W7XqlPM; "The Chamber of Commerce Has Hit a Big Film Jackpot," *Las Vegas Sun* (June 18, 1956), 4; Las Vegas Chamber of Commerce Board of Directors Meeting Minutes, August 29, 1956, Kaufman Papers, Box 1, Folder 2; Don English, interview with author, August 2, 2005.

68. Gragg, "Never Accorded," 32.

69. "40 Million Get Glimpse of Las Vegas," *Las Vegas Sun* (July 7, 1958), 2.

70. A. E. Cahlan, "From Where I Sit," *Las Vegas Review-Journal* (May 2, 1951), 6.

71. Al Freeman to Dick Kollmar, July 23, 1955, Sands Hotel Collection, Box 46, Folder 4.

72. Al Freeman to Jack Entratter, October 9 and November 17, 1955; Notice of NBC-TV Show "Wide, Wide World" telecast from Sands, November 28, 1955, Sands Hotel Collection, Box 51, Folder, 8.

73. John G. Stephens, *From My Three Sons to Major Dad: My Life as a TV Producer* (Lanham, Md.: The Scarecrow Press, 2005), 34; "The Millionaire" at the Sands, November 18, 1959, Sands Hotel Collection, Box 50, Folder 7. For other examples of the Entratter-Freeman treatment, see Cecil Barker to Jack Entratter, October 7, 1959; Jack Entratter to All Departments, October 28, 1959, Sands Hotel Collection, Box 51, Folder 5; Betty White to Al Freeman, October 27, 1959, Sands Collections, Box 1, Folder 5.

74. Gragg, "Never Accorded," 37–39.

75. *Variety* (February 8, 1956); *Variety's Film Reviews*, vol. 10 (New York: R. R. Bowker, 1983), n.p.; Bosley Crowther, "Las Vegas Visit," *New York Times* (March 14, 1956), 39; Sam Lesner to Al Freeman, n.d., Sands Hotel Collection, Box 65.

76. "Where I Stand," *Las Vegas Sun* (February 18, 1956), 1.

77. Forrest Duke, "The Visiting Fireman," *Las Vegas Sun* (June 18, 1956), 9.

78. Larry Gragg, "Defending a City's Image: Las Vegas Opposes the Making of *711 Ocean Drive*, 1950," *Popular Culture Review* 22, no. 1 (2011): 7–15.

79. Larry Gragg, "Protecting a City's Image: The Death of Las Vegas Beat, 1961," *Studies in Popular Culture* 34, no. 1 (2011): 1–22.

80. Remarks by Maxwell Kelch, Livewire Kick-off Luncheon, January 15, 1953, Kaufman Papers, Box 1, Folder 2.

81. Larry Gragg, "Live Wire Fund," *ONE: Online Nevada Encyclopedia*, accessed January 5, 2017, http://www.onlinenevada.org/articles/live-wire-fund.

82. Alan Jarlson, "On the Town," *Las Vegas Review-Journal* (July 16, 1953), 5. An audit of the Hotel Last Frontier operations revealed that in 1950 the owners spent nearly $150,000 on advertising and promotion which was almost a tenth of all expenses. See Hotel Last Frontier Las Vegas, Nevada, Report on Operations, January 1951, Frontier Hotel and Casino Collection, 1942–1988, Box 1, Folder 2, Special Collections and Archives, University Libraries, University of Nevada, Las Vegas.

83. "Resort Hotels Promotional Drive Spurred," *Las Vegas Review-Journal* (January 5, 1951), 1; Las Vegas News Bureau Memo, January 3, 1958, Sands Hotel Collection, Box 7, Folder 1.

84. Gragg, "Never Accorded," 44.

85. "Knowing How to Get 'Job' Done," *Las Vegas Sun* (January 4, 1957), 6.

86. "It Seems to Us," *Las Vegas Review-Journal* (January 5, 1956), 4.

CHAPTER 3

1. Richard English, "The Million-Dollar Talent War," *Saturday Evening Post* (October 24, 1953), 25, 68, and 69.

2. Gladwin Hill, "Klondike in the Desert," *New York Times* (June 7, 1953), SM14; Jim Bacon, "Las Vegas New Nightlife Capital," *Syracuse Herald-American* (August 30, 1953), 1.

3. "Las Vegas: 'It Just Couldn't Happen,'" *Time* (November 23, 1952), 30.

4. Paul Anka, with David Dalton, *My Way* (New York: St. Martin's Press, 2013), 166–67.

5. The best biography of Liberace is Darden Asbury Pyron, *Liberace: An American Boy* (Chicago: University of Chicago Press, 2001). Also, see "Kidding on the Keys," *Life* (December 7, 1953), 88; Larry Gragg, *Bright Light City: Las Vegas in Popular Culture* (Lawrence: University Press of Kansas, 2013), 127–30.

6. Liberace, *An Autobiography* (New York: G. P. Putnam's Sons, 1973), 175; William A. Henry III, "Show Business: A Synonym for Glorious Excess," *Time* (February 16, 1987), 82.

7. Richard Gehman, *Sinatra and the Rat Pack* (New York: Belmont Productions, Inc., 1961), 9.

8. Doc Stacher quoted in James Kaplan, *Frank: The Voice* (New York: Doubleday, 2010), 656.

9. Anka, *My Way*, 166.

10. "Joe E. Lewis, Nightclub Comic Noted for Garrulousness, Dies," *New York Times* (June 5, 1971), 32.

11. Photo caption: "Lili St. Cyr," *Las Vegas Review-Journal* (May 3, 1954), 7.

12. Dorothy Kilgallen, "Broadway," *Boston American* (September 7, 1955), 35.

13. Ralph Pearl, "Vegas Daze and Nites," *Las Vegas Sun* (August 5, 1959), 4.

14. Les Devor, "Vegas Vagaries," *Las Vegas Review-Journal* (April 30, 1954), 5.

15. Dick Odessky, "Talk of the Town," *Las Vegas Sun* (June 17, 1953), 9.

16. Erskine Johnson, "Betty Hutton Blames Hollywood For Keeping Her Out of Spotlight," *Sacramento Bee* (August 7, 1953), 13. Also see Sean Flannelly, "Talk of the Town," *Las Vegas Sun* (July 9, 1953), 11.

17. Aline Mosby, "Mae West Shows Something for the Girls: 'Beefcake,'" *Las Vegas Review-Journal* (July 28, 1954), 9; "Mae West," *Billboard* (August 7, 1954), 46; Ralph Pearl, "Vegas Daze and Nites," *Las Vegas Sun* (August 6, 1954), 6; Les Devor, "Vegas Vagaries," *Las Vegas Review-Journal* (December 14, 1954), 5.

18. "Frontier Hotel Spends 100G for Talent in Year; Plans Expansion," *Billboard* (October 16, 1943), 5.

19. Entertainment Histories, David Fluke Papers on Las Vegas Entertainers, 1946–1983, Box 1, Folder 23, Special Collections and Archives, University Libraries, University of Nevada, Las Vegas.

20. "$7,000,000 in Hotel Showbiz," *Billboard* (February 10, 1945), 28.

21. Al Fischler, "Las Vegas as Showbiz Mint," *Billboard* (August 31, 1946), 3 and 43.

22. "Five-Million-Dollar Flamingo Resort Hotel Opens," *Las Vegas Review-Journal* (December 26, 1946), 3. Also, see Gragg, *Bright Light City*, 118–19.

23. Bob Thomas, "Las Vegas Is Transformed into New Barbary Coast," *Laredo (Tex.) Times* (December 31, 1946), 14.

24. "Las Vegas Strikes It Rich," *Life* (May 26, 1947), 99; Seymour Korman, "Las Vegas Now a Year Round Desert Resort," *Chicago Daily Tribune* (July 27, 1952), F9; Octavus Roy Cohen, *A Bullet for My Love* (New York: Macmillan, 1950), 11.

25. Dick Odessky, "Talk of the Town," *Las Vegas Sun* (April 20, 1953), 4.

26. Les Devor, "Vegas Vagaries," *Las Vegas Review-Journal* (April 30, 1954), 5; Al Freeman (for Les Devor), "Vegas Vagaries," *Las Vegas Review-Journal* (July 23, 1954), 5.

27. Alan Jarlson, "On the Town," *Las Vegas Review-Journal* (April 21, 1953), 5.

28. Hank Greenspun, "Where I Stand," *Las Vegas Sun* (July 7, 1956), 1.

29. Dick Pearce, "Pleasure Palaces," *Harper's*, February 1955, 81; Casey Shawhan and James Bassett, "Costly Floor Shows Frost Las Vegas Gambling Cake," *Oakland Tribune* (July 21, 1953), D10.

30. John Gunther, "Inside Las Vegas," *Washington Post and Times Herald* (August 19, 1956), AW18.

31. Dick Odessky, "Talk of the Town," *Las Vegas Sun* (June 1, 1953), 7.

32. Dick Odessky, "Talk of the Town," *Las Vegas Sun* (June 11, 1953), 10.

33. Gilbert Millstein, "Mr. Coward Dissects Las Vegas," *New York Times Magazine* (June 26, 1955), 41–42.

34. *Wide, Wide World*, NBC, December 4, 1955, script, 60–64 and 64a, Sands Hotel Collection, Box 51, Folder 8.

35. Clair C. Stebbins, "Daytime Sun and Nighttime Fun: That's the Routine at Las Vegas," *Sunday Times Signal* (Zanesville, Ohio) (February 11, 1951), section 2, 8.

36. Vic Damone, with David Chanoff, *Singing Was the Easy Part* (New York: St. Martin's Press, 2009), 164.

37. James Perkins to Folks, February 12, 1952, James Perkins Collection, 1951–1952 Box 1, Special Collections and Archives, University Libraries, University of Nevada, Las Vegas.

38. "Duke, Duchess Take In Las Vegas Sights," *Las Vegas Sun* (March 20, 1959), 1; Ralph Pearl, "Vegas Daze and Nites," *Las Vegas Sun* (March 20, 1959), 4.

39. Joel Grey, with Rebecca Paley, *Master of Ceremonies: A Memoir* (New York: Flatiron Books, 2016), 96; Eddie Fisher, with David Fisher, *Been There, Done That: An Autobiography* (New York: St. Martin's Press, 2000), 117; Damone, *Singing*, 112.

40. Lee Zhito, "Las Vegas Set to Spend Big on Top Names," *Billboard* (June 10, 1950), 3, 44, and 47.

41. "From Where I Sit," *Las Vegas Review-Journal* (August 15, 1954), 4.

42. "Jack Entratter, Action Tuesday, October 4," Sands Hotel Collection, Box 4, Folder 1.

43. English, "Talent War," 73.

44. "Hal Braudis Dies after Operation," *Las Vegas Sun* (November 6, 1955), 1; Alan Jarlson, "Show Booker Hal Braudis Gambles With Talent—and Usually Wins," *Las Vegas Review-Journal* (March 8, 1953), 8; Les Devor, "Vegas Vagaries," *Las Vegas Review-Journal* (September 8, 1954), 5; Les Devor, "Vegas Vagaries," *Las Vegas Review-Journal* (November 21, 1954), 7; "Thunderbird Hotel Plans Birthday Party Celebration," *Las Vegas Review-Journal* (September 3, 1950), 2.

45. Alan Balboni, "The Italians," in *The Peoples of Las Vegas: One City, Many Faces*, ed. Jerry L. Simich and Thomas C. Wright (Reno: University of Nevada Press, 2005), 149; "Frank Sennes, Sr.," *Variety* (February 4, 1993), accessed June 24, 2017, http://variety.com/1993/scene/people-news/frank-sennes-sr-103727/; "Frank Sennes to Op Miami Colonial Inn," *Billboard* (November 4, 1950), 47; "Sennes to Coast; Rocky Takes Over," *Billboard* (July 11, 1953), 13; Murray Hertz, "Sun Dial," *Las Vegas Sun* (October 10, 1960), 13.

46. Les Devor, "Vegas Vagaries," *Las Vegas Review-Journal* (October 12, 1954), 5; Alan Jarlson, "The Bright Lights," *Las Vegas Review-Journal* (July 5, 1953), 22; Maxine Lewis, "Speaking of Publicity," *Las Vegas Sun* (September 26, 1959), 6.

47. "Sean Flannelly's The Morning After," *Las Vegas Sun* (January 25, 1954), 7.

48. Tom Austin and Ron Kase, *Bill Miller's Riviera: America's Showplace in Fort Lee, New Jersey* (Charleston, S.C.: The History Press, 2011), 67–90; K. J. Evans, "Bill Miller," in *The First 100: Portraits of the Men and Women Who Shaped Las Vegas*, ed. A. D. Hopkins and K. J. Evans (Las Vegas: Huntington Press, 1999), 216–19; "Lena Horne Breaks Record at N.Y. Opening," *Jet* (May 14, 1953), 58.

49. "Miller Adds Sahara Buying," *Billboard* (March 7, 1953), 15; Evans, "Miller," 218.

50. Forrest Duke, "Bill Miller, Associate Take Over Dunes Hotel," *Las Vegas Sun* (March 2, 1956), 1; "Miller Quits Dunes; Riddle New President," *Las Vegas Sun* (January 18, 1957), 1; Judith Miller, "Cuba on the Edge," *Pundicity*, July 2015, accessed June 25, 2017, http://www.judithmiller.com/17552/cuba-on-the-edge; Ed Reid, "Miller Says Havana No Threat to Vegas," *Las Vegas Sun* (January 26, 1958), 12; "Complete Deal to Reopen New Frontier," *Las Vegas Sun* (March 12, 1959), 1.

51. Les Devor, "Vegas Vagaries," *Las Vegas Review-Journal* (February 16, 1955), 5.

52. Les Devor, "Vegas Vagaries," *Las Vegas Review-Journal* (July 8, 1956), 3; Evans, "Bill Miller," 218.

53. Larry Gragg, "Jack Entratter: The Greatest Las Vegas Impresario," *Nevada in the West* 4, no. 3 (2013): 4–9.

54. Shawhan and Bassett, "Costly Floor Shows," D10; James Bacon, "Las Vegas Takes Over as Top Spot in U.S. Show Biz," *Panama City (Fla.) News-Herald* (August 16, 1953), 10.

55. Bob Thomas, "Las Vegas Talent War Skyrockets Salaries," *Newport (R.I.) Daily News* (December 30, 1954), 7; Vernon Scott, "Las Vegas' Richest Year Sees 3 Plush Gambling Palaces Fold," *Sun* (Yuma, Ariz.) (January 17, 1956), 16.

56. Thomas, "Vegas Talent War," 7.

57. "'One-Man Revolt' in New Vegas Dunes Setup; Names for Names' Sake Are Out," *Variety* (November 17, 1954), 1.

58. "Vegas Passes First Test of Talent Deal," *Billboard* (May 1, 1954), 12.

59. "Van Johnson Scores Well at Sands Date," *Billboard* (April 25, 1953), 42; Ronald L. Davis, *Van Johnson: MGM's Golden Boy* (Oxford: University Press of Mississippi, 2001), 152.

60. Ronald Reagan, with Richard G. Hubler, *Where's the Rest of Me?* (New York: Duell, Sloan and Pearce, 1965), 247–48; Nancy Reagan, with William Novak, *My Turn: The Memoirs of Nancy Reagan* (New York: Random House, 1989), 125–27; "Sean Flannelly's The Morning After," *Las Vegas Sun* (February 17, 1954), 6.

61. Aline Mosby, "Vegas Shows Are First in Cost, Talent, Size," *Las Vegas Review-Journal* (April 3, 1953), 1.

62. Alan Jarlson, "On the Town," *Las Vegas Review-Journal* (March 13, 1955), 5.

63. Larry Gragg, "'Noel Coward Wows 'Em in Café Town': The Impact of Noel Cowards' 1955 Performance at the Desert Inn," *Nevada Historical Society Quarterly* 53, no. 2 (2010): 108–26.

64. Ralph Pearl, "Vegas Daze and Nites," *Las Vegas Sun* (January 17, 1956), 13.

65. "Jeff Chandler," *Billboard* (May 28, 1955), 33.

66. "Replacement Due for Wally Cox at Dunes," *Las Vegas Sun* (July 16, 1955), 1; Wally Cox (for Ralph Pearl), "Vegas Daze and Nites," *Las Vegas Sun* (July 21, 1955), 8.

67. Roland L. Bessette, *Mario Lanza: Tenor in Exile* (Portland, Ore.: Amadeus Press, 1999), 159–67; Derek Mannering, *Mario Lanza: Singing to the Gods* (Jackson: University Press of Mississippi, 2005), 127–30.

68. See Larry Gragg, "'They Weren't My Kind of Audience': Elvis Presley's First Appearance in Las Vegas in 1956," *Nevada in the West* 6, no. 4 (2015): 4–9.

69. Bob Clements, "Inside Las Vegas," *Las Vegas Sun* (March 7, 1954), 5.

70. Ibid.

71. Ibid.; Alan Jarlson, "On the Town," *Las Vegas Review-Journal* (October 23, 1953), 5.

72. "El Rancho's Cabaret Proves A Natural for Late Evening Trade," *Las Vegas Sun* (February 12, 1955), 7; Forrest Duke, "The Visiting Fireman," *Las Vegas Review-Journal* (December 22, 1960), 4; Freddie Whiteman, "Loungin' Around," *Las Vegas Review-Journal* (February 8, 1957), 5.

73. The best sources on Prima's life are Garry Boulard, *Louis Prima* (Urbana: University of Illinois Press, 2002); Tom Clavin, *That Old Black Magic: Louis Prima, Keely Smith,*

and the Golden Age of Las Vegas (Chicago: Chicago Review Press, 2010); *Louis Prima: The Wildest*, prod. Joe Lauro and dir. Don McGlynn, 90 mins. (Blue Sea Productions, 1999); David Kamp, "They Made Vegas Swing," *Vanity Fair*, December 1999, 346–78.

74. Erskine Johnson, "Closing 3 Las Vegas Casinos Wrecks Gravy Train for Stars," *Sun* (Yuma, Ariz.) (February 9, 1956), 17.

75. Scott Shea quoted in Clavin, *Old Black Magic*, 85.

76. Quoted in Boulard, *Louis Prima*, 111–12.

77. "Nightclubs: The Wages of Vulgarity," *Time* (September 7, 1959), 50.

78. Alan Jarlson, "On the Town," *Las Vegas Review-Journal* (May 8, 1953), 5.

79. Frank Kane, *A Short Bier* (New York: Dell Publishing, 1960), 58; "The Belles of Las Vegas," *Real Men*, December 1958, 26–29.

80. Lloyd Shearer, "Chorus Girls," *Parade Magazine, Independent Press-Telegram* (Long Beach, Calif.) (June 2, 1957), 27.

81. Paul Price, "Dateline—Las Vegas," *Las Vegas Sun* (July 2, 1960), 3.

82. Les Devor, "Vegas Vagaries," *Las Vegas Review-Journal* (June 29, 1954), 5. For an exception, see "Sean Flannelly's The Morning After," *Las Vegas Sun* (December 26, 1953), 4.

83. "Snake Eyes in Las Vegas," *Time* (September 19, 1955), 97.

84. Les Devor, "Vegas Vagaries," *Las Vegas Review-Journal* (January 7, 1955), 5.

85. George Stamos, "The Great Resorts of Las Vegas: How They Began," *Las Vegas Sun Magazine* (July 15, 1979), 6.

86. Esper Esau, *Las Vegas' Golden Era: Memoirs, 1954–1974* (Indianapolis: Dog Ear Publishing, 2016), 50. This book is an excellent introduction to the entertainment world of Las Vegas in the 1950s from an insightful eyewitness.

87. Larry Gragg, "'Big Step to Oblivion for Las Vegas?': The 'Battle of the Bare Bosoms,' 1957–1959," *Journal of Popular Culture* 43, no. 5 (2010): 1012.

88. "Donn Arden's Art," *Los Angeles Times* (July 15, 1988), 6; "Master of the Spectacular," *Escapade*, December 1959, 56; "Bare Bosoms Will Engulf Strip Hotels," *Las Vegas Review-Journal* (July 30, 1958), 1.

89. "Dazzling Revue at the Stardust," *Dallas Morning News* (July 7, 1958), section 2, 6.

90. Gragg, "'Big Step,'" 1004–22.

91. "Paris Come-On in Vegas," *Life* (June 6, 1960), 51–52, 54, and 57.

92. Ralph Pearl, "Vegas Daze and Nites," *Las Vegas Sun* (June 9, 1959), 4.

CHAPTER 4

1. Hedda Hopper, "Tall English Girls Star in Las Vegas Lido Show," *Chicago Daily Tribune* (August 13, 1958), B1; Erskine Johnson, "Hollywood Today," *Eureka (Calif.) Humboldt Standard* (July 10, 1958), 2.

2. Las Vegas City Commission Minutes, November 5, 1958, vol. 11, 233, Special Collections and Archives, University Libraries, University of Nevada, Las Vegas. For a discussion of this long-held notion, see Alice Kessler-Harris, *A Woman's Wage: Historical Meanings and Social Consequences* (Lexington: University Press of Kentucky, 2014).

3. Joanne L. Goodwin, "'She Works Hard for Her Money': A Reassessment of Las Vegas Women Workers, 1945–1985," in *The Grit Beneath the Glitter: Tales From the Real Las Vegas*, ed. Hal K. Rothman and Mike Davis (Berkeley: University of California Press, 2002), 247.

4. Anne Martin, "These United States—VIII, Nevada: Beautiful Desert of Buried Hopes," *Nation* (July 26, 1922), 89–90.

5. Harper Leech, "Boulder Dam a Cuss Word in Nevada Peaks," *Chicago Daily Tribune* (April 20, 1928), 17.

6. "Women Jurors Called Unfit," *Clark County Review* (December 9, 1921), 1.

7. Emilie N. Wanderer and Joanne L. Goodwin, *"A Thousand to One": The Story of Emilie N. Wanderer the First Woman to Practice Law in Las Vegas* (Las Vegas Women Oral History Project, University of Nevada, Las Vegas, 2005), 20. Shortly after Wanderer arrived, Nelle Price also began a law practice in the town. See "One of City's First Female Attorneys Dies," *Las Vegas Sun* (June 30, 1998), accessed May 7, 2017, https://lasvegassun.com/news/1998/jun/30/one-of-citys-first-female-attorneys-dies/.

8. Goodwin, "She Works Hard for Her Money," 255.

9. Louise Kapp Howe, *Pink Collar Workers: Inside the World of Women's Work* (New York: G. P. Putnam's Sons, 1977), 21; William H. Chafe, *Women and Equality: Changing Patterns in American Culture* (New York: Oxford University Press, 1978), 31; Andrew J. Dunar, *America in the Fifties* (Syracuse: Syracuse University Press, 2006), 197; J. Ronald Oakley, *God's Country: America in the Fifties* (New York: Dembner Books, 1986), 299; "Women Hold Third of Jobs," *Life* (December 24, 1956), 31.

10. Elaine Tyler May, *Homeward Bound: American Families in the Cold War Era* (New York: Basic Books, 2008), 1–18.

11. Wini Breines, *Young, White, and Miserable: Growing Up Female in the Fifties* (Boston: Beacon Press, 1992), 47–53.

12. "Vegas among Nation's Boom Towns," *Las Vegas Sun* (April 11, 1954), 10; "Tourists Dump Total $164 Millions Here," *Las Vegas Sun* (July 10, 1955), 1; Goodwin, "She Works Hard for Her Money," 251; Eugenia Kaledin, *Mothers and More: American Women in the 1950s* (Boston: Twayne Publishers, 1984), 63; Joanne L. Goodwin, *Changing the Game: Women at Work in Las Vegas, 1940–1980* (Reno: University of Nevada Press, 2014), 7.

13. Joanne L. Goodwin, "Mojave Mirages: Gender and Performance in Las Vegas," *Women's History Review* 111, no. 1 (2002): 116.

14. This is based on an examination of ads in the *Las Vegas Review-Journal* in February 1950 and February 1960.

15. Ed Reid, *City without Clocks* (Englewood Cliffs, N.Y.: Prentice-Hall, 1961), 168.

16. Claytee D. White, "'Eight Dollars a Day and Working in the Shade': An Oral History of African American Migrant Women in the Las Vegas Gaming Industry," in *African American Women Confront the West, 1600–2000*, ed. Quintard Taylor and Shirley Ann Wilson Moore (Norman: University of Oklahoma Press, 2003), 276–89.

17. Joy Garner, email to author, January 11, 2018; "Our Barmaids a Problem?" *Las Vegas Sun* (September 7, 1958), 18.

18. "Last Douglas Alley Citadel of Masculinity Falls; Women Are Dealing at Bank Club!" *Nevada State Journal* (May 28, 1952), 8; "Reno Gambler Raps Bill to Bar Women," *Sacramento Bee* (February 19, 1949), 14; "Bill to Ban Women Dealers Is Withdrawn," *Reno Evening Gazette* (March 17, 1949), 1; "Don't Replace Men with Women Dealers, Legion Members Urge," *Nevada State Journal* (March 25, 1953), 9; Ralph J. Roske, *Las Vegas: A Desert Paradise* (Tulsa, Okla.: Continental Heritage Press, 1986), 121.

19. "500 Vegas Dealers Reported Organized," *Nevada State Journal* (May 31, 1949), 1. This fledgling effort at organization was not particularly successful, and dealers have struggled ever since in their battles with casino owners.

20. Colin McKinlay, "City Dads Halt Gal Dealers," *Las Vegas Review-Journal* (November 7, 1958), 1.

21. City Commission Minutes, November 5, 1958, 233–34; "Women Hiring Causing Exodus of Dealers to Vegas—Legion," *Las Vegas Sun* (December 7, 1953), 8.

22. "Reno Casino Men Oppose Banning Women Dealers," *Las Vegas Sun* (November 10, 1958), 2.

23. City Commission Minutes, November 5, 1958, 235.

24. "Male Dealers in 'Bitter Protest' to Gambling Gals in Vegas Clubs," *Las Vegas Review-Journal* (November 6, 1958), 3.

25. "Dear Hank from M.R.S.," *Las Vegas Sun* (November 21, 1958), 6.

26. Caption: "Signs of Trouble," *Las Vegas Review-Journal* (November 16, 1958), 1.

27. Eugene P. Moehring, *Resort City in the Sunbelt: Las Vegas 1930–2000* (Reno: University of Nevada Press, 2000), 201.

28. Irene B. Scholl Rostine, "Our Turn: Working Women in the Las Vegas Valley, 1940–1980" (master's thesis, University of Nevada, Las Vegas, 2013), 67–89.

29. "Women behind the Strip Scenes," *Las Vegas Sun* (November 11, 1956), 13; Rostine, "Our Turn," 101–5; Goodwin, "She Works Hard for Her Money," 254.

30. Sean Flannelly, "Talk of the Town," *Las Vegas Sun* (July 21, 1953), 7; Wesley Juhl, "Businesswoman, Philanthropist Kitty Rodman Dies," *Las Vegas Review-Journal* (February 28, 2014), accessed January 28, 2017, http://www.reviewjournal.com/news /businesswoman-philanthropist-kitty-rodman-dies.

31. This was increasingly a field open to women nationally. In 1950 women made up 32 percent of all journalists, though most worked on "women's pages." See Kathleen A. Cairns, *Front-Page Women Journalists, 1920–1950* (Lincoln: University of Nebraska Press, 2003), xi.

32. Kimberly Wilmot Voss and Lance Speere, "Where She Stands: Ruthe Deskin and the *Las Vegas Sun*," *Nevada Historical Society Quarterly* 55, nos. 1–4 (2012): 91–92.

33. A. D. Hopkins, "Florence Lee Jones," in *The First 100: Portraits of the Men and Women Who Shaped Las Vegas*, ed. A. D. Hopkins and K. J. Evans (Las Vegas: Huntington Press, 1999), 92–94; Mary Ellen Glass, *John F. Cahlan: Reminiscences of a Reno and Las Vegas, Nevada Newspaperman, University Regent, and Public-Spirited Citizen* (Reno: University of Nevada Oral History Program, 1970), 298–99.

34. C. C. Wright, "Early Resident Helps Wed Pahrump to Civilization, *Pahrump Valley Times* (February 20, 2015), accessed January 23, 2017, http://pvtimes.com/community/early-resident-helps-wed-pahrump-civilization.html; Jamie McKee, "Alice Key," *Nevadan* (February 25, 1990), T3, 6, and 7.

35. "Ousted Ada Bassett Blast Harmon," *Las Vegas Sun* (March 20, 1959), 1; "Woman Appointed Vegas Assistant Manager," *Las Vegas Sun* (March 7, 1952), 1; Spencer and Georgia Butterfield Collection, 1912–1975, Box 1, Folder 8, Special Collections and Archives, University Libraries, University of Nevada, Las Vegas; Ruthe Deskin and Alan Jarlson, "Las Vegas Lowdown," *Las Vegas Sun* (February 4, 1960), 10; "It Seems to Us," *Las Vegas*

Review-Journal (September 10, 1956), 4; "Lodwick Quits as City's Clerk, Takes New Job," *Las Vegas Sun* (August 23, 1958), 3; "Interracial Marriages Now Okay in Las Vegas," *Las Vegas Sun* (April 21, 1959), 9.

36. Wanderer and Goodwin, *"A Thousand to One,"* 43.

37. "Appoints Mrs. Dorothy to State Parole Board," *Las Vegas Sun* (July 24, 1959), 1.

38. "Maude Frazier Denies Plans to Quit," *Las Vegas Sun* (March 12, 1959), 1 and 2; "A Bouquet for Miss Frazier," *Las Vegas Sun* (April 8, 1960), 20. Also, see James W. Hulse, "Maude Frazier: Pioneering Educator and Lawmaker," in *The Maverick Spirit: Building the New Nevada*, ed. Richard O. Davies (Reno: University of Nevada Press, 1998), 12–22.

39. "What Goes On behind the Scenes at Vegas Strip Hotel?" *Las Vegas Review-Journal* (January 3, 1954), 18; photo caption, *Las Vegas Sun* (October 7, 1952), 13; "Sans Souci Hostesses Named for Jamaica Room, Restaurant," *Las Vegas Sun* (October 23, 1957), 17; Les Devor, "Vegas Vagaries," *Las Vegas Review-Journal* (September 22, 1954), 5.

40. "Women behind the Scenes."

41. "Desert Inn Gets New Publicity Chief; Ruth Brady Resigns," *Las Vegas Sun* (August 10, 1950), 2; Alan Jarlson, "On the Town," *Las Vegas Review-Journal* (January 12, 1953), 5; "Bill Willard," *Las Vegas Sun* (March 2, 1953), 2; Les Devor, "Vegas Vagaries," *Las Vegas Review-Journal* (December 2, 1954), 5; Les Devor, "Vegas Vagaries," *Las Vegas Review-Journal* (March 3, 1954), 5; "3:00 A.M. and All's Well," *Las Vegas Sun* (April 4, 1955), 24; "Maxine Lewis Tropicana Pub. Thumper," *Las Vegas Review-Journal* (August 28, 1957), 3. Nationally, women held 11 percent of the jobs in public relations in 1950, but they held 23 percent a decade later. See Dunar, *America in the Fifties*, 196.

42. "Abe Schiller in New Post," *Las Vegas Review-Journal* (January 15, 1952), 6; Les Devor, "Vegas Vagaries," *Las Vegas Review-Journal* (June 21, 1956), 5; "Maxine Lewis."

43. "Millicent: Socially Speaking," *Las Vegas Sun* (November 11, 1956), 14; "Mrs. Melba Moore Named to Top Operational Post at Hacienda," *Las Vegas Sun* (June 12, 1956), 13. Bayley's wife Judy inherited the property upon his death in 1964 and ran the Hacienda until her death seven years later.

44. Janis L. McKay, *Played Out on the Strip: The Rise and Fall of Las Vegas Casino Bands* (Reno: University of Nevada Press, 2016), 55; Janis McKay, email to author, February 6, 2017.

45. "Top Nitery Acts," *Las Vegas Sun* (June 6, 1959), 4.

46. Bob Thomas, "Las Vegas Talent War Skyrockets Salaries," *Newport (R.I.) Daily News* (December 30, 1954), 7; Maxine Lewis Flamingo Bookings, 1948–1951, Special Collections and Archives, University Libraries, University of Nevada, Las Vegas; James Bacon, "Las Vegas Takes Over as Top Spot in U.S. Show Biz," *Kingsport (Tenn.) Times-News* (August 16, 1953), B3; Maria Riva, *Marlene Dietrich* (New York: Ballantine Books, 1994), 634.

47. James P. Kraft, *Vegas at Odds: Labor Conflict in a Leisure Economy, 1960–1985* (Baltimore: Johns Hopkins University Press, 2010), 40.

48. Judy Jones, Memoirs, unpublished, 17.

49. Tab Tabet, "Sundial," *Las Vegas Sun* (June 1, 1959), 10.

50. Alan Jarlson, "The Bright Side," *Las Vegas Review-Journal* (June 21, 1953), 22.

51. Oral History with Dottie and Don Tomlin, conducted by Ron Tomlin, 2002, Dottie Dee Dancers Collection, 1940s–2002, Box 1, Folder 4, Special Collections and Archives, University Libraries, University of Nevada, Las Vegas.

52. Les Devor, "Vegas Vagaries," *Las Vegas Review-Journal* (April 4, 1956), 5.

53. "Wild Women of Las Vegas: Morals Take a Back Seat amid Sizzling Desert Sin," *Pose*, April 1955, 16–17.

54. Wallace Turner, "Las Vegas: Trickery at Casinos Goes On Despite Close Scrutiny," *New York Times* (November 19, 1963), 34. See also Larry Gragg, *Bright Light City: Las Vegas in Popular Culture* (Lawrence: University Press of Kansas, 2013), 158–79.

55. Mike Weatherford, *Cult Vegas: The Weirdest! The Wildest! The Swingin'est Town on Earth!* (Las Vegas: Huntington Press, 2001), 219 and 221.

56. Ad, *Las Vegas Review-Journal* (July 17, 1951), 2; ad, *Las Vegas Review-Journal* (April 14, 1952), 5; ad, *Las Vegas Review-Journal* (December 23, 1954), 3.

57. "DA Closes New Strip Burlesque Club," *Las Vegas Sun* (February 18, 1953), 3; Alan Jarlson, "On the Town," *Las Vegas Review-Journal* (February 24, 1953), 5; Alan Jarlson, "On the Town," *Las Vegas Review-Journal* (July 30, 1953), 5.

58. Ralph Pearl, "Vegas Daze and Nites," *Las Vegas Sun* (September 14, 1957), 8; "Burlesque Parlor Loses Grog License; to Peddle Soft Drinks with G-Strings." *Las Vegas Review-Journal* (February 28, 1958), 3.

59. Ad, *Las Vegas Sun* (April 17, 1953), 2; ad, *Las Vegas Review-Journal* (December 30, 1956), 2; ad, *Las Vegas Sun* (March 1, 1957), 2; ad, *Las Vegas Sun* (May 23, 1958), 4; ad, *Las Vegas Sun* (July 1, 1959), 5.

60. Ted Schwarz and Mardi Rustam, *Candy Barr: The Small-Town Texas Runaway Who Became a Darling of the Mob and the Queen of Las Vegas Burlesque* (Lanham, Md.: Taylor Trade Publishing, 2008), 197; Ralph Pearl, "Vegas Daze and Nites," *Las Vegas Sun* (August 22, 1958), 4.

61. "Tempest Storm in Legal Spat Over Her 'Chest,'" *Las Vegas Review-Journal* (September 24, 1952), 2; Ralph Pearl, "Vegas Daze and Nites," *Las Vegas Sun* (October 16, 1957), 4.

62. Ralph Pearl, "Vegas Daze and Nites," *Las Vegas Sun* (October 11, 1958), 7.

63. Quoted in Kelly DiNardo, *Gilded Lili: Lili St. Cyr and the Striptease Mystique* (New York: Backstage Books, 2007), 97–98.

64. Katharine Best and Katharine Hillyer, *Las Vegas: Playground U.S.A.* (New York: David McKay, 1955), 74.

65. "Strip 'Artist' Lili Just a Nuisance at Desert Resort," *Independent* (Long Beach, Calif.) (October 16, 1952), 8.

66. Hank Greenspun, "Where I Stand," *Las Vegas Sun* (January 23, 1960), 2.

67. Gordon Gassaway, "Southern Nevada Picturesque Paradise for the Wandersome," *Los Angeles Times* (February 24, 1918), VI2.

68. Michael Johnson, "Transforming the 'Old West' into 'Modern Splendor': The Suppression of Brothel Prostitution in Las Vegas," presentation at the Biennial Conference on Nevada History, Las Vegas, Nevada, May 24, 2006; Marie Katherine Rowley, "'So Much for Fond Five-Dollar Memories': Prostitution in Las Vegas, 1905–1955" (master's thesis, University of Nevada, Las Vegas, 2012), 19 and 21.

69. Rowley, "Five-Dollar Memories," 37–51; Eugene P. Moehring and Michael S. Green, *Las Vegas: A Centennial History* (Reno: University of Nevada Press, 2005), 104 and 118; Jamie Coughtry and R. T. King, eds., *George L. Ullom, Politics and Development in Las Vegas, 1930s–1970s* (Reno: University of Nevada Oral History Program, 1989), 48;

"Bordello Owner Gives Up," *Las Vegas Sun* (September 15, 1951), 1; "Vice House Catered to Teen-agers," *Las Vegas Sun* (April 30, 1954), 1.

70. "Clippingers Get 3 Years," *Las Vegas Sun* (August 22, 1954), 1; Bob Considine, "The Inside Story of Las Vegas," *PIC*, July 1955, 70–71.

71. "Prostitutes, Panderers Flocking to Las Vegas," *Las Vegas Review-Journal* (February 1, 1953), 1.

72. Ed Reid, "Fate of Roxie Operation Remains County Problem," *Las Vegas Sun* (August 1, 1954), 1; Henry Delahunt, "Find Explosive 'Black Books,'" *Las Vegas Sun* (June 5, 1960), 1.

73. "County Seeks Strong Law to Battle Vice on Strip," *Las Vegas Sun* (February 9, 1960), 2; "Teenager Tells of Life of Shame on Vegas Strip," *Las Vegas Sun* (May 25, 1960), 2; "Nab Call-Girl Quintet in Motel, Hotel Raids," *Las Vegas Sun* (November 12, 1960), 6.

74. Lloyd Shearer, "Chorus Girls," *Parade Magazine* in *Independent-Press-Telegram* (Long Beach, Calif.) (June 2, 1957), 27. *Life* magazine reached a similar conclusion: "For chorus girls the best place in the country is Las Vegas." The magazine learned that Las Vegas's attraction for dancers did not diminish in the 1960s. See "Showgirl Shangri-La," *Life* (June 21, 1954), 47; "The Audacious New Swimsuits," *Life* (January 8, 1965), 57.

75. "Paris Come-On in Vegas," *Life* (June 6, 1960), 51–52, 54, and 57.

76. Gale Baker, *Neon Queens: Fifty Years of Las Vegas' "Finest Feathered Femmes,"* (Auburn, Calif.: eBookstand Books, 1999), 25; "Showgirl Shangri-La," 47; Virginia James Papers, 1949–1982, Box 1, Folders 2, 4, and 5, Special Collections, University Libraries, University of Nevada, Las Vegas; Reid, *City without Clocks*, 158–59.

77. Lisa Gioia-Acres, *Showgirls of Las Vegas* (Charleston, S.C.: Arcadia Publishing, 2013), 75; Earl Wilson, "Chorine Life in Vegas Differs from Other Show Spots Says Hoofer," *Las Vegas Review-Journal* (August 16, 1953), 18; Valda Esau, "From Paris to Las Vegas," unpublished memoir, 2–4; Reid, *City without Clocks*, 158–59.

78. "Showgirl Shangri-La," 48 and 50; Wilson, "Chorine Life," 18; Joan Ryba, interview with author, April 9, 2011; Jones, Memoirs, 21; "'Good Life' on Las Vegas Strip Told by Chorines," *Las Vegas Sun* (June 9, 1957), 3; Forrest Duke, "Typical Vegas Chorus Girl Has Busy Schedule," *Las Vegas Sun* (May 12, 1957), 19.

79. Lissa Townsend Rodgers, "Stories from the Chorus Line," *Vegas Seven* (February 11, 2016), accessed January 29, 2017, http://vegasseven.com/2016/02/11/showgirls-tales-from-the-chorus-line/.

80. Jones, Memoirs, 21; Fluff LeCoque Interview, *The Real Las Vegas* (May 22, 1996), 2, Special Collections and Archives, University Libraries, University of Nevada, Las Vegas; Ryba interview.

81. Ryba interview; Virginia James Oral History Video, Special Collections and Archives, University Libraries, University of Nevada, Las Vegas.

82. Jones, Memoirs, 44–45; Ryba interview; Joy Garner, interview with author, November 17, 2017.

83. Esau, "Paris to Las Vegas," 5.

84. Quoted in Goodwin, *Changing the Game*, 93. Also, see James Oral History Video.

85. Wilson, "Chorine Life," 18.

86. Lynn M. Zook, *Gambling on a Dream: The Classic Las Vegas Strip* (self-published,

2016), Kindle edition, LOC 318; Betty Bunch, *High Heels and Headdresses: Memoirs of a Vintage Vegas Showgirl* (Las Vegas: Stephens Press, 2011), Kindle edition, LOC 160; Judy Jones interview with author, March 22, 2011.

87. Bunch, *High Heels*, LOC 716 and 744.

88. Oral History with Dottie and Don Tomlin; Zook, *Gambling on a Dream*, LOC 318; Goodwin, *Changing the Game*, 93.

89. Ryba interview; Jones, Memoirs, 44–45; Garner interview; Baker, *Neon Queens*, 32.

90. "The Las Vegas I Remember: Interview with Tracy Heberling," KNPR, Las Vegas, June 20, 2005.

91. "Good Life."

92. Quoted in Kraft, *Vegas at Odds*, 38.

93. Esau, "Paris to Las Vegas," 5; "The Las Vegas I Remember: Interview with Tracy Heberling."

94. Goodwin, *Changing the Game*, 92–93; Jones, Memoirs, 41; Joyce Marshall, Interview with Betty Bunch (Las Vegas Women in Gaming and Entertainment Oral History Project, UNLV Libraries, 1997), 23.

95. Linda Chase, *Picturing Las Vegas* (Layton, Utah: Gibbs Smith, 2009), 92–93.

96. "The Belles of Las Vegas," *Real Men*, December 1958, 26–29.

97. Bill Willard, "Talk of Our Town," *Las Vegas Sun* (January 5, 1951), 4.

98. Goodwin, "She Works Hard," 255; Goodwin, *Changing the Game*, 87 and 90.

99. "Where I Stand," *Las Vegas Sun* (November 14, 1958), 1–2.

100. "Where I Stand," *Las Vegas Sun* (February 6, 1960), 1.

101. "A Timely Recollection," *Las Vegas Sun* (July 24, 1954), 4.

102. "Where I Stand," *Las Vegas Sun* (November 14, 1958), 1–2.

103. "Where I Stand," *Las Vegas Sun* (January 26, 1955), 1 and 13.

104. City Commission Minutes, November 5, 1958, 233–34; "Women Hiring Causing Exodus of Dealers to Vegas—Legion," *Las Vegas Sun* (December 7, 1953), 8.

105. Wanderer and Goodwin, "A Thousand to One," 51.

106. Rodgers, "Stories from the Chorus Line"; Garner interview.

CHAPTER 5

1. Daniel Mark Epstein, *Nat King Cole* (Boston: Northeastern University Press, 2000), 269–77.

2. "Did Bias Banish Nat's TV Show?" *Jet* (March 4, 1965), 60.

3. "The Nat King Cole Show," September 24, 1956, YouTube, accessed September 5, 2015, https://www.youtube.com/watch?v=26qgK40xcb8; script for September 24, 1957, Nat "King" Cole Show, Sands Hotel Collection, Box 14, Folder 8.

4. Quoted in Maria Cole, with Louie Robinson, *Nat King Cole: An Intimate Biography* (New York: William Morrow, 1971), 105–6.

5. Johnny Mathis, interview with author, September 2, 2015.

6. Harry Belafonte, with Michael Shnayerson, *My Song: A Memoir* (New York: Alfred A. Knopf, 2011), 179; Horne quoted in Alan Pomerance, *Repeal of the Blues* (Secaucus, N.J.: Citadel Press, 1988), 120.

7. Maxine Lewis Flamingo Bookings, 1948–1951, Special Collections and Archives, University Libraries, University of Nevada, Las Vegas.

8. "Pick Best of Entertainers for Sands Shows," *Las Vegas Review-Journal* (December 15, 1952), 20; William L. Taub, *Forces of Power* (New York: Grosset and Dunlap, 1979), 7.

9. Maria Cole, *Nat King Cole*, 105–6; Leslie Gourse, *Unforgettable: The Life and Mystique of Nat King Cole* (New York: St. Martin's Press, 1991), 166.

10. Eartha Kitt, *Thursday's Child* (New York: Duell, Sloan and Pearce, 1956), 243.

11. "Show Reviews," *Las Vegas Sun* (November 24, 1951), 4; Ralph Pearl, "Vegas Daze and Nites," *Las Vegas Sun* (November 26, 1955), 5.

12. Mathis interview.

13. "Delta Boys to Close with Amos 'n' Andy," *The Afro-American* (Baltimore) (May 18, 1946), 5; Carl Jones Interview, Perfect Sound Forever, January 2001, accessed October 11, 2015, http://www.furious.com/perfect/deltarhythmboys.html.

14. "Delta Rhythm Boys," *Billboard Music Year Book* (1944), 253; "Delta Rhythm Boys Are Feted," *Plaindealer* (Kansas City, Kans.) (June 28, 1946), 10.

15. William H. Stevens to Gloster B. Current, August 17, 1948, NAACP Records, Las Vegas File, Part II, Box C105, Library of Congress, Washington, D.C.

16. Red Callender and Elaine Cohen, *Unfinished Dream: The Musical World of Red Callender* (London: Quartet Books, 1985), 71; Lionel Hampton, with James Haskins, *Hamp: An Autobiography* (New York: Amistad Press, 1993), 45.

17. Sammy Davis, Jane Boyer, and Burt Boyer, *Sammy: An Autobiography, With Material Newly Revised from Yes I Can and Why Me?* (New York: Farrar, Straus and Giroux, 2000), 74.

18. Belafonte, *My Song*, 105.

19. See "Harrison's Guest House," National Register of Historic Places Registration Form, April 7, 2014; photo captions in James Goodrich, "Negroes Can't Win," *Ebony*, March 1954, 50.

20. "The Other Side," *The Voice* (March 25, 1954), 2.

21. Fred Bronson, "The Years in Music: The Charts of 40, 30, 20 and 10 Years Ago," *Billboard*, December 26, 1998–January 2, 1999, 64; "Johnny Mathis Jams in Debut," *Chicago Defender* (August 4, 1958), 17.

22. Les Devor, "Vegas Vagaries," *Las Vegas Review-Journal* (August 6, 1958), 5; Mathis interview.

23. See Stan Irwin Oral History, 2009, Special Collections and Archives, University Libraries, University of Nevada, Las Vegas; Nadine Cohodas, *Queen: The Life and Music of Dinah Washington* (New York: Pantheon Books, 2004), 220–21 and 353.

24. Mathis interview.

25. Maria Cole, *Nat King Cole*, 106.

26. John Chilton, *Let the Good Times Roll: The Story of Louis Jordan and His Music* (Ann Arbor: University of Michigan Press, 1994), 191.

27. Eartha Kitt, *Confessions of a Sex Kitten* (New York: Barricade Books, 1991), 55. Also, see Callender and Cohen, *Unfinished Dream*, 72.

28. Joyce Marshall, Interview with Betty Bunch (Las Vegas Women in Gaming and Entertainment Oral History Project, UNLV Libraries, 1997), 28.

29. Arnold Shaw, *Belafonte: An Unauthorized Biography* (Philadelphia: Chilton Company, 1960), 106.

30. Davis, Boyer, and Boyer, *Sammy,* 75–76. Also, see the experience of Lena Horne in Callender and Cohen, *Unfinished Dream,* 72.

31. Goodrich, "Negroes Can't Win," 46.

32. John L. Williams, *Miss Shirley Bassey* (London: Quercus, 2010), 157; Michael Sullivan, *There's No People Like Show People: Confessions of a Showbiz Agent* (London: Quadrant Books, 1982), 165. Interracial relationships also threatened to end lives, as Las Vegas veteran Sammy Davis Jr. feared when rumors surfaced that he had an affair with actress Kim Novak. After Harry Cohn, the president of Columbia Pictures who had Novak under contract, learned of the rumors, he apparently called upon some mobsters to tell Davis to end it. Sammy took the threat seriously and quickly married black singer Loray White at the Sands Hotel in January 1958. See Sam Kashner, "The Color of Love," *Vanity Fair* (September 3, 2013), accessed December 22, 2015, http://www.vanityfair.com/style/1999/03/sammy-davis-kim-novak-dating; Gary Fishgall, *Gonna Do Great Things: The Life of Sammy Davis, Jr.* (New York: Scribner, 2004), 109–18; Davis, Boyer, and Boyer, *Sammy,* 320–21.

33. "Discrimination Out West Grows with Rise in Colored Population," *Chicago Defender* (March 7, 1953), 4; Alice A. Dunnigan, "Human Rights Committee Shows Racial Bias on Increase in the West," *Plaindealer* (Kansas City, Kans.) (August 30, 1957), 34.

34. Goodrich, "Negroes Can't Win," 51; William G. Nunn, "An Interracial Dream," *Pittsburgh Courier* (June 4, 1955), 1; "Where I Stand," *Las Vegas Sun* (June 1, 1955), 1. Bill Moore, architect of the Hotel Last Frontier and native Texan, agreed that the segregation in Las Vegas resembled the situation in his home state. See Perry Kaufman Interview Notes, Kaufman Papers, Box 1, Folder 29.

35. Grant Sawyer, Gary E. Elliott, and R. T. King, *Hang Tough! Grant Sawyer, An Activist in the Governor's Mansion* (Reno: University of Nevada Oral History Program, 1993), 98. Late in the decade, Hank Greenspun summed up the perspective of a number of the owners, who continued to believe "any degree of racial integration will harm the economy." "Have We Outgrown Pettiness?" *Las Vegas Sun* (March 24, 1960), 30.

36. Chilton, *Let the Good Times Roll,* 151.

37. "Here's Reaction from Strip on NAACP Plan," *Las Vegas Review-Journal* (March 17, 1960), 1 and 3.

38. Roger Kahn, *Memories of Summer: When Baseball Was an Art, and Writing about It a Game* (New York: Hyperion, 1997), 259–60. I wish to thank Professor Michael Green for sharing this example. The next year, the Sands Hotel hosted the Giants team, black players included, to a dinner after an exhibition game in Las Vegas. See *Sands Times,* July 1955, 2.

39. Davis, Boyer, and Boyer, *Sammy,* 99; Donald Bogle, *Dorothy Dandridge: A Biography* (New York: Amistad Press, 1997), 174; Mathis interview.

40. Chilton, *Let the Good Times Roll,* 151; *Invisible Las Vegas: The Untold Story of the West Las Vegas Community,* prod. and dir. Stan Armstrong, 60 mins. (Desert Rose Production, 2007).

41. Claytee White, "Nevada," in *Black America: A State-by-State Historical Encyclopedia,* ed. Alton Hornsby, vol. 2 (Westport, Conn.: Greenwood Press, 2011), 506; Leslie

Gourse, *Every Day: The Story of Joe Williams* (London: Quartet Books, 1985), 70. See also Cohodas, *Queen*, 174.

42. Michael Lyle, "Black Community Pushed to End Racial Discrimination in Las Vegas," *Las Vegas Review-Journal* (February 15, 2014), accessed October 11, 2015, http://www.reviewjournal.com/news/black-community-pushed-end-racial-discrimination-las-vegas.

43. Helen Crozier Greenwood, "West Las Vegas," *Las Vegas Sun* (February 1, 1956), 16; "Bill Willard," *Las Vegas Sun* (December 16, 1955), 23.

44. Gloster B. Current to William H. Stevens, July 28, 1948, NAACP Records, Las Vegas File, Part II, Box C105.

45. William H. Stevens to Gloster B. Current, August 7, 1948; William H. Stevens to Gloster B. Current, August 17, 1948, NAACP Records, Las Vegas File, Part II, Box C105.

46. Joey Bishop, "My Small War Against Prejudice," *Ebony*, April 1961, 64 and 66.

47. Bailey quoted in Elizabeth Patrick Nelson, "The Black Experience in Southern Nevada, Part II," *Nevada Historical Society Quarterly* 22, no. 3 (1979): 218.

48. "Entertainment Row," *Jet* (September 3, 1959), 29.

49. *Live at the Sands, November 1961*, CD, prod. Charles Pignone (Bristol Productions, 2006).

50. "Along the NAACP Battlefront," *Crisis*, December 1945, 356. See James Kaplan, *Frank: The Voice* (New York: Doubleday, 2010), 249–54 and 352–53, for a discussion of Sinatra's "contempt for the thickheaded smugness of racist America."

51. "Relationships of Sinatra with Blacks That Book about Him Does Not Highlight," *Jet* (October 13, 1986), 57.

52. James Kaplan, *Sinatra: The Chairman* (New York: Doubleday, 2015), 27.

53. Tina Sinatra, with Jeff Coplon, *My Father's Daughter: A Memoir* (New York: Simon and Schuster, 2000) 96; Kaplan, *Chairman*, 343; Pomerance, *Repeal of the Blues*, 132.

54. Eckstine also credited Beldon Katleman with a willingness to break down barriers. See Billy Eckstine Oral History, 1987, and Forrest Duke Oral History, 1977, both in Special Collections and Archives, University Libraries, University of Nevada, Las Vegas; Epstein, *Cole*, 233.

55. Mathis interview.

56. Jones, Memoirs, 46.

57. "Hazel Scott Fights Jim Crow at Las Vegas," *Jet* (April 24, 1952), 61–62.

58. "Hazel Scott Wins Point in Civil Rights Suit," *Seattle Times* (December 30, 1949), 7.

59. Taub, *Forces of Power*, 7; Jean-Claude Baker, *Josephine: The Hungry Heart* (New York: Random House, 1993), 319.

60. Belafonte, *My Song*, 142 and 177.

61. Maria Cole, *Nat King Cole*, 106; Gourse, *Unforgettable*, 165.

62. Maria Cole, *Nat King Cole*, 108.

63. Forrest Duke, "The Visiting Fireman," *Las Vegas Sun* (December 3, 1955), 7.

64. Louie Robinson, "The Life and Death of Nat King Cole," *Ebony*, April 1965, 128.

65. Quoted in *Nat King Cole: Afraid of the Dark*, prod. and dir. Jon Brewer, 94 mins. (Jon Brewer Production, 2014).

66. Gourse, *Every Day*, 71.

67. Kitt, *Thursday's Child*, 244.

68. Bogle, *Dorothy Dandridge*, 238; Williams, *Shirley Bassey*, 157; Sullivan, *Confessions*, 164.

69. Ralph Pearl, "Vegas Daze and Nites," *Las Vegas Sun* (December 1, 1955), 11; "Riviera Shop Talk," photo caption, *Las Vegas Sun* (February 5, 1956), 24.

70. Bogle, *Dorothy Dandridge*, 238.

71. "Scott Fights Jim Crow," 61–62; Bill Willard to Mike Kaplan and Al Sharper, April 5, 1952, Bill Willard Collection, 1887–1999, Box 1, Folder 1, Special Collections and Archives, University Libraries, University of Nevada, Las Vegas.

72. Belafonte, *My Song*, 108–9. Bob Bailey, Las Vegas entertainer and civil rights leader recalled in 1979 that Sammy Davis Jr. jumped into the Sands pool. See Nelson, "Black Experience," 218.

73. Dr. William H. "Bob" Bailey, *Looking Up: Finding My Voice in Las Vegas* (Las Vegas: Stephens Press, 2009), 140.

74. Jamie Coughtry and R. T. King, *Lubertha Johnson: Civil Rights Efforts in Las Vegas, 1940s–1960s* (Reno: University of Nevada Oral History Program, 1988), 34.

75. Goodrich, "Negroes Can't Win," 46.

76. "Scott Fights Jim Crow," 61–62.

77. Bill Willard to Mike Kaplan and Al Sharper, April 5, 1952, Bill Willard Collection, 1887–1999, Box 1, Folder 1.

78. "Baker Beats Bias," 62; Jamie Coughtry and R. T. King, *Woodrow Wilson: Race, Community and Politics in Las Vegas, 1940s–1980s* (Reno: University of Nevada Oral History Program, 1990), 42; Claytee D. White, Interview with J. David Hoggard (Las Vegas: African American Collaborative, Oral History Research Center, University Libraries, University of Nevada Las Vegas, 2012), 21 and 48.

79. "Vegas Daze and Nites," *Las Vegas Sun* (June 7, 1955), 4.

80. Quintard Taylor, "From Esteban to Rodney King: Five Centuries of African American History in the West," in *The American West: The Reader*, ed. Walter Nugent and Martin Ridge (Bloomington: University of Indiana Press, 1999), 288; Goodrich, "Negroes Can't Win," 49–50.

81. The best account of the Nevada Biltmore is by Bob Stoldal, "The Black Biltmore," *Desert Companion*, Summer 2009, 8–13. See also Frank Wright, *Nevada Yesterdays: Short Looks at Las Vegas History* (Las Vegas: Stephens Press, 2005), 115.

82. Stoldal, "Black Biltmore," 8–13. Hunter claimed he had purchased the Biltmore from Snowden. See "New Deal for Biltmore Hotel Revealed Today," *Las Vegas Review-Journal* (June 14, 1949), 1; "Nevada Biltmore Foreclosure Set," *Reno Evening Gazette* (July 14, 1949), 1.

83. Stoldal, "Black Biltmore," 11–13; "New Deal"; "Biltmore Foreclosure Set."

84. "Luxury Motel Planned for Strip, Wilbur Clark Says," *Las Vegas Review-Journal* (August 15, 1952), 6.

85. "Los Angeles Attorney Hugh Macbeth Succumbs," *Washington Afro-American* (October 30, 1956), 19; "In the Matter of International Spa, Inc." *Securities and Exchange Commission: Decisions and Reports*, vol. 36 (Washington, D.C.: Government Printing Office, 1956), 618–25; "Interracial Resort Planned for Las Vegas," *Jet* (December 18, 1952), 8; "Plan Resort for All Races," *Billboard* (December 6, 1952), 1.

86. "In the Matter," 618–25.

87. Ibid.; "Vegas Operation Stopped by SEC," *Reno Evening Gazette* (January 23, 1956), 2.

88. "New Resort Hotel Planned in Vegas," *Reno Evening Gazette* (October 21, 1954), 2; "Sell Stock for Las Vegas' 1st Cooperative Hotel," *Jet* (October 27, 1955), 17.

89. "Resort Hotel Slated on Salt Lake Highway," *Las Vegas Review-Journal* (August 20, 1954), 1; "Work Expected to Begin Soon on Westside Hotel," *Las Vegas Review-Journal* (September 5, 1954), 1.

90. "Progress!" *The Voice* (April 15, 1954), 2.

91. "Las Vegas to Get $1,200,000 Interracial Hotel," *Jet* (April 22, 1954), 1; "Realtor and Hotel Man, Moulin Director," and "Famed Restaurateur Turns Hotel Man," *Las Vegas Sun* (May 25, 1955), 18; "Nevada Licenses Las Vegas Hotel; Louis Is Partner," *Sacramento Bee* (May 7, 1955), 16; Gary Elliott, "The Moulin Rouge Hotel: Critical Appraisal of a Las Vegas Legend," unpublished paper, 6.

92. "Sammy Davis, Jr. and Lena Horne May Play Opener at Louis Hotel," *Chicago Defender* (December 11, 1954), 6.

93. "Joe Louis, Former Champion of the Ring, Now Is Official Greeter at New Vegas Hotel," *Nevada State Journal* (May 27, 1955), 11.

94. Evelyn Cunningham, "'It's Unbelievable,' Says Evelyn after Tour of Moulin Rouge Hotel," *Pittsburgh Courier* (June 4, 1955), 5.

95. Bailey, *Looking Up*, 104–5.

96. There are short articles on these men in the *Las Vegas Review-Journal* (May 26, 1955), 19–21.

97. "Well Known Las Vegans Manage Moulin Casino," *Las Vegas Sun* (May 25, 1955), 20; "Pit Boss," *Las Vegas Review-Journal* (May 26, 1955), 21.

98. "Westside News," *Las Vegas Review-Journal* (May 30, 1955), 12; "Westside News," *Las Vegas Review-Journal* (June 28, 1955), 15; "Westside News," *Las Vegas Review-Journal* (July 4, 1955), 11.

99. "Where I Stand," *Las Vegas Sun* (June 1, 1955), 1.

100. Alan Jarlson, "Inside Las Vegas," *Las Vegas Sun* (May 25, 1955), 9.

101. Al Monroe, "Celebs at Opening of Joe Louis' Moulin Rouge," *Chicago Defender* (June 4, 1955), 18.

102. Nunn, "Interracial Dream," 1.

103. "Gerri Major's Society," *Jet* (June 16, 1955), 40.

104. Evelyn Cunningham, "The Women," *Pittsburgh Courier* (June 4, 1955), 9.

105. Bailey, *Looking Up*, 109; "Moulin Rouge Third Show Is Luring Crowds," *Las Vegas Review-Journal* (June 24, 1955), 9; Claytee D. White, Interview with Anna Bailey Oral History (Las Vegas: Las Vegas Women's Oral History Project, Gaming and Entertainment Series, University of Nevada, Las Vegas, 1997), 35.

106. Les Devor, "Vegas Vagaries," *Las Vegas Review-Journal* (August 17, 1955), 5.

107. "Moulin Rouge Defendant in $46,000 Suit for Pay," *Las Vegas Review-Journal* (May 2, 1955), 2; "Moulin Rouge Reorganization Indicated," *Las Vegas Review-Journal* (July 28, 1955), 2.

108. "Why the Moulin Rouge Went Broke," *Jet* (October 20, 1955), 19–20.

109. "Moulin Rouge Chief to Sands, Dunes," *Las Vegas Review-Journal* (August 31, 1955), 1; "City Threatens Moulin Rouge License over Ownership Fuss," *Las Vegas Review-Journal* (October 5, 1955), 1.

110. "Financial Troubles Piling Up at Moulin Rouge," *Pittsburgh Courier* (October 8, 1955), 15. See the ads in the *Las Vegas Review-Journal* (September 2, 1955), 13–15.

111. "City Threatens Moulin Rouge," 3; Les Devor, "Vegas Vagaries," *Las Vegas Review-Journal* (October 7, 1955), 13.

112. "Slim Spending," 2.

113. George E. Pitts, "After Twelve," *Pittsburgh Courier* (October 22, 1955), 15.

114. Robert M. Ratcliffe, "Behind the Headlines," *Pittsburgh Courier* (October 22, 1955), 9.

115. Pitts, "After Twelve"; "Why the Moulin Rouge Went Broke," 18.

116. "Why the Moulin Rouge Went Broke," 22; "Financial Troubles Piling Up at Moulin Rouge," 15; Ratcliffe, "Behind the Headlines."

117. "Moulin Rouge Executive Denies Reports," *Las Vegas Review-Journal* (October 7, 1955), 1; "Moulin Rouge Re-Financing Is Sought after Casino Is Closed Last Evening," *Las Vegas Review-Journal* (October 7, 1955), 1.

118. "Propose Stock Promotion to Reopen Moulin Rouge," *Las Vegas Sun* (January 10, 1956), 1 and 13; "Moulin Rouge Creditors Meet Here Tomorrow," *Las Vegas Sun* (January 16, 1956), 5 and 10.

119. See Eugene P. Moehring, *Resort City in the Sunbelt: Las Vegas, 1930–2000* (Reno: University of Nevada Press, 2000), 183.

120. Elliott, "The Moulin Rouge," 7; Earnest N. Bracey, *The Moulin Rouge and Black Rights in Las Vegas* (Jefferson, N.C.: McFarland , 2009), 57. A good collection of speculation on the causes of the closing of the Moulin Rouge, from racism to skimming to concerns of mob-owned Strip hotels about losing money to the upstart new hotel, is in *The Misunderstood Legend of the Las Vegas Moulin Rouge*, prod. and dir. Stan Armstrong and Gary Lipsman, 105 mins. (Desert Rose Productions, 2014). The documentary has an excellent collection of images and interviews with people who worked at the Moulin Rouge.

CHAPTER 6

1. "Hazel Scott Fights Jim Crow at Las Vegas," *Jet* (April 24, 1952), 61; "Jo Baker Beats Bias," *Jet* (May 29, 1952), 62; Franklin H. Williams, "Sunshine and Jim Crow," *The Crisis*, April 1954, 205.

2. James Goodrich, "Negroes Can't Win in Las Vegas," *Ebony*, March 1954, 45; "Mayor Backs Las Vegas Race Bars," *Chicago Defender* (May 1, 1954), 20.

3. William G. Nunn, "An Interracial Dream," *Pittsburgh Courier* (June 4, 1955), 1.

4. Roosevelt Fitzgerald, "The Evolution of a Black Community in Las Vegas: 1905–1940," unpublished manuscript, 1–7, Special Collections and Archives, University Libraries, University of Nevada, Las Vegas; Eugene P. Moehring, "Profile of a Nevada Railroad Town: Las Vegas, 1910," *Nevada Historical Society Quarterly* 34, no. 4 (1991): 468; Helen M. Blue and Jamie Coughtry, *Clarence Ray: Black Politics and Gaming in Las Vegas, 1920s–1980s* (Reno: University of Nevada Oral History Program, 1991), 21, 23, 36, and 39.

5. "Pioneer Las Vegan Sees Town Grow," *Las Vegas Sun* (February 9, 1965), 4; Blue and Coughtry, *Clarence Ray*, 36.

6. "A Good Record," *Las Vegas Age* (May 22, 1930), 2.

7. Fitzgerald, "Black Community," 2.

8. Stanley A. Steward, *Where Sin Abounds: A Religious History of Las Vegas* (Eugene, Ore.: Wipf and Stock, 2012), 13–14; "Colored Annex to Restricted District," *Las Vegas Review-Journal* (October 9, 1934), 5; Fitzgerald, "Black Community," 7.

9. Craig F. Swallow, "The Ku Klux Klan in Nevada during the 1920s," *Nevada Historical Society Quarterly* 24, no. 3 (1981): 213–20; A. E. Cahlan, "From Where I Sit," *Las Vegas Sun* (November 8, 1965), 20.

10. Michael Hiltzik, *Colossus: Hoover Dam and the Making of the American Century* (New York: Free Press, 2010), 314–15.

11. Robert V. Nickel, "Dollars, Defense, and the Desert: Southern Nevada's Military Economy and World War II," *Nevada Historical Society Quarterly* 47, no. 4 (2004): 303–8; William T. Dobbs, "Southern Nevada and the Legacy of Basic Magnesium Incorporated," *Nevada Historical Society Quarterly* 34, no. 1 (1991): 273–303.

12. "200 Negro Workers Walk off Jobs at BMI Plant Today," *Las Vegas Review-Journal*, October 10, 1944, 1; Coughtry and King, *Woodrow Wilson*, 17.

13. Hiltzik, *Colossus*, 314–15.

14. Fitzgerald, "Black Community," 17; Eric N. Moody, "The Early Years of Casino Gambling in Nevada, 1931–1945" (Ph.D. diss., University of Nevada, Reno, 1997), 269.

15. "Bar on Westside Ordered Closed," *Las Vegas Review-Journal* (July 1, 1943), 3.

16. Claytee White, "The March That Never Happened: Desegregating the Las Vegas Strip," *Nevada Law Review* 5, no. 1 (2004): 73; Marion Earl Oral History, 1972; Boysie Ensley Oral History, 1972, Kaufman Papers.

17. Fitzgerald, "Black Community," 17; "The Only Thing That Seems to Fit," *Las Vegas Review-Journal* (November 20, 1934), 6.

18. Richard English, "The Boom Came Back," *Collier's* (August 22, 1942), 36.

19. Dobbs, "Legacy of Basic Magnesium," 284; C. B. McClelland and Company, *Report of Las Vegas, Nevada, Housing Survey, December 1947* (Riverside, Calif.: McClelland, 1947), 7.

20. Coughtry and King, *Lubertha Johnson*, 12; Dobbs, "Legacy of Basic Magnesium," 287.

21. "Fire Spurs Westside Housing Drive," *Las Vegas Review-Journal* (June 9, 1943), 3.

22. Elizabeth Nelson Patrick, "The Black Experience in Southern Nevada," *Nevada Historical Society Quarterly* 22, no. 2 (1979): 136n11.

23. Perry Kaufman, "The Best City of Them All: A History of Las Vegas, 1930–1960 (Ph.D. diss., University of California, Santa Barbara, 1974), 328; "Colored Folk Discuss Jobs," *Las Vegas Age* (December 19, 1931), 3; "Noted Colored Lecturer Is to Speak in Vegas," *Las Vegas Age* (April 13, 1932), 1; "Negroes Will Get Jobs on Project," *Las Vegas Age* (June 18, 1932), 4.

24. Kaufman, "Best City," 331–39; "Colored Vets Organize Post," *Las Vegas Age* (August 18, 1932), 1; "Colored G.O.P. Voters Meet," *Las Vegas Age* (September 2, 1932), 1; "Colored Club Asks Jobs for Members," *Las Vegas Review-Journal* (March 28, 1936), 3.

25. Las Vegas City Commission Minutes, October 16, 1939, vol. 4, 207, Special Collections and Archives, University Libraries, University of Nevada, Las Vegas; "Colored Residents Win Legal Battle," *Las Vegas Review-Journal* (October 17, 1939), 2.

26. A. McCants to Roy Wilkins, May 29, 1941, NAACP Records, Las Vegas File, Box C105, Folder 3.

27. Wm. H. Stevens to Mrs. Black, April 24, 1946; Wm H. Stevens to Gloster Current, December 4, 1946, NAACP Records, Las Vegas File, Box C105, Folder 3.

28. Gloster B. Current to W. H. Stevens, September 15, 1947; Wm. H. Stevens to Gloster B. Current, December 29, 1947, NAACP Records, Las Vegas File, Box C105, Folder 3.

29. Wm. H. Stevens to Walter White, August 14, 1946, NAACP Records, Las Vegas File, Box C105, Folder 3.

30. "Nevada Citizens Gird to Fight for Civil Rights," *Chicago Defender* (February 18, 1939), 4; "Race Bill Dropped By Solons Tuesday," *Nevada State Journal* (February 15, 1939), 1; Claytee White, "Nevada," in *Black America: A State-by-State Historical Encyclopedia*, ed. Alton Hornsby Jr. (Westport, Conn.: Greenwood, 2011), 501.

31. Verlene Stevens, "Race in Las Vegas," *Crisis*, September 1946, 271.

32. Coughtry and King, *Woodrow Wilson*, 27; Jamie Coughtry, *John F. Cahlan: Fifty Years in Journalism and Community Development* (Reno: University of Nevada Oral History Program, 1987), 117.

33. Lubertha Johnson Interview, 1972, Kaufman Papers, Box 1, Folder 29.

34. Roosevelt Fitzgerald, "A Demographic Impact of Basic Magnesium on Southern Nevada," 15, unpublished manuscript, Special Collections and Archives, University Libraries, University of Nevada, Las Vegas; "Where I Stand," *Las Vegas Sun* (December 22, 1952), 2; "Tourists Dump Total $164 Millions Here," *Las Vegas Sun* (July 10, 1955), 1; "Over 15,000 Residences Built in Las Vegas Area Since 1950 Census, 87 Per Cent Increase," *Las Vegas Sun* (September 12, 1955), 3.

35. Claytee D. White, An Interview with Hazel Geran (Las Vegas: African American Collaborative, Oral History Research Center at UNLV, 2012), 4; "Vegas Pay Hikes Outstrip Cost of Living Increase," *Las Vegas Sun* (June 1, 1957), 1.

36. White, "Nevada," 507.

37. "Vegas Public Housing Moves Step Closer to Reality," *Las Vegas Review-Journal* (June 25, 1950), 2; Minutes, Urban Renewal Area Advisory Committee, October 11, 1957, Donald Clark Collection, 1953–1972, Box 1, Folder 18, Special Collections and Archives, University Libraries, University of Nevada, Las Vegas (hereafter Donald Clark Collection).

38. Patrick, "The Black Experience," 137; Claytee D. White, Interview with Alma Whitney (Las Vegas: African American Collaborative, Oral History Research Center, University Libraries, University of Nevada Las Vegas, 1997), 6; Greg McCurdy, Interview with Lovey McCurdy (Las Vegas: African American Collaborative, Oral History Research Center, University Libraries, University of Nevada Las Vegas, 2012), 1; Claytee D. White, Interview with Marzette Lewis (Las Vegas: African American Collaborative, Oral History Research Center, University Libraries, University of Nevada Las Vegas, 2012), 9.

39. "Westside Shacks Are Being Razed," *Las Vegas Review-Journal* (September 22, 1944), 2; "Westside Slum Clearance Starts," *Las Vegas Review-Journal* (April 10, 1945), 7.

40. "Work toward Equitable Settlement of Zaugg Tract Dispute," *Las Vegas Sun* (March 15, 1952), 3; "Westside Slum Clearance Project Will Open Today," *Las Vegas Sun* (August 14, 1952), 1.

41. Alexander von Hoffman, "A Study in Contradictions: The Origins and Legacy of the Housing Act of 1949," *Housing Policy Debate* 11, no. 2 (2000), 310; "Vegas Slum Clearance to Go Ahead despite Truman Cutback Order," *Las Vegas Sun* (August 2, 1950), 3.

42. "Wheels to Start Turning on Vegas Slum Clearance," *Las Vegas Sun* (December 23, 1950), 1.

43. "Residents to Fight Location of Westside Housing Project," *Las Vegas Sun* (April 13, 1951), 1; "'Politics' Charged in Housing Uproar," *Las Vegas Sun* (April 13, 1951), 1; "Tempers Flare in Housing Session," *Las Vegas Review-Journal* (April 19, 1951), 2; Adam Yacenda, "Bitter Wrangling Highlights Rezoning Fight over Westside Housing Project," *Las Vegas Sun* (April 19, 1951), 1 and 3.

44. Jeff McColl, "City Grants Westside Zoning Appeal," *Las Vegas Review-Journal* (April 24, 1951), 3.

45. Jerry Smothers, "Marble Manor 'Different World,'" *Las Vegas Review-Journal* (October 5, 1952), 8.

46. A. E. Cahlan, "From Where I Sit," *Las Vegas Review-Journal* (September 28, 1952), 4; Smothers, "Marble Manor."

47. "Slum Clearance Plan for Vegas Gets Okeh," *Las Vegas Review-Journal* (June 20, 1956), 1.

48. Eugene Moehring, "C. D. Baker and the Modernization of Postwar Las Vegas," *Nevada Historical Society Quarterly* 60, nos. 1–4 (2017): 53–54.

49. "Move 600 in Westside When Freeway Goes In," *Las Vegas Sun* (July 5, 1957), 9.

50. Report of NAACP Housing Committee Report, 1958, 1–2, NAACP Records, Las Vegas File, Box C81.

51. "'Open Occupancy' Request to Be Made by Dr. West," *Las Vegas Review-Journal* (June 11, 1958), 2.

52. "Agree to View Proposed Housing Area," *Las Vegas Sun* (June 12, 1959), 2; Bonanza Home Owners Association to Mayor Pro-Tem Reed Whipple, June 16, 1959, Donald Clark Collection, Box 1, Folder 15; Las Vegas City Commission Minutes, July 15, 1959, vol. 11, 464; "LV Housing Petition Due Today," *Las Vegas Sun* (August 3, 1959), 1 and 2; "Vegas Approves Slum Clearance," *Las Vegas Sun* (October 16, 1959), 1 and 2; "$1,650,000 Federal Aid OK'd for Slum Clearance," *Las Vegas Sun* (September 21, 1960), 6; "Majority of Residents Favor Slum Clearance," *Las Vegas Sun* (October 28, 1960), 8; "Housing Authority Lets Contract on 125 Homes," *Las Vegas Sun* (November 16, 1960), 6.

53. Claytee D. White, Interview with Ruby Duncan (Las Vegas: African American Collaborative, Oral History Research Center, University Libraries, University of Nevada, Las Vegas, 2012), 15–16; White, Interview with Lewis, 12.

54. White, "Nevada," 505–6; Carol A. Crotta, "Architecture of Paul Revere Williams, Born 120 Years Ago, Still 'Remarkable,'" *Los Angeles Times* (July 19, 2014), accessed June 3, 2016, http://www.latimes.com/home/hometours/la-hm-paul-williams-20140719-story.html; "Model Homes in Berkley Plaza Open," *Las Vegas Sun* (March 21, 1953), 5; "First Families Move into Berkley Square," *Las Vegas Sun* (October 3, 1954), 6.

55. B. Leon Green, Interview with Eddie Wright, Jr. and Johnie B. Wright (Las Vegas: African American Collaborative, Oral History Research Center, University Libraries, University of Nevada Las Vegas, 2012), 38.

56. *The National Conference and the Reports of the State Advisory Committees to the U.S. Commission on Civil Rights,* 1959 (Washington, D.C.: Government Printing Office, 1960), 239–40. One solution for those seeking home loans was the Westside Credit Union, where NAACP activist Woodrow Wilson served as secretary-treasurer. See Harry J. Moore, "News and Views of Westside," *Las Vegas Review-Journal* (December 8, 1958), 9.

57. For example, see Lionel Hampton, with James Haskins, *Hamp: An Autobiography* (New York: Amistad Press, 1993), 45.

58. McCurdy, Interview with Lovey McCurdy, 1.

59. "Westside Asks City Dads for Better Streets," *Las Vegas Review-Journal* (August 8, 1945), 4; "City to Provide Long Sought Street Paving, Curbs, Gutters," *Las Vegas Sun* (July 31, 1955), 16.

60. Coughtry and King, *Lubertha Johnson,* 33 and 50.

61. Moehring, "C.D. Baker," 8; "Lighting, Paving Installation Set for Westside Area," *Las Vegas Sun* (February 6, 1954), 2.

62. White, Interview with Marzette Lewis, 9.

63. Eugene P. Moehring, *Resort City in the Sunbelt: Las Vegas, 1930–2000* (Reno: University of Nevada Press, 2000), 177.

64. Claytee D. White, Interview with Agnes Marshall (Las Vegas: African American Collaborative, Oral History Research Center, University Libraries, University of Nevada Las Vegas, 2012), 6; Green, Eddie Wright, Jr. and Johnie B. Wright, 73.

65. Quincy T. Mills, *Cutting Along the Color Line: Black Barbers and Barber Shops in America* (Philadelphia: University of Pennsylvania Press, 2013), 172.

66. Claytee D. White, Interview with Jerry Eppenger (Las Vegas: African American Collaborative, Oral History Research Center, University Libraries, University of Nevada Las Vegas, 2007), 11; John Grygo, Interview with Nathaniel Whaley (Las Vegas: African American Collaborative, Oral History Research Center, University Libraries, University of Nevada Las Vegas, 2012), 44; White, Interview with Ruby Duncan, 21.

67. Claytee D. White, Interview with Shirley Edmond (Las Vegas: African American Collaborative, Oral History Research Center, University Libraries, University of Nevada Las Vegas, 2007), 3; Claytee D. White, Interview with Thelma Turner (Las Vegas: African American Collaborative, Oral History Research Center, University Libraries, University of Nevada Las Vegas, 2012), 14 and 18; White, Jerry Eppenger, 14.

68. Steward, *Where Sin Abounds,* 16–17.

69. Ibid., 13–15, 38, and 54–56; White, "Nevada," 513.

70. White, Interview with Shirley Edmond, 5; Claytee D. White, Interview with Ruth Eppenger D'Hondt (Las Vegas: African American Collaborative, Oral History Research Center, University Libraries, University of Nevada Las Vegas, 2012), 6.

71. Green, Eddie and Johnie Wright, 14; White, Shirley Edmond, 2; John Grygo and Claytee D. White, Interview with Jocelyn Oats (Las Vegas: African American Collaborative, Oral History Research Center, University Libraries, University of Nevada Las Vegas, 2012), 4.

72. Goodrich, "Negroes Can't Win," 48.

73. Two useful interpretations of this leadership group have emerged. Claytee White has pointed out, "the leaders of the relentless series of pushes for equal rights were outsiders who toiled for civil liberties for a period and would then step aside to allow others with new ideas and novel strategies to take the reins of the struggle. Each migratory wave brought new leadership that pushed the black community toward the goal of full integration." White, "March That Never Happened," 74. Michael Green borrows W. E. B. Du Bois's concept of a needed "talented tenth" to characterize the professionals who led the fight against discrimination in the late 1950s. Green, "*Brown*, Integration, and Nevada," in *With All Deliberate Speed: Implementing Brown v. Board of Education*, ed. Brian J. Daugherity and Charles C. Bolton (Fayetteville: University of Arkansas Press, 2008), 295.

74. "NAACP Hears Details of Mississippi Lynch," *Las Vegas Review-Journal* (September 15, 1955), 2; "Local NAACP Calls Meeting over Slaying of Youth in South," *Las Vegas Sun* (October 1, 1955), 6; "'Mississippi Justice Protest' Meeting Set by NAACP Here Sunday," *Las Vegas Sun* (November 19, 1955), 10.

75. "Westside Parents to Air Dismissal of Elman Rape Charge," *Las Vegas Review-Journal* (November 12, 1953), 3; "NAACP Sets Own Meeting Tonight over Rape Case Dismissal," *Las Vegas Sun* (November 13, 1953), 1–2.

76. "Delegates at Capitol on Civil Rights," *Las Vegas Sun* (March 4, 1953), 7; "Opponents Win in Battle over Civil Rights," *Nevada State Journal* (March 17, 1953), 2.

77. "City Attorney Asked for Civil Rights Law Ruling," *Las Vegas Review-Journal* (August 6, 1953), 1.

78. Howard W. Cannon to Mayor and Board of City Commissioners, October 21, 1953; Howard W. Cannon to Mayor and Board of City Commissioners, November 30, 1953, Kaufman Papers, Box 1, Folder 18.

79. "NAACP Asks Convention Men to Boycott Vegas," *Las Vegas Review-Journal* (March 15, 1954), 1.

80. James McMillan, Gary E. Elliott, and R. T. King, *Fighting Back: A Life in the Struggle for Civil Rights* (Reno: University of Nevada Oral History Program, 1997), 81–82.

81. "Club Owners 'On Carpet' at City Hall," *Las Vegas Sun* (July 17, 1959), 1; Charles I. West and James B. McMillan to Operators of Grievances of the Dealers, September 1, 1959, Donald Clark Collection, Box 1, Folder 4; "Remove Casino Pickets," *Las Vegas Sun* (September 7, 1959), 1. Ironically, liberal attorney Ralph Denton, who often worked with West and McMillan, represented Zee Louie in this case. See Ralph Denton, Michael S. Green, and R. T. King, eds., *A Liberal Conscience: Ralph Denton, Nevadan* (Reno: University of Nevada Oral History Program, 2001), 153.

82. Dr. J. B. McMillan and Dr. C. I. West to Oran Gragson, n.d., Kaufman Papers, Box 1, Folder 18; Las Vegas City Commission Minutes, November 18, 1959, vol. 11, 588–89.

83. James B. McMillan to Clyde Port, December 3, 1959; E. E. Winters to Dr. James B. McMillan, January 6, 1960, Donald Clark Collection, Box 1, Folder 4.

84. Dr. William H. "Bob" Bailey, *Looking Up: Finding My Voice in Las Vegas* (Las Vegas: Stephens Press, 2009), 134–38; Claytee White, An Interview with Alice Key (UNLV: Las Vegas Women in Gaming and Entertainment Oral History Project, 1998), 51.

85. McMillan, Elliott, and King, *Fighting Back*, 80–81; "Newspaper Committee Report," 1958, NAACP Records, Las Vegas File, Box C81.

86. "Bill Willard," *Las Vegas Sun* (December 16, 1955), 23; "NAACP Plan Party for Sunday," *Las Vegas Review-Journal* (December 24, 1957), 15.

87. NAACP Las Vegas Branch Annual Report, 1960, Donald Clark Collection, Series 1, NAACP, 1959–1962, Box 1, Folder 3.

88. "Westsiders Irate over Exploitation," *Las Vegas Sun* (August 26, 1950), 1; Patrick, "Black Experience in Southern Nevada," 135.

89. "Westsiders Irate," 1.

90. See, for example, Green and King, *Liberal Conscience*, 198.

91. Coughtry and King, *Woodrow Wilson*, 76; Coughtry and King, *George L. Ullom*, 95.

92. Steward, *Where Sin Abounds*, 64; Green, Eddie and Johnie Wright, 54.

93. P. S. Walker Interview, Kaufman Papers, Box 1, Folder 29. Roosevelt Fitzgerald vigorously rejected this interpretation, arguing that black votes "could not be had for a picnic offering cheap whiskey and sizzling barbeque." See Fitzgerald, "Impact of BMI," 17.

94. "Malone Pal Seen Doling Free Money on Westside," *Las Vegas Sun* (October 30, 1952), 1. For Graham's background, see C. Elizabeth Raymond, *George Wingfield: Owner and Operator of Nevada* (Reno: University of Nevada Press, 1992), 165.

95. Moehring, *Resort City*, 184.

96. David Hoggard, Chairman, Legislative Committee Report, 1958, NAACP Records, Las Vegas File, Box C81; NAACP Las Vegas Branch Annual Report, 1960, Donald Clark Collection, Series 1, NAACP, 1959–1962, Box 1, Folder 3.

97. "Text of Gov. Sawyer's Message to 1960 Nevada Legislature," *Nevada State Journal* (January 20, 1960), 2; Sawyer, Elliott, and King, *Hang Tough*, 96–98.

98. Claytee White, "Nevada," 507; McMillan, Elliott, and King, *Fighting Back*, 84.

99. Taylor Branch, *Parting the Waters: America in the King Years, 1954–63* (New York: Simon and Schuster, 1989), 271–84; McMillan, Elliott, and King, *Fighting Back*, 91; "NAACP Asks Boycott of Resistant Stores," *Evening Star* (Washington, D.C.) (March 17, 1960), B5.

100. McMillan, Elliott, and King, *Fighting Back*, 92–93; Coughtry and King, *Woodrow Wilson*, 82; Coughtry and King, *Lubertha Johnson*, 57; Claytee White, Interview with J. David Hoggard (Las Vegas: African American Collaborative, Oral History Research Center, University Libraries, University of Nevada Las Vegas, 2012) 17.

101. "NAACP in Threat of Vegas Race Segregation Protest," *Las Vegas Sun* (March 17, 1960), 2. McMillan knew the significance of his threat. The new convention center had just opened in 1959, and Las Vegas was depending upon it to increase dramatically the income of the resort hotels.

102. "Here's Reaction from Strip on NAACP Plan," *Las Vegas Review-Journal* (March 17, 1960), 1 and 3.

103. "NAACP in Threat," 17.

104. McMillan, Elliott, and King, *Fighting Back*, 93; Oran Gragson Interview, "The Las Vegas I Remember," KNPR, Las Vegas, Nevada, July 12, 2005.

105. McMillan, Elliott, and King, *Fighting Back*, 94–95.

106. "Racial Showdown Nears in LV," *Las Vegas Sun* (March 23, 1960), 1; Coughtry and King, *Woodrow Wilson*, 84.

107. McMillan, Elliott, and King, *Fighting Back*, 95–97; "Where I Stand," *Las Vegas Sun* (March 25, 1960), 1.

108. Hank Greenspun Interview, Kaufman Papers, Box 2, Folder 29.

109. Belafonte, *My Song*, 251.

110. Alan Jarlson, "Vegas Color Barrier Lifted after Parley," *Las Vegas Sun* (March 26, 1960), 1.

111. Coughtry and King, *Lubertha Johnson*, 58; Coughtry and King, *Woodrow Wilson*, 86.

112. See White, Hoggard, 17.

113. "NAACP in Threat," 1.

CHAPTER 7

1. The former federal courthouse in Las Vegas now is the site of the National Museum of Organized Crime and Law Enforcement, or the Mob Museum.

2. Mary Ellen Glass, *Robbins E. Cahill: Recollections of Work in State Politics, Government, Taxation, Gaming Control, Clark County Administration, and the Nevada Resort Association*, vol. 3 (Reno: University of Nevada Oral History Program, 1977), 973.

3. *Hearings before a Special Committee to Investigate Organized Crime in Interstate Commerce*, part 10 (Washington, D.C.: Government Printing Office, 1950), 68–70.

4. Alan Balboni, "Moe Dalitz: Controversial Founding Father of Las Vegas," in *The Maverick Spirit: Building the New Nevada*, ed. Richard O. Davies (Reno: University of Nevada Press, 1999), 25.

5. Edward A. Olsen, *My Careers as a Journalist in Oregon, Idaho, and Nevada; in Nevada Gaming Control; at the University of Nevada* (Reno: University of Nevada Oral History Program, 1972), 225.

6. Glass, *Robbins E. Cahill*, 3:756. A good place to start in a study of organized crime in Las Vegas is Sally Denton and Roger Morris, *The Money and the Power: The Making of Las Vegas and Its Hold on America, 1947–2000* (New York: Knopf, 2001).

7. "Gambling Is Hit at Meeting by Speakers Here," *Reno Evening Gazette* (February 5, 1931), 12; "Nevada's Two False Steps," *Los Angeles Times* (March 22, 1931), 4.

8. Doug J. Swanson, *Blood Aces: The Wild Ride of Benny Binion, the Texas Gangster Who Created Las Vegas* (New York: Viking, 2014), 106.

9. See Eric N. Moody, "The Early Years of Casino Gambling in Nevada, 1931–1945," (Ph.D. diss., University of Nevada, Reno, 1997), 256–67; Jeff Burbank, "Red Rooster," *ONE: Online Nevada Encyclopedia*, accessed April 27, 2017, http://www.onlinenevada.org /articles/red-rooster.

10. Larry Gragg, *Bright Light City: Las Vegas in Popular Culture* (Lawrence: University Press of Kansas, 2013), 62–63.

11. Ibid., 64; "Gamblers Go to Las Vegas," *Los Angeles Times* (June 1, 1939), A.

12. Gragg, *Bright Light City*, 61–62; Kevin Starr, *The Dream Endures: California Enters the 1940s* (New York: Oxford University Press, 1997), 168. See also George Creel, "Unholy City," *Collier's* (September 2, 1939), 13.

13. Larry Gragg, *Benjamin "Bugsy" Siegel: The Gangster, the Flamingo, and the Making of Modern Las Vegas* (Santa Barbara, Calif.: Praeger, 2015), 76.

14. Ibid., 1–93.

15. Quotes in Ibid., 118 and 126.

16. Susan Berman, *Lady Las Vegas: The Inside Story behind America's Neon Oasis* (New York: TV Books, 1996), 77.

17. Swanson, *Blood Aces*, 137 and 238.

18. Bob Considine, "The Inside Story of Las Vegas," *PIC*, July 1955, 68.

19. "Moe Sedway Will on File Shows $297,546 Estate in Clark County," *Las Vegas Sun* (February 9, 1952), 1; "Death Takes Moe Sedway in Florida," *Las Vegas Sun* (January 4, 1952), 1.

20. "Death Takes Sedway"; *State of California Third Progress Report of the Special Crime Study Commission on Organized Crime* (Sacramento: Crime Study Commission, January 31, 1950), 22; "Moe Sedway's Sombrero Hits Ring's Center," *Nevada Courier* (April 8, 1947), 1 and 3; Brigham Townsend, "Making the Rounds," *Las Vegas Review-Journal* (May 6, 1946), 4; *Hearings*, Part 10, 65–68; "Where I Stand," *Las Vegas Sun* (January 4, 1952), 1.

21. "Underworld Links with Nevada's Legal Gambling Shocks Senate Investigators," *Lima (Ohio) News* (November 16, 1950), 5; "U.S. Opens Probe of Gangland; Mickey Cohen on Solon's List," *Oakland Tribune* (November 16, 1950), 1; "Gamblers Are Gamblers," *Chicago Daily Tribune* (November 21, 1950), 16; "Disposition of Siegel Hotel Under Inquiry," *Galveston (Tex.) News* (November 16, 1950), 8.

22. Lee Bernstein, *The Greatest Menace: Organized Crime in Cold War America* (Amherst: University of Massachusetts Press, 2002), 62.

23. Joseph Bruce Gorman, *Kefauver: A Political Biography* (New York: Oxford University Press, 1971), 78.

24. Bernstein, *Greatest Menace*, 61–78; Gorman, *Kefauver*, 102.

25. Estes Kefauver, "What I Found in the Underworld," *Saturday Evening Post* (April 7, 1951), 71; Estes Kefauver, "Crime in America," *Kingsport (Tenn.) News* (July 31, 1951), 3; Estes Kefauver, *Crime in America* (Garden City, N.Y.: Doubleday, 1951), 229–37; *The Kefauver Committee Report on Organized Crime* (New York: Didier Publishers, 1951), 71–75.

26. *Kefauver Committee Report*, 74; Kefauver, *Crime in America*, 229.

27. Dan Fowler, "What Price Gambling in Nevada?" *Look* (June 15, 1954), 49–52; Lester Velie, "Las Vegas: The Underworld's Secret Jackpot," *Reader's Digest*, October 1959, 138.

28. Fred J. Cook, "Treasure Chest of the Underworld: Gambling, Inc.," *Nation* (October 22, 1960), 301.

29. Sid W. Meyers, *The Great Las Vegas Fraud* (Chicago: Mayflower Press, 1958), 47, 68, and 85.

30. John D. MacDonald, *The Only Girl in the Game* (Greenwich, Conn.: Fawcett Publications, 1960), 32.

31. *Las Vegas Shakedown*, prod. William F. Broidy and dir. Sidney Salkow, 79 mins. (William F. Broidy Pictures, 1955).

32. Bob Considine, "Pierre Lafitte Got 'Tape' to Trip Nevada Racketeers," *Charleston (W.Va.) Gazette* (January 27, 1955), 7.

33. Sergio Lalli, "Cliff Jones: 'The Big Juice,'" in *Players: The Men Who Made Las Vegas*, ed. Jack Sheehan (Reno: University of Nevada Press, 1997), 23–34; "Cliff Jones Rapped at Meeting," *Las Vegas Sun* (August 6, 1952), 1.

34. Len Lefkow, "Lieut. Gov. Cited in Probe of Racket Link at Thunderbird," *Las Vegas Sun* (October 13, 1954), 1; Hank Greenspun Interview Notes, 1972, Kaufman Papers, 1930–1974, Box 1, Folder 29.

35. Bugsy Siegel FBI Files, 62-81518-125, 62-81518-288, 62-2837-150, FBI Records: The Vault, accessed May 7, 2017, http://vault.fbi.gov/Bugsy%20Siegel.

36. "McCarran Discloses Action in Tax Case," *New York Times* (December 30, 1952), 6; "McCarran Denies Try to Harm Newspaper," *Reno Evening Gazette* (December 30, 1952), 1; "McCarran Admits Aid to Gangster-Run Hotel," *Independent* (Long Beach, Calif.) (December 30, 1952), 5.

37. "Where I Stand," *Las Vegas Sun* (April 2, 1952), 1.

38. Jerome E. Edwards, *Pat McCarran, Political Boss of Nevada* (Reno: University of Nevada Press, 1982), 157.

39. Mary Ellen Glass, *Norman H. Biltz: Memoirs of the "Duke of Nevada"* (Reno: University of Nevada Oral History Program, 1969), 75. Jerome E. Edwards concluded, "It is impossible to avoid the conclusion that McCarran was ultimately the instigator of the boycott. Either he directly gave the word, or someone acting in his name did so" (Edwards, *McCarran*, 162).

40. Special Agent in Charge, Salt Lake City, to Director, FBI, May 28, 1952, Hank Greenspun FBI Files, 62-97009-19, Internet Archive, accessed May 9, 2017, https://archive .org/details/HermanHankM.Greenspun (hereafter Greenspun FBI Files).

41. Mary Ellen Glass, *Lester Ben "Benny" Binion: Some Recollections of a Texas and Las Vegas Gambling Operator* (Reno: University of Nevada Oral History Program, 1976), 52; Swanson, *Blood Aces*, 197–98; Michael J. Ybarra, *Washington Gone Crazy: Senator Pat McCarran and the Great American Communist Hunt* (Hanover, N.H.: Steerforth Press, 2004), 676.

42. L. B. Nichols to Mr. Tolson, March 29, 1952, Greenspun FBI Files, 62-97007-7X.

43. "Settlement Closes SUN Damage Suit," *Las Vegas Sun* (February 14, 1953), 1; Ybarra, *Washington Gone Crazy*, 697.

44. "Nevada Lieut. Governor Grilled in Gaming Probe," *Oakland Tribune* (October 27, 1954), 10; Considine, "Pierre Lafitte," 1 and 7; "'Mike Fright' Seizes Nevada," *Independent* (Long Beach, Calif.) (February 23, 1955), 4; Lalli, "Cliff Jones," 23–34; Robert Lacey, *Little Man: Meyer Lansky and the Gangster Life* (Boston: Little, Brown, 1991), 218.

45. *Nevada Tax Commission v. Hicks*, Supreme Court of Nevada, May 3, 1957, Justia, U.S. Law, accessed May 7, 2017, http://law.justia.com/cases/nevada/supreme-court /1957/3949-1.html; "Ban Hicks, Jones from T-Bird," *Las Vegas Sun* (April 2, 1955), 1.

46. Chet Sobsey, "The Boiling Pot," *Las Vegas Sun* (January 8, 1956), 6. Merrill's quote is in *Tax Commission v. Hicks*.

47. George Wolf with Joseph DiMona, *Frank Costello: Prime Minister of the Underworld* (New York: William Morrow, 1974).

48. "Manners and Morals," *Time* (November 28, 1949), 11.

49. Wolf, *Frank Costello*, 253–55; Selwyn Raab, *Five Families: The Rise, Decline, and Resurgence of America's Most Powerful Mafia Empires* (New York: Thomas Dunne Books, 2006), 108–10. The police apprehended Gigante, but at his trial for attempted murder, Costello claimed he did not get a good look at the shooter. When the jury found Gigante not guilty, the gunman quietly thanked Costello. See Raab, *Five Families*, 110.

50. Wayne Phillips, "Costello's Stake in Nevada Sifted," *New York Times* (June 13, 1957), 26; "Note to Costello Cited by Nevada," *New York Times* (June 29, 1957), 8.

51. "Another Pair of Bigtime Boys Lolling about Strip," *Las Vegas Review-Journal* (August 10, 1954), 1; Glass, *Robbins E. Cahill*, 3:812; "US Tax Claim May Cut Kastel-Tropicana Link," *Las Vegas Sun* (August 21, 1957), 1.

52. "N.Y. Police Link Note on Costello with Tropicana Casino Winnings," *Las Vegas Review-Journal* (June 12, 1957), 1.

53. Mary Ellen Glass, *Robbins E. Cahill: Recollections of Work in State Politics, Government, Taxation, Gaming Control, Clark County Administration, and the Nevada Resort Association*, vol. 2 (Reno: University of Nevada Oral History Program, 1977), 591.

54. "Where I Stand," *Las Vegas Sun* (May 2, 1951), 2.

55. Bob Considine, "Rich Nevada Oasis Must Be Seen to Be Believed, Newsman Says," *Charleston (W.Va.) Gazette* (January 23, 1955), 2.

56. Moody, "Early Years of Casino Gambling," 41–63 and 434–49; Mary Ellen Glass, *Robbins E. Cahill: Recollections of Work in State Politics, Government, Taxation, Gaming Control, Clark County Administration, and the Nevada Resort Association*, vol. 1 (Reno: University of Nevada Oral History Program, 1977), 294; 3:943–45, 1022; Mary Ellen Glass, *Robbins E. Cahill: Recollections of Work in State Politics, Government, Taxation, Gaming Control, Clark County Administration, and the Nevada Resort Association*, vol. 4 (Reno: University of Nevada Oral History Program, 1977), 1412–15; Gary E. Elliott, *Senator Alan Bible and the Politics of the New West* (Reno: University of Nevada Press, 1994), 22; Jeff Burbank, *License to Steal: Nevada's Gaming Control System in the Megaresort Age* (Reno: University of Nevada Press, 2000), 16.

57. "'Hoodlums Have Us Licked,' Says County Board," *Las Vegas Sun* (December 9, 1952), 1.

58. "Freedman Denied Gambling License for Sands Hotel," *Las Vegas Review-Journal* (August 6, 1952), 3. On Freedman's background, see George Fuermann, *Houston: Land of the Big Rich* (New York: Doubleday, 1951), 166–69.

59. Gus Russo, *The Outfit: The Role of Chicago's Underworld in the Shaping of Modern America* (New York: Bloomsbury, 2001), 309. Factor's half brother Max became a dominant player in the cosmetics industry with his Max Factor and Company.

60. Jack Sheehan, *Quiet Kingmaker of Las Vegas: E. Parry Thomas* (Las Vegas: Stephens Press, 2009), 76; Gus Russo, *Supermob: How Sidney Korshak and His Criminal Associates Became America's Hidden Power Brokers* (New York: Bloomsbury, 2007), 48–50 and 218; Michael Newton, *Mr. Mob: The Life and Crimes of Moe Dalitz* (Jefferson, N.C.: McFarland and Company, 2007), 167; Dwayne Kling, *The Rise of the Biggest Little City: An Encyclopedic History of Reno Gaming, 1931–1981* (Reno: University of Nevada Press, 2000), 42.

61. Joseph Stocker, "Las Vegas's Golden Boy," *American Legion Magazine*, December 1953, 24, 25, and 46.

62. David G. Schwartz, "JFK in Las Vegas," *Vegas Seven* (July 2, 2013), accessed May 25, 2017, http://vegasseven.com/2013/07/02/jfk-las-vegas-2/.

63. "Weeding Out Hoodlums in Las Vegas," *Las Vegas Sun* (February 12, 1960), 10.

64. Doc Stacher quoted in Russo, *Supermob*, 202.

65. "Tax Commission Counsel Threatened with Death," *Las Vegas Sun* (March 31, 1955), 1; "15 Million Gaming Empire Periled," *Las Vegas Review-Journal* (February 4, 1955), 2; "Tax Unit Blasts Gambling," *Las Vegas Review-Journal* (July 17, 1956), 8.

66. "Workers Fret Over Police Requirement of New Regulation," *Las Vegas Sun* (July 24, 1951), 2; "Police Tighten Policy Regarding Casino Employees," *Las Vegas Sun* (May 29, 1952), 1–2; John Gunther, "Inside Las Vegas," *Washington Post and Times Herald* (August 12, 1954), AW5.

67. "Hood Joe Sica Set to Test Law on Con Registry," *Las Vegas Sun* (March 27, 1958), 1.

68. "From Where I Sit," *Las Vegas Review-Journal* (August 24, 1954), 4.

69. "Las Vegas Police Give 'Rousting' Welcome to Visiting Chicagoans," *Las Vegas Review-Journal* (January 16, 1953), 1; "Accardo's Vegas Vacation Ends after Few Hours," *Las Vegas Review-Journal* (January 18, 1953), 1; Alan Jarlson, "On the Town," *Las Vegas Review-Journal* (January 18, 1953), 5.

70. "Underworld Pair Told to 'Stay Out of Vegas,'" *Las Vegas Review-Journal* (March 3, 1955), 3.

71. Ronald A. Farrell and Carole Case, *The Black Book and the Mob: The Untold Story of the Control of Nevada's Casinos* (Madison: University of Wisconsin Press, 1995), 23–31.

72. Mary Ann Culver Oral History, 1981; Irwin Molasky Oral History, 1999, Special Collections and Archives, University Libraries, University of Nevada, Las Vegas.

73. William D. "Butch" Leypoldt Interview Notes, 1972, Kaufman Papers, Box 1, Folder 2. Lloyd Bell, who served as undersheriff in the 1950s, agreed with Leypoldt's assessment. See Lloyd Bell Interview Notes, 1972, Kaufman Papers, Box 1, Folder 2.

74. Greenspun Interview Notes, 1972; Ed Oncken Interview Notes, 1972, Kaufman Papers, Box 1, Folder 2.

75. Mary Ellen Glass, *Charles H. Russell: Reminiscences of a Nevada Congressman, Governor, and Legislator* (Reno: University of Nevada Oral History Program, 1967), 74.

76. Sawyer, Elliott, and King, *Hang Tough!*, 85.

77. Glass, *Robbins E. Cahill*, 2:591.

78. Ibid., 2:334 and 3:850.

79. Ibid., 2:343 and 3:768. FBI quote in Russo, *Supermob*, 208.

80. Balboni, "Dalitz," 33–43; John L. Smith, *Sharks in the Desert: The Founding Fathers and Current Kings of Las Vegas* (Fort Lee, N.J.: Barricade Books, 2005), 49.

CHAPTER 8

1. Richard Perez-Pena, "Gladwin Hill Dies at 78," *New York Times* (September 20, 1992), B8; Douglas Brinkley, *Cronkite* (New York: Harper Collins, 2012), 93–97.

2. Gladwin Hill, "Watching the Bombs Go Off," *New York Times* (June 9, 1957), 353.

3. A. Constandina Titus, *Bombs in the Backyard: Atomic Testing and American Politics* (Reno: University of Nevada Press, 1986), 27. Titus's work is the best single source on atomic testing in Nevada. Others include Howard Ball, *Justice Downwind: America's Atomic Testing Program in the 1950's* (New York: Oxford University Press, 1986); Barton C. Hacker, *Elements of Controversy: The Atomic Energy Commission and Radiation Safety in Nuclear Weapons Testing, 1947–1974* (Berkeley: University of California Press, 1994); Richard Miller, *Under the Cloud: The Decades of Nuclear Testing* (New York: Free Press, 1986).

4. "Where I Stand," *Las Vegas Sun* (April 19, 1952), 1.

5. Russell D. Buhite, *Douglas MacArthur: Statecraft and Stagecraft in America's East Asian Policy* (Lanham, Md.: Rowman and Littlefield, 2008), 136–37; A. M. Rosenthal, "U.N. Circles Wary on Atom Bomb Use," *New York Times* (December 1, 1950), 5.

6. Titus, *Bombs in the Backyard*, 55–57.

7. Terrence R. Fehner and F. G. Gosling, *Origins of the Nevada Test Site* (Washington: U.S. Department of Energy, 2000), 55–56; "U.S. Will Test Atomic Bombs in Vegas Area," *Nevada State Journal* (January 12, 1951), 1; "Vegas Range to Speed A-Weapons," *Las Vegas Review-Journal* (January 12, 1951), 1.

8. A. Constandina Titus, "A-Bombs in the Backyard: Southern Nevada Adapts to the Nuclear Age, 1951–1963," *Nevada Historical Society Quarterly* 26, no. 4 (1983): 240.

9. Titus, *Bombs in the Backyard*, 60; "So. Nevada Atomic Games Will 'Save Lives in Battle'—Gen. Swing," *Las Vegas Sun* (September 20, 1951), 1; "Wherever You Look There's Danger in Las Vegas," *Life* (November 12, 1951), 38; "Army Conducts Tests of Its Own with Atom Bomb," *Las Vegas Sun* (March 6, 1955), 6; "Marines Learn Value of Foxholes under Atom Shot," *Las Vegas Sun* (May 2, 1952), 2.

10. "Atomic Fall-Out Dusts Las Vegas," *New York Times* (March 23, 1955), 14; Anthony Leviero, "Tank Resistance to Blast Hailed," *New York Times* (May 7, 1955), 7; "Second Spring A-Test Fired; Light Viewed 700 Miles Away," *Las Vegas Review-Journal* (March 24, 1953), 1; "Marines Maneuver in Atomic Cloud Shadow," *Las Vegas Review-Journal* (April 19, 1953), 1.

11. "Jets Chase 'A' Clouds to 'Capture' Dread Fallout," *Las Vegas Sun* (September 13, 1957), 18.

12. "Paratroopers Feel Fury of New A-Blast," *Las Vegas Review-Journal* (September 2, 1957), 1; "Check Man's Reactions to A-Blast," *Las Vegas Review-Journal* (September 3, 1957), 1; "Desert Rock GIs Back Use of Atom Weapons in War," *Las Vegas Review-Journal* (March 29, 1955), 10.

13. "Human Guinea Pigs Hail Survival of Atom Blast," *Las Vegas Review-Journal* (March 25, 1953), 6; "5 Air Officers Test 'Guinea Pigs,'" *Las Vegas Sun* (July 20, 1957), 1.

14. "Second Spring A-Test Fired; Light Viewed 700 Miles Away," *Las Vegas Review-Journal* (March 24, 1953), 1; "Pigs Star in Atom Test," *Las Vegas Review-Journal* (May 8, 1953), 1.

15. Charles J. V. Murphy, "A-Bomb vs. House," *Life* (March 30, 1953), 21; *Operation Cue*, film, Federal Civil Defense Administration, 1955. Some of the documentary films made by or with the cooperation of the Federal Civil Defense Administration meant to reassure Americans often became objects of ridicule. In 1954 *The House in the Middle*, a documentary short, showed the effects of an atomic test on three houses on the periphery of the blast. While the other two had not been painted and were surrounded by dry grass and litter went up in flames, the house in the middle had been freshly painted and featured a clean yard and survived the heat effects of a blast. See *The House in the Middle* on YouTube, accessed July 8, 2018, https://www.youtube.com/watch?v=pGJcwaUWNZg. An excellent recent account of the Doom Towns and the context for the tests is Andrew G. Kirk, *Doom Towns: The People and Landscapes of Atomic Testing, A Graphic History* (New York: Oxford University Press, 2017).

16. Gladwin Hill, "'Town' Does Well in Atomic Blast," *New York Times* (May 7, 1955), 6.

17. "Atomic Tests Light Up Four States," *Life* (February 12, 1951), 25; "AEC Investigates Reports of Blast Damage," *Las Vegas Review-Journal* (February 2, 1951), 2.

18. Timothy Cole, "Growing Up Nuclear: Las Vegas Children and the Bomb," (Ph.D. diss., University of Calgary, 2006), 46–50; Donna Smith interview, in Nevada Test Site Oral History Project, ed. Mary Palevsky, Robert Futrell, and Andrew Kirk, 9, November 4, 2006, accessed June 19, 2016, http://digital.library.unlv.edu/api/1/objects/nts/1324 /bitstream.

19. Ernest Williams interview, in Nevada Test Site Oral History Project, ed. Mary Palevsky, Robert Futrell, and Andrew Kirk, 32, March 26, 2004, accessed June 18, 2016, http://digital.library.unlv.edu/api/1/objects/nts/1296/bitstream.

20. A. O. Sulzberger Jr., "'55 Atomic Bomb Tests in Nevada Are Recalled by a Former Soldier," *New York Times* (May 14, 1979), D8.

21. Cole, "Growing Up Nuclear," 50–53.

22. "Heck, We're Not Scared!" *Las Vegas Review-Journal* (January 12, 1951), 1. See also Titus, "A-Bombs in the Backyard," 247.

23. Mary Ellen Glass, *John Cahlan: Reminiscences of a Reno and Las Vegas, Nevada Newspaperman, University Regent, and Public-Spirited Citizen* (Reno: Oral History Program, University of Nevada, Reno, 1970), 151–52; Florence Lee Jones Cahlan, Oral History, 1973, Special Collections and Archives, University Libraries, University of Nevada, Las Vegas.

24. "Where I Stand," *Las Vegas Sun* (January 30, 1951), 1 and 3.

25. "It Seems to Us," *Las Vegas Review-Journal* (January 15, 1951), 10.

26. "Heck, We're Not Scared," 1.

27. Paul Boyer, *By the Dawn's Early Light: American Thought and Culture at the Dawn of the Atomic Age* (Chapel Hill: University of North Carolina Press, 1994), 334; Allan M. Winkler, *Life under a Cloud: American Anxiety about the Atom* (New York: Oxford University Press, 1993), 91.

28. Gladwin Hill, "3rd Atom Test Lights Nevada Dawn; Peaks Stand Out in Weird Glare," *New York Times* (February 2, 1951), 1.

29. Robert R. Brunn, "'This . . . Should Arouse the Most Solemn Reflections,'" *Christian Science Monitor* (July 2, 1951), 9.

30. Glen M. Feighery, "'A Light Out of This World': Awe, Anxiety, and Routinization in Early Nuclear Test Coverage, 1951–1953," *American Journalism* 28, no. 3 (2011): 17–18.

31. Richard P. Taffe, "I'm Not Afraid of the A-Bomb," *Collier's* (January 26, 1952), 1.

32. Gladwin Hill, "Mightiest Atom Blast of Tests Unleashed on Nevada Desert," *New York Times* (June 5, 1953), 1.

33. Gladwin Hill, "Atomic Boom Town in the Desert," *New York Times* (February 11, 1951), 158.

34. Gladwin Hill, "Effect of A-Bomb is Found Limited," *New York Times* (March 30, 1955), 16.

35. Gladwin Hill, "Less Fall-Out Predicted," *New York Times* (May 14, 1957), 19.

36. Gladwin Hill, "Atomic-Test Area Calm on Fall-Out," *New York Times* (June 9, 1957), 6.

37. Gladwin Hill, "Radiation in Test Put at Safe Level," *New York Times* (July 5, 1958), 5. There have been significant questions raised about the credibility of the *New York Times*'s reporting on atomic testing both in Nevada and in the Pacific. For example, see Beverly Deepe Keever, *News Zero: The New York Times and the Bomb* (Monroe, Maine: Common Courage Press, 2004).

38. "Board Conceals Radiation Peril, Says A-Scientist," *San Diego Union* (March 27, 1953), 2.

39. "Pall Closes Town after Atom Blast," *Oregonian* (May 20, 1953), 1; "AEC Checks Utah Atomic Area, Denies Harm Done," *Ogden (Utah) Standard-Examiner* (May 21, 1953), 1; "A.E.C. Denies Rays Killed Utah Sheep," *New York Times* (January 17, 1954), 46. See also Sarah Alisabeth Fox, *Downwind: A People's History of the Nuclear West* (Lincoln: University of Nebraska Press, 2014), 50–89; John G. Fuller, *The Day We Bombed Utah: America's Most Lethal Secret* (New York: New American Library, 1984).

40. "Japanese Furor Eases," *New York Times* (September 27, 1954), 7; "Four Exposed to Excessive Radiation at Atomic Site," *Las Vegas Sun* (January 21, 1956), 1.

41. "Maladies Afflict Animals Near 'A' Test Site," *Las Vegas Sun* (June 6, 1957), 1 and 12.

42. "Are Nuclear Tests Safe?," *Las Vegas Review-Journal* (June 13, 1957), 4. Leisl Carr Childers offers a cogent discussion of the challenges the tests posed for rancher Floyd Lamb in her book *The Size of the Risk: Histories of Multiple Use in the Great Basin* (Norman: University of Oklahoma Press, 2015), 75–102.

43. "Editor Starts A-Ban Picketing Here," *Las Vegas Sun* (June 18, 1957), 3; "AEC Picket Gives Up 22 Pounds to Cause," *Las Vegas Review-Journal* (June 30, 1957), 3; "Atom Test Foe Plans a Fast," *New York Times* (June 9, 1957), 51; Ammon Hennacy, "Picketing Atomic Tests in Las Vegas," *Catholic Worker*, July–August, 1957, 7.

44. "11 Protesting A-Tests Nabbed," Cleveland *Plain Dealer* (August 6, 1957), 29; "A Call to Non-Violent Action against Nuclear Weapons," n.d., Nevada Desert Experience Records, 1957–2007, Box 1, Folder 17, Special Collections and Archives, University Libraries, University of Nevada, Las Vegas; George Dugan, "Halt in Big 3 Atom Tests Urged By World Council of Churches," *New York Times* (August 6, 1957), 1.

45. "Ranchers Renew A-Test Ban Plea," *Las Vegas Sun* (September 4, 1957), 1 and 8.

46. "Program to Curb Fallout Offered," *Los Angeles Times* (June 13, 1956), 19; *The Biological Effects of Atomic Radiation: Summary Reports from a Study by the National Academy of Sciences* (Washington: National Academy of Sciences—National Research Council, 1956), 30; Jacob Darwin Hamblin, "'A Dispassionate and Objective Effort': Negotiating the First Study on the Biological Effects of Atomic Radiation," *Journal of the History of Biology* 40, no. 1 (2007): 147–77; Robert A. Divine, *Blowing on the Wind: The Nuclear Test Ban Debate, 1954–1960* (New York: Oxford University Press, 1978), 78–80.

47. Gladwin Hill, "2,000 Join Pauling in Bomb Test Plea," *New York Times* (June 4, 1957), 17.

48. "A Searching Inquiry into Nuclear Perils," *Life* (June 10, 1957), 24.

49. Atomic Energy Commission, Meeting Minutes, May 22, 1953, Alice P. Broudy Papers on Broudy v. United States, 1948–2006, Box 76, Folder 3, Special Collections and Archives, University Libraries, University of Nevada, Las Vegas (hereafter Broudy Papers).

50. Atomic Energy Commission Minutes, February 23, 1955, 117–23, Broudy Papers Box 76, Folder 4.

51. Harry S. Truman, *Memoirs by Harry S. Truman*, vol. 2: *Years of Trial and Hope* (Garden City, N.Y.: Doubleday, 1956), 312.

52. See Paul Jacobs, "Clouds from Nevada," *The Reporter* (May 16, 1957), 14; Miller, *Under the Cloud*.

53. Interview with Dina Titus, September 28, 2004, 3 and 8, in Test Site Oral History Project.

54. Divine, *Blowing on the Wind*, 53 and 55; Harry S. Truman, "Truman Predicts Fall-Out Answer," *New York Times* (May 28, 1957), 17.

55. Atomic Test Effects in the Nevada Test Site Region (United States Atomic Energy Commission, 1955), accessed August 13, 2016, https://www.fourmilab.ch/etexts/www/atomic_tests_nevada/#12.

56. "The Facts about A-Bomb 'Fall-Out': Not a Word of Truth in Scare Stories over Tests," *U.S. News and World Report* (March 25, 1955), 21–26.

57. *Plumbbob Off-Site Rad-Safety*, 19–20, Broudy Papers, Box 76, Folder 4.

58. "Nevada A-Fallout Reports 'Exaggerated,' Meet Told," *Las Vegas Sun* (July 18, 1957), 1; "Doctor Confirms AEC Statements," *Las Vegas Sun* (September 2, 1957), 6.

59. Garber Davidson, "Las Vegans Enjoy Those Atom Jolts," *Los Angeles Times* (February 11, 1951), 3.

60. Coates quoted in "Vegans Don't Scare Easily Los Angeles Reporter Learns," *Las Vegas Review-Journal* (February 7, 1951), 3.

61. Hill, "Atomic Boom Town," 158.

62. Daniel Lang, "Our Far-Flung Correspondents: Blackjack and Flashes," *New Yorker* (September 20, 1952), 101–9.

63. *Luskey's Official Las Vegas Criss Cross Directory* (Santa Ana, Calif.: Luskey Brothers and Company, 1956), 10; Katharine Best and Katharine Hillyer, *Las Vegas: Playtown U.S.A.* (New York: David McKay, 1955), 159; "Las Vegas: Dice, Dollars and Doom Town," *Fortnight*, June 1955, 46; ad, *Las Vegas Sun* (May 29, 1957), 15; Angela Moor, "Operation Hospitality: Las Vegas and Civil Defense, 1951–1959," *Nevada Historical Society Quarterly* 51, no. 4 (2008): 293.

64. John O'Brian and Jeremy Borsos, *Atomic Postcards: Radioactive Messages from the Cold War* (Chicago: University of Chicago Press, 2011), 108–13; Titus, *Bombs in the Backyard*, 94.

65. "Lili St. Cyr Weds Actor Ted Jordan," *San Mateo (Calif.) Times* (February 22, 1955); Larry Gragg, "'They Weren't My Kind of Audience': Elvis Presley's First Appearance in Las Vegas in 1956," *Nevada in the West* 6, no. 4 (2015): 6.

66. *Las Vegas: Playground U.S.A.* (Las Vegas: Las Vegas News Bureau, 1956), YouTube, accessed February 1, 2017, https://www.youtube.com/watch?v=5029W7XqlPM.

67. A. Constandina Titus, "Cultural Fallout in the Atomic Age," in *History and Humanities: Essays in Honor of Wilbur S. Shepperson*, ed. Francis X. Hartigan (Reno: University of Nevada Press, 1989), 131–32.

68. Dick Odessky, "Talk of the Town," *Las Vegas Sun* (April 15, 1953), 10.

69. Michael Scheibach, *Atomic Narratives and American Youth: Coming of Age with the Atom, 1945–1955* (Jefferson, N.C.: McFarland and Company, 2003), 173.

70. Ibid., 164; Ferenc Morton Szasz, *Atomic Comics: Cartoonists Confront the Nuclear World* (Reno: University of Nevada Press, 2012), 81.

71. Oak Ridge Associated Universities Health Physics Historical Instrumentation Museum Collection, accessed July 24, 2016, http://www.orau.org.

72. Joyce A. Evans, *Celluloid Mushroom Clouds: Hollywood and the Atomic Bomb* (Boulder, Colo.: Westview Press, 1998), 75–112.

73. Kenneth Frogley Oral History, n.d., Special Collections and Archives, University Libraries, University of Nevada, Las Vegas.

74. "Bill Willard," *Las Vegas Sun* (December 13, 1952), 5.

75. William Writley to Al Freeman, June 15, 1953, Sands Hotel Collection, Box 66.

76. Don English, interview with author, August 2, 2005.

77. Gladwin Hill, "Atomic Test Gets Elaborate Plans," *New York Times* (April 17, 1955), 42.

78. Val Peterson to Al Freeman, March 14, 1955, Box 49, Folder 3, Sands Collection.

79. Al Freeman to Jack Entratter, April 4, 1955, Box 49, Folder 3, Sands Collection; Dick Odessky, *Fly on the Wall: Recollections of Las Vegas' Good Old, Bad Old Days* (Las Vegas: Huntington Press Publishing, 1999), 86.

80. Al Freeman to Jack Entratter, March 28, 1955, Box 49, Folder 3, Sands Collection.

81. Jake Freedman to Our Press, Atomic Test Observers, and Government Friends, April 26, 1955, Box 49, Folder 3, Sands Collection.

82. Al Freeman to Jack Entratter, May 11, 1955, Box 49, Folder 3, Sands Collection.

83. For example, see "Mightiest Atom Test Rocks, Fires Desert," *Oakland Tribune* (July 5, 1957), 3.

84. Al Freeman to Jack Entratter, May 7, 1957, Box 7, Folder 2, Sands Collection; Les Devor, "Vegas Vagaries," *Las Vegas Review-Journal* (May 22, 1957), 5; Al Freeman, ed., *Sands Times*, December 1958, 5.

85. Donald E. English interview, in Test Site Oral History Project, 3; "The Las Vegas I Remember: Interview with Don English," Transcript, KNPR, Las Vegas, 2005.

86. Quoted in Lawrence J. Mullen, *Las Vegas: Media and Myth* (Lanham, Md.: Lexington Books, 2007), 12.

87. "A-Ballet," *Las Vegas Review-Journal* (June 7, 1953), 14; "Angel's Dance," *Parade* (June 28, 1953), 2.

88. Jane Ann Morrison, "News Bureau Showed Sexy Sells," *Las Vegas Review-Journal* (May 7, 2012), accessed August 17, 2016, http://www.reviewjournal.com/life/las-vegas -history/news-bureau-showed-sexy-sells. Actually, English was not the first to do this. Four years earlier, Last Frontier publicist Harvey Diederich had a photo of Candy King, with cotton in a mushroom shape attached to her bathing suit, sent over the wire services, and most papers printed it with the caption: "It's Atomic." See "Bill Willard," *Las Vegas Sun* (March 9, 1953), 3; "It's Atomic," *El Paso (Tex.) Herald Post* (March 24, 1953), 6.

89. "The Las Vegas I Remember: Interview with Don English"; "There's Danger in Las Vegas," 37; O'Brian and Borsos, *Atomic Postcards*, 73.

90. "The Las Vegas I Remember: Interview with Don English."

91. Best and Hillyer, *Playtown U.S.A.*, 164.

92. U.S. Committee on Interstate and Foreign Commerce, Subcommittee on Oversight and Investigations, *"The Forgotten Guinea Pigs": A Report on Health Effects of Low-Level*

Radiation Sustained as a Result of the Nuclear Weapons Testing Program Conducted by the United States Government (Washington, D.C.: Government Printing Office, 1980), III.

93. *Advisory Committee on Human Radiation Experiments Final Report* (Washington, D.C.: Government Printing Office, 1995), 455. The threat to test site workers did not end when testing went underground. In December 1970 a ten-kiloton underground test broke through the surface, exposing nearly a hundred workers to radiation. See Larry and Alan Jones, *The Baneberry Disaster: A Generation of Atomic Fallout* (Reno: University of Nevada Press, 2017).

94. A. O. Sulzberger Jr., "Bomb-Test Records Found Inconclusive," *New York Times* (May 29, 1980), D19; Carl J. Johnson, "Cancer Incidence in an Area of Radioactive Fallout Downwind From the Nevada Test Site," *Journal of the American Medical Association* 251, no. 2 (January 13, 1984), 230–36.

95. *Human Radiation Experiments Final Report*, 482; Gary Turkak, "Atomic 'Time Bombs,'" *VFW: Veterans of Foreign Wars Magazine*, April 1998, 22–23.

96. Fox, *Downwind*, 160. The federal government did, however, decide to compensate veterans who participated in the tests and residents of the counties in Utah, Nevada, and Arizona nearest the Test Site who developed over a dozen types of cancer associated with radiation exposure. See Turkak, "'Time Bombs,'" 24; Sarah Kershaw, "Suffering Effects of 50's A-Bomb Tests," *New York Times*, Sept. 5, 2004, N19.

97. English interview, in Test Site Oral History Project, 13.

98. Best and Hillyer, *Playtown U.S.A.*, 159.

CHAPTER 9

1. Ad, January 19, 1960, *Las Vegas Sun*, 5.

2. "Gala Opening for 'Big Four,'" *Dallas Morning News* (January 22, 1960), Section 3, 7; Cecil Smith, "Nothing Serene at Summit Meeting," *Los Angeles Times* (January 25, 1960), A8; Ralph Pearl, *Las Vegas Is My Beat* (Toronto: Bantam Books, 1974), 59.

3. Shirley MacLaine, *My Lucky Stars: A Hollywood Memoir* (New York: Bantam, 1996), 77.

4. Les Devor, "Vegas Vagaries," *Las Vegas Review-Journal* (January 21, 1960), 18; Ralph Pearl, "Vegas Daze and Nites," *Las Vegas Sun* (January 22, 1960), 4.

5. Robert Legare, "Meeting at the Summit: Sinatra and His Buddies Bust 'Em Up in Vegas," *Playboy* (June 1960), 34–37, 48, and 97–100.

6. James Kaplan and the Editors of *Life*, *The Rat Pack: The Original Bad Boys* (New York: Life Books, 2013), 70.

7. Bob Thomas, "Filming of 'Ocean's 11' Actually Being Started," *Press-Telegram* (Long Beach, Calif.) (January 18, 1960), 18; Lawford quote in Nancy Sinatra, *Frank Sinatra: My Father* (New York: Pocket Books, 1986), 135; Shawn Levy, *Rat Pack Confidential* (New York: Anchor Books, 1998), 108.

8. Philip K. Scheuer, "Las Vegas Swarms with Movie Stars," *Los Angeles Times*, February 2, 1960, 23; Hedda Hopper, "Film Companies Rock Desert City," *Los Angeles Times* (February 8, 1960), C10.

9. Gene Tuttle, "'Oceans' Eleven' World Premier Proves One of the Greatest," *Los Vegas Review-Journal* (August 4, 1960), 5; Ralph Pearl, "Vegas Daze and Nites," *Las Vegas Sun*

(August 5, 1960), 4; Philip K. Scheuer, "Sinatra Premieres 'Ocean's Eleven,'" *Los Angeles Times* (August 5, 1960), A7; Monique Van Dooren, "Actress Prefers 'Quiet' New York to Vegas," *Daily Reporter* (Dover, Ohio) (August 24, 1960), 11.

10. Graham Payn and Sheridan Morley, eds., *The Noël Coward Diaries* (London: Weidenfeld and Nicolson, 1982), 270; Lauren Bacall, *By Myself and Then Some* (New York: Harper, 2006), 249; Rat Pack, Part 1: Humphrey Bogart Sings!, July 9, 1955, accessed December 17, 2017, https://www.youtube.com/watch?v=WPV58b6es68; James Kaplan, *Sinatra: The Chairman* (New York: Doubleday, 2015), 57; Stephen Humphrey Bogart, *Bogart: In Search of My Father* (New York: Dutton, 1995), 55. While this version seems the most plausible, there are various origin stories about the Rat Pack.

11. Kaplan, *Chairman*, 235.

12. Paul O'Neil, "The 'Clan' Is the Most," *Life* (December 22, 1958), 116.

13. Ibid., 121.

14. Ibid.

15. Richard Gehman, "The Enigma of Frank Sinatra," *Good Housekeeping*, July 1960, 60; Tom Allen, "Question: Will Clan (Not Klan) Be Political Issue?" *Sunday World-Herald (Omaha) Magazine* (August 28, 1960), 4.

16. "Frank Sinatra—John Kennedy Las Vegas, Jan 1960," YouTube, accessed December 29, 2017, https://www.youtube.com/watch?v=3_cYfaOXb_U&t=63s; Allen, "Question," 4.

17. Steven Watts, *JFK and the Masculine Mystique: Sex and Power on the New Frontier* (New York: Thomas Dunne, 2016), 88; Kaplan, *Rat Pack*, 87.

18. There is a short home movie of Kennedy's visit on YouTube: "JFK in Las Vegas 1960 & Ocean's Eleven Set," accessed December 29, 2017, https://www.youtube.com/watch?v=d-9EbdEga5I.

19. Forrest Duke, "The Visiting Fireman," *Las Vegas Review-Journal* (January 31, 1960), 3; "Vegans Plan Gala Monday Reception for Sen. Kennedy," *Las Vegas Sun* (February 2, 1960), 1; "Kennedy Admits Primaries Hold Key to His Nomination Plans," *Las Vegas Sun* (February 9, 1960), 1; Bart Lytton Oral History Interview: JFK1, June 18, 1966, 7–9, John F. Kennedy Presidential Library and Museum.

20. Gary Fishgall, *Gonna Do Great Things: The Life of Sammy Davis, Jr.* (New York: Scribner, 2003), 155.

21. April 1, 1960, memo to Hoover, in *The Sinatra Files: The Secret FBI Dossier*, ed. Tom Kuntz and Phil Kuntz (New York: Three Rivers Press, 2000), 132–33.

22. Quoted in Kaplan, *Rat Pack*, 88.

23. Judith Exner, as told to Ovid Demaris, *Judith Exner: My Story* (New York: Grove Press, 1977), 86; James N. Giglio, *The Presidency of John F. Kennedy* (Lawrence: University Press of Kansas, 2006), 149–50.

24. Max Rudin, "Fly Me to the Moon: Reflections on the Rat Pack," *American Heritage* 49, no. 8 (1998), 54.

25. Forrest Duke, "The Visiting Fireman," *Las Vegas Review-Journal* (February 18, 1960), 5.

26. "Confirm Mafia's 'Nevada Scheme,'" *Las Vegas Sun* (January 30, 1960), 1; "Apalachin's Mob Is In—and Its Secret Is Out," *Life* (January 25, 1960), 25; Ronald Farrell and Carole Case, *The Black Book and the Mob: The Untold Story of the Control of Nevada*

Casinos (Madison: University of Wisconsin Press, 1995), 37. Three years later, Sinatra surrendered his gaming license for the Cal-Neva Lodge at Lake Tahoe, where he was one of the owners, because he had permitted Sam Giancana, one of the men included in the Black Book, to be on the property. See "Sinatra Gives Up Gaming License," *Reno Evening Gazette* (October 8, 1963), 1.

27. *Ocean's Eleven*, prod. and dir. Lewis Milestone, 127 mins. (Warner Brothers, 1960).

28. Dave Calvert, "Similar Hats on Similar Heads: Uniformity and Alienation at the Rat Pack's Summit Conference of Cool," *Popular Music* 34, no. 1 (2015), 12.

29. Watts, *JFK and the Masculine Mystique*, 84–85; Calvert, "Similar Hats," 15; Karen McNally, *When Frankie Went to Hollywood: Frank Sinatra and American Male Identity* (Urbana: University of Illinois Press, 2008), 175.

30. Sinatra, *Sinatra, My Father*, 133.

31. Calvert, "Similar Hats," 14.

32. Quotes in Sinatra, *Sinatra, My Father*, 133; Watts, *JFK and the Masculine Mystique*, 376n17.

33. Legare, "Meeting at the Summit," 48; Forrest Duke, "The Visiting Fireman," *Las Vegas Review-Journal* (February 2, 1960), 3.

34. Legare, "Meeting at the Summit," 98; Calvert, "Similar Hats," 15–16.

35. Ralph Pearl, "Vegas Daze and Nites," *Las Vegas Sun* (August 9, 1960), 4.

36. Paul Anka, with David Dalton, *My Way: An Autobiography* (New York: St. Martin's Press, 2013), 2 and 64.

37. Johnny Mathis interviews with author, September 15, 2015; November 8, 2017.

38. Forrest Duke, "The Visiting Fireman," *Las Vegas Review-Journal* (February 2, 1960), 3.

39. Kaplan, *Chairman*, 297 and 340.

40. Forrest Duke, "Vegas' Zillion-$ Five," *Variety* (February 24, 1960), 111.

41. Larry Gragg, "'Noel Coward Wows 'Em in Café Town': The Impact of Noel Coward's 1955 Performance at the Desert Inn," *Nevada Historical Society Quarterly* 53, no. 2 (2010): 121.

42. "Irma Premiere is Brought to Close Early This Morn," *Las Vegas Review-Journal* (June 27, 1950), 2; "Film Beauty Mobbed by Unruly Premiere Crowd," *Las Vegas Sun* (February 13, 1952), 1; "Vegas Enjoys Publicity Boon via TV, Premiere," *Las Vegas Sun* (February 22, 1956), 1; "Gala 'Joker Is Wild' Premiere," *Las Vegas Sun* (August 25, 1957), 6.

43. Garry Boulard, *Louis Prima* (Urbana: University of Illinois Press, 1989), 107 and 113.

44. Forrest Duke, "The Visiting Fireman," *Las Vegas Review-Journal* (January 28, 1960), 3; Forrest Duke, "The Visiting Fireman," *Las Vegas Review-Journal* (February 1, 1960), 3.

45. Kaplan, *Chairman*, 229; Mike Connolly, "Mr. Hollywood," *Independent* (Pasadena, Calif.) (October 11, 1958), 8.

46. David G. Schwartz, "JFK in Las Vegas," *Vegas Seven* (July 2, 2013), accessed December 30, 2017, http://vegasseven.com/2013/07/02/jfk-las-vegas-2/; photo caption: "Senator Kennedy Visits," *Las Vegas Review-Journal* (November 10, 1957), 1.

47. Sammy Davis, Jr., *Hollywood in a Suitcase* (New York: Morrow, 1980), 84.

48. Legare, "Meeting at the Summit," 35.

49. Quotes are in Deana Martin, with Wendy Holden, *Memories Are Made of This: Dean Martin through His Daughter's Eyes* (New York: Three Rivers Press, 2004), 91; Sinatra, *Sinatra, My Father*, 135; George Stamos Jr., "The Great Resorts of Las Vegas: How They Began," *Las Vegas Sun Magazine* (June 17, 1979), 8; Tracey Davis and Nina Bunche Pierce, *Sammy Davis, Jr.: A Personal Journey with My Father* (Philadelphia: Running Press, 2014), 85; Joy Garner, interview with author, November 27, 2017; Pearl, *Las Vegas*, 61.

50. Legare is a good example in his "Meeting at the Summit," 34.

51. Watts, *JFK and the Masculine Mystique*, 79; Tom Santopietro, *Sinatra in Hollywood* (New York: Thomas Dunne, 2008), 285; Lawrence J. Quirk and William Schoell, *The Rat Pack: Neon Nights and the Kings of Cool* (New York: Perennial, 2002), 184; Ronald Brownstein, *The Power and the Glitter: The Hollywood-Washington Connection* (New York: Pantheon Books, 1990), 155.

52. Richard Lacayo, "Ring-A-Ding Ding," *Time*, May 25, 1998, 73.

53. Angie Dickinson quoted in Michael Starr, *Mouse in the Rat Pack: The Joey Bishop Story* (New York: Taylor, 2002), 62.

54. John M. Findlay, *People of Chance: Gambling in American Society from Jamestown to Las Vegas* (New York: Oxford University Press, 1986), 144.

55. John M. Findlay, *Magic Lands: Western Cityscapes and American Culture after 1940* (Berkeley: University of California Press, 1992), 91.

56. Gladwin Hill, "Disneyland Gets Its Last Touches," *New York Times* (July 9, 1955), 32. Two good biographies of Walt Disney include discussions of his amusement park: Neal Gabler, *Walt Disney: The Triumph of the American Imagination* (New York: Random House, 2006); Steven Watts, *The Magic Kingdom: Walt Disney and the American Way of Life* (Columbia: University of Missouri Press, 2006).

57. Julian Halevy, "Disneyland and Las Vegas," *Nation* (June 7, 1958), 513.

58. Caskie Stinnett, "Las Vegas: Where Anything Is Forgivable Except Restraint," *Holiday*, May 1967, 32.

59. Charles Champlin, "Making the World Safe for Frivolity," *Los Angeles West Magazine* (October 19, 1969), 68, 74, and 75.

60. Stinnett, "Las Vegas."

AFTERWORD

1. Las Vegas Convention and Visitors Authority, Historical Las Vegas Visitor Statistics (1970–2017), accessed February 1, 2018, http://www.lvcva.com/includes/content/images/media/docs/Historical-1970-to-2017.pdf.

2. The best account of Sarno's work is David G. Schwartz, *Grandissimo: The First Emperor of Las Vegas* (Las Vegas: Winchester Books, 2013).

3. There are two full-length biographies of Kerkorian: Dial Torgerson, *Kerkorian: An American Success Story* (New York: Dial Press, 1974); William C. Rempel, *The Gambler: How Penniless Dropout Kirk Kerkorian Became the Greatest Deal Maker in Capitalist History* (New York: Dey Street Books, 2018).

4. "Las Vegas: The Game is Illusion," *Time* (July 11, 1969), 32.

5. Eugene Moehring and Michael Green labeled Wynn's work as the "Mirage Revolution." See Moehring and Green, *Las Vegas: A Centennial History* (Reno: University

of Nevada Press, 2005), 210. While many developers succeeded, as in the 1950s, there was a series of failed projects after 1960. For a good summary of those efforts, see Arnold M. Knightly, "A History of Landmarks Never Built," *Las Vegas Review-Journal* (August 31, 2014), accessed February 10, 2018, https://www.reviewjournal.com/news/a-history-of-landmarks-never-built/.

6. John L. Scott, "The Clan Cuts Up at Sands Outing," *Los Angeles Times* (April 16, 1966), 20.

7. Richard Goldstein, "A White Boy with Black Hips," *New York Times* (August 10, 1969), D22.

8. Robert Hilburn, "Fan to Fan: What's Happened to Elvis," *Los Angeles Times* (February 6, 1972), Y44.

9. Ron Rosenbaum, "Do You Know Vegas?" *Esquire*, August 1982, 64; Robert Windeler, "The Most Successful Performer in Vegas History? Not Frank, Not Elvis—It's Wayne Newton," *People Weekly* (April 30, 1979), 89.

10. Richard Joseph, "Las Vegas Now Bigger and Brassier Than Ever," *Chicago Daily Tribune* (January 31, 1965), F6.

11. Peter Bart, "Celebrating the Celine Machine," *Daily Variety* (March 31, 2003), 3.

12. Gary Dretzka, "The Magic of Las Vegas," *Chicago Daily Tribune* (July 7, 1996), Section 8, 1.

13. Phil Gallo, "Dion Ends 'Day' in Vegas with $400 mil.," *Daily Variety* (December 14, 2007), 4.

14. Sandy Smith, "How Top Gangsters Siphon Off $6 Million a Year at Las Vegas," *Chicago Sun-Times*, July 10, 1966, 1.

15. "F.B.I. Harassment Charged in Nevada," *New York Times* (September 2, 1966), 1 and 32; Peter R. Kann, "Nevada Agency Denies Casinos in Las Vegas 'Skimmed' Large Sums," *Wall Street Journal* (September 2, 1966), 1.

16. Geoff Schumacher, *Howard Hughes: Power, Paranoia and Palace Intrigue* (Las Vegas: Stephens Press, 2008), 29.

17. Wallace Turner, "Howard Hughes Captures Imagination of Las Vegas as He Fashions Nevada Empire," *New York Times* (January 14, 1968), 69; Bob Considine, "Desert Develops Skyline," *Lowell (Mass.) Sun* (January 15, 1968), 5.

18. "Nevada May Bar Spilotro From Clubs," *Chicago Daily Tribune* (June 26, 1978), 6.

19. For an account of these prosecutions, see Kenneth J. Peak and William N. Ousley, "The FBI's 'Strawman': Breaking the Kansas City Mob's Connection to Las Vegas," *Missouri Historical Review* 104, no. 2 (2010): 106–7.

20. Trip Gabriel, "From Vice to Nice: The Suburbanization of Las Vegas," *New York Times* (December 1, 1991), SM79.

21. Jeffrey J. Sallaz, "Civil Rights and Employment Equity in Las Vegas Casinos: The Failed Enforcement of the Casino Consent Decree, 1971–1986," *Nevada Historical Society Quarterly* 47, no. 4 (2004): 283–93; Eugene P. Moehring, *Resort City in the Sunbelt: Las Vegas, 1930–2000* (Reno: University of Nevada Press, 2000), 186–99.

22. Moehring, *Resort City*, 202.

23. Jim Seagrave, interview with author, April 1, 2006; Dick Odessky, *Fly on the Wall: Recollections of Las Vegas' Good Old, Bad Old Days* (Las Vegas: Huntington Press, 2010), 47.

24. John Katsilometes, "A Look Back at the Advertising Magic of 'What Happens Here, Stays Here,'" *Las Vegas Sun* (October 5, 2011), accessed February 10, 2018, https://lasvegassun.com/blogs/kats-report/2011/oct/05/look-back-advertising-magic -what-happens-here-stay/.

25. Bruce Bégout, *Zeropolis: The Experience of Las Vegas*, trans. Liz Heron (London: Reaktion Books, 2003), 11, 22, 29, and 84.

26. Mario Puzo, *Inside Las Vegas* (New York: Grosset and Dunlap, 1976), 18.

27. Ibid., 24.

28. Ibid., 20.

29. Ibid., 16 and 55.

30. Rob Schultheis, "Yes!! It's . . . Las Vegas!!!!! An Unabashed Frolic in the City Where Dreams Work Overtime and Inhibitions Take a Holiday," *National Geographic Traveler*, May/June 1991, 107–14.

31. "Year of the Tiger," *Las Vegas*, prod. Daniel Arkin, dir. Perry Lang, 60 mins. (Gary Scott Thompson Productions, 2003); "Pilot," *Las Vegas*, prod. Preston Fischer, dir. Michael W. Watkins, 60 mins. (Gary Scott Thompson Productions, 2003).

32. Edward Allen, "Penny Ante," in *Literary Las Vegas: The Best Writing About America's Most Fabulous City*, ed. Mike Tronnes (New York: Henry Holt, 1995), 315.

Bibliography

MANUSCRIPT COLLECTIONS

Lacey, Robert, Collection, 1980–1989. Nevada State Museum, Las Vegas.

McCarran, Patrick, Papers. Nevada Historical Society, Reno.

NAACP Records, Las Vegas File. Library of Congress.

Special Collections and Archives, University Libraries, University of Nevada, Las Vegas.
    Broudy, Alice P. Papers on Broudy v. United States, 1948–2006.
    Butterfield, Spencer and Georgia, Collection, 1912–1975.
    Clark, Donald, Collection, 1953–1972.
    Clark, Wilbur and Toni, Collection, 1947–1991.
    Dottie Dee Dancers Collection, 1940s–2002.
    Dunes Hotel Collection, 1955–1991.
    Fluke, David, Papers on Las Vegas Entertainers, 1946–1983.
    Frontier Hotel and Casino Collection, 1942–1988.
    James, Virginia, Papers, 1949–1982.
    Kaufman, Perry, Papers, 1930–1974.
    Las Vegas Chamber of Commerce Records, 1911–2014.
    Las Vegas City Commission Minutes, 1911–1960.
    Lewis, Maxine, Flamingo Bookings, 1948–1951.
    Nevada Biltmore Hotel Collection, 1942–1986.
    Nevada Desert Experience Records, 1957–2007.
    Perkins, James, Collection, 1951–1952.
    Real Las Vegas Interviews, 1996.
    Sands Hotel Collection, 1952–1979.
    Union Pacific Railroad Collection, 1902–1969.
    Willard, Bill, Collection, 1887–1999.

ORAL HISTORIES

Blue, Helen M. and Jamie Coughtry. *Clarence Ray: Black Politics and Gaming in Las Vegas, 1920s–1980s.* Reno: University of Nevada Oral History Program, 1991.

Cahlan, Florence Lee Jones. Oral History. University Libraries, University of Nevada, Las Vegas, 1973.

Coughtry, Jamie. *John F. Cahlan: Fifty Years in Journalism and Community Development* Reno: University of Nevada Oral History Program, 1987.

Coughtry, Jamie, and R. T. King. *George L. Ullom: Politics and Development in Las Vegas, 1930s–1970s*. Reno: University of Nevada Oral History Program, 1989.

Coughtry, Jamie, and R. T. King. *Lubertha Johnson: Civil Rights Efforts in Las Vegas, 1940s–1960s*. Reno: University of Nevada Oral History Program, 1988.

———. *Woodrow Wilson: Race, Community and Politics in Las Vegas, 1940s–1980s*. Reno: University of Nevada Oral History Program, 1990.

Culver, Mary Ann. Oral History. University Libraries, University of Nevada, Las Vegas, 1981.

Denton, Ralph, Michael S. Green, and R. T. King. *A Liberal Conscience: The Oral History of Ralph Denton, Nevadan*. Reno: University of Nevada Oral History Program, 2001.

Duke, Forrest. Oral History. University Libraries, University of Nevada, Las Vegas, 1977.

Eckstine, Billy. Oral History. University Libraries, University of Nevada, Las Vegas, 1987.

Ensley, Boysie. Oral History. University Libraries, University of Nevada, Las Vegas, 1972.

Frogley, Kenneth. Oral History. University Libraries, University of Nevada, Las Vegas, n.d.

Glass, Mary Ellen. *Charles H. Russell: Reminiscences of a Nevada Congressman, Governor, and Legislator*. Reno: University of Nevada Oral History Program, 1967.

———. *John F. Cahlan: Reminiscences of a Reno and Las Vegas, Nevada Newspaperman, University Regent, and Public-Spirited Citizen*. Reno: University of Nevada Oral History Program, 1970.

———. *Lester Ben "Benny" Binion: Some Recollections of a Texas and Las Vegas Gambling Operator*. Reno: University of Nevada Oral History Program, 1976.

———. *Norman H. Biltz: Memoirs of the "Duke of Nevada."* Reno: University of Nevada Oral History Program, 1969.

———. *Robbins E. Cahill: Recollections of Work in State Politics, Government, Taxation, Gaming Control, Clark County Administration, and the Nevada Resort Association*. 4 vols. Reno: University of Nevada Oral History Program, 1977.

Green, B. Leon. Interview with Eddie Wright, Jr., and Johnie B. Wright. Las Vegas: African American Collaborative, Oral History Research Center, University Libraries, University of Nevada, 2012.

Grygo, John, and Claytee D. White. Interview with Jocelyn Oats. Las Vegas: African American Collaborative, Oral History Research Center, University Libraries, University of Nevada, 2012.

Irwin, Stan. Oral History. Las Vegas: University Libraries, University of Nevada, 2009.

James, Virginia. Oral History Video. Las Vegas: University Libraries, University of Nevada,.

"The Las Vegas I Remember: Interview with Don English." KNPR. Las Vegas, Nevada, June 20, 2005.

"The Las Vegas I Remember: Interview with Tracy Heberling." KNPR. Las Vegas, Nevada, June 20, 2005.

"The Las Vegas I Remember: Interview with Oran Gragson." KNPR, Las Vegas, Nevada, July 12, 2005.

Bart Lytton Oral History Interview. JFK1, June 18, 1966. John F. Kennedy Presidential Library and Museum.

Marshall, Joyce. Interview with Betty Bunch. Las Vegas: Las Vegas Women in Gaming and Entertainment, Oral History Project, University of Nevada, 2009.

McCurdy, Greg. Interview with Lovey McCurdy. Las Vegas: African American Collaborative, Oral History Research Center, University Libraries, University of Nevada, 2012.

McMillan, James, Gary E. Elliott, and R. T. King. *Fighting Back: A Life in the Struggle for Civil Rights*. Reno: University of Nevada Oral History Program, 1997.

Molasky, Irwin. Oral History. Las Vegas: University Libraries, University of Nevada, 1999.

Nevada Test Site. Oral History Project. Las Vegas: University Libraries, University of Nevada, 2008.

Olsen, Edward A. *My Careers as a Journalist in Oregon, Idaho, and Nevada; in Nevada Gaming Control; and at the University of Nevada*. Reno: University of Nevada Oral History Program, 1972.

Sawyer, Grant, Gary E. Elliott, and R. T. King. *Hang Tough! Grant Sawyer, An Activist in the Governor's Mansion*. Reno: University of Nevada Oral History Program, 1993.

Wanderer, Emilie N., and Joanne L. Goodwin. *"A Thousand to One": The Story of Emilie N. Wanderer, the First Woman to Practice Law in Las Vegas*. Las Vegas: Las Vegas Women Oral History Project, University of Nevada, 2005.

White, Claytee D. Interview with Agnes Marshall. Las Vegas: African American Collaborative, Oral History Research Center, University Libraries, University of Nevada, 2012.

———. Interview with Alice Key. Las Vegas: Las Vegas Women in Gaming and Entertainment, Oral History Project, University Libraries, University of Nevada, 1998.

———. Interview with Alma Whitney. Las Vegas: African American Collaborative, Oral History Research Center, University Libraries, University of Nevada, 1997.

———. Interview with Anna Bailey. Las Vegas: Las Vegas Women's Oral History Project, Gaming and Entertainment Series, University of Nevada, 1997.

———. Interview with Hazel Geran. Las Vegas: African American Collaborative, Oral History Research Center, University Libraries, University of Nevada, 2012.

———. Interview with J. David Hoggard. Las Vegas: African American Collaborative, Oral History Research Center, University Libraries, University of Nevada, 2012.

———. Interview with Jerry Eppenger. Las Vegas: African American Collaborative, Oral History Research Center, University Libraries, University of Nevada, 2007.

———. Interview with Marzette Lewis. Las Vegas: African American Collaborative, Oral History Research Center, University Libraries, University of Nevada, 2012.

———. Interview with Nathaniel Whaley. Las Vegas: African American Collaborative, Oral History Research Center, University Libraries, University of Nevada, 2012.

———. Interview with Ruth Eppenger D'Hondt. Las Vegas: African American Collaborative, Oral History Research Center, University Libraries, University of Nevada, 2012.

———. Interview with Shirley Edmond. Las Vegas: African American Collaborative, Oral History Research Center, University Libraries, University of Nevada, 2007.

———. Interview with Thelma Turner. Las Vegas: African American Collaborative, Oral History Research Center, University Libraries, University of Nevada, 2007.

INTERVIEWS BY AUTHOR
Diederich, Harvey. August 10, 2005.
English, Don. August 2, 2005.
Garner, Joy. November 17, 2017.
Jones, Judy. March 22, 2011.
Mathis, Johnny. September 2, 2015, and November 8, 2017.
Payne, Don. August 2, 2005.
Ryba, Joan. April 9, 2011.
Seagrave, Jim. April 1, 2006.

UNPUBLISHED MANUSCRIPTS
Cole, Timothy. "Growing Up Nuclear: Las Vegas Children and the Bomb." Ph.D. dissertation, University of Calgary, 2006.
Elliott, Gary. "The Moulin Rouge Hotel: Critical Appraisal of a Las Vegas Legend." University Libraries, University of Nevada, Las Vegas.
Esau, Valda. "From Paris to Las Vegas." Memoir in author's collection.
Fitzgerald, Roosevelt. "A Demographic Impact of Basic Magnesium on Southern Nevada." University Libraries, University of Nevada, Las Vegas.
———. "The Evolution of a Black Community in Las Vegas: 1905–1940." University Libraries, University of Nevada, Las Vegas.
Johnson, Michael. "Transforming the 'Old West' into 'Modern Splendor': The Suppression of Brothel Prostitution in Las Vegas." Paper presented at the Biennial Conference on Nevada History, Las Vegas, Nevada, May 24, 2006.
Jones, Judy. Memoirs in author's collection.
Kaufman, Perry. "Best City of Them All: A History of Las Vegas, 1930–1960." Ph.D. dissertation, University of California, Santa Barbara, 1960.
Moody, Eric N. "The Early Years of Casino Gambling in Nevada, 1931–1945." Ph.D. dissertation, University of Nevada, Reno, 1997.
Rostine, Irene B. Scholl. "Our Turn: Working Women in the Las Vegas Valley, 1940–1980." Master's thesis, University of Nevada, Las Vegas, 2013.
Rowley, Marie Katherine. "'So Much for Fond Five-Dollar Memories': Prostitution in Las Vegas, 1905–1955." Master's thesis, University of Nevada, Las Vegas, 2012.
Ver Hulst, Leta Lafay. "The Creation of the Las Vegas Image: A Case Study of Harvey Diederich." Master's thesis, University of Nevada, Las Vegas, 1999.

NEWSPAPERS

Afro-American (Baltimore)
Anderson (Ind.) Daily Bulletin
Boston American
Boston Sunday Advertiser
Charleston (W.Va.) Gazette
Chicago Daily Tribune
Chicago Defender
Clark County (Nev.) Review
Daily Reporter (Dover, Ohio)
Daily Variety
Dallas Morning News
El Paso (Tex.) Herald Post
Evening Star (Washington, D.C.)
Evening World-Herald (Omaha, Neb.)
Eureka (Calif.) Humboldt Standard
Galveston News
Illinois State Journal-Register
Independent (Pasadena)
Independent Telegram (Long Beach, Calif.)
Kingsport (Tenn.) Times
Laredo (Tex.) Times
Las Vegas Age
Las Vegas Review-Journal
Las Vegas Sun
Lima (Ohio) News
Los Angeles Times
Lowell (Mass.) Sun
Morning Advocate (Baton Rouge)
Nevada Courier
Nevada State Journal

Newport (R.I.) Daily News
Oakland Tribune
Ogden (Utah) Standard-Examiner
Oregonian
Panama City (Fla.) News-Herald
Pahrump (Nev.) Valley Times
Pioche (Nev.) Record
Pittsburgh Courier
Plain Dealer (Cleveland)
Plaindealer (Kansas City, Kans.)
Post-Standard (Syracuse)
Press-Telegram (Long Beach, Calif.)
Reno Evening Gazette
Sacramento Bee
Salt Lake Tribune
San Diego Union
San Mateo (Calif.) Times
Seattle Times
Springfield (Mass.) Union
Sun (Yuma, Ariz.)
Sunday Times Signal (Zanesville, Ohio)
Syracuse Herald-American
New York Times
Times-Picayune (New Orleans)
Vegas Seven
Voice (Las Vegas)
Wall Street Journal
Washington Afro-American
Washington Post
World-Herald (Omaha)

GOVERNMENT DOCUMENTS

Advisory Committee on Human Radiation Experiments Final Report. Washington, D.C.: Government Printing Office, 1995.

The Biological Effects of Atomic Radiation: Summary Reports from a Study by the National Academy of Sciences. Washington, D.C.: National Academy of Sciences, National Research Council, 1956.

Greenspun, Hank. FBI Files. FBI Records: The Vault. https://archive.org/details/HermanHankM.Greenspun.

Hearings before a Special Committee to Investigate Organized Crime in Interstate Commerce, Part 10. Washington, D.C.: Government Printing Office, 1950.

"In the Matter of International Spa, Inc." *Securities and Exchange Commission: Decisions and Reports*, vol. 36. Washington, D.C.: Government Printing Office, 1956: 618–25.

McClelland and Company. *Report of Las Vegas, Nevada, Housing Survey, December 1947.* Riverside, Calif.: McClelland, 1947.

The National Conference and the Reports of the State Advisory Committees to the U.S. Commission on Civil Rights, 1959. Washington, D.C.: Government Printing Office, 1960.

Siegel, Bugsy. FBI Files. FBI Records: The Vault. http://vault.fbi.gov/Bugsy%20Siegel.

State of California Third Progress Report of the Special Crime Study Commission on Organized Crime. Sacramento: Crime Study Commission, January 31, 1950.

U.S. Committee on Interstate and Foreign Commerce, Subcommittee on Oversight and Investigations. *"The Forgotten Guinea Pigs": A Report on Health Effects of Low-Level Radiation Sustained as a Result of the Nuclear Weapons Testing Program Conducted by the United States Government.* Washington, D.C.: Government Printing Office, 1980.

BOOKS

Al, Stefan. *The Strip: Las Vegas and the Architecture of the American Dream.* Cambridge, Mass.: MIT Press, 2017.

Allen, Edward. "Penny Ante." In *Literary Las Vegas: The Best Writing about America's Most Fabulous City,* edited by Mike Tronnes. New York: Henry Holt, 1995.

Anka, Paul with David Dalton. *My Way.* New York: St. Martin's Press, 2013.

Austin, Tom, and Ron Kase. *Bill Miller's Riviera: America's Showplace in Fort Lee, New Jersey.* Charleston, S.C.: History Press, 2011.

Bailey, William H. "Bob." *Looking Up: Finding My Voice in Las Vegas.* Las Vegas: Stephens Press, 2009.

Baker, Gale. *Neon Queens: Fifty Years of Las Vegas' "Finest Feathered Femmes."* Auburn, Calif.: eBookstand Books, 1999.

Baker, Jean-Claude. *Josephine: The Hungry Heart.* New York: Random House, 1993.

Balboni, Alan. "The Italians." In *The Peoples of Las Vegas: One City, Many Faces,* edited by Jerry L. Simich and Thomas C. Wright. Reno: University of Nevada Press, 2005.

———. "Moe Dalitz: Controversial Founding Father of Las Vegas." In *The Maverick Spirit: Building the New Nevada,* edited by Richard O. Davies. Reno: University of Nevada Press, 1999.

Ball, Howard. *Justice Downwind: America's Atomic Testing Program in the 1950's.* New York: Oxford University Press, 1986.

Barber, Alicia. *Reno's Big Gamble: Image and Reputation in the Biggest Little City.* Lawrence: University Press of Kansas, 2008.

Bégout, Bruce. *Zeropolis: The Experience of Las Vegas.* Translated by Liz Heron. London: Reaktion Books, 2003.

Beidler, Philip D. *The Island Called Paradise: Cuba in History, Literature, and the Arts.* Tuscaloosa: University of Alabama Press, 2014.

Belafonte, Harry, with Michael Shnayerson. *My Song: A Memoir.* New York: Alfred A. Knopf, 2011.

Berman, Susan. *Lady Las Vegas: The Inside Story behind America's Neon Oasis*. New York: TV Books, 1996.

Bernstein, Lee. *The Greatest Menace: Organized Crime in Cold War America*. Amherst, Mass.: University of Massachusetts Press, 2002.

Bessette, Roland L. *Mario Lanza: Tenor in Exile*. Portland, Ore.: Amadeus Press, 1999.

Best, Katharine, and Katharine Hillyer. *Las Vegas: Playtown U.S.A.* New York: David McKay, 1955.

Bogart, Stephen Humphrey. *Bogart: In Search of My Father*. New York: Dutton, 1995.

Bogle, Donald. *Dorothy Dandridge: A Biography*. New York: Amistad Press, 1997.

Boulard, Garry. *Louis Prima*. Paperback ed. Urbana: University of Illinois Press, 2002.

Boyer, Paul. *By the Dawn's Early Light: American Thought and Culture at the Dawn of the Atomic Age*. Paperback ed. Chapel Hill: University of North Carolina Press, 1994.

Bracey, Earnest N. *The Moulin Rouge and Black Rights in Las Vegas*. Jefferson, N.C.: McFarland, 2009.

Branch, Taylor. *Parting the Waters: America in the King Years, 1954–63*. Paperback ed. New York: Simon and Schuster, 1989.

Breines, Wini. *Young, White, and Miserable: Growing Up Female in the Fifties*. Boston: Beacon Press, 1992.

Brinkley, Douglas. *Cronkite*. New York: HarperCollins, 2012.

Brownstein, Ronald. *The Power and the Glitter: The Hollywood-Washington Connection*. New York: Pantheon Books, 1990.

Bubb, Daniel. *Landing in Vegas: Commercial Aviation and the Making of a Tourist City*. Reno: University of Nevada Press, 2012.

Buhite, Russell D. *Douglas MacArthur: Statecraft and Stagecraft in America's East Asian Policy*. Lanham, Md.: Rowman and Littlefield, 2008.

Bunch, Betty. *High Heels and Headdresses: Memoirs of a Vintage Vegas Showgirl*. Las Vegas: Stephens Press, 2011.

Burbank, Jeff. *License to Steal: Nevada's Gaming Control System in the Megaresort Age*. Paperback ed. Reno: University of Nevada Press, 2000.

Cairns, Kathleen A. *Front-Page Women Journalists, 1920–1950*. Lincoln: University of Nebraska Press, 2003.

Callender, Red, and Elaine Cohen. *Unfinished Dream: The Musical World of Red Callender*. London: Quartet Books, 1985.

Chafe, William H. *The Unfinished Journey: America Since World War II*. 8th ed. New York: Oxford University Press, 2015.

———. *Women and Equality: Changing Patterns in American Culture*. New York: Oxford University Press, 1978.

Chase, Linda. *Picturing Las Vegas*. Layton, Utah: Gibbs Smith, 2009.

Chilton, John. *Let the Good Times Roll: The Story of Louis Jordan and His Music*. Ann Arbor, Mich.: University of Michigan Press, 1994.

Clavin, Tom. *That Old Black Magic: Louis Prima, Keely Smith, and the Golden Age of Las Vegas*. Chicago: Chicago Press Review, 2010.

Cohen, Lizabeth. *A Consumer's Republic: The Politics of Mass Consumption in Postwar America*. New York: Alfred A. Knopf, 2001.

Cohen, Octavus Roy. *A Bullet for My Love*. New York: Macmillan, 1950.

Cohodas, Nadine. *The Life and Times of Dinah Washington*. New York: Pantheon Books, 2004.

Cole, Maria, with Louie Robinson. *Nat King Cole: An Intimate Biography*. New York: William Morrow, 1971.

Damone, Vic, with David Chanoff. *Singing Was the Easy Part*. New York: St. Martin's Press, 2009.

Davis, Sammy, Jr. *Hollywood in a Suitcase*. New York: Morrow, 1980.

Davis, Sammy, Jr., Jane Boyer, and Burt Boyer. *Sammy: An Autobiography: With Material Newly Revised from Yes I Can and Why Me?* New York: Farrar, Straus and Giroux, 2000.

Davis, Tracey, and Nina Bunche Pierce. *Sammy Davis, Jr.: A Personal Journey with My Father*. Philadelphia: Running Press, 2014.

Demaris, Ovid. *Judith Exner: My Story*. New York: Grove Press, 1977.

Devine, Robert A. *Blowing on the Wind: The Nuclear Test Ban Debate, 1954–1960*. New York: Oxford University Press, 1978.

Diggins, John Patrick. *The Proud Decades: America in War and in Peace, 1941–1960*. New York: W. W. Norton, 1988.

DiNardo, Kelly. *Gilded Lili: Lili St. Cyr and the Striptease Mystique*. New York: Backstage Books, 2007.

Dunar, Andrew J. *America in the Fifties*. Syracuse: Syracuse University Press, 2006.

Edwards, Jerome E. *Pat McCarran, Political Boss of Nevada*. Reno: University of Nevada Press, 1982.

Elliott, Gary E. *The New Western Frontier: An Illustrated History of Greater Las Vegas*. Carlsbad, Calif.: Heritage Media, 1999.

———. *Senator Alan Bible and the Politics of the New West*. Reno: University of Nevada Press, 1994.

English, T. J. *Havana Nocturne: How the Mob Owned Cuba—And Then Lost It to the Revolution*. New York: William Morrow, 2007.

Epstein, Daniel Mark. *Nat King Cole*. Paperback ed. Boston: Northeastern University Press, 2000.

Esau, Esper. *Las Vegas' Golden Era: Memoirs, 1954–1974*. Indianapolis: Dog Ear Publishing, 2016.

Evans, Joyce A. *Celluloid Mushroom Clouds: Hollywood and the Atomic Bomb*. Boulder, CO: Westview Press, 1998.

Evans, K. J. "Bill Miller." In *The First 100: Portraits of the Men and Women Who Shaped Las Vegas*. Ed. A. D. Hopkins and K. J. Evans. Las Vegas: Huntington Press, 1999.

Farrell, Ronald A., and Carole Case. *The Black Book and the Mob: The Untold Story of the Control of Nevada's Casinos*. Madison: University of Wisconsin Press, 1995.

Fehner, Terrence R., and F. G. Gosling. *Origins of the Nevada Test Site*. Washington, D.C.: U.S. Department of Energy, 2000.

Findlay, John M. *Magic Lands: Western Cityscapes and American Culture after 1940*. Berkeley: University of California Press, 1992.

———. *People of Chance: Gambling in American Society from Jamestown to Las Vegas*. New York: Oxford University Press, 1986.

Fisher, Eddie, with David Fisher. *Been There, Done That: An Autobiography.* Paperback ed. New York: St. Martin's Press, 2000.

Fishgall, Gary. *Gonna Do Great Things: The Life of Sammy Davis, Jr.* New York: Scribner, 2004.

Fox, Sarah Alisabeth. *Downwind: A People's History of the Nuclear West.* Lincoln: University of Nebraska Press, 2014.

Fuermann, George. *Houston: Land of the Big Rich.* New York: Doubleday and Company, 1951.

Fuller, John G. *The Day We Bombed Utah: America's Most Lethal Secret.* New York: New American Library, 1984.

Gabler, Neal. *Walt Disney: The Triumph of the American Imagination.* New York: Random House, 2006.

Gallup, George H. *The Gallup Poll: Public Opinion, 1935–1971,* vol. 2. New York: Random House, 1972.

Gehman, Richard. *Sinatra and the Rat Pack.* Paperback ed. New York: Belmont Productions, 1961.

Giglio, James N. *The Presidency of John F. Kennedy.* 2nd ed. Lawrence: University Press of Kansas, 2006.

Gioia-Acres, Lisa. *Showgirls of Las Vegas.* Charleston, S.C.: Arcadia Publishing, 2013.

Glass, Mary Ellen. *Nevada's Turbulent '50s: Decade of Political and Economic Change.* Reno: University of Nevada Press, 1981.

Goodwin, Joanne, L. *Changing the Game: Women at Work in Las Vegas, 1940–1980.* Reno: University of Nevada Press, 2014.

———. "'She Works Hard for Her Money': A Reassessment of Las Vegas Women Workers, 1945–1985." In *The Grit Beneath the Glitter: Tales From the Real Las Vegas,* edited by Hal K. Rothman and Mike Davis. Berkeley: University of California Press, 2002.

Gorman, Joseph Bruce. *Kefauver: A Political Biography.* New York: Oxford University Press, 1971.

Gourse, Leslie. *Every Day: The Story of Joe Williams.* London: Quartet Books, 1985.

———. *Unforgettable: The Life and Mystique of Nat King Cole.* New York: St. Martin's Press, 1991.

Gragg, Larry. "'Avoid Advertising the Obvious . . . Gambling': The Chamber of Commerce Promotion of Las Vegas in the 1950s." In *All In: Gambling in the Twentieth Century United States,* edited by Jonathan D. Cohen and David G. Schwartz. Reno: University of Nevada Press, 2018.

———. *Benjamin "Bugsy" Siegel: The Gangster, the Flamingo, and the Making of Modern Las Vegas.* Santa Barbara, Calif.: Praeger, 2015.

———. *Bright Light City: Las Vegas in Popular Culture.* Lawrence: University Press of Kansas, 2013.

Green, Michael S. "*Brown,* Integration, and Nevada," In *With All Deliberate Speed: Implementing Brown v. Board of Education,* edited by Brian J. Daugherity and Charles C. Bolton. Fayetteville: University of Arkansas Press, 2008.

———. *Nevada: A History of the Silver State.* Paperback ed. Reno: University of Nevada Press, 2015.

Grey, Joel, with Rebecca Paley. *Master of Ceremonies: A Memoir.* New York: Flatiron Books, 2016.

Hacker, Barton C. *Elements of Controversy: The Atomic Energy Commission and Radiation Safety in Nuclear Weapons Testing, 1947–1974.* Berkeley: University of California Press, 1994.

Halberstam, David. *The Fifties.* Paperback ed. New York: Random House, 1993.

Hampton, Lionel, with James Haskins. *Hamp: An Autobiography.* Paperback ed. New York: Amistad Press, 1993.

Hiltzik. Michael. *Colossus: Hoover Dam and the Making of the American Century.* New York: Free Press, 2010.

Hine, Thomas. *Populuxe.* New York: Alfred A. Knopf, 1986.

Hopkins, A. D. "Florence Lee Jones." In *The First 100: Portraits of the Men and Women Who Shaped Las Vegas,* edited by A. D. Hopkins and K. J. Evans. Las Vegas: Huntington Press, 1999.

Howe, Louise Kapp. *Pink Collar Workers: Inside the World of Women's Work.* New York: G. P. Putnam's Sons, 1977.

Hulse, James W. "Maude Frazier: Pioneering Educator and Lawmaker." In *The Maverick Spirit: Building the New Nevada,* edited by Richard O. Davies. Reno: University of Nevada Press, 1999.

Jakle, John A. *The Tourist: Travel in Twentieth-Century North America.* Lincoln: University of Nebraska Press, 1985.

Kahn, Roger. *Memories of Summer: When Baseball Was an Art, and Writing about It a Game.* New York: Hyperion, 1997.

Kaledin, Eugenia. *Mothers and More: American Women in the 1950s.* Boston: Twayne Publishers, 1984.

Kane, Frank. *A Short Bier.* New York: Dell Publishing, 1960.

Kaplan, James. *Frank: The Voice.* New York: Doubleday, 2010.

———. *Sinatra: The Chairman.* New York: Doubleday, 2015.

Kaplan, James, and the Editors of *Life. The Rat Pack: The Original Bad Boys.* New York: Life Books, 2013.

Keever, Beverly Deepe. *News Zero: The New York Times and the Bomb.* Monroe, Maine: Common Courage Press, 2004.

Kefauver, Estes. *Crime in America.* Garden City, N.Y.: Doubleday and Company, Inc., 1951.

The Kefauver Committee Report on Organized Crime. New York: Didier Publishers, 1951.

Kessler-Harris, Alice. *A Woman's Wage: Historical Meanings and Social Consequences.* Updated ed. Lexington: University Press of Kentucky, 2014.

Kirk, Andrew G. *Doom Towns: The People and Landscapes of Atomic Testing, a Graphic History.* New York: Oxford University Press, 2017.

Kitt, Eartha. *Confessions of a Sex Kitten.* New York: Barricade Books, 1991.

———. *Thursday's Child.* New York: Duell, Sloan and Pearce, 1956.

Kling, Dwayne. *The Rise of the Biggest Little City: An Encyclopedic History of Reno Gaming, 1931–1981.* Reno: University of Nevada Press, 2000.

Kraft, James P. *Vegas at Odds: Labor Conflict in a Leisure Economy, 1960–1985.* Baltimore: Johns Hopkins University Press, 2010.

Kuntz, Tom, and Phil Kuntz, eds. *The Sinatra Files: The Secret FBI Dossier.* New York: Three Rivers Press, 2000.

Lacey, Robert. *Little Man: Meyer Lansky and the Gangster Life.* Boston: Little, Brown, 1991.

Lalli, Sergio. "Cliff Jones: 'The Big Juice.'" In *Players: The Men Who Made Las Vegas,* edited by Jack Sheehan. Reno: University of Nevada Press, 1997.

Leuchtenburg, William. *A Troubled Feast: American Society Since 1945.* Updated ed. Boston: Little, Brown, 1983.

Levy, Shawn. *Rat Pack Confidential.* Paperback ed. New York: Anchor Books, 1998.

Liberace. *An Autobiography.* New York: G. P. Putnam's Sons, 1973.

Mannering, Derek. *Mario Lanza: Singing to the Gods.* Jackson: University of Mississippi Press, 2005.

Martin, Deana, with Wendy Holden. *Memories Are Made of This: Dean Martin through His Daughter's Eyes.* Paperback ed. New York: Three Rivers Press, 2004.

May, Elaine Tyler. *Homeward Bound: American Families in the Cold War Era.* Rev. ed. New York: Basic Books, 2008.

MacLaine, Shirley. *My Lucky Stars: A Hollywood Memoir.* Paperback ed. New York: Bantam, 1996.

MacDonald, John D. *The Only Girl in the Game.* Greenwich, Conn.: Fawcett Publications, 1960.

McKay, Janis. *Played Out on the Strip: The Rise and Fall of Las Vegas Casino Bands.* Reno: University of Nevada Press, 2016.

McNally, Karen. *When Frankie Went to Hollywood: Frank Sinatra and American Male Identity.* Urbana: University of Illinois Press, 2008.

Mullen, Lawrence J. *Las Vegas: Media and Myth.* Lanham, Md.: Lexington Books, 2007.

Meyers, Sid W. *The Great Las Vegas Fraud.* Chicago: Mayflower Press, 1958.

Miller, Richard. *Under the Cloud: The Decades of Nuclear Testing.* New York: Free Press, 1986.

Mills, Quincy T. *Cutting along the Color Line: Black Barbers and Barber Shops in America.* Philadelphia: University of Pennsylvania Press, 2013.

Moehring, Eugene P. *Resort City in the Sunbelt: Las Vegas, 1930–2000.* 2nd ed. Reno: University of Nevada Press, 2000.

———. *Reno, Las Vegas, and the Strip: A Tale of Three Cities.* Reno: University of Nevada Press, 2014.

———. *The University of Nevada Las Vegas: A History.* Reno: University of Nevada Press, 2007.

Moehring, Eugene P., and Michael S. Green. *Las Vegas: A Centennial History.* Reno: University of Nevada Press, 2005.

Newton, Michael. *Mr. Mob: The Life and Crimes of Moe Dalitz.* Jefferson, N.C.: McFarland and Company, 2007.

1959 Las Vegas Report. Las Vegas: Las Vegas Research and Statistical Bureau, 1959.

Oakley, J. Ronald. *God's Country: America in the Fifties*. New York: Dembner Books, 1986.

O'Brian, John, and Jeremy Borsos. *Atomic Postcards: Radioactive Messages from the Cold War* Chicago: University of Chicago Press, 2011.

Odessky, Dick. *Fly on the Wall: Recollections of Las Vegas' Good Old, Bad Old Days*. Las Vegas: Huntington Press, 1999.

Oshinsky, David M. *A Conspiracy So Immense: The World of Joseph McCarthy*. New York: Free Press, 1983.

Patterson, James T. *Great Expectations: The United States, 1945–1974*. New York: Oxford University Press, 1996.

Payn, Graham, and Sheridan Morley, eds. *The Noël Coward Diaries*. London: Weidenfeld and Nicolson, 1982.

Pearl, Ralph. *Las Vegas Is My Beat*. Paperback ed. Toronto: Bantam Books, 1974.

Pomerance, Alan. *Repeal of the Blues*. Secaucus, N.J.: Citadel Press, 1988.

Popp, Richard K. *The Holiday Makers: Magazines, Advertising, and Mass Tourism in Postwar America*. Baton Rouge: Louisiana State University Press, 2012.

Puzo, Mario. *Inside Las Vegas*. New York: Grosset and Dunlap, 1976.

Pyron, Darden Asbury. *Liberace: An American Boy*. Paperback ed. Chicago: University of Chicago Press, 2001.

Quirk, Lawrence J. and William Schoell. *The Rat Pack: Neon Nights and the Kings of Cool*. Paperback ed. New York: Perennial, 2002.

Raab, Selwyn. *Five Families: The Rise, Decline, and Resurgence of America's Most Powerful Mafia Empires*. Paperback ed. New York: Thomas Dunne Books, 2006.

Ralli, Paul. *Viva Vegas*. Culver City, Calif.: Murray and Gee, 1953.

Raymond, C. Elizabeth. *George Wingfield: Owner and Operator of Nevada*. Reno: University of Nevada Press, 1992.

Reagan, Nancy, with William Novak. *My Turn: The Memoirs of Nancy Reagan*. New York: Random House, 1989.

Reagan, Ronald, with Richard G. Hubler. *Where's the Rest of Me?* New York: Duell, Sloan and Pearce, 1965.

Reid, Ed. *City without Clocks*. Englewood Cliffs, N.Y.: Prentice-Hall, 1961.

Richardson, Heather Cox. *To Make Men Free: A History of the Republican Party*. New York: Basic Books, 2014.

Riva, Maria. *Marlene Dietrich*. Paperback ed. New York: Ballantine Books, 1994.

Roske, Ralph. *Las Vegas: A Desert Paradise*. Tulsa, Okla.: Continental Heritage Press, 1986.

Rothman, Hal K. *Devil's Bargains: Tourism in the Twentieth-Century American West*. Lawrence: University Press of Kansas, 1998.

Rovner, Eduardo Sáenz. *The Cuban Connection: Drug Trafficking, Smuggling, and Gambling in Cuba from the 1920s to the Revolution*. Translated by Russ Davidson. Chapel Hill: University of North Carolina Press, 2008.

Russo, Gus. *The Outfit: The Role of Chicago's Underworld in the Shaping of Modern America* New York: Bloomsbury, 2001.

———. *Supermob: How Sidney Korshak and His Criminal Associates Became America's Hidden Power Brokers*. Paperback ed. New York: Bloomsbury, 2007.

Santopietro, Tom. *Sinatra in Hollywood*. New York: Thomas Dunne, 2008.

Scheibach, Michael. *Atomic Narratives and American Youth: Coming of Age with the Atom, 1945–1955*. Jefferson, N.C.: McFarland, 2003.

Schumacher, Geoff. *Howard Hughes: Power, Paranoia and Palace Intrigue*. Las Vegas: Stephens Press, 2008.

———. *Sun, Sin and Suburbia: An Essential History of Modern Las Vegas*. Rev. and expanded ed. Reno: University of Nevada Press, 2015.

Schwartz, David G. *Grandissimo: The First Emperor of Las Vegas*. Las Vegas: Winchester Books, 2013.

———. *Roll the Bones: The History of Gambling, Casino Edition*. Las Vegas: Winchester Books, 2013.

———. *Suburban Xanadu: The Casino Resort on the Las Vegas Strip and Beyond*. New York: Routledge, 2003.

Schwartz, Ted, and Mardi Rustam. *Candy Barr: The Small-Town Texas Runaway Who Became A Darling of the Mob and the Queen of Las Vegas Burlesque*. Lanham, Md.: Taylor Trade Publishing, 2008.

Shaw, Arnold. *Belafonte: An Unauthorized Biography*. Philadelphia: Chilton Company, 1960.

Sheehan, Jack. *Quiet Kingmaker of Las Vegas: E. Parry Thomas*. Las Vegas: Stephens Press, 2009.

Sinatra, Nancy. *Frank Sinatra: My Father*. Paperback ed. New York: Pocket Books, 1986.

Sinatra, Tina, with Jeff Coplon. *My Father's Daughter: A Memoir*. New York: Simon and Schuster, 2000.

Smith, John L. *Sharks in the Desert: The Founding Fathers and Current Kings of Las Vegas*. Fort Lee, N.J.: Barricade Books, 2005.

Starr, Kevin. *The Dream Endures: California Enters the 1940s*. New York: Oxford University Press, 1997.

Starr, Michael. *Mouse in the Rat Pack: The Joey Bishop Story*. New York: Taylor, 2002.

Stephens, John G. *From My Three Sons to Major Dad: My Life as a TV Producer*. Lanham, Md.: Scarecrow Press, 2005.

Steward, Stanley A. *Where Sin Abounds: A Religious History of Las Vegas*. Eugene, Ore.: Wipf and Stock, 2012.

Stouffer, Samuel A. *Communism, Conformity, and Civil Liberties: A Cross-Section of the Nation Speaks Its Mind*. 1955. Reprint, Gloucester, Mass.: Peter Smith, 1963.

Stover, John. *American Railroads*. Chicago: University of Chicago Press, 2008.

Sullivan, Michael. *There's No People Like Show People: Confessions of a Showbiz Agent*. London: Quadrant Books, 1982.

Swanson, Doug J. *Blood Aces: The Wild Ride of Benny Binion, the Texas Gangster Who Created Las Vegas*. New York: Viking, 2014.

Szasz, Ferenc Morton. *Atomic Comics: Cartoonists Confront the Nuclear World*. Reno: University of Nevada Press, 2012.

Taub, William L. *Forces of Power*. New York: Grosset and Dunlap, 1979.

Taylor, Quintard. "From Esteban to Rodney King: Five Centuries of African American History in the West." In *The American West: The Reader*, edited by Walter Nugent and Martin Ridge. Bloomington: University of Indiana Press, 1999.

Titus, A. Constandina. *Bombs in the Backyard: Atomic Testing and American Politics.* Reno: University of Nevada Press, 1986.

Torgerson, Dial. *Kerkorian: An American Success Story.* New York: Dial Press, 1974.

Truman, Harry S. *Years of Trial and Hope.* Vol. 2 of *Memoirs by Harry S. Truman.* Garden City, N.Y.: Doubleday, 1956.

Watts, Steven. *JFK and the Masculine Mystique: Sex and Power on the New Frontier.* New York: Thomas Dunne, 2016.

———. *The Magic Kingdom: Walt Disney and the American Way of Life.* Paperback ed. Columbia: University of Missouri Press, 2006.

Weatherford, Mike. *Cult Vegas: The Weirdest! The Wildest! The Swingin'est Town on Earth!* Las Vegas: Huntington Press, 2001.

White, Claytee D. "'Eight Dollars a Day and Working in the Shade': An Oral History of African American Migrant Women in the Las Vegas Gaming Industry." In *African American Women Confront the West, 1600–2000*, edited by Quintard Taylor and Shirley Ann Wilson Moore. Norman: University of Oklahoma Press, 2003.

———. "Nevada." In *Black America: A State-by-State Historical Encyclopedia*, vol. 2. Edited by Alton Hornsby Jr. Westport, Conn.: Greenwood Press, 2011.

Williams, John L. *Miss Shirley Bassey.* London: Quercus, 2010.

Winkler, Allan M. *Life under a Cloud: American Anxiety about the Atom.* New York: Oxford University Press, 1993.

Wolf, George, with Joseph DiMona. *Frank Costello: Prime Minister of the Underworld.* New York: William Morrow and Company, 1974.

Wright, Frank. *Nevada Yesterdays: Short Looks at Las Vegas History.* Las Vegas: Stephens Press, 2005.

Ybarra, Michael J. *Washington Gone Crazy: Senator Pat McCarran and the Great American Communist Hunt.* Paperback ed. Hanover, N.H.: Steerforth Press, 2004.

Zook, Lynn. *Gambling on a Dream: The Classic Las Vegas Strip.* Self-published, 2016.

ARTICLES

"Along the NAACP Battlefront." *Crisis,* December 1945.

"Apalachin's Mob Is In—And Its Secret Is Out." *Life,* January 25, 1960.

"Atomic Tests Light Up Four States." *Life,* February 12, 1951.

"The Audacious New Swimsuits." *Life,* January 8, 1965.

Beebe, Lucius. "Las Vegas," *Holiday,* December 1952.

"The Belles of Las Vegas." *Real Men,* December 1958.

Bine, Al. "Paging 'Mr. Las Vegas.'" *California Living,* February 4, 1973.

Bishop, Joey. "My Small War against Prejudice." *Ebony,* April 1961.

Bronson, Fred. "The Years in Music: The Charts of 40, 30, 20 and 10 Years Ago." *Billboard,* December 26, 1998–January 2, 1999.

Brunn, Robert R. "'This . . . Should Arouse the Most Solemn Reflections.'" *Christian Science Monitor,* July 2, 1951.

Calvert, Dave. "Similar Hats on Similar Heads: Uniformity and Alienation at the Rat Pack's Summit Conference of Cool," *Popular Music* 34, no. 1 (2015): 1–21.

Considine, Bob. "The Inside Story of Las Vegas." *PIC,* July 1955.

Cook, Fred J. "Treasure Chest of the Underworld: Gambling, Inc." *Nation,* October 22, 1960.

Creel, George. "Unholy City." *Collier's,* September 2, 1939.

Day, Ned. "The Selling of Las Vegas." *Las Vegan Magazine,* August 1984.

"Did Bias Banish Nat's TV Show?" *Jet,* March 4, 1965.

Dobbs, William T. "Southern Nevada and the Legacy of Basic Magnesium Incorporated." *Nevada Historical Society Quarterly* 34, no. 1 (1991): 273–303.

English, Richard. "The Boom Came Back." *Collier's,* August 22, 1942.

———. "The Million-Dollar Talent War." *Saturday Evening Post,* April 14, 1953.

"The Facts about A-Bomb 'Fall-Out': Not a Word of Truth in Scare Stories over Tests." *U.S. News and World Report,* March 25, 1955.

Feighery, Glen M. "'A Light Out of This World': Awe, Anxiety, and Routinization in Early Nuclear Test Coverage, 1951–1953." *American Journalism* 28, no. 3 (2011): 9–34.

Fischler, Al. "Las Vegas as Showbiz Mint." *Billboard,* August 31, 1946.

Fowler, Dan. "What Price Gambling in Nevada?" *Look,* June 15, 1954.

"Frank Sennes, Sr." *Variety,* February 4, 1993. http://variety.com/1993/scene/people-news-frank-sennes-sr-103727/.

"Frank Sennes to Op Miami Colonial Inn." *Billboard,* November 4, 1950.

"Frontier Hotel Spends 100G for Talent in Year; Plans Expansion." *Billboard,* October 16, 1943.

Gehman, Richard. "The Enigma of Frank Sinatra." *Good Housekeeping,* July 1960.

"Gerri Major's Society." *Jet,* June 16, 1955.

Goodrich, James. "Negroes Can't Win in Las Vegas." *Ebony,* March 1954.

Goodwin, Joanne L. "Mojave Mirages: Gender and Performance in Las Vegas." *Women's History Review* 111, no. 1 (2002): 115–32.

Gragg, Larry. "'Big Step to Oblivion for Las Vegas?': The 'Battle of the Bare Bosoms,' 1957–1959." *Journal of Popular Culture* 43, no. 5 (2010): 1004–22.

———. "Defending a City's Image: Las Vegas Opposes the Making of *711 Ocean Drive,* 1950." *Popular Culture Review* 22, no. 1 (2011): 7–15.

———. "El Sonador and the Struggle to Develop Resort Hotels in Las Vegas in the 1930s." *Nevada in the West* 6, no. 1 (2015): 4–9.

———. "Jack Entratter: The Greatest Las Vegas Impresario." *Nevada in the West* 4, no. 3 (2013): 4–9.

———. "'A Long Struggle and Many Disappointments': Las Vegas' Failure to Open a Resort Hotel, 1905–1940." *Nevada Historical Society Quarterly* 58, nos. 1–4 (2015): 44–65.

———. "'Never Accorded the Recognition He Deserved': Al Freeman, Sands Hotel Publicist, 1952–1972." *Nevada Historical Society Quarterly* 51, no. 1 (2008): 25–55.

———. "'Noel Coward Wows 'Em in Café Town': The Impact of Noel Coward's 1955 Performance at the Desert Inn." *Nevada Historical Society Quarterly* 53, no. 2 (2010): 108–26.

———. "Protecting a City's Image: The Death of *Las Vegas Beat,* 1961." *Studies in Popular Culture* 34, no. 1 (2011): 1–22.

———."Selling 'Sin City': Successfully Promoting Las Vegas during the Great Depression, 1935–1941." *Nevada Historical Society Quarterly* 49, no. 2 (2006): 83–106.

———. "'They Weren't My Kind of Audience': Elvis Presley's First Appearance in Las Vegas in 1956." *Nevada in the West* 6, no. 4 (2015): 4–9.

Halevy, Julian. "Disneyland and Las Vegas." *Nation*, June 7, 1958.

Hamblin, Jacob Darwin. "'A Dispassionate and Objective Effort': Negotiating the First Study on the Biological Effects of Atomic Radiation." *Journal of the History of Biology* 40, no. 1 (2007): 147–77.

Harmon, Mella Rothwell. "Getting Renovated: Reno Divorces in the 1930s." *Nevada Historical Society Quarterly* 42, no. 1 (1999): 46–68.

"Hazel Scott Fights Jim Crow at Las Vegas." *Jet*, April 24, 1952.

"Haymes Affair Has MCA and Sands Hotel in Frenzy." *Billboard*, August 15, 1953.

Hennacy, Ammon. "Picketing Atomic Tests in Las Vegas." *Catholic Worker*, July–August, 1957.

Henry, William A. III. "Show Business: a Synonym for Glorious Excess." *Time*, February 16, 1987.

"Interracial Resort Planned for Las Vegas." *Jet*, December 18, 1952.

"In the Armed Forces." *Billboard*, January 16, 1943.

Jacobs, Paul. "Clouds from Nevada." *The Reporter*, May 16, 1957.

"Jo Baker Beats Bias." *Jet*, May 29, 1952.

Johnson, Carl J. "Cancer Incidence in an Area of Radioactive Fallout Downwind From the Nevada Test Site." *Journal of the American Medical Association* 251, no. 2 (January 13, 1984): 230–36.

Kamp, David. "They Made Vegas Swing." *Vanity Fair*, December 1999.

Kashner, Sam. "The Color of Love." *Vanity Fair*, September 3, 2013. http://www.vanityfair.com/style/1999/03/sammy-davis-kim-novak-dating.

Kefauver, Estes. "What I Found in the Underworld." *Saturday Evening Post*, April 7, 1951.

Lacayo, Richard. "Ring-A-Ding Ding." *Time*, May 25, 1998.

Lang, Daniel. "Our Far-Flung Correspondents: Blackjack and Flashes." *New Yorker*, September 20, 1952.

"Las Vegas: Dice, Dollars and Doom Town." *Fortnight*, June 1955, 46.

"Las Vegas: 'It Just Couldn't Happen.'" *Time*, November 23, 1952.

"Las Vegas: Nice People Live on Divorce, Gambling." *Newsweek*, April 20, 1953.

"Las Vegas Strikes it Rich." *Life*, May 26, 1947.

"Las Vegas: The Game Is Illusion." *Time*, July 11, 1969.

"Las Vegas to Get $1,200,000 Interracial Hotel." *Jet*, April 22, 1954.

Legare, Robert. "Meeting at the Summit: Sinatra and His Buddies Bust 'Em Up in Vegas." *Playboy*, June 1960.

"Lena Horne Breaks Record at N.Y. Opening." *Jet*, May 15, 1953.

"Mae West." *Billboard*, August 7, 1954.

"Manners and Morals." *Time*, November 28, 1949.

Martin, Anne. "These United States—VIII, Nevada: Beautiful Desert of Buried Hopes." *Nation*, July 26, 1922.

Miller, Judith. "Cuba on the Edge." *Pundicity,* July 2015. Accessed June 25, 2017. http://www.judithmiller.com/17552/cuba-on-the-edge.

"Miller Adds Sahara Buying." *Billboard,* March 7, 1953.

Moehring, Eugene P. "C.D. Baker and the Modernization of Postwar Las Vegas." *Nevada Historical Society Quarterly* 60, nos. 1–4 (2017): 37–58.

———. "Profile of a Nevada Railroad Town: Las Vegas, 1910." *Nevada Historical Society Quarterly* 34, no. 4 (1991): 466–87.

Moor, Angela. "Operation Hospitality: Las Vegas and Civil Defense, 1951–1959." *Nevada Historical Society Quarterly* 51, no. 4 (2008): 292–310.

Murphy, Charles J. V. "A-Bomb vs. House." *Life,* March 30, 1953.

"Nevada Brings It into Open and Gets Rich." *Life,* June 19, 1950.

Nickel, Robert V. "Dollars, Defense, and the Desert: Southern Nevada's Military Economy and World War II." *Nevada Historical Society Quarterly* 47, no. 4 (2004): 303–27.

"Nightclubs: The Wages of Vulgarity." *Time,* September 7, 1959.

O'Neil, Paul. "The 'Clan' Is the Most." *Life,* December 22, 1958.

"'One-Man Revolt' in New Vegas Dunes Setup; Names for Names' Sake Are Out." *Variety,* November 17, 1954.

"Paris Come-On in Vegas." *Life,* June 6, 1960.

Patrick, Elizabeth Nelson. "The Black Experience in Southern Nevada." *Nevada Historical Society Quarterly* 22, no. 2 (1979): 128–40.

———. "The Black Experience in Southern Nevada, Part II." *Nevada Historical Society Quarterly* 22, no. 3 (1979): 209–20.

Peak, Kenneth J., and William N. Ousley. "The FBI's 'Strawman': Breaking the Kansas City Mob's Connection to Las Vegas." *Missouri Historical Review* 104, no. 2 (2010): 94–114.

Pearce, Dick. "Pleasure Palaces." *Harper's,* February 1955.

"Plan Resort for All Races." *Billboard,* December 6, 1952.

"Relationships of Sinatra with Blacks That Book about Him Does Not Highlight." *Jet,* October 13, 1986.

Robinson, Louie. "The Life and Death of Nat King Cole." *Ebony,* April 1965.

Rosenbaum, Ron. "Do You Know Vegas?" *Esquire,* August 1982.

Rudin, Max. "Fly Me to the Moon: Reflections on the Rat Pack." *American Heritage* 49, no. 8 (1998): 52–65.

Sallaz, Jeffrey J. "Civil Rights and Employment Equity in Las Vegas Casinos: The Failed Enforcement of the Casino Consent Decree, 1971–1986." *Nevada Historical Society Quarterly* 47, no. 4 (2004): 283–302.

Schultheis, Rob. "Yes!! It's . . . Las Vegas!!!!! An Unabashed Frolic in the City Where Dreams Work Overtime and Inhibitions Take a Holiday." *National Geographic Traveler,* May–June 1991.

Schwartz, David G. "JFK in Las Vegas." *Vegas Seven,* July 2, 2013. Accessed December 30, 2016. http://vegasseven.com/2013/07/02/jfk-las-vegas-2/.

———. "The Long, Hot Summer of '55." *Vegas Seven,* August 6, 2015. http://vegasseven.com/2015/08/06/long-hot-summer-55/.

———. "The Tiffany of the Strip." *Vegas Seven,* March 30, 2017. http://vegasseven .com/2017/03/30/tropicana-the-tiffany-of-the-strip/.

"A Searching Inquiry into Nuclear Perils." *Life,* June 10, 1957.

"Sell Stock for Las Vegas' 1st Cooperative Hotel." *Jet,* October 27, 1955.

"Sennes to Coast; Rocky Takes Over." *Billboard,* July 11, 1953.

"$7,000,000 in Hotel Showbiz." *Billboard,* February 10, 1945.

"Showgirl Shangri-La." *Life,* June 21, 1954.

"Snake Eyes in Las Vegas." *Time,* September 19, 1955.

Stevens, Verlene. "Race in Las Vegas." *Crisis,* September 1946.

Stinnett, Caskie. "Las Vegas: Where Anything Is Forgivable Except Restraint." *Holiday,* May 1967.

Stocker, Joseph. "Las Vegas' Golden Boy." *American Legion Magazine,* December 1953.

Stoldal, Bob. "The Black Biltmore." *Desert Companion,* Summer 2009: 8–13.

Stout, Wesley. "Nevada's New Reno." *Saturday Evening Post,* October 31, 1942.

Swallow, Craig F. "The Ku Klux Klan in Nevada during the 1920s." *Nevada Historical Society Quarterly* 24, no. 3 (1981): 203–20.

Taffe, Richard P. "I'm Not Afraid of the A-Bomb." *Collier's,* January 26, 1952.

"Taunted Tiger Mars Marilyn." *Life,* September 6, 1954.

Titus, A. Constandina. "A-Bombs in the Backyard: Southern Nevada Adapts to the Nuclear Age, 1951–1963." *Nevada Historical Society Quarterly* 26, no. 4 (1983): 235–54.

———. "Cultural Fallout in the Atomic Age." In *History and Humanities: Essays in Honor of Wilbur S. Shepperson,* edited by Francis X. Hartigan. Reno: University of Nevada Press, 1989.

Turkak, Gary. "Atomic 'Time Bombs.'" *VFW: Veterans of Foreign Wars Magazine,* April 1998.

"An Unfrumptious Wedding." *Time,* September 25, 1953.

"Unhappy Cuba's Cockeyed Week." *Life,* March 10, 1958.

"Van Johnson Scores Well at Sands Date." *Billboard,* April 25, 1953.

"Vegas Passes First Test of Talent Deal." *Billboard,* May 1, 1954.

Velie, Lester. "Las Vegas: The Underworld's Secret Jackpot." *Reader's Digest,* October 1959.

Von Hoffman, Alexander. "A Study in Contradictions: The Origins and Legacy of the Housing Act of 1949." *Housing Policy Debate* 11, no. 2 (2000): 299–326.

Voss, Kimberly Wilmot, and Lance Speere. "Where She Stands: Ruthe Deskin and the Las Vegas Sun." *Nevada Historical Society Quarterly* 55, nos. 1–4 (2012): 87–105.

"Wherever You Look There's Danger in Las Vegas." *Life,* November 12, 1951.

White, Claytee. "The March That Never Happened: Desegregating the Las Vegas Strip." *Nevada Law Review* 5, no. 1 (2004): 71–83.

"Why the Moulin Rouge Went Broke." *Jet,* October 20, 1955.

"Wilbur's Dream Joint." *Time,* May 8, 1950.

"Wild Women of Las Vegas: Morals Take a Back Seat amid Sizzling Desert Sun." *Pose,* April 1955.

"Wild, Woolly and Wide-Open." *Look,* August 14, 1940.

Williams, Franklin H. "Sunshine and Jim Crow." *The Crisis,* April 1954.

"Women Hold Third of Jobs." *Life,* December 24, 1956.

Zhito, Lee. "Las Vegas Set to Spend Big on Top Names." *Billboard,* June 10, 1950.

FILMS

Armstrong, Stan, and Gary Lipsman, dirs. *The Misunderstood Legend of the Las Vegas Moulin Rouge.* Desert Rose Productions, 2014.

———. *Invisible Las Vegas: The Untold Story of the West Las Vegas Community.* Desert Rose Productions, 2007.

Brewer, Jon, dir. *Nat King Cole: Afraid of the Dark.* Jon Brewer Production, 2014.

A Last Frontier: Las Vegas, Nevada. Bengal Pictures, 1950. Accessed January 4, 2017. http://www.youtube.com/watch?v=9361U5Sd81A.

Las Vegas: Playground U.S.A. Las Vegas News Bureau, 1956. Accessed November 12, 2016. https://www.youtube.com/watch?v=5029W7XqlPM.

Las Vegas Recreation Unlimited. MacDonald Film Productions, 1956. Accessed January 4, 2017. http://youtube.com/watch?v=jnsjf8PLzY.

McGlynn, Don, dir. *Louis Prima: The Wildest.* Blue Sea Productions, 1999.

Milestone, Lewis, dir. *Ocean's Eleven.* Warner Brothers, 1960.

Salkow, Sidney, dir. *Las Vegas Shakedown.* William F. Broidy Pictures, 1955.

Weissenbeck, Barbara, and Gerald Benesch, eds. *The Carsony Brothers: From Vienna to Las Vegas.* Filmwerkstatt Wien, 2014. Accessed December 14, 2016. http://www.youtube.com/watch?v=1ANgN1bsYak.

Index

Bacall, Lauren, 34, 57, 168, 177
Bailey, Bob, 96, 100, 120; and Moulin
  Rouge, 104, 105, 106; and *Talk of the
  Town*, 75, 122
Bailey, Pearl, 104, 107
Baker, Charles Duncan, 26, 27, 118–19, 136
Baker, Josephine, 89, 98, 101
Baker, Nancy Williams, 82, 83
Ball, Lucille, 44, 82, 165
Bally's, 181
Balzar, Fred, 129
Bankhead, Tallulah, 57, 174
Barber, Alicia, 193n12
Bardoli, Martha, 153
Barr, Candy, 34, 79–80
Bart, Peter, 181
bartenders, 73
Basic Magnesium Industries (BMI) plant,
  11, 110–12, 113–14
Basie, Count, 104
Bassett, Ada, 75
Bassey, Shirley, 93, 99
Batista, Fulgencio, 24
Battaglia, John, 141–42
Bayley, Warren "Doc," 77, 143, 204n43
Bégout, Bruce, 185
Beidler, Philip D., 25
Belafonte, Harry, 52, 77, 89, 95, 104, 126;
  and fight against discrimination, 98,
  99, 100; hotels' treatment of, 91, 92–93
Bell, Lloyd, 73
Bennett, Tony, 25, 52
Benny, Jack, 46–47, 106, 174
Benzell, Mimi, 63
Berkley, Thomas, 118
Berkley Square, 117–18
Berle, Milton, 47, 51, 53, 62, 165, 172
Berman, Charles, 131
Berman, David "Davie," 131–32
Bernstein, Leonard, 23
Berry, Chuck, 3
Best, Katharine, 16–17, 80, 163–64
Bible, Alan, 35, 139

Billboard, 55, 63, 64
Biltz, Norman, 136
Binion, Benny, 17, 18, 131, 136, 157
Bischoff, Willie, 141–42
Bishop, Joey, 96; and Rat Pack, 165, 167,
  170–71, 172, 175
Bisno, Alexander, 103, 104, 106
Black Book, 142–43, 171
black entertainers, 88–108; discriminatory
  treatment of, 88–89, 90–91, 92, 93,
  94, 96, 100, 211n72; fight against
  discrimination by, 98–99, 100, 101;
  hotels' payments to, 89; and NAACP,
  95–96; and Westside, 91–92, 119,
  122–23; white performers' support for,
  96–97. *See also* African Americans;
  entertainers
Bluebell Girls, 68
Bogart, Humphrey, 34, 57, 168
Bolger, Ray, 45, 61
Bonanza Village, 115
Borst, Lyle, 152
Boston Blackie, 46
Boswell, Connee, 25, 77
Boswell, Sonny, 105
Boulard, Garry, 174
Boulder Club, 11–12, 18
Boulder Dam, 7, 10–11, 32, 110, 112
Bowron, Fletcher, 130
Boyd, Sam, 17, 18, 49, 129
Boyle, Hal, 41
Bracey, Earnest, 108
Bracken, Walter, 110
Brady, Ruth, 36, 76
Brasselle, Keefe, 60
Braudis, Hal, 59–60, 61, 96
Breakfast with Dorothy and Dick, 46
British Medical Research Council, 153–54
Brooks, Bob, 12
Brown, Les, 107, 108
Brown Derby, 119
Brunn, Robert R., 150–51
Bryant, Lucille, 72

Prima, Louis, 61, 65–66, 168
production shows, 60, 67, 181
Progressive Civic Service League, 120
promotional efforts, 30–50; around
atomic tests, 156–58, 159–64; around
celebrities, 34–35, 44–45; attracting
gamblers, 36–37; budget for, 49,
197n82; by Chamber of Commerce,
30, 31–32, 40, 45, 49–50, 145, 157;
cheesecake photos, 33–34; courting
of columnists, 36; by Desert Inn,
41, 42–44, 45, 157; by Flamingo, 44,
157; marketing slogans, 184; around
movies and television, 44–49; "place
promotion," 193n12; planting stories,
33; promotional films, 45, 157; by
publicity and advertisement firms,
31, 32–33; around Rat Pack, 173–74;
by Sands, 38–39, 44–45, 47, 157–58,
159–60, 173–74; stunts, 37–38, 184; by
travel agents, 31. *See also* publicists
Proser, Monte, 59, 62
prosperity: of 1950s, 5–6
prostitution, 7, 80–81, 85
publicists: Brady as, 36, 76; columnists
courted by, 36; Diederich as, 36,
37–38, 173, 183, 229n88; Fischer as, 35,
36–37; Freeman as, 35, 36–37, 38–39,
44, 46, 47, 48; Irwin as, 30, 36, 37, 92,
173 McDonald as, 36, 173; Murphy
as, 36, 42, 173; recruitment of, 35;
sexuality sold by, 78–79; Taylor as,
35, 76; women as, 76, 204n41. *See also*
promotional efforts
Puzo, Mario, 185

racial discrimination, 109–27; against
black entertainers, 88–89, 90–91, 92,
93, 94, 96; black entertainers' fight
against, 98–99, 100, 101; blacks' fight
against, 95–96, 100, 101–2, 112–13,
121–22, 124–27, 125, 183; at El Rancho
Vegas, 90–91, 92, 93; at Flamingo,

125; hotels' agreement to end, 126–27;
at Last Frontier, 90, 95, 100; in Las
Vegas, 93–94, 109–10, 111, 124–27,
184, 209nn34–35; NAACP and fight
against, 113, 121; at Riviera, 96, 98; at
Sahara, 92; at Sands, 91–92, 97–98; at
Thunderbird, 88, 92–93, 100; tourists
blamed for, 94; white entertainers'
opposition to, 96–97. *See also* African
Americans
Racket Squad, 46
Raft, George, 168
Ramona Room, 55, 56, 65, 98, 101
Rand, Sally, 34, 102
Randall, Tracy, 79
Ratcliffe, Bea, 76
Rat Pack, 165–77; ad libs and heckling by,
174–75; hotels' promotion of, 173–74;
and Kennedy, 169–70, 175; and Las
Vegas appeal, 175–76, 177; national
publicity about, 168–69; and *Ocean's
Eleven*, 165, 167–68, 170, 172, 173,
174, 175; origin of term, 168; popular
appeal of, 176; racial and ethnic gags
of, 171–72
Ray, Clarence, 109
Ray, Johnnie, 45, 62
Raye, Martha, 102
Reader's Digest, 52
Reagan, Ronald, 63
Real Men, 84
Red Cross, 50
Red Skelton Show, 46
Reed, Helen Scott, 75–76
Reese, Della, 65
Regan, Neil, 32–33
Reid, Ed, 72, 82, 182
Reno, NV, 26, 133, 140; casinos in, 73–74,
124, 171
Reno Evening Gazette, 75
Resnick, Charlie, 131
Reynolds, Debbie, 45
Richman Harry, 55